BY LISE OLSEN

Code of Silence

The Scientist and the Serial Killer

THE SCIENTIST
AND THE
SERIAL KILLER

THE SCIENTIST AND THE SERIAL KILLER

THE SEARCH FOR HOUSTON'S LOST BOYS

LISE OLSEN

RANDOM HOUSE
NEW YORK

Published in the United States by Random House, an imprint and division of Penguin Random House LLC, New York.

RANDOM HOUSE and the HOUSE colophon are registered trademarks of Penguin Random House LLC.

Photographs courtesy of Dr. Sharon Derrick, Pat Paul, Texas A&M University–Corpus Christi, and the *Houston Chronicle;* additional photos from Harris County archives, Pasadena and Houston police files, Reagan and Vidor High School yearbooks, or taken by the author

Portraits of the Lost Boys and neighborhood map by Nancy Rose

Title page and part opener map: Houston area map, The National Atlas of the United States of America, 1970 (Courtesy of the University of Texas Libraries, the University of Texas at Austin)

Hardback ISBN 9780593595688
Ebook ISBN 9780593595695

Printed in the United States of America on acid-free paper

randomhousebooks.com

9 8 7 6 5 4 3 2 1

ScoutAutomatedPrintCode

First Edition

Book design by Caroline Cunningham

To the memory of the Lost Boys

CONTENTS

PART II: Sex, Drugs, and Other Pieces of the Puzzle

PART III: Mistaken Identities

PART IV: Patterns and Contradictions

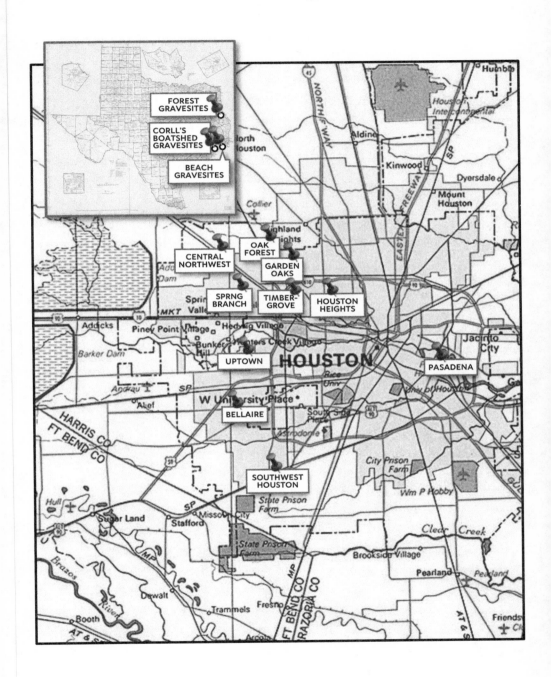

LIST OF ILLUSTRATIONS

AUTHOR'S NOTE

THIS IS THE STORY of Sharon Derrick's quest to restore the identities of Houston's Lost Boys and an account of the lives of those teenaged boys and young men from more than a hundred people who remember them, and from every news article, archive, and public record I could find. Many people I interviewed had never before shared painful and deeply personal memories in these pages. Each friend, relative, and witness has independent recollections about these murder victims' lives, different ideas about the meanings of half-century-old conversations and encounters, and their own interpretations of what happened and why.

No one alive today knows the Lost Boys' full stories or exactly how many lives were erased by these killers. But these pages reveal secrets about these crimes and about previously unidentified and uncounted victims. All of those I interviewed helped build this account of a deeply troubling tale that remains relevant and resonates through time.

PART I

DISAPPEARANCES AND DISCOVERIES

CHAPTER 1

THE DEATH OF A KILLER

PASADENA, TEXAS, AUGUST 8, 1973

ELMER WAYNE HENLEY, JR., woke with a jolt as cold steel clicked against his wrists.

He'd caught only three hours' sleep, and now the first rays of dawn were creeping through patterned drapes that shrouded the living room windows. The seventeen-year-old lifted his shaggy head and locked eyes with Dean Corll, a man he revered as a mentor, now clamping handcuffs on him. "Hey, what are you doing?" he said.

Corll towered above him, sober and scowling. "You pissed me off by bringing that *girl* here," Corll growled, his gray eyes never shifting from the teen's frightened face.

Henley, who went by Wayne, dared glance only briefly at the people he'd brought to this sparsely furnished place to party, now hog-tied and handcuffed beside him on the stubbly shag carpet: fifteen-year-old Rhonda Williams and twenty-year-old Tim Kerley. Fighting a fog of intoxication, he didn't remember being manhandled or tied up. The living room where he and his friends had passed out held only a few chairs clustered around a black-and-white TV, along with the beer bottles, paint cans, and detritus from their late-night revels.

"Wake up, bitch!" Corll said, kicking at the tiny young woman, half hidden in a veil of curly hair, who still slept despite the cuffs on her wrists and ropes around her ankles.

"You blew it," Corll told Wayne. "I'm going to teach you a lesson."

By the summer of 1973, Wayne had abandoned the crowded Houston Heights bungalow he shared with his mother, grandmother, and three younger brothers to live with Corll, a thirty-three-year-old electrician. Wayne had a key and came and went from this low-slung home along muddy Vince Bayou in the city of Pasadena, a mostly blue-collar suburb that hugged Houston's industrial Ship Channel. He admired Corll, a clean-cut U.S. Army veteran who held a steady job and, at least to Wayne's eyes, seemed so superior to his father and namesake, Elmer Wayne Henley, Sr., a laborer who often got drunk and beat Wayne's mother, and had repeatedly fired a gun at him.

Now Wayne and his friends were locked inside the nightmare he had helped Corll create.

Rhonda and Tim immediately awoke, but neither could speak, since Corll had slapped duct tape across their mouths. He fixed them with his penetrating stare and grabbed a boxy transistor radio, placed it between their bodies, and cranked up the volume, blasting music from an AM station. Then Corll hoisted Wayne to his feet and pushed him, shirtless and sweating, into the cramped kitchen with its Formica dinette set. Still wasted from a long night of partying, Wayne stood no chance in a fight against Corll, who was stronger and well armed. Corll usually enjoyed hosting parties for teens and kept his house stocked with pills, paint, pot, and beer. The night before, he'd expected Wayne to bring over Tim. But he'd already fallen asleep by the time they went to pick up Rhonda, and had awoken furious to see *a girl* in his house.

Wedged up against dark stained cabinets where the others could not hear his humiliation, Wayne begged for forgiveness. "I'll do anything you want me to if you take off the cuffs."

Dean Corll brandished both a .22 revolver and a saber, a replica of one used by the Japanese military, with a curving eighteen-inch blade.

Wayne didn't have to fake his fear: He groveled and made more promises. They were alone in the kitchen negotiating for about thirty minutes before Corll relented. "I'm going to let you loose, but I'll keep the gun and knife."

When they returned to the living room together, Wayne, now free, watched Corll deadlift two-hundred-pound Tim Kerley and tote him, still tied up and handcuffed, down a narrow hallway and into a nearly empty spare bedroom. The floor inside had already been covered in a thick sheet of polyurethane and held a rectangular sheet of plywood. Corll dropped Tim with a thud, tying him face-down and spread-eagled to the board. Then Corll waved his saber. "I'll lop off your arm if you move," he said.

Corll returned to the living room for Rhonda, now fully awake and terrified though groggy from the beer and pills Wayne had slipped her the night before. Corll hauled the petite fifteen-year-old to the spare room and laid her faceup beside Tim. He bound her with practiced precision, using braided ropes and more handcuffs, to the board. That handcrafted oddity was Corll's own invention, a sheet of thick marine-grade plywood nearly the size of a twin bed with holes through which handcuffs could be fastened and ropes could be laced to immobilize any unlucky house guest. Some later called it the "torture board."

Corll slashed at Tim's clothes with the saber and stripped him. Then he handed Wayne the blade and ordered him to cut off Rhonda's clothes as well.

Immobilized, Rhonda was dazed after snatches of drugged sleep but recognized the danger she and Tim faced. Unable to speak with tape across her mouth, she used her eyes to plead with Wayne. The two had known each other since early childhood and only recently begun to date. They had grown up together in a picturesque neighborhood called the Heights—a place she considered a "ten-speed society," where kids walked or rode bikes everywhere and hung out on esplanades, parks, and ballfields. But inside that seemingly idyllic community, Rhonda inhabited a private hell: Her father regularly beat and bloodied her. So, whenever he began to drink heavily, she'd learned to sneak out of her two-story white house with its tall columns. That's how she'd ended up at Corll's place. She'd summoned

Wayne for help and he'd scaled an exterior wall to reach her second-floor bedroom, climbed inside the window like a lover from a romance novel, and spirited her here. She did not want to believe her hero would betray her now.

Wayne leaned over Rhonda and whispered not to worry, yet Corll's commands held sway. He didn't question orders; he'd become "Dean's little soldier." With a few slashes of the saber, he cut away her blue jeans and panties, never breaking the skin. He tried not to watch as Corll fumbled with Tim beside them.

Tim was terrified. He'd watched Corll change from a quiet intelligent introvert into a glaring, tense madman. "It was like a man growling, taking a deep breath, expanding his eyes, and going into this second personality," he later explained. He was sure Corll planned to kill him, but tried to keep Corll talking.

Corll urged Wayne to go ahead and rape Rhonda. Instead, he stood. He paced. He dithered. He'd had sex with Rhonda before, but never like this. At least twice, he left the bedroom in search of acrylic paint from one of the cans still strewn throughout the house. He sprayed fumes into a brown paper sack, placed the bag full of intoxicants over his mouth and huffed, trying to numb himself. A paint-thinner high came on quickly, though it didn't last as long as expensive drugs and burned out more brain cells. Briefly, everything would go smooth, as if Wayne were only slipping through the world. By the last time Wayne returned from "bagging," the fumes had done their work. He was stumbling and incoherent, yet he still knew exactly what Corll had planned.

Corll was hovering and poking at Tim, who kept squirming despite the ropes and cuffs that bound him. Trying not to look at them, Wayne politely requested Corll's permission to remove the tape from Rhonda's mouth, and his request was granted.

Wayne slumped down beside Rhonda in a stupor. With her mouth free, she begged for help. "Aren't you going to do anything?" she asked, not caring if Corll heard.

Slowly, Wayne rose again. Instead of seeking another fix, this time he lurched toward the shiny .22 revolver Corll had abandoned on top of a dresser, the only furniture in this unwelcoming room. He grabbed the gun and pointed it at Corll.

"I'm not going to let you do this anymore," he said. "I can't have you kill all my friends."

Corll immediately stood, towering six inches above Wayne's scrawny five-feet-six frame. Tim, still strapped to the plywood, watched as the somewhat flabby thirty-three-year-old seemed to transform. "I saw him change into a different person. His body swelled up; his eyes got big. He was a completely different personality. I would call it demonic," Tim would long remember.

Dean Corll raised his arms and charged, delivering another taunt: "Kill me, Wayne, kill me!"

Wayne did not hesitate. He raised the revolver and fired. His first shot struck Corll in the forehead, just above the left eyebrow. The second copper-nosed bullet caught the thick muscle of Corll's left shoulder. Neither of these wounds by itself would have been fatal, and Corll kept moving as Wayne kept on shooting. The third bullet blasted through Corll's thickened midsection, struck the liver, and lodged in the stomach, halting his advance.

Corll spun and staggered.

Wayne sidestepped and kept shooting as Corll, mortally wounded, tripped on the long, tightly wound cord of a rotary telephone, lurched, and crumpled onto the hallway floor. The last three bullets struck him in the back. All six chambers of the .22 were empty.

Wayne wept and shook as blood from Corll's warm corpse dripped down the wall and pooled on the shag carpet. "I hope he would be proud of me," Wayne muttered as his bewildered friends, still bound to the board, watched through the doorway. In some strange way, he figured maybe this killing really had pleased Dean Corll.

Slowly, Wayne returned to the spare room to release his friends. He unlocked the handcuffs, untied the ropes, and freed Tim, then Rhonda. At her request, he searched for a sleeping bag and used it to cover the carnage.

For a few minutes, he and his friends sat dazed amid the remnants of their party: the bags, the empty spray paint cans, the joints, the beer bottles. And the body. Then Wayne picked up the rotary phone with its long cord still dangling between the legs of the dead man and dialed the dispatcher at the Pasadena Police Department. It was just after 8 A.M.

"I shot a man," he said.

Patrolman A. B. Jamison arrived at 8:30 A.M. in his black-and-white sedan. The house at 2020 Lamar didn't stand out in the look-alike block of working-class homes built in the aftermath of World War II for workers in the plants. But tangled vines threaded through its evergreen bushes and the dusty grass needed trimming. Inside, Jamison found the naked form of a dead man he rapidly identified as Dean Arnold Corll, a white male aged thirty-three, facedown in the hall. There was no whodunit here. The murder weapon was sitting on the sidewalk beside the confessed killer—seventeen-year-old Elmer Wayne Henley, Jr.—its blue metal barrel glinting in the sun. Jamison summoned homicide detectives but assumed their work would be quick; Corll, an electronics specialist for Houston Lighting & Power, had been shot dead with his own gun by a scrawny teen who was obviously still high and claimed self-defense.

Wayne Henley was "crying and seemed emotional," Jamison wrote in his report.

His victim, a U.S. Army veteran, had no criminal history and had been renting this small house from his father. A deed showed that Arnold Corll, also an electrician, had owned the three-bedroom place in Pasadena since the 1950s.

The Corlls had blended into Pasadena, a place of contradictions. Harris County's second-largest city was overwhelmingly white—the KKK's Texas headquarters was on Red Bluff Road—yet many working-class Hispanic families were arriving, attracted by an abundance of plant work and affordable bungalows. The city rodeo was popular with locals, but urban cowboys competing on mechanical bulls in a honky-tonk called Gilley's had drawn national attention. The blue-collar city's longtime regional reputation—and its persistent scent of rotten eggs and gasoline—was irrevocably tied to massive refineries and chemical plants along the serpentine ship channel. Meanwhile, on its rural southern side, farmers still grew strawberries.

Dean Corll seemed ordinary to his neighbors, who included a federal government employee and a Pasadena police patrolman. They described him as friendly, a "swell guy," as one reporter wrote. But Corll's toolbox-toting everyman exterior concealed a cipher.

The wood-frame house on 2020 Lamar was his thirtieth address in five years.

Police, who probed check records and credit reports and interviewed landlords, soon discovered that Corll's long list of recent residences spanned the booming Houston metro area. He'd inhabited high-rise apartments near the upscale Houston Galleria mall; warren-like complexes along the city's buzzing 610 Loop; obscure trailer parks; and garage apartments and "rent houses" all across the historic Houston Heights, where he had once operated Corll's Candy Kitchen, one of a series of candy factories, and had often handed out homemade pralines, caramels, and other confections to kids at elementary schools.

His last home was painted green with a darker emerald trim. He'd accumulated very little furniture: a full-sized bed covered in a patchwork quilt and striped comforter, two dressers, a Formica table, and a couple of chairs. His pet goldfish still swam through the water in its tank.

Investigators from the Harris County Medical Examiner's Office concluded after surveying the scene that "the decedent was having a sex party." They figured the victim, Dean Corll, was likely into S&M. On the floor of the spare bedroom, they examined that eight-foot-long sheet of plywood, still connected to four sets of handcuffs, and studied "several artificial articles used by the gay boys," as one wrote. Ample evidence of that party was strewn all over the living room, yet, surprisingly, authorities would later determine Corll had died with no alcohol or drugs in his system.

Inside his own bedroom, Corll had amassed an eye-popping collection of pornography, sex toys, and erotic curios and oddities. An oversized gray steel toolbox with a scarlet interior contained a fourteen-inch double-headed "firm rubber" dildo, a collection of thin glass rods, and "a suppository type object." An unexplained gas mask had been discarded atop the quilt on his rumpled bed. The evidence of what the investigators considered sexual perversion or an orgy was everywhere, but didn't immediately suggest serial rape or murder. By phone, one investigator privately told colleagues: "Man, you're not going to believe this one. This is the weirdest scene I've ever made."

On his dresser, Corll displayed a framed Polaroid photo of a doe-eyed teenager standing near the patterned black-and-white drapes that still covered the living room's front windows. In that photo, the boy's muscular frame was hidden beneath an oversized T-shirt, his long hair tucked behind his ears and his mouth set in a straight line. Police later identified this handsome boy as fifteen-year-old Billy Lawrence, an aspiring football player from a bucolic Houston neighborhood called Garden Oaks. Billy Lawrence had made a new friend named Elmer Wayne Henley, Jr., that spring—and then disappeared in June, though his father, a pressman at the *Houston Post,* had not yet reported him missing.

Wayne, still shirtless, barefoot, and dazed, was sitting outside on a stoop with his friends when Patrolman Jamison arrived. He seemed in shock. Though reeling from the intoxicants in his system and the murder he'd just committed, the Texas teenager minded his manners, addressing the officer as "sir." As a small boy, he'd played in the Heights Little League and made good grades before dropping out of junior high at fourteen, around the time his parents separated. The divorce went through in March 1970.

From 1971 to 1973, Wayne had been hanging out with this middle-aged mystery man, guzzling beer and moonshine, smoking pot, and huffing spray-paint fumes. He preferred Corll to his father, who had once shot at Wayne after he bragged that he, only a kid, was bringing home more cash.

Even before he killed Dean Corll, Wayne seemed unhinged in the summer of 1973. Many other Americans were engrossed in the details of the ongoing investigations of a burglary at the Watergate Hotel that seemed poised to take down the Nixon administration, or excited about the upcoming "Battle of the Sexes" tennis match between Billie Jean King and Bobby Riggs at the Houston Astrodome, then the world's largest air-conditioned stadium. Wayne Henley was preoccupied with personal concerns. That summer, he had been practicing shooting pistols at a range, learning judo moves, and claiming his life was in danger. He confided his dark ambitions to a few close friends: He wanted to be "a hitman." One night, Wayne ran around a Heights park chasing friends and yelling, "I'm going to give you to Dean."

Henley's green eyes were glazed as he spoke to Jamison. He slurred his words and cried as he confessed to killing Corll. Then he told the patrolman he had something else to get off his chest.

"Dean told me about a warehouse he had rented," Wayne said, the word coming out as *warhouse* in his Texas twang. Then he offered a chilling claim: That shed was filled with the bodies of murdered boys. "And I can show you where it is."

CHAPTER 2

A ROOMFUL OF MYSTERIES

HARRIS COUNTY MEDICAL EXAMINER'S OFFICE,
2006

Dr. Sharon Derrick
PHOTO TEXAS A&M UNIVERSITY–CORPUS CHRISTI

DR. SHARON DERRICK, PH.D., tugged open the sliding metal door and felt a blast of cold air as she stepped inside the long-term storage vault at the Harris County ME's office, a three-story brick edifice on the edge of Texas Medical Center. The careful and determined scientist entered the chamber, kept at a bone-chilling 40 degrees, filled with body bags and cardboard cartons containing the remains and effects of more than a hundred unidentified people—the department's oldest and most perplexing unsolved identity cases. Some of these people's remains had been collected after accidents or found on roadsides without wallets or witnesses. Many were victims of unsolved murders or suicides who had long ago been autopsied, but still had nooses stored in their body bags or bullet holes in their skulls. A few had been discovered without any possessions at all; others remained here with their cowboy boots, wallets, party dresses, lockets, or wallets beside them.

Derrick, forty-nine years old and standing all of five feet three, edged past the rows of bagged corpses reclining on rows of metal shelves that stretched far above her head all the way to the ceiling. The thin plastic of her disposable autopsy gown offered little protection from the cold, but she felt a thrill of anticipation. For Derrick, an aspiring forensic anthropologist, this room contained enticing mysteries. By examining these boxes, bones, and bodies, she hoped to discover clues that could unlock the lost identities of these men, women, and children, though the conditions here were decidedly uninviting. It didn't help that the room's vintage 1980s heating and cooling system constantly leaked: "There was condensation dripping down from the ceiling so when you went in there you got wet. The body bags had a sheen on them."

Time seemed suspended or irrelevant in this frigid, surreal space. Even in the 2000s, the chamber still resembled the set of a 1960s TV detective drama, with mint-green walls and a darker emerald acrylic floor. Derrick could easily pull out sliding removable metal trays to zip open and examine the contents of each of the body bags and then use labels to locate records for the corresponding medicolegal cases and autopsy photos in the office's vast paper archives or in its computerized scanned records. But these shelves were so full of long-term occupants that many newer arrivals remained stored on gurneys, which meant Derrick had to weave her way through them, pushing some aside in order to unzip other bags and inspect their contents. Some corpses still looked like waxy sleeping versions of the people whose lives had been tragically lost. Others, after as many as four decades, had begun to assume rather unworldly forms. "I was not having any problems with current fleshed remains . . . but these people were just awful looking—big cauliflower-like growths, waxy fish skin . . . for someone who had never worked in that area it was disturbing," she remembers.

Derrick, an ambitious working mom, was already an experienced bioarchaeologist with a Ph.D. But she was new to the Harris County Medical Examiner's Office in the spring of 2006 and had only recently begun training to become a full-fledged forensic anthropologist. She was eager to prove herself in her newly chosen field, though some relatives worried about her, wondering aloud how she could spend so much time with the dead. "Maybe it's a quirk in my personality," she'd say. Born into a family of musicians, Derrick had gravitated early toward science, and she found a talent for focusing intently and clinically on bones and bodies to unlock their secrets. To succeed, she had to be hyperalert: Key clues to a lost identity could be as subtle as the shape of the molars inside a skull, a faded label hidden inside a pair of pants, a telling tattoo, the curve of a pelvis, or the precise form and length of a long bone.

One of her first assignments at the ME's office was to inventory and examine the bones and bodies connected to cold cases, most of which had been found before DNA was available as a tool for identifications, and to collect samples for new genetic tests. The eventual goal was to "clear out" the mysterious unidentified remains inside this institutional cavern—and return at least some people to their families for proper burial. That task seemed overwhelming. In addition to the one hundred unnamed individuals here, three hundred more had been buried in graves marked only with numbers in the Harris County Cemetery, established in 1904 on a desolate patch of land along Oates Road on what was then the "Poor Farm" and became the last resting place for both the anonymous and the unclaimed dead.

Prior to her arrival at one of America's largest medical examiner's offices, Derrick had probed and exhumed the contents of many centuries-old graves. As a grad student, she'd viewed skulls and skeletons of early settlers and of Native Americans on digs across Texas and had studied the way cradleboards created holes in the backs of the skulls of infants in ancient Caddo burial mounds. That work had been deeply engrossing. After earning her doctorate in 2002, Derrick had chosen to study more modern deaths and leave prehistory to others. Her first job had been leading a team at the Harris County Health Department that reviewed troubling unnatural deaths among children, in an effort to find ways to prevent tragedies like teen suicides and fatal child abuse. It was during that period she'd met Dr. Luis A. Sanchez, M.D., a forensic pathologist for Harris County, and when he later became Chief Medical Examiner, she had convinced him to employ her in order to help tackle this very problem: the backlog of unidentified dead.

She had sought out Sanchez at meetings, buttonholed him with smiles and small talk, and engaged him in discussions of how an anthropologist—like her—could help resolve Harris County's lost identity cases. Her arguments seemed to sink in, especially after a San Antonio medical examiner's official failed to consult an anthropologist, publicly declared an unidentified woman's skeleton to be male, and earned embarrassing publicity for his gaffe.

Derrick had already excavated archaeological graves and attended autopsies with no signs of queasiness. Yet her introduction to the unusual occupants of the ME's long-term storage chamber felt unsettling. "I had not worked with a lot of bodies where only refrigerated decomposed flesh remained," she recalls. Despite its fluorescent lighting and frequent cleanings, the room still seemed dark. "It was creepy."

But she felt a surge of excitement about her mission here. Like others in the business of investigating untimely or unnatural death, Derrick saw the restoration of identities as one of the highest callings of forensic science. Rediscovering lost names for these people, she knew, could provide answers and sometimes solace to waiting families and, in some cases, revive or resolve stalled murder investigations. Indeed, forensic anthropologists' efforts to supply names to the deceased often represent "the victim's last chance to be heard, to reveal a major insight into how a person lived or perhaps how she died," wrote Douglas Ubelaker, a senior scientist at the Smithsonian Institution who was one of the pioneers in his field. "Sometimes their last words speak not only for the victim but for society and we ignore them at our peril."

These bones and bodies were part of a tremendous problem that some called the nation's "Silent Mass Disaster." Across the country, remains belonging to more than forty thousand lost identity cases were stored in morgues and unmarked graves with only case numbers to mark their time on earth. Criminal justice experts warned the tremendous backlog of unsolved cases allowed too many murder victims to remain unidentified—and serial killers to remain undetected. In many other U.S. counties, records and remains of unknown persons were often buried and forgotten, and got lost or misplaced over time. But when Derrick first arrived in 2006, Harris County ME had documentation on more than four hundred open identification cases, what some called John, Jane, and Baby Does. (That outdated terminology had been banned by the decree of Chief Medical Examiner Sanchez, who considered the use of "Doe" unprofessional and dehumanizing to the dead.)

Harris County has one of the nation's oldest professional county medical examiner's offices—and one of the biggest backlogs of unidentified remains. The office, founded in 1957, had been led for many years by a legendary chief medical examiner with a law degree from Boston College and a medical degree from Harvard: Dr. Joseph Jachimczyk (pronounced YA-him-chick). Many of the bones and bodies had been stored here under "Dr. Joe" and later by his successors in the hopes that one day new clues—or scientific breakthroughs—would help restore their identities.

DNA had been available for criminal investigations since the late 1980s, but into the 1990s and early 2000s it remained difficult to extract usable DNA profiles for identification purposes from such cold cases. Fortunately, by the time Derrick arrived in 2006, DNA tests and lab techniques had gotten more powerful. Tiny amounts of different types of DNA could be extracted and then replicated from inside molars or the shafts of long bones to produce genetic profiles that could then be compared to potential relatives (or descendants), even for decades-old or degraded remains. (Indeed, mitochondrial DNA collected from ancient mummies and Ice Men had been analyzed.) Still, obtaining DNA profiles from older remains could be costly and time-consuming for a cash-strapped county government—especially if an exhumation was required to retrieve a tissue or bone sample. Many of these cold cases seemed hopeless.

Harris County's oldest unsolved identity case from June 1964 involved the torso of a dark-haired man, nicknamed Old Stubby, who'd been decapitated and dismembered, likely with a hatchet or an ax, and discarded in a ditch near the Jones Creek Bridge in an apparent organized crime hit. The files were full of tips that had led nowhere, including the rumor that Old Stubby might have been a mafia boss, perhaps tied to Jimmy Hoffa, the powerful Teamsters union president who disappeared in 1975. After decades of attempts ended in failure, Dr. Joe and most of the staff attended a ceremony in the county cemetery in November 1984, after which Old Stubby's remains were interred in one of the many plots marked with square stones and etched with case numbers. "In my heart of hearts, I feel we've done everything humanly possible," Jachimczyk told a reporter that day. "Now I'll know that whoever he is and whatever he did, at least he's had a decent burial. If the shoe were on the other foot, God forbid, I hope someone would put me away, too." Eleven years later, Dr. Joe retired, leaving these unresolved identifications to the next generation.

DERRICK KNEW THAT SOME lost souls stuck in storage were the victims of serial killers. *The Texas Chainsaw Massacre*'s cinematic carnage was fiction, but Angel Maturino Resendiz, the mentally disturbed Railroad Killer; Henry Lee Lucas, the violent pathological liar known as the Confession Killer; and a demented serial strangler named Carl Eugene Watts all claimed victims in Houston. Next to the vault filled with body bags, an adjacent room contained shelves filled with dozens of boxes containing unidentified skeletal remains, property, and clothing, many of which had been relocated there in 1985 after the county's original morgue closed.

In one of her early forays, Derrick spotted a series of corrugated brown shipping boxes on a shelf just below her eye level. They were labeled with the year 1973. "I immediately gravitated toward those three boxes," she recalls. When she peeked inside, she knew right away that these "were boxes of young male bones. One had what looked like a complete set of skeletal remains." Her discovery felt personal and intensely disturbing. "Each of them said 'Houston Mass Murders,' and I immediately clicked back to when I was in high school." She recognized this real-life Texas horror story: These were the victims of Dean Corll, the so-called Candy Man, who'd gained the title of the nation's most prolific modern killer in August 1973.

Those cartons contained the bones and effects of the Lost Boys, some of the twenty-seven adolescent boys and young men known to have been killed by Corll and his two teenaged henchmen in the 1970s. Derrick felt stunned. *They still have remains from that case? Those boys still haven't been identified?*

Many of Corll's victims came from a neighborhood she knew well: Houston Heights.

SHARON MCCORMICK (DERRICK), A child of the 1960s and 1970s herself, grew up in a bucolic family compound north of the Austin city limits in a house her father built. She was by far the youngest of the five McCormick siblings. Yet this coddled child, through happenstance, had been affected early and often by violent death.

Her paternal grandfather, S. C. McCormick, whom she never knew, had been shot and killed in June 1920 by a Black man while serving an arrest warrant as a volunteer deputy sheriff in Wharton County. The homicide in that sparsely populated and heavily segregated rice-growing area had unleashed a mob of 250 who carried out a horrifying round of retaliatory murders, gunning down the triggerman and his brother and lynching two of their friends. Young Sharon McCormick heard those disturbing tales from her father, who'd been only a boy at the time. In the aftermath, her father rapidly relocated more than fifty miles northeast to Houston, where he later dropped out of school to work as a tile setter to support his widowed mother. Yet in a way, murder had enabled her parents to meet, since otherwise her father might never have left Wharton at all.

Her mom and dad were married in a church in the Heights, where her mother's family, the Morses, had lived for three generations.

WHEN SHE FIRST LEARNED of the devastation that could be caused by a single prolific killer, Sharon was a charming child who played the flute, wore plaid jumpers, and pulled her hair up into long side ponytails. Her older brother was attending the University of Texas at Austin and her sister was working there on the day Charles Whitman climbed into the UT bell tower and opened fire in August 1966, killing fourteen and wounding another thirty-one—shocking the nation with the highest death toll caused by a mass shooter in a single incident up to that time. Sharon knew a student whose fiancé died in the melee—that young woman's finger had been blown off when she reached for her beloved.

A few years later, in her junior high days, another friend's sister committed suicide, prompting Sharon, preternaturally curious about death, to pose probing questions that adults seemed reluctant to answer.

As an older teen, Sharon often stayed up late at slumber parties with her best friend Susan, watching *Saturday Night Live* and late-night horror films on TV. Their favorite was a campy 1967 spoof by director Roman Polanski called *The Fearless Vampire Killers,* featuring actors with oily pompadours and capes cavorting through a haunted castle. One over-the-top scene featured the actress Sharon Tate sprouting fangs and taking a bite from the exposed neck of her hapless would-be savior (a role Polanski played). The on-screen chemistry Sharon McCormick noticed between those two actors was real: Tate married Polanski in 1968.

Teenaged Sharon McCormick knew Tate only from TV, yet she felt a strong connection—they shared the same name and similar roots. Sharon Tate spent her formative years in Texas too. As an eight-month-old, Tate had been named Miss Tiny Tot in a Dallas pageant. She'd moved often as the daughter of a U.S. Army officer, attending high schools in Pasadena and Dallas, and as an actress, she displayed a decidedly Texan sense of style. In the film, her blond updo, impeccable makeup, and glamor held up no matter what the vampires or stooge-like vampire hunters did or said. That familiar film lost all of its allure in August 1969, when Tate, eight months pregnant with her first child, was slain by real monsters: members of the Manson family who invaded her California home in one of their infamous "creepy crawly" raids and painted the word PIG on a wall in the dead actress's blood. Sharon McCormick felt those losses deeply. "We had watched that movie so many times, and then she was killed . . ."

Sharon attended David Crockett High School in Austin from 1970 to 1973, marching in the band and later switching to drill team to perform in go-go boots as a "Tex-Ann." Her musically inclined family was astonished by her choice: the youngest McCormick had never mastered the flute and wasn't much better at dancing. All of her parents' musical genes seemed to have gone to her brothers, two of whom played in bands professionally, while she struggled to keep a beat. But the fun of her high school years was marred by yet another tragedy right after Christmas 1972. Some of her classmates were en route home from a Baptist youth gathering in New Mexico when an eighteen-wheel cattle truck jackknifed on a bridge, striking their bus and killing sixteen teens and three adults. One of the victims had been in Sharon's gym class. She inherited clothing from another dead girl who happened to share her size. A boy she knew was left grieving for his twin, and another survivor showed up at school in a wheelchair with a broken leg. Some five thousand people attended a public memorial service in Austin, then a city of 250,000. Crockett High, named for Davy Crockett, a frontiersman and perhaps the most famous of the fighters killed at the Alamo, erected a monument to those who died on that bus.

But young Sharon McCormick felt a particularly strong jolt from homicidal violence on the sweltering summer morning in August 1973 when she ran out to grab the family's rolled-up copy of the *Austin American-Statesman*. She unfurled the newspaper and was struck to see yearbook photos of handsome boys about her own age on the front page. All of them were dead. They had all been tortured, raped, and killed by a man named Dean Corll. Teenaged Sharon went on to read all she could about Corll's crimes. The term "serial killer" did not yet exist, so police kept calling them the "Houston Mass Murders" and journalists began referring to the victims as the "Lost Boys." Heartbreaking interviews appeared with some boys' parents; others remained nameless. Two of Corll's accomplices were teenagers too: Wayne Henley and David Brooks.

This tragedy didn't seem at all distant to her. These murdered teens were mostly from the Heights, the same neighborhood where her parents had met and her grandparents had lived. Her paternal aunt and uncle and a band of boy cousins still hosted family gatherings at their bungalow in Oak Forest, a neighborhood just north of there. Sharon devoured those stories and stared at the boys' school portraits. From that moment, she began forging a personal connection with the Lost Boys that deepened over time. "They were all so young," she recalled. "And some looked like the handsome long-haired boys I liked to date in high school."

The news about that Houston case kept getting worse. In a few days of gruesome excavations, the body count swelled to twenty-seven males, aged thirteen to twenty. Texas Rangers, local news reporters, and national anchors all began describing this as the deadliest documented murder spree in modern American history: Corll had surpassed even the death toll of Juan Vallejo Corona, convicted in 1971 of slaying twenty-five migrant farmworkers and burying their bodies in California peach orchards. The Houston Mass Murders quickly went international. Pope Paul VI sent his sympathy to victims' families, while the Vatican newspaper described the slayings as a horror "in the domain of the devil." The Kremlin issued a statement distributed by United Press International that condemned American decadence. By early 1974, Truman Capote, a celebrity writer considered a true crime expert after *In Cold Blood*, turned up in a dark gray suit and matching fedora on assignment to cover the case for *The Washington Post*.

Still, many things about Dean Corll remained unclear: Had Corll killed only twenty-seven victims, as authorities concluded after ending searches for graves in just four days? Or were there at least forty, as Henley's defense attorney later claimed? Houston's police chief and Harris County's DA had pushed to quickly close the cases and end the barrage of negative attention as a "Murdertown" on a place so proud of its status as America's Space City and as the Oil Capital of the World.

As decades passed, the many mysteries surrounding Dean Corll only deepened: The *whodunit* transformed into a *whowerethey*.

OF COURSE, IN HER school days, Sharon McCormick never dreamed she'd play any role in that infamous murder case. In college, she initially focused on a possible career in journalism or in anthropology, and then deferred those career plans after falling in love with Al Derrick, a co-worker at a popular Austin café, a hot spot frequented by Willie Nelson and other outlaw country musicians. She was a hostess; he was a busboy. Back then, Al wore his hair long and charmed her with tales of crazy adventures, including a summer of camping, hiking, and scuba diving on remote beaches in Hawaii. Al's more rebellious older brother had run away twice—hopping on a plane by himself and traveling out of state. But like most teenagers, Al and his brother survived their risk-taking years. These Lost Boys had been deprived of the chance to live into their own adulthoods.

Now, years later, as an aspiring forensic anthropologist, Sharon Derrick was in a position to help them. She soon became engaged in this compelling upside-down murder mystery: The serial killer had been quickly identified, but for three decades, the identities of some of his victims remained unknown.

Derrick felt a pang of sorrow as she lifted the lids of the boxes and got her first look at the weathered bones and scraps of clothing inside that had belonged to boys who, like her, were teens in the 1970s, but never got any older. She could easily imagine their world: Texas in the Age of Aquarius—when teens wore bell-bottom jeans and hip boots and listened to Creedence Clearwater Revival, her own favorite band of that era. She knew that DNA and other advanced forensic techniques available to her hadn't been around in the 1970s. But even in the 2000s, DNA was primarily useful as an identification tool only *after* an unidentified person's closest prospective relatives had already been discovered and convinced to cooperate. To verify any ID, Derrick would also have to locate parents or siblings, close relatives who would share similar patterns with a decedent's nuclear or mitochondrial DNA profile. The ranges needed to establish what scientists call "relatedness" varied, but generally mothers or fathers are preferred since a child inherits 50 percent of their DNA from each parent; Derrick knew that would be challenging, given the age of these cases.

Still, it perplexed her that these particular teens had not been identified long ago. Most of Corll's known victims had been kidnapped and killed in a relatively compact area: the Heights and surrounding neighborhoods like Spring Branch, Garden Oaks, and Oak Forest. All of her life, Derrick had visited relatives in those same places. Certainly the Heights, which had again become fashionable in the 2000s, had experienced a slump in the 1970s, but even in those tough years, many Heights families still owned their bungalows and knew their neighbors. *Why had no one ever recognized these boys and reclaimed them?*

Some of the boys' belongings seemed straight out of a 1970s time capsule. She spotted scraps of bedraggled bell-bottom jeans, a shirt with a peace sign on its pocket, and what looked like a surfer's knotted jute bracelet tucked beside bones inside those boxes. One of the 1973 boxes contained a particularly confusing mixture of bones and odd items, including a stray piece of women's hosiery as well as other bones that seemed to come from more than one teenager or perhaps an unrelated homicide case. Another held the bones of a boy who once wore a T-shirt with an elaborate U.S. Marine Corps decal with the hand-drawn black letters LA4MF, possibly sketched by someone in a unit deployed to Vietnam. That insignia, one veteran later told her, might refer to a dark joke: "Late for my funeral." Inside that same box was a pair of faded Catalina swimming trunks with red, blue, and gold stripes that eventually earned this murder victim a nickname in the press: Swimsuit Boy.

Despite efforts in the 1970s and subsequent advances in forensics, no one had been able to use this evidence to find these victims' families and restore their names. Derrick knew her own attempts to reexamine these bones and get a lab to extract DNA samples might be the last hope. Some mothers and fathers, likely in their seventies now, could still be waiting and able to provide comparison DNA samples. But time was running out to obtain answers for people who had loved these boys most and known them best. Without more clues—and prospective relatives willing to cooperate—the task might prove impossible. Still Derrick, a fundamentally optimistic person, remained full of hope. "I felt such compassion for them and for their families," she remembers. "I thought that if I had the ability to give their identities back to them, that would feel good." Derrick drew inspiration from her own mother, a bold and determined woman with five children, who had never been able to attend college but had somehow managed to become an Austin schoolteacher and eventually an administrative assistant by working hard, projecting confidence—and aiming high.

Derrick turned her attention to the third box, which held what seemed like the most promising collection of clues. It contained skeletal remains and a fairly complete set of clothing, including that shirt with the peace sign, a dark long-sleeved uniform jacket like the ones gas station attendants wore back when Americans rarely pumped their own, and a pair of well-worn leather boots.

Something about that case called to Derrick. She would begin her quest with this boy—and his boots.

DERRICK HAD HER OWN private office in the Harris County ME's brick building in the Texas Medical Center and, from the beginning, had to borrow time to work on cold cases in between newly arriving assignments, including examining the unidentified remains of recent or recently discovered accident, homicide, and suicide victims. The first bone case she handled turned out to be a "trophy skull" that someone had hauled home after World War II as a souvenir and stashed away for half a century.

As the weeks and months passed, identifying the Lost Boys turned into her mission, an unofficial second job. Derrick became deeply enmeshed in their lives, reading the small, often blurred font of copies of carbon copies of typewritten case reports, deciphering hand-written notes, and gazing at autopsy photos late into the night in bed at home. She kept the school portraits and family snapshots of missing and murdered boys on her computer, frequently gazing at their faces. When she reflected years later on the bond she formed with the victims, she sounded a little like a girl with a crush: "These boys are sort of in my age bracket, right, and they're the kind of boys that I was always attracted to in high school. So now they're still living for me—only they're forever fifteen, sixteen, and seventeen like those boys in the pictures. When I talk to their families, it's like they're really still here. And I know that sounds really weird, but they're here for me, and I can't even picture them with silver hair and older. They died beautiful and young."

Derrick came to consider the Lost Boys and their elusive relatives part of her own world. To her, they were not mere case numbers. They were individuals who deserved to be restored to their families and friends. She made her own copies of the 1973 Houston homicide reports and took them home. Night after night, she scanned type-written passages, scribbled her own notes, and identified clues that might help her tie a set of lonely bones to a missing boy. Soon the story became so familiar that she could quote portions of detectives' narratives by heart.

CHAPTER 3

THE BODIES IN THE BOATSHED

HOUSTON, AUGUST 8, 1973

DETECTIVE DAVID MULLICAN PULLED up to Lamar Drive in a boxy black-and-white sedan on the morning of August 8. He didn't bother with a siren. By then, Officer Jamison had already loaded Wayne Henley, along with Tim and Rhonda, into the back of his patrol car; he briefed Mullican, handed over the murder weapon, then hauled them down to police headquarters. The police in Pasadena, an industrialized community of ninety thousand—a fraction of Houston's size—would take the lead on what initially seemed like a routine case.

The three youths soon arrived at the station, a no-frills brick building inside the city's municipal complex, and were immediately taken before a magistrate, who'd been summoned that day specifically to advise them of their rights. All agreed to cooperate without an attorney present. Then they waited, sweating and anxious, while Mullican surveyed the crime scene and then returned to separately interview each one.

In those interviews, Rhonda Williams and Tim Kerley mostly backed up Wayne Henley's story of self-defense, each painting him as the fearless boy who'd faced down a monster and saved them. Tim, a Southern Baptist raised on sermons of fire and brimstone, described Dean Corll as demonic. Rhonda saw Wayne, whom she'd first met as a little girl, as a hero. But there were murky undertones to the typed sworn statements that they each signed that morning.

Other kids in the Heights knew Rhonda as a wild beauty and the hard-partying daughter of a notorious neighborhood drunk. In her version of events, Wayne had responded to her pleas and delivered them from Dean Corll. After Corll finally fell, "Tim started yelling 'Thank you for saving my life!'" Rhonda said, and then both boys— not her—began to cry. Wayne hadn't wanted to kill his friend, she said. "Wayne told us that it was a matter of either us being killed by Dean or him killing Dean." But Rhonda did not mention another story to Pasadena detectives that day which might have cast doubt on Wayne's heroic status: Frank Aguirre, her previous boyfriend and fiancé, had mysteriously disappeared back in March 1972 after finishing his shift at the Long John Silver's restaurant on Yale Street in the Heights and then accepting an invitation to party with Wayne. Nor did Rhonda reveal right away that her current beau had told her several times to "forget about Frank because he was never coming back."

Tim agreed that Wayne Henley had saved his life: Corll was attempting to rape and murder him, before Wayne gunned him down. "I knew Dean was going to kill us. . . . It was going to be my time." But once Tim was alone, the burly twenty-year-old shared a troubling prelude to that homicidal encounter.

On the night of August 7, he'd driven Wayne Henley to 2020 Lamar in his VW Beetle, a gift from doting parents who hoped their talented son would straighten out, stop drinking, and become a preacher or maybe a pianist in a gospel group. (He'd already wrecked his previous car in a drunk-driving crash.) They'd partied at Corll's awhile, then gone to the Heights to pick up Rhonda in the wee hours of August 8. Before returning to Pasadena, Wayne had given one of his seemingly nonsensical speeches. "He was talking to me and asking me if I knew of any young white men that were fairly good-looking and could be missing without anybody raising too much of a fuss," Tim said. "Another time he said if I wasn't his friend, he could get $1,500 for me. . . . I was kinda messed up and really wasn't paying much attention to what he was saying, but he said that I was the only one who knew about this and that he better not hear of me saying anything to anybody." Tim said he closed that conversation by telling Wayne: "I didn't know anybody I would do that to, but that I didn't care what he did as long as nothing happened to me."

Tim's statement didn't make much sense to Pasadena investigators, not at first anyway.

Wayne would quickly be cleared of Dean Corll's murder: The homicide by multiple gunshot wounds was declared to be justifiable, a clear-cut case of self-defense. Indeed, Wayne might have gone free if only he'd remained silent. But Wayne Henley had always been a talker.

It was about ninety minutes after Corll's violent death when Wayne hunkered down in a booth in the squad room to face the steady gaze of Detective Sergeant David Mullican. A seasoned homicide investigator, Mullican was a dark-haired, authoritative man in his thirties who wore long sideburns and had served in the military; superficially he resembled Dean Corll. The officer, skilled at using his small-town East Texas roots to charm people, easily established a rapport with Wayne, who quickly came to see the officer as more of an advisor than an adversary.

Wayne told Mullican that he first met Dean Corll in 1970 through his junior high chum David Brooks, who at sixteen had gotten a gleaming lime-green Corvette as a gift from Corll. "Dean was a lot older than me," Wayne said. "David was always riding around in Dean's car and everything. I was only fourteen back then and I thought this was great." Wayne wanted in.

His father was gone by then and Wayne was hustling for ways to help keep his mother, grandmother, and little brothers afloat. At first, he sold stolen goods to Corll for cash. But then he matter-of-factly told Mullican that Dean Corll also "belonged to an organization out of Dallas that bought and sold boys, ran whores and stuff like that. Dean told me that he would pay me two hundred dollars for every boy I could get for him and maybe more if they were real good-looking boys. . . . I decided that I could use the money to get better things for my people so one day I went over to Dean's apartment on Schuler Street and told him I would find a boy for him."

Wayne was vague, at first, about which boys he'd found for Corll.

Detective Mullican pretended to calmly accept these ramblings, though he initially assumed the far-fetched stories must be a troubled teen's dark fantasy. Mullican, who had children of his own, had a quick mind and an intense crime-fighting focus that kicked in as he learned more about this confounding case. He and his partner, Detective Sidney Smith, soon realized that this matter was far more complex than the fatal shooting of a pervert, the terse summary police dispatchers had provided to beat reporters earlier that morning.

Wayne's hands shook. He suffered from asthma and his breathing was heavy, but he seemed to get more comfortable as he kept talking. He told Mullican that Dean Corll had specifically requested he bring Tim Kerley in order to have "unnatural sex acts with him." Then Wayne returned to a topic he'd mentioned at the crime scene. "Dean told me about a warehouse he had over on Hiram Clark where he had killed some boys and buried them after he had sex with them."

That same afternoon Detective Mullican typed up different versions of Elmer Wayne Henley's statement on a manual typewriter, as Henley kept adding details and his story grew more complex and conflicted.

Wayne had lived nearly his entire life in his maternal grandparents' squat bungalow in the Heights, where his parents had moved to raise him and his three younger brothers. He hesitated to mention that several boys he'd grown up with had recently disappeared. But he later told Mullican that he feared neighborhood friends had been killed and buried in Corll's rented warehouse stall. He first named David Hilligiest, his friend since preschool days who'd gone missing in 1971, along with Malley Winkle (both boys lived only a block or two from the Henleys' place) and then Charles Cobble and Marty Jones, teens his own age, who shared a Heights apartment. Later he mentioned more former Hamilton Junior High classmates: Frank Aguirre and Mark Scott, both missing since 1972.

Mullican finished his first round of questions, compared Wayne's statements (different versions, one with suspected murder victims' names and one without) to those made by Rhonda and Tim, and then contacted the Houston Police Department. HPD officials quickly responded. Incredibly, Houston officers had not noticed any unusual cluster of adolescent abductions in the Heights, though the boys Henley named had been reported missing. Only the recent disappearances of Charles Cobble and his roommate Marty Jones, two weeks prior, were the subject of an open HPD homicide case. Officers were investigating that matter as a possible drug-related double murder, since both teens had called their parents to say they were in trouble and needed money fast. That case had a personal connection to HPD: Marty was the cousin of a Houston homicide detective.

Mullican remained skeptical about Wayne Henley's credibility. But as he pondered the teen's strange claims, he began to wonder if the state's largest police force had missed a massive murder spree until the killer himself had been gunned down on his turf. Wayne clearly saw himself as the savior of his friends. Yet Mullican thought Wayne knew far too much about these missing boys.

DETECTIVES MULLICAN AND SMITH began making necessary arrangements. They would need Houston officers' cooperation and the owner's consent (or a warrant) to search the rented stall inside metal commercial storage units on Silver Bell Drive where Wayne Henley claimed Dean Corll had created a clandestine cemetery. By 5 P.M. on the day of Corll's death everything came together; Mullican and Smith drove Wayne in their squad car toward the Southwest Boat and Storage Facility, an unremarkable address on a dead-end street. Smith wore dark oversized sunglasses to protect his eyes against the blazing afternoon sun as they headed west across the Houston city limits. Patrolmen and several HPD homicide detectives were already waiting, their attention finally attracted by the names of so many missing teens.

The owner, an elderly woman who occupied a ramshackle house on-site, described Dean Corll as a pleasant client who paid his bills on time—and had recently inquired about renting another unit, since his space had gotten full. She didn't have the key, but gave officers permission to break in after learning Corll had been killed. Then she pointed out Stall No. 11 inside an oversized L-shaped metal barn.

Wayne Henley's story of a shed full of bodies still seemed impossible to believe, until a Houston policeman lifted a bolt cutter to remove the padlock and swung open the door and Mullican caught a whiff from the interior: the unmistakable "odor of decaying flesh."

Wayne Henley blanched and reeled around, refusing to enter.

The scent of human death, cloyingly sweet and simultaneously sour, grew stronger as Mullican and other officers entered the confined space at 5:30 P.M. that Wednesday. Inside, investigators encountered a strange mixture of errata: bags of lime, two short-handled shovels, a garden rake with a broken handle, and assorted metal washtubs. Way in the back was a Chevy Camaro, stripped to its shell. (A check of the plate revealed it had been reported stolen that February from a suburban Katy, Texas, auto dealership.) Near the entrance, a boy's red bike with a long banana-style seat tilted against the wall. The floor surrounding the bike was lined with a strip of royal-blue carpet, and just beyond, officers noticed that portions of the hard-packed dirt and oyster-shell floor appeared "cracked and

Officers entering Corll's boatshed in 1973

raised," as one wrote. The earth here had been disturbed and de-formed into a series of odd-shaped humps.

Inside the stifling shed, a cluster of homicide detectives wore suits, though some doffed their jackets in the afternoon heat. The temperature on that long August afternoon hit 90 degrees. The sweating officers initially figured they were here to supervise, exam-ine evidence, take photos, and write reports. Low-risk inmates known as trusties wearing bright white coveralls had been sprung from the Harris County Jail to dig up the hard-packed clay soil with garden spades and wheelbarrows. At the time, the Harris County Medical Examiner's Office, busy with the Bayou City's usual influx of unnatural deaths, lacked sufficient funds and manpower to dis-patch its own death investigators to any one scene full time. Soon detectives wearing neatly pressed shirts and wide striped ties would be forced to step into the holes to assist the diggers.

HPD homicide detective Karl Siebeneicher sported a polished pair of dress shoes that quickly became stained with sticky, foul-smelling soil. Siebeneicher was filled with dread. He knew he might soon unearth the remains of his missing cousin Marty: Wayne Hen-ley had hinted to Mullican that both Marty Jones, eighteen, and Charles Cobble, seventeen, had been buried here in a single grave, with their bodies "tied together in a single piece of plastic."

Another homicide detective, Larry Earls, began to chain-smoke, anything to get rid of the pervasive scent—and taste—of decay from corpses that seemed to be actively decomposing inside this shed. His hands soon became so filthy that he had someone else put the cigarettes in his mouth. Corll had been renting this stall since De-cember 1970. But based on the dates of their missing persons cases, some of the freshest graves had been dug in July or early August—only days or weeks before, in the hottest days of Houston's long and brutal summers.

A crowd of reporters and gawkers, alerted by dispatches on squawking police radio channels, soon gathered at the isolated property, only blocks away from one of the buzzing and glowing ar-rays of towers and coils of Houston Lighting & Power's southwest switching station, an outpost where Corll had sometimes worked.

There was no police tape to keep curiosity seekers from stepping onto private property to peer inside the shed's open doors. As word spread, mayors and police officers and other dignitaries uninvolved in the case arrived to tour the gruesome scene. Some journalists boldly stepped inside to snap photos and film video as trusties poked their shovels into cracks in the soil beyond the blue carpet. One digger gagged from the smell, turned away from his grisly task, and asked to be taken back to jail. For the first thirty minutes, others steadily filled wheelbarrows with piles of shells from the floor and bits of Houston's unusually dense, clay-rich, sticky gumbo soil beneath.

To homicide detectives, the smell of human decomposition was unmistakable, evoking other scenes of violent death and heartbreak and simultaneously triggering a rise of bile in the back of the throat. Mentally, a few began to brace themselves for the sight of murdered children—among the most disturbing spectacles that may appear at a crime scene. But even veteran officers were entirely unprepared for the horrors they would find beneath this uneven ground. Though they'd read about other prolific so-called "mass murderers," the concept of a "serial killer," a violent criminal who stalked and slew other human beings for sexual motives, was as yet undiscovered. An FBI agent's invention of that term was a decade away. None but the war veterans among them had previously seen so many young men felled by violence in one place.

At a depth of about 18 inches, they spotted the first corpse wrapped in a clear plastic bag near the front of the shed. These remains retained the shape of a young boy's body, his decayed face bound in layers of tape. In life he'd been slim, but this corpse had bloated from waste gases accumulated after a few searing August days. Even inside that relatively fresh grave, the murdered boy's face was unrecognizable. His pale blond hair, altered by the clay and decomposition gases, had turned strawberry red, complicating his identification. But the bike beside his grave had a license number affixed to the frame. This dead boy was not one of the Houston teenagers Wayne Henley had already named. That red bicycle, with a customized handlebar and modified seat, belonged to thirteen-year-old James Stanton Dreymala, reported missing from his south Houston home on August 3, 1973—only five days before.

Stanton, as family and friends called him, had set out around dusk that Friday on his unusual bike, which he'd found and rebuilt with a neighborhood buddy. He told his mother he planned to visit a nearby convenience store to gather returnable glass bottles and redeem them for a nickel deposit apiece. He'd already saved enough to take his first girlfriend to the new James Bond movie, *Live and Let Die.* He wanted to impress the girl he'd met at church camp by collecting more for a special gift. He'd pedaled down the street toward a corner store and disappeared, much later making calls home and to friends to say he'd been invited to a party.

There was one small mercy for Stanton's devastated parents: They would not have to wait long before authorities identified their son. Fingerprints collected by investigators from bicycle handlebars and from furniture inside his childhood bedroom did not clearly match those on this body, which had decomposed rapidly in Houston's intense heat. But the dental records his parents supplied did. None of the fingertips from the other boys' remains recovered here would yield any usable prints. Some waxy and disintegrating corpses, wrapped in plastic, tied with nylon ropes, and doused with lime, had been stashed away here for more than two years. Many had been stripped before burial, with bodies buried faceup or contorted in a fetal position.

Inside this strange packaging, some boys were only bones.

Police now had proof to corroborate Henley's horrific tale. They also knew the identity of the mastermind: Dean Corll. The investigative challenge would be in determining the victims' identities and in discovering how Corll managed to snatch so many teens from the same Houston neighborhoods without attracting suspicion or raising alarm. Even on that first night, diggers found more bodies than the victims Wayne Henley had named.

Officers tolerated the mass of camera-toting journalists swarming around the crime scene. They knew that there might be a hope, however slim, of making IDs from such ravaged remains only if parents of missing boys saw the news stories and produced names and dental records that the Harris County Medical Examiner's Office could use as evidence.

THE DIGGING CONTINUED AS the daylight faded to dusk. Wayne Henley, at that point officially under arrest only for Dean Corll's murder, leaned on the hood of a police cruiser just outside the shed, chain-smoking cigarettes provided by officers or by reporters and watching events unfold with a dazed expression. His hair long and his eyes wild, Henley turned his gaze away from the metal door as police officers and jail trusties began to unearth the graves of boys he knew. For hours, Henley waited on foot or ensconced in patrol cars. At one point, he hunched over the hood of a cruiser and buried his face in his hands as he responded to questions hollered out by journalists in what seemed like a parody of a press conference.

Wayne Henley seemed stoic and emotionless—or maybe still high—until one sympathetic reporter bought him a Pepsi and another, Jack Cato, the star newsman for Houston's KPRC Channel 2, loaned him an enormous oversized radio car phone to call home. That mobile phone was a novelty; Cato was pretty much the only Houston journalist who had one. The station kept filming as Henley, again covering his face in one hand, told one of his little brothers to fetch their mother. He and his mother didn't immediately realize that their conversation was being recorded (she later tried to sue the station) and would soon be featured on broadcasts worldwide.

"Mama?" he said, for the first time sounding like a scared teenager.

"Who's this?" she answered, sounding confused.

"This is Wayne, Mama."

"Yes, this is Mama, baby," she answered, her voice warming and her accent as thick as her eldest's.

"Mama?"

"Yes?"

"I killed Dean!" The word came out *kilt* in Henley's Texas twang. Henley reassured his worried mama that he was already with the police, and there was no need for her to come, though a large crowd of spectators surrounded him. The seventeen-year-old, pumped up by adrenaline and bravado, still seemed to consider himself a hero—though officers and reporters noticed how much Wayne knew about these hidden graves and the murder victims inside them. He remained there, watching and listening as the ravaged bodies of teenagers were zipped into body bags, placed in hearses, and hauled away to the Harris County morgue.

Police and inmates unearthed evidence of what modern forensic scientists would call a "mass fatality event": a cluster of unnatural deaths so large that the resources of local agencies were overwhelmed. Homicide detectives, who continued to watch and sometimes helped inmates dig, piled the evidence they encountered on clean sheets of plastic. Stray bones. Pairs of boots encrusted in clay. Shreds of towels stuffed inside mouth cavities. Skulls with bullet holes. Nooses wrapped around what remained of boys' necks. They were caught by surprise by the unprecedented number of murder victims and rushed to recover them even after the national evening news and radio stations began to broadcast the names of the likely murdered teens supplied by Henley. In all the chaos, no one contained leaks so that families could be privately informed of the devastating news that their son might be one of the murder victims inside this shed of horrors; instead, some learned from neighbors, news broadcasts, or journalists banging at their doors.

All of the murder victims' remains had been hideously altered by decomposition, yet it was obvious that many were heartbreakingly young: skinny kids who had once worn blue jeans, fringed leather jackets, and T-shirts with psychedelic patterns or rebellious logos. One Houston news photographer trained his lens on the diggers and caught the moment when a skull was placed atop a heap of dirt in a wheelbarrow as onlookers gaped.

The sun set just after 8 P.M. that Wednesday, and another shift of officers and inmates continued to excavate, bringing in portable spotlights for illumination. In a spot labeled Hole No. 5, they uncovered two more skeletons. Some scraps of cloth and shoes inside that hole appeared to match Henley's dead neighbors: Malley Winkle, sixteen, and David Hilligiest, thirteen—boys who had disappeared on Memorial Day weekend 1971 on their way to a swimming pool. Officers recovered a grimy gray-and-white-striped swimming suit like one Malley had owned, as well as what looked like David's tennis shoes and scraps of his striped yellow shirt. Confoundingly, that same hole held the insurance cards of two different missing Houston boys, Donald and Jerry Waldrop, a pair of brothers, ages fifteen and thirteen, who'd vanished on their way to a bowling alley in January 1971. Diggers discovered more clothing with another set of remains in a spot labeled Hole No. 6 that night. But most bodies appeared to have been stripped before burial. More stray shoes and clothing had been stuffed into sacks and stored alongside the sacks of lime, stray pieces of furniture, and other items in the shed.

Hearts heavy and heads full of visions of early violent death, homicide investigators began to wonder: *Had these teens been buried beside any of their own clothing and possessions? Or had the killers—it was hard to believe Corll had acted alone—scrambled everything?*

By the time they finally called for a break at 11:50 P.M. on that first terrible night, the body count had reached eight. And there were still more hidden graves to unearth. . . .

ELMER WAYNE HENLEY, JR.'S mother, Mary, already knew that the radio phone conversation with her son had been recorded for broadcast on the *NBC Nightly News* when the first journalist knocked at her door on the afternoon of August 8. "She invited me in," remembers Craig Smyser, a cub reporter for the *Houston Chronicle,* fresh out of college at that time. Excited about his first scoop, he quickly accepted her invitation to watch the show alongside Wayne's little brothers.

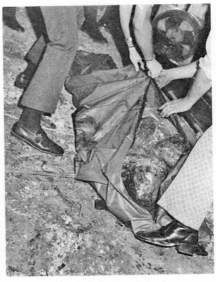

Inside Corll's boatshed, August 1973

"She lived in a Heights classic house—it was tiny," he said. "When you walked in the door you were immediately in the living room and she had a couch that faced the television set."

Mary Henley seemed proud that her eldest was going to be famous. "And she talked to me and told me what a nice kid Elmer Wayne Henley was." Wearing a bathrobe and slippers, she offered a tray of cookies and a glass of instant lemonade to Smyser as they settled down to watch Wayne in his network TV debut. His brothers and his grandmother joined them, all gathered together on a battered couch and a bed converted into a divan in the living room in their house on West 27th Street.

At the time, his mother—and Smyser—still believed that Henley had saved his friends and killed only one person, Dean Corll, in self-defense. "Dean treated Wayne like a son. And Wayne loved him like a father," she told Smyser. "I knew Dean must've done something terrible to Wayne to make Wayne shoot him." Even to Smyser, an inexperienced cub reporter, she seemed naïve. "She was a nice woman; she was caring for her family and her kids. . . . She was overwhelmed and didn't have any concept of what had happened. I think as far as she was concerned, Elmer Wayne Henley had done what he had to do in the circumstances."

THE HENLEYS' NEIGHBORS DOROTHY and Fred Hilligiest, the parents of David Hilligiest, one of the missing boys Wayne had named, lived only about five doors down.

Fred Hilligiest worked long hours striping streets for the City of Houston and made extra money by running a side business that did similar work in private parking lots. Dorothy, an organized mother of six, ran their household, getting groceries, running errands, conducting home repairs, and ferrying around her children. (With David missing, she still had two at home; the three eldest were married and on their own.) A caring woman who knew her neighbors and their troubles, she had often worried about the Henley boys, who seemed adrift following their parents' 1970 divorce. Well before that, signs and sounds of strife, drinking, and domestic violence had emanated from the Henleys' small house.

Sometimes Dorothy had stopped to offer Wayne's little brothers rides on rainy days when she spotted them walking home from school. She'd done so only a few days before the horrific finds in the boatshed, and Wayne had greeted her near the back porch, thanking her for her kindness. Then, as they sometimes did, Wayne and Mrs. Hilligiest lingered outside to discuss David's long, unexplained absence. Her missing son, two years younger, had been one of Wayne's earliest playmates, though the boys had parted ways when David began Catholic elementary school at St. Rose of Lima. Though David had been missing for two years by then, Wayne said he believed her son was near, adding, "David could be under our noses and we might not even know it."

"I'll never give up," Dorothy had responded. The energetic, determined woman didn't mention she'd been feeling hopeless that summer, as if "there was a cloud that would never lift."

The date that would have been their missing son's sixteenth birthday arrived on July 30, 1973, without any news. Her husband awoke early that morning with tears on his pillow. He'd been crying in his sleep without knowing why. "It's David's birthday and I've been feeling extra low too," she'd said.

The Hilligiests normally watched the evening news, but Wednesday, August 8, was no ordinary day for them. Dorothy Hilligiest had just lost her younger sister to a sudden illness, and the couple spent hours attending the funeral and mourning with family. When they reached home, they sat on the sofa exhausted and never turned on the TV. Mr. Hilligiest had already gone to bed when a friend called Dorothy at 10:20 P.M. to ask whether she'd seen the broadcasts.

"No," she answered, explaining why.

"They found a bunch of bodies out here at this boathouse," her friend said.

Dorothy Hilligiest didn't want to believe that any of the corpses stashed in Southwest Houston could be David's, but her friend urged her to call Channel 11, and a reporter connected her to the HPD homicide division.

The detective, sounding spent, immediately asked if she was alone.

"Why?" she responded.

"Well, Mrs. Hilligiest, we feel pretty sure that one of these is your boy," he said, adding that he had already pulled David's missing persons file as part of an active and expanding investigation.

"What makes you think that?"

"This Henley boy named him."

"My God, what's happening out there?" she asked.

"Well, it's a homosexual thing," the detective replied.

Dorothy Hilligiest felt shocked, as if she'd suddenly been hit in the head. She never asked why the officer called her son's murder "a homosexual thing." After hanging up, she roused her husband just before midnight.

During that terribly long, sad day, Mrs. Hilligiest had heard a rumor about their neighbor being involved in a shooting. Now that odd fact clicked into place alongside Wayne Henley's puzzling recent remarks about David being nearby. The Hilligiests both remembered how eagerly Wayne had volunteered to help put up flyers in the search for David and his friend Malley more than two years before. And now it appeared that he'd known all along that they were dead.

The pair jumped into their Ford Galaxie, flipped on the headlights, and drove toward the boatshed, hoping to see their son's burial site for themselves. Dorothy figured they might be able to help HPD officers distinguish David's body from his friend's, given that David was much smaller, darker-haired, and younger than Malley. They had no idea the shed held so many graves. But digging had been suspended at 11:55 P.M., and the 4500 block of Silver Bell Drive had been blocked off. They had to turn around.

WAYNE HENLEY SPENT THAT night in Pasadena's air-conditioned jail, where he complained so mightily about the chill that officers transferred him to a padded cell that was marginally warmer. His buzz had finally worn off by the time Mullican summoned him to the squad room for more questioning the next morning. Later, his defense attorney would argue he'd been too exhausted and drugged up after Corll's death to understand his rights to remain silent or to request an attorney when the magistrate had delivered the Miranda warning.

Mullican planned to keep Wayne talking, since he alone appeared able to unlock the dead man's secrets. Public records had revealed little about Dean Corll, who kept his phone numbers unlisted, moved every few months, and collected his mail at a P.O. box. Corll swapped vehicles often and had been spotted driving a convertible, a GTX muscle car, a tan sedan, and a succession of white vans that collectively seemed beyond the limit of his paychecks as a supervisor at Houston Lighting & Power, even with the line of credit he'd established. "No matter how much you talked to him, you didn't know him," Wayne Henley later reflected. "Dean searched for a climax he never found."

The efforts to exhume more bodies were continuing that day. And if Dean Corll really had been a mass murderer—the term still used in 1973 for those who killed more than once—perhaps only Corll's killer, Elmer Wayne Henley, Jr., could confirm the true death toll. Around 9 A.M., Mullican hauled Wayne Henley out of his padded cell and offered him a chair and a cup of coffee. Wayne, whose asthma was flaring up, had trouble catching his breath; Mullican suggested relief might come if he only told the truth, adding that HPD officers were already interviewing eighteen-year-old David Brooks, the former Hamilton Junior High classmate through whom Wayne claimed to have met Corll.

Henley took another breath. "Now I can tell the whole story," he said.

They were again sitting face-to-face when Wayne acknowledged that he'd been involved in "unnatural sex practices, torture, and killings of young boys with Corll for at least two years."

Wayne named more childhood friends and former schoolmates as murder victims, and for the first time began to coldly disclose how he'd helped exterminate them. He still claimed to be uninvolved in the murders of David Hilligiest and Malley Winkle, but admitted that he'd shot Charles Cobble in the head with Dean's pistol and helped Dean choke Marty Jones. He also described killing two other longtime friends. "We choked Mark Scott and Frank Aguirre and buried them at High Island . . . I don't remember the dates on all these because there has been too many of them." David, Malley, Charles, Mark, and Frank were all from the Heights.

He provided names and details of other teenagers' murders, implicating himself in at least eight. Three of those boys had inexplicably disappeared that summer: Michael Baulch, Billy Lawrence, and Homer Garcia, all only fifteen. Michael Baulch also grew up in the Heights and his older brother had attended school with Wayne Henley. Billy Lawrence, from a neighborhood north of the Heights, had recently befriended Wayne. And Homer Garcia, an honor student at Houston's prestigious Bellaire High, happened to take a class at the same driving school.

Wayne didn't mention it then, but Michael's brother Billy Baulch was missing too. He did admit that he "shot and killed Johnny Delome," another Heights boy who had disappeared with Billy, his best friend. In addition to the bodies in the boatshed, Wayne confided he knew of more graves concealed deep in the East Texas piney woods, near where Corll's father owned a log cabin on Lake Sam Rayburn, the state's largest reservoir, and of bodies buried in the sand along a remote stretch of beach on the Gulf of Mexico.

Henley signed a typed version of that second damning confession in a police lieutenant's office with a picture window on August 9, 1973. Four Pasadena officers and a *Houston Chronicle* reporter acted as witnesses.

INSCRUTABLE BEHIND HIS JOHN Lennon–style wire-rimmed glasses, David Brooks had shown up voluntarily at HPD earlier that same day. His father had independently contacted a Houston police officer he knew soon after news broke about the boatshed bodies to arrange the meeting. With his father beside him, the eighteen-year-old warily answered detectives' questions about his long "friend-ship" with Dean Corll, but repeatedly and vehemently insisted that he'd never killed anyone. Like Wayne, David considered himself merely a cooperating witness and not a murder suspect.

David Brooks was never as forthcoming as Wayne Henley. He seemed more intelligent, perhaps because his bespectacled gaze was sharp and his Texas accent less syrupy. He, like Wayne, had dropped out of school, though he'd managed a year at Waltrip High. He'd often been seen in the Heights squiring his girlfriend around in the Corvette he'd gotten from Corll or at the wheel of one of Corll's boxy panel vans. He was known, in certain teenaged circles, as Corll's sidekick, and a reliable purveyor of pills and pot. Dean Corll had provided shelter, money, and the 1969 Corvette to David, whose parents were also divorced, in exchange for sexual services and for "keeping his mouth shut about what he had seen," he told Houston police.

Dean Corll had long served as a substitute for David's parents. By the time David arrived at HPD for questioning, he hadn't seen his mother, a nurse who lived in Beaumont, for more than five years. After a long estrangement, he'd only recently reconciled with his fa-ther, Alton Brooks, a contractor and World War II veteran with mil-itary tattoos, who'd divorced David's mother in 1963, remarried, and seemed to prefer the company of his other children. Yet David Brooks had clearly been trying to break away from Corll and Wayne Henley that summer. He'd moved out of Corll's place and married his teenaged girlfriend, Bridget, a Catholic girl from Reagan High who was heavily pregnant with his child. He and Bridget had been living in their own apartment in Spring Branch, though he'd seemed nervous, barring the door at night and keeping a shotgun handy. He'd also taken a job. "I now work for the Alton Brooks Paving Com-pany, which is owned by my father," he told police.

Confronted by homicide detectives with questions about the pa-rade of corpses still being hauled out of Corll's shed, David denied being involved in any murders but declared "there were several times that Dean told me about killing people." Only in his second statement, a day later, did he admit to being present at some slayings and provide names and clues that led investigators to files on more missing teens: James Glass, who'd disappeared with his friend Danny Yates after attending a revival at an evangelical church in the Heights in December 1970; and Ruben Haney, who vanished after making plans to see a movie in August 1971. Brooks named addresses where Corll had committed murders, but offered only the vaguest descriptions of other victims: "a Mexican boy," "two boys strapped down on his bed," "a boy in a bathtub."

In the first forty-eight hours, detectives working in Pasadena and in Houston had persuaded Wayne Henley and David Brooks to supply leads or names for about a dozen murder victims. Soon the body count would more than double that.

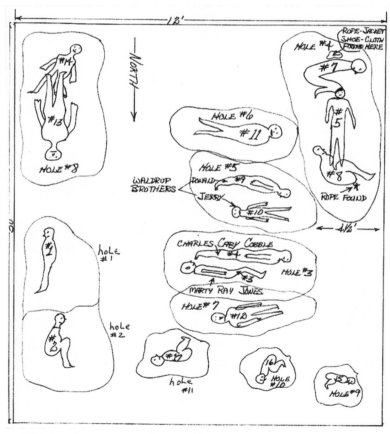

PPD's diagram of the boatshed burials

Sometime on Thursday, August 9, two detectives—one from Houston and one from Pasadena—independently diagrammed the boatshed scene, sketching out locations of what they called "holes" containing one, two, or even three bodies. Ultimately, officers drew eleven different holes containing at least seventeen decaying bodies or skeletal remains crammed into a space twelve feet wide and thirty feet long. Both sketched out crude cartoons to show which bodies had been buried flat and which had been crouched in fetal positions. Nearly all were nude. Some graves overlapped. Meanwhile, others photographed the contents of each hole. In all the confusion, officers never managed to establish a formal search grid. Years later, it became almost impossible to match crudely drawn graves in those diagrams with unlabeled crime scene photos and autopsy case numbers.

The very last set of skeletal remains found inside the shed belonged to a boy who'd been buried beside a brightly colored striped swimming suit and a pair of what looked like black cowboy boots.

Before sunset, a bulldozer driver was brought in by the City of Houston to re-cover the shed floor with crushed oyster shells and to grade it smooth for the owners to reuse—though Wayne Henley kept insisting more bodies were still buried inside. Rookie Houston police detective D. R. James told the press: "If there's nineteen in here, we missed two, but we've been over every inch of this ground, some of it twice."

Wayne Henley was not there to object. By that time, he'd been hauled a hundred miles away and was leading Det. Mullican and another group of officers to more clandestine graves in the woods near Corll's family cabin.

A SMALL TEAM AT the Harris County Medical Examiner's Office, including an enterprising twenty-two-year-old administrative secretary named Pat Paul, simultaneously embarked on the terrible task of trying to identify all of those boys' bodies and bones even as grief-stricken Houston families clamored for answers. In August 1973, the office was jammed inside the cramped basement of the county's

Ben Taub Hospital, a major trauma center in the growing Texas Medical Center complex. To visitors and employees, the crowded underground space felt like a glorified rabbit warren. The entrance lacked any reception room; it was near Paul's shared admin area and the investigators' narrow office with its oversized (and outdated) wall-sized Harris County roadmap. Down a winding hall was the office's lone autopsy suite, although, when necessary, pathologists could deploy a second table and perform two forensic examinations simultaneously. In the back, adjacent to the hospital's freight elevator, was the morgue's overstuffed cold storage vault. Some body bags from other unsolved identity cases had to be stacked on top of each other to make room for the influx.

Before joining the ME's office in 1969, Pat Paul had only seen a single corpse—her grandmother's in an open casket at the funeral. At first, Paul averted her eyes whenever she passed the open door of the autopsy suite, deeper inside the warren of rooms. That space with its metal tables, oversized scales, and sharp knives was the domain of the pathologists, physicians with medical degrees, and their autopsy assistants, known as dieners. Initially deployed to answer phones and type reports, Paul quickly adapted to the office's sights, smells, and hardships. By August 1973, she'd seen victims arrive after plane crashes, car fires, and plant explosions, though she'd never experienced anything as overwhelming as the arrivals of bodies from Corll's boatshed.

The lights on the oversized rectangular office phones on her desk kept flashing red with calls. Distressed parents from Houston and from all over the United States were phoning the ME's office and Paul logged every message in longhand. Fortunately, she knew how to handle people in acute emotional distress. For years, her family ran Paul's Ice House, at 10000 Telephone Road, a beloved outdoor bar that doubled as a community gathering place. Raised beside four bossy older brothers, Paul had learned early how to talk to anyone—inebriated or sober—inside that icehouse, its seating area crowded with pool tables and dartboards and illuminated after sunset mainly by neon beer signs. "You're a therapist when it comes to a beer joint. Everyone tells you their story and their problems."

Paul had long dreamed of becoming an ME investigator—her mother, after all, had been one of Harris County's first female deputy sheriffs, toiling three years in its perennially overcrowded jail. She so far had been rebuffed. "There's no female police officers. We don't need a female," the ME's all-male cadre of investigators insisted. The huge influx of unidentified teenagers' remains in August 1973 gave Paul her chance. She became the main staff liaison between investigators, doctors, and the teenaged victims' families, though all that extra work didn't earn her a real promotion. Officially she remained a receptionist; it would be three more years before the ME formally named her an investigator. "I was doing everything," she recalls. "I just didn't have the title. I went and did all the investigative work. I just didn't get paid for it."

She soon learned about more missing Houston boys than the number of bodies that had been found. Paul kept calling Houston police and accumulated a thick stack of about two hundred reports of active missing persons and runaways from HPD's juvenile division from 1970 to 1973. She was ordered to try to call every next of kin's number, though many phones were disconnected. She and others working on IDs faced a huge challenge: Most of these teenaged boys' bodies were badly decomposed or skeletal. In that state, their bones looked a lot alike: Nearly all were local boys roughly 13 to 17. Each one had a family somewhere, she knew. "I worked my ass off for these kids. Somebody somewhere loved them. It used to drive me crazy."

As part of ID investigations, every missing boy's parent was asked if his or her son had ever seen a dentist or broken a bone. Fortunately, several missing teens had recently had their teeth checked. Paul and others concentrated on family dentists who could supply diagrams or X-rays, data that could be scientifically and precisely compared to teeth found in the corpses or skulls to verify an ID. If and when X-rays or charts were obtained, investigators would provide images of a missing boy's teeth (or broken bones) to office pathologists and to Dr. Paul Stimson, D.D.S., a professor at the University of Texas dental school who was considered a big dog in the 1970s world of forensic odontology (and who was still around when Derrick began to dig into the files). Stimson could use his expertise to compare the shape, position, and size of teeth in dental records to autopsy photos and X-rays of teeth in skulls, even though some teeth had gotten dislodged or lost in the burial and excavation process. Similarly, X-rays of bones any missing boys might have broken could be used by forensic pathologists for identifications if similar fractures showed up in X-rays of remains. Some radiographs revealed more complications: "We have X-rays on the rest of the bodies, and some are disjointed," Dr. Joe said as he sorted through the cases that first terrible week. "We have many bones and we don't know which go with which bodies."

Soon Houston parents whose children's names had already appeared as likely murder victims in newspapers and on broadcasts began to drop by, in obvious distress and loudly demanding answers. Some insisted on viewing remains, saying their son must be in the morgue because "Elmer Wayne Henley said so."

Under office protocols, Paul and others were ordered never to allow family members to view corpses; autopsy photos of faces were rarely shared unless decomposition was minimal. She sometimes responded to frustrated fathers (few mothers visited the morgue back then) by gently asking: "How can we be sure Henley's telling the truth when we know he helped kill your kids?" Once in a while, Ben Taub Hospital's busy emergency room staff would mistakenly direct parents seeking the morgue to the sally port beside the ER, instead of the ME's official basement door. There was no security guard posted, so misdirected relatives might accidentally take the freight elevator to the morgue's rear service door. The odd office geography meant some anguished parents might encounter a gauntlet of bagged bodies waiting on gurneys to be processed before finding anyone alive to assist them.

Walter Scott, a brash and physically imposing man with an ego bolstered by his status as a small business owner in the Heights, was an early and frequent visitor. He loudly expressed outrage about the seemingly haphazard regard for his son, Mark, whom Wayne Henley had named early as a murder victim. Mark Scott was one of Wayne's junior high classmates. But as the days ticked by, Mark's body remained unidentified. Walter Scott became a regular, frequently phoning and visiting Paul, and demanding to see the ME himself. "He gave us the most pressure of anybody," Paul recalls. "I'd walk in at 8 A.M. and he'd be sitting in the hall in the basement, then he would come in and sit in the front office for hours." At first, Walter Scott felt absolutely sure his eldest boy's body must be one of those encased in plastic and stashed away on forlorn piles inside the morgue's cold storage chamber. At six feet, his son had been taller, as well as blonder, than most other named murder victims. Scott repeatedly asked to view photos of remains and of property connected with taller un-identified boys—at least three were estimated to have been about six feet tall, based primarily on the length of their leg bones. For a while, he carried around photos of an unidentified victim in his pocket, but ultimately rejected them all.

Handwritten notes on telephone memo pads show Walter Scott left message after message for investigators. His son Mark had worn a Timex watch; he had a necklace that seemed to be missing; he had a scar on his leg from when David Brooks had shot him with a pellet gun, an injury that had been treated at the Heights Hospital.

Paul never found any such necklace or watch among effects re-covered with Corll's victims, and she knew that the power of a pellet gun to inflict a wound varied. If the pellet had struck only the flesh or tissue of the leg, there would be no nick at all. And even if a pellet directly hit the bone, whether it would make any mark depended on the power behind that pellet, the number of pumps, and how close the shot was. In any case, pathologists had not noticed any such nick on the unidentified teens' leg bones they'd examined.

Over time, the budding investigator began to wonder whether Scott's feverish search was motivated by shame or by guilt rather than simply grief. But Paul lacked time to focus on any one case.

Too many other Houstonians were looking for their lost sons and brothers too.

CHAPTER 4

THE BOY ON THE BIKE

HOUSTON, 1971–1973

RANDY HARVEY RODE OFF on his yellow bike on Tuesday March 9, 1971, with his knees bobbing above its frame. At fifteen, he topped six feet. Although his bicycle was too small and had no gears, Randy was used to the two-mile ride to the Fina station, where he pumped gas for minimum wage while wearing a long-sleeved uniform jacket under the sweltering Texas sun. His downstrokes were swift as he peddled past the brightly lit 7-Eleven, then crossed busy North Shepherd Drive, a major thoroughfare crammed with a line of used-car lots, taverns, and businesses. The safest route led west toward White Oak Bayou, passing the cowboy church on 11th Street, where charismatic guitar-toting preachers labored to save the souls of teens drawn to pot. In December 1970, two other teenaged boys had vanished after attending an antidrug revival at that church, the Evangelistic Temple, only a few blocks from Randy's home. But they lived in another neighborhood and attended a Spring Branch school. Randy likely didn't know them.

Randy lived on the gritty commercial western edge of the Heights in a rental shared with his sister and mother on the same block as the Coin-Operated Launderama, the Our Motor Co. used-car lot, and the Starlite Lounge. Other, fancier sections of the Heights still held rows of Victorian homes and smaller but solid bungalows. The

Heights, originally developed in the 1880s as an independent city with its own schools and streetcars, had been built on slightly higher ground than the rest of swampy Houston so that its residents could reduce the risk of malaria. The enclave, settled by the forebears of some of Houston's most prominent families, was just two miles wide and three miles long. By the 1970s, though, the ninety-year-old neighborhood was showing its age. Towering live oaks planted along the esplanade in the heart of the original townsite still stood, but some mansions erected by founding families sat dark and empty, their windows gaping maws. The area had been annexed by sprawling Houston, a Big Oil boomtown of more than a million, and was crisscrossed by highways, bridges, and railroad tracks. The fast-growing city never bothered to adopt any zoning, and many of the Heights' older bungalows, particularly along its thoroughfares, had been razed and replaced with boxy brick apartment buildings, junkyards, car lots, and random businesses. Still, it remained a relatively close-knit community where Randy and his kid sister knew many neighborhood teens, who generally attended the same junior high schools: Hamilton or Hogg.

The Harveys' apartment occupied the backside of a house painted bright pink that sat on North Shepherd Drive, a bustling commercial street that connected the Heights with the rest of Houston. That location was convenient for the family: Randy and his sister could easily walk to school, or visit hangouts like the Burger King or Merchant Park Lanes bowling alley. Like other Heights parents, their mother liked to unwind after work at a neighborhood watering hole, her favorite being the Sahara Lounge. But even late at night, when the *whoosh* of passing cars and trucks finally slowed, the family's sleep could be disrupted by heavy thuds, whistles, and rumbles of trains pulling petroleum tanker cars or heavy freight along the railroad tracks.

Randy worked part time at a Fina station located on busy Ella Boulevard near the humming 610 Loop. Though close to the highway, the station was also only a block or two from the Little Thicket, a ten-acre park that had once been part of a larger estate, and some of Houston's original log cabins still stood under stands of pines nearby. Randy had no fear of riding his bike through sometimes heavy commercial traffic toward the station. Once he reached White Oak Bayou, he could follow shady unpaved trails threading through the trees. He had no idea any danger lurked on that familiar path. A fifteen-year-old with no father at home, he was used to taking care of himself. He wore his hair long over the collar, and considered himself a rebel—a hippie.

IN 1956, RANDY'S BIRTH year, Beat poet Allen Ginsberg wrote "Howl," a poetic manifesto that denounced conformity and capitalism and praised "angelheaded hipsters burning for the ancient heavenly connection to the starry dynamo in the machinery of night." Ginsberg's lyrical celebration of wasted days and midnight wanderings lauded those who "lounged hungry and lonesome through Houston seeking jazz or sex or soup," and who sought adventures in peyote, wine-drunkenness, and nakedness. Though gay sex remained illegal in almost every state, Ginsberg boldly exalted acts of heterosexual and homosexual ecstasy.

All across the United States, fans of some of those same footloose, long-haired, pro-sexual-liberation ideals set out to remake themselves as hippies.

Some counterculture celebrities visited or lived within Houston city limits. Into the 1960s, author Larry McMurtry was writing novels, teaching creative writing at Rice University, and entertaining unusual guests in his Houston home, a stop for Ken Kesey and his Merry Pranksters on their 1964 psychedelic bus tour. And in 1969, a group of renegade Texans formed a band in Houston they called ZZ Top and began growing out their hair and beards, laying down licks, and incorporating grunts and laughs into hits like "La Grange," a song glorifying a Central Texas whorehouse that topped the charts in 1973.

In 1968, Joan Didion attempted to capture the quicksilver hippie movement in an essay for *The Saturday Evening Post* linking episodes she witnessed in San Francisco's Haight-Ashbury neighborhood. Didion had been dispatched to cover what some viewed as a fading fad, but instead described a wave of nihilism that seemed dangerously attractive, particularly to teens. Inspired by W. B. Yeats's 1911 poem "The Second Coming," Didion found that hippies were emerging in an epoch when "things fall apart; the centre cannot hold." The hippie movement, Didion wrote, was birthed in "a country of bankruptcy notices and public-auction announcements and commonplace reports of casual killings and misplaced children and abandoned homes and vandals who misspelled even the four-letter words they scrawled." Fundamentally, being a hippie was mostly about getting lost, she concluded after meeting youths from distant states who were congregating in California. "Adolescents drifted from city to torn city, sloughing off both the past and the future as snakes shed their skins, children who were never taught and would never now learn the games that held the society together. People were missing. Children were missing. Parents were missing. Those left behind filed desultory missing persons reports, then moved on themselves."

RANDY HARVEY, LIKE OTHER young Houstonians, caught glimpses on TV or in magazines of glossy portraits of proud public pot smokers and scantily clad braless girls roaming the streets of Haight-Ashbury in the 1967 Summer of Love. But his path to declaring himself a hippie in 1971 Houston was simpler. At fifteen, the lanky teen grew his hair long and in that way declared himself free. For a young man—really, still a boy—the act of growing your hair was the obvious first step toward a deeper rebellion. Long hair served as a beacon to alert Texas allies that you were one of them, though it could also attract negative attention from peers, parents, and police. Boys like Randy had to be ready to defend themselves.

Some young Texans who called themselves hippies found God and joined wanderers known as Jesus People, traveling around in robes, casting off all possessions, and severing ties with family and former friends. Others formed communes and lived off the land. On Texas campuses, more political long-haired youths joined the Students for a Democratic Society and protested the Vietnam War.

Many teens hated President Nixon for his war on drugs, his bellicosity, and his stench of corruption. But some Texas hippies supported the war. Dodging the draft or moving to California was optional. Getting stoned and making love on a mattress in a dimly lit room, catching a rock concert at the Sam Houston Coliseum, where Jimi Hendrix, Three Dog Night, and the Grateful Dead all performed in 1970, or hitchhiking to the beach in Galveston was infinitely easier.

In the Heights, clusters of long-haired boys and girls gathered on sidewalks in front of hippie-friendly households to strum guitars, channel flower power, and explore Texan brands of rebellion. They listened to DJs on the 610 AM radio station KILT and bought vinyl at record stores (which doubled as head shops), went for cones at the locally owned Heap-o-Cream on Yale and cheap meals at relatively new fast-food chains like the Burger King on Shepherd or the Jack in the Box on 20th Street, "where even if you only had a dollar you could still get the taco special," remembers Johnny Holton, a Heights boy who counted himself among Houston's hippies in the 1970s.

These days, Johnny Holton lives out in the suburbs and drives an SUV. He and his wife, Cindy Bazar Holton, who grew up in the adjacent Oak Forest neighborhood, are grandparents, though they still look like aging hippies. They regularly make the long drive to the Heights to visit old haunts or one of the many fashionable new cafés. They wish they could afford to move back, but even the smaller Heights bungalows, like the one where Johnny grew up, have been renovated and command high prices. One vintage gas station on Yale is now a glitzy restaurant and bar that serves up microbrews and lattes; the dive pool hall on 11th Street has been converted into a bakery catering to pets. And yet the watering hole his hard-drinking father favored seems virtually unchanged; it still has the same vintage manual pull-tab cigarette machine lighting up a dark corner. Holton marvels at how close those places are to addresses where some of Corll's murder victims were abducted, tortured, and killed.

He could easily have been one of them. Accepting a ride or a party invitation or smoking pot in public in the Heights esplanade was common for Holton and his hippie friends. "You would take a ride from people you barely knew," Johnny recalls. He sometimes partied with Charles Cobble, a former classmate at Reagan High who was killed by Corll.

Some kids who could not afford pot would inhale fumes from pressurized spray paint, model-plane glue, or cooking spray cans for their intoxicating effects. "It killed your brain cells, but it was whatever was the cheapest," recalls Johnny's wife, Cindy, who hung out in the Heights and knew another boy Corll killed. Teens inhaled fumes from spray paint, glue, or solvents to get high or to try to enhance their sexual experience. Cindy knew a boy who died after "huffing" too much aerosol cooking spray.

Randy Harvey, like many other Houston hippies, roamed the Heights on his bike and on foot—or, if he was lucky enough to have the money, in cars. Depending on their preferences, teens could attend revivals at that church near the White Oak Bayou, roller-skate under a rotating disco ball at the Rainbow Rink, or pay ten cents to swim in the Olympic-sized pool at a private club run by Czech immigrants that also offered Friday night dances. In the 1960s and early 1970s, the Heights had its own candy factory, which had been operated at three different locations by Mary Corll and her son, Dean, the friendly neighborhood candy man.

RANDY WAS SUPPOSED TO finish work at the Fina station before sunset on March 9, 1971. It was a school night and his mother and little sister were waiting at home.

Like other Heights parents in those days, hardworking Frances Conley, a single mom, rarely worried about her fifteen-year-old son being out on his bike all day or even after dark. Even younger neighborhood kids were routinely allowed to walk alone to friends' houses, pools, and parks at least until the streetlights came on at sunset, around 8 P.M. in the summertime. Away from Shepherd Drive's commercial strip with its teeming taverns and used-car lots, most of the Heights still seemed like a safe enclave—at least on the surface.

Checking in with parents posed logistical problems. While some

Texas Medical Center physicians were toting around gadgets called "beepers" or "pagers," and NASA's Mission Control could contact men on the moon, ordinary Space City residents lacked such connectivity. Some Heights families could not afford home phones, running to a nearby washateria for the pay phone or borrowing a neighbor's in an emergency. Though answering machines had been invented by 1971, they were expensive and required reel-to-reel tape. In order for a teen like Randy to call home, he'd first have to find a working pay phone and have the right coins. Then, only if his home phone was working and someone answered could he leave a message.

When Randy wasn't home by morning, his mother may have figured that her son had spent the night with a friend and forgotten to call. No one immediately alerted the police. Houston officers weren't always helpful, especially with teens considered "hippies." Some of Randy Harvey's long-haired classmates had been hassled or arrested for little or no reason. Under Texas law, kids as young as seventeen were basically treated like adults and the punishment meted out even for smoking pot or petty theft could be severe in the juvenile justice system.

Randy Harvey had once been questioned by HPD for allegedly stealing a classmate's stereo. Another boy he knew, Malley Winkle, had been arrested with a group of kids stealing bicycles and shipped off to the state's massive juvenile prison complex in Gatesville, where he was locked up for a month. It was a terrible place: In 1974, a federal judge found that Texas juvenile authorities there routinely used beatings, solitary confinement, chemical crowd-control devices, drugs, and other forms of cruel and unusual punishment that violated the Eighth Amendment of the U.S. Constitution.

That Thursday, after Randy had been missing for more than forty-eight hours, Frances Conley phoned HPD, who generally would not take a report any sooner. She told a patrolman that her son and his bike had simply vanished. He had left home with only his work clothes: a pair of bell-bottom jeans, a T-shirt, and a navy jacket with a red lining. The officer seemed sure that Randy had simply taken off. But where?

Later he loaded the standard missing persons report into a manual typewriter and pecked out two sentences: "Subject missing for 2 days. Mother has no idea where or with whom subject is staying." Randell Lee Harvey, fifteen, was classified as a runaway; the report was stuffed in a filing cabinet on the fourth floor of the department's juvenile division with all the rest. In 1971 alone, 5,632 juveniles were reported missing in Houston, nearly all labeled runaways. The division was short-staffed; its best investigations typically involved calling parents once or twice to see if teens returned on their own.

The overabundance of runaway cases, and the city's troublesome teens in general, were viewed as an irritant by Police Chief Herman B. Short. For eight years, the Houston Police Department, in the last gasps of the Jim Crow era, had been overseen by Short, an oversized man with a crew cut who was a friend and a fan of segregationist Alabama governor George Wallace. (He'd been photographed at banquets seated at the governor's table.) Slowly, segregation days were coming to a shuddering halt in Houston. The Coloreds Only signs at drinking fountains were coming down; HPD officers were banned from using the "*n* word" over the radio, and local teens were making diverse friends in newly desegregated classes, on sports teams, and in military service. Still, the department's few Black officers regularly heard that slur. Progressive Houstonians considered Chief Short behind the times or even dangerous.

Short liked to boast that on his watch, Houston had experienced none of the violent riots that had plagued larger cities, but he was hated by Houston civil rights leaders for his callous treatment of youthful protesters. In 1967, the chief had ordered officers to use deadly force to break up a demonstration at the historically Black Texas Southern University by firing into a dorm filled with students and a handful of outside activists. (Through sheer luck, no students died, but a rookie police officer got killed by a ricocheting bullet of the same caliber used by his colleagues.) After a series of unsolved arsons for which the KKK claimed credit and after newspapers published photos of uniformed officers wearing white hoods, Houston activists called for an investigation in 1970 into how many HPD officers secretly belonged to the Klan. In response, Short told newspapers, "I am not a Klansman, and I know of no police officer who is a Klansman. You can't fault a man, however, for praising God, country, and obedience to law and order. That's what we all stand for." Short retained the favor of Houston mayor Louie Welch, who'd first assumed office in 1964 and didn't bother to hide his family's own KKK connections. But many other Houstonians distrusted HPD.

LENORE HARVEY WAS ONLY thirteen when her big brother disappeared. She and Randy shared the same long face, square jaw, and broad grin, though her hair was red and his was dark. He often struggled to tame that mane, which tended to frizz in Houston's hothouse humidity. Often she'd seen him stand in front of the mirror, contemplating a cowlick and repeating the teenaged mantra, "I hate my hair! I hate my hair!" The two were close, but Lenore was shy while Randy was tough and seemingly ready for anything. Lenore considered Randy cool. "All I can say is, he was a hippie. But he was our hippie," she later said.

She knew that plenty of teens like her brother longed for a life away from drudgery, like pumping gas for minimum wage. Many dreamed of the adventures embodied by Janis Joplin, the Port Arthur native whose 1971 hit promised "Freedom's just another word for nothing left to lose." Some Houston teens regularly hitchhiked, and a popular destination was the beach about fifty miles south on the Gulf Freeway. "Sometimes, somebody would come along in a van, stop, throw open a door, and offer a ride to Galveston and you took it," remembered Mike Morse, Derrick's beloved first cousin, who grew up near the Heights.

Lenore never believed Randy had intentionally left home. He had no money, had never mentioned any plans, and had taken none of his stuff. Like any other station attendant, his clothes stank of sweat and gas after a shift (though their mother would later learn from Randy's boss that he'd never even made it to work that day). Weirder than that, Randy had left his records behind. Lenore thought of him whenever she heard one of his favorite songs. He loved a mixture of music: Jimi Hendrix, Iron Butterfly, Janis Joplin. Other teens argued

whether the Rolling Stones or the Beatles were better; Randy preferred the Zombies, a British psychedelic pop band.

At the family apartment inside the hot-pink house, Lenore waited
for Randy's return. Their older sister, Donna, already lived on her
own, so Lenore was stuck there with their mother, who juggled two
or three jobs. Their father had left long before. Without Randy, the
house grew sadder and quieter. The blooms dropped off the azalea
bushes, the school year dragged to an end, and sweltering spring
heat arrived, without any word. If Randy was out on an adventure,
following the hippie trail to California, Lenore wondered: *Why
didn't he ever call her or at least send a postcard?*

AT THE NORMALLY JOYOUS start of the summer break, two more
boys from the Heights vanished on their way to a swimming pool.
Malley Winkle, sixteen, and his neighbor, David Hilligiest, thirteen,
walked off that Saturday in May to join David's brother at the SPJST
Lodge, a civil fraternity founded by Czech immigrants. The group
owned twelve acres over on Beall Street, where they had built the
Olympic-sized swimming pool that they allowed local kids (as
members' friends) to use.

Lenore knew both boys. Malley Winkle was her brother's age. She
and half of the girls in the neighborhood had a crush on the tall,
slim teen, who had a cowlick and dreamy blue eyes, though Malley
had never really got around to officially dating anyone.

Malley's mom, Selma Winkle, was a widow raising two boys on
her own; she worked long hours as an evening-shift nurse at Houston's busy Sharpstown hospital. Her eldest, a charming child whom
teachers fawned over and gave high marks for conduct, had worked
as a busboy and done odd jobs to help her after dropping out. He'd
recently gotten into some trouble and ended up on probation, but
his mother didn't think he'd run away. His friend David Hilligiest
didn't seem to fit the picture of a runaway at all.

At thirteen, David, who wore his short hair slicked back, was still
basically an overactive kid. He enjoyed doodling, sometimes still
climbed furniture for fun, and was very attached to his mother and

siblings. He'd been all ready to leave on a family vacation to Kerrville in the Texas Hill Country on the day he disappeared. The twenty dollars he'd saved as pocket money for that trip and his packed suitcase stayed behind in his bedroom.

The two boys were last seen wearing street clothes and carrying swimming trunks and towels for the mile-long walk to the pool at 1435 Beall Street. David's ten-year-old brother and a friend were already there, but the older boys never arrived. The Hilligiests were alarmed and quickly called Houston Police. "The police couldn't get it on the news or anything because I didn't have any proof he'd been abducted. I didn't have any proof of an enemy. There wasn't much for them to go on. So, they classified him as a runaway," Dorothy Hilligiest later told one of the many reporters who visited her home for an interview.

Over time, the Hilligiests printed up five hundred flyers with the boys' photos, consulted a psychic and a medium, hired a detective, and offered a $1,000 reward for "ANYONE KNOWING THE WHEREABOUTS OF EITHER OR BOTH OF THESE BOYS MISSING SINCE May 29, 1971." Malley's kid brother saw the boys accept a ride from someone in a white van. Later, the Hilligiests provided the plate of a Pontiac GTX seen cruising neighborhood streets. Even if HPD officers had found time to connect that plate number or the van to Dean Corll, he likely would not have attracted any interest. Many parents already knew him as the neighborhood's mild-mannered "Candy Man."

For a while, Malley Winkle and his mom had both worked part time at Corll's candy factory behind Helms Elementary for extra cash. "Dean Corll knew all the boys in this neighborhood. All the boys looked up to him like he was a king, he was the most well-loved man in the neighborhood. He was very neat, very clean, very determined, a good man," Selma Winkle recalled. David and many other kids visited that shop, where Corll kept a pool table and a plastic frog that he'd rigged so that its eyes lit up whenever the phone rang.

In 1974, when Selma Winkle heard court testimony about what Corll and the others had done to her son and other victims, she became hysterical, calling out, "Henley is an animal! He should be hanged!" before being offered a sedative and escorted out. But at the time no one seemed to notice Corll's illicit activities or realize that in the eight months between December 1970 and August 1971, eight boys had vanished from spots within or adjacent to the Heights.

THE FIRST TWO, JAMES Glass and Danny Yates, fourteen, disappeared after attending that antidrug revival at the Evangelistic Church on 11th Street. In the middle of the service, James's brother, Willie, "saw them walk up an aisle, as if they were going to the restroom. And that was it. They basically vanished into thin air." Danny Yates's big brother, Bradley, who stayed home from the revival that day because of a cough, had a more complicated recollection. If police had asked, Bradley says he could have described Dean Corll as a stranger who'd offered him and those boys beers, a ride, and his phone number only a few days before they vanished. He believes Corll had arranged to meet them. "They weren't lured away," he said. "It was a setup."

The next to disappear were the sons of Everett Waldrop, an enterprising construction worker from Georgia who'd recently arrived to help erect high-rise apartments in Houston's building boom. Donald, fifteen, and Jerry, thirteen, went missing on January 30, 1971, after leaving their Heights bungalow bound for a friend's house and for Merchant Park Lanes, the bowling alley in a commercial strip on North Shepherd Drive. Everett Waldrop immediately told police he believed his boys had been picked up by a "homosexual [who] gathers kids and takes movies." One of the names he supplied was a friend of Dean Corll's. For the next eight months, Waldrop basically "camped on that police department door," he later told a *Houston Chronicle* reporter. "I was there about as much as the chief was. But all they did was say 'Why are you down here? You know your boys are runaways.' They treated me like I was some kind of idiot."

Randy Harvey, fifteen, was the fifth boy to go missing in only six months; he lived very near Merchant Park Lanes. Malley Winkle and David Hilligiest were the sixth and seventh. The next, in August

1971, was Ruben (Watson) Haney, a seventeen-year-old dropout from the Heights who sold copies of the underground *Space City* newspapers near the neighborhood's 11th Street pool hall.

Like that, Dean Corll had abducted eight boys in a compact area and killed them without attracting attention from police. Houston parents were searching for their own kids in 1971; but they were unaware that a charismatic and violent pedophile was stalking teenagers in the Heights and nearby neighborhoods.

BY 1971, KIDS ALL across the United States were being bombarded with a clean up America message—"Give a hoot! Don't pollute!"— the slogan of Woodsy Owl, rolled out that September. Back in 1967, the FBI had harnessed the power of humming, room-sized computers to launch the National Crime Information Center or NCIC. Even in the 1970s, cops could trade teletype messages and consult printouts from computer databases to share information about fugitives, missing persons, or suspects in unsolved crimes. But no database of missing persons was available to the public, and no missing kids' photos appeared on milk cartons. The mantra "Stranger Danger" became popular only after a six-year-old disappeared in the heart of New York City in 1979.

Child predators across the United States operated in a shadowy no-man's-land where loose or nonexistent laws allowed them to escape detection and punishment. More than a decade after Corll's crimes, in 1984, Congress would found the nonprofit National Center for Missing and Exploited Children, which began to provide assistance on new and cold cases involving murdered, missing, and unidentified minors, eventually including investigators, forensic artists, and a database of missing children's photos and unknown dead children's facial reconstructions. In 1994, the National Sex Offender Registry would be established, initially named for Jacob Wetterling, an eleven-year-old Minnesota boy who'd been abducted while riding his bike with friends to a convenience store. Wetterling's presumed 1989 murder remained unsolved until 2016 when a longtime suspect was arrested and led police to a clandestine grave on a farm, only minutes from where Jacob had been snatched. The sex offender registry would later be publicized and broadened by supplemental laws named after still more slaughtered children.

In 1996, Amber Alerts followed, named for a Texas girl who'd been snatched by a stranger in a black pickup while riding her bike in the parking lot of a grocery store in Arlington, a Dallas suburb. Amber Hagerman, a nine-year-old with a spray of freckles on her nose and a thick fringe of bangs, was found murdered four days after the abduction. Those "Amber Alerts" would compel investigators to rapidly evaluate many other missing persons reports and to notify the public about missing children (or younger teens) who left unexpectedly, abandoned cherished possessions, or were last seen with strangers. By 2023, that system had contributed to the recovery of more than eleven hundred others; yet Amber's killer has never been caught.

All of those meaningful reforms were inspired by terrible tragedies carried out in the decades after Corll's murder spree came to light. Back in the early 1970s, though, discussion of child pornography or potentially dangerous sexual predators remained taboo, particularly when boys were their targets. In those days, Harris County prosecutors might prioritize rape cases but tended to define that felony narrowly as a violent sexual attack carried out by a stranger on an adult woman. Sexual assaults of children or teens, often committed by relatives or acquaintances, tended to be underreported and rare prosecutions often ended in plea bargains. Taking girls or women across state lines for immoral purposes had been banned since 1910 under a federal law, the Mann Act, also called the White Slave Traffic Act. But no such law protected adolescent boys. Under age of consent laws, boys and girls over sixteen who were sexually exploited were considered consenting adults or, sometimes, blamed as juvenile delinquents.

Certainly, the nation's overwhelming number of hippies and runaways, along with the antiwar movement and the development of the interstate highway system, fostered a footloose youthful segment of American society estranged from relatives and other authority figures. In major cities like Houston, San Francisco, and Los Angeles, groups of teenaged hippies, people exploring their sexual orientations, runaways, hitchhikers, so-called juvenile delinquents, drug users, and sex workers were forming alternative fringe communities. Unfortunately, some members of those groups were treated by police and society as if they were invisible or disposable. Cultural divides made it easier for predators who sought to exploit—or kill—teens. By 1977, only one major police agency had created a unit that specialized in investigating rampant sexual exploitation of children and adolescents: the Los Angeles Police Department.

BY SEPTEMBER 1971, AFTER his first year of homicidal operations, Dean Corll had kidnapped and killed at least ten people, some unknown even to his teenaged accomplices, David Brooks and Wayne Henley. Corll continued to pluck teens off of the streets in the Heights, but for the next two years, the three of them would roam widely looking for targets, trolling newer tree-lined suburbs outside the 610 Loop, like Spring Branch, Garden Oaks, and Oak Forest. More unexplained disappearances were reported in Bellaire and West University, relatively upscale communities. Over time, the hidden death toll tripled.

Even by August 1973, worried moms, gossipy locals, and neighborhood patrolmen did not realize that so many Houston boys between the ages of twelve and twenty had abruptly disappeared from the Heights and surrounding neighborhoods. Most of the relevant missing persons reports still described boys or young men as having "run away" after walking or biking to or from an ordinary teenagers' hangout, like a mall, pool, bowling alley, skating rink, or friend's home. Houston Police had no personal computers back then to track crime trends. But there were patterns: Many missing kids knew Wayne Henley or David Brooks, or had attended Hamilton Junior High School. Some had shopped or worked at Dean Corll's candy company. And other boys had been chased or even attacked by Corll and managed to survive, but opted not to contact police out of fear, distrust, well-known discrimination against hippies and homosexuals, or the simple conviction they would never be believed.

The detective hired by the Hilligiests to investigate the disappearance of their son David and his friend Malley developed what
seemed like an outlandish theory: The boys might have been taken
by a cult or kidnapped by a homosexual porn ring run by an underworld figure called Chicken Joe. Once the desperate parents accompanied an investigator to a stakeout at a bar in Montrose, the city's
most gay-friendly neighborhood, hoping to spot their child. Chicken
Joe never materialized, yet over time, stories of Corll's involvement
in a "boy porn" ring would persist.

The truth was complex and twisted. A monster was stalking the
Heights and other neighborhoods with assistance from teenaged
accomplices. "Everyone knew there was good guys and bad guys,"
David Hilligiest's younger brother Stanley recalled. "We played cops
and robbers, but never thought it affected us." All that time, a real
killer lived just down the street.

On August 8, 1973, Lenore Harvey and many other teens listened
to AM radio or watched on black-and-white TVs with rabbit-ear
antennas when news broke that Elmer Wayne Henley, Jr., had killed
Dean Corll, the former Heights candy man.

Lenore thought instantly of her brother, whose former classmates
were Wayne Henley and David Brooks. *Was Randy buried in that
boatshed too?* Her school crush, Malley Winkle, and his friend David
Hilligiest were among the first to be identified. Their smiling school
photos appeared on the front pages of the *Houston Post* and the
Houston Chronicle. But Randy's name and photo never appeared.
Lenore Harvey and her mother had moved a few blocks away from
their apartment in that hot-pink house and no longer used the number listed on Randy's missing persons report. No police officer or
reporter visited the Harvey home. Lenore wanted to find her brother
so badly that on October 1, she showed up at the morgue by herself,
asking to view murder victims' clothing. At fifteen, she was too
young, really, to act as her brother's representative. She was turned
away, but she didn't give up.

On May 10, 1974, Lenore walked down the street to use a drug-
store pay phone. She rifled through the white pages, found the Harris County Medical Examiner's Office number, deposited ten cents,

and dialed. When Lenore finally got through, the harried employee was polite, but could likely tell Lenore was a child by the lilt of her voice. Lenore's name and some information about Randy were scribbled down on a memo pad.

But messages about missing boys were piling up. Some were filed away; others got lost.

Lenore Harvey's 1974 message to the morgue

CHAPTER 5

THE CHIEF STRIKES BACK

HOUSTON CITY HALL, 1973

O N MONDAY, AUGUST 13, 1973, Houston police chief Herman Short called a 10 A.M. press conference at the police headquarters—not to update the public on the ongoing homicide investigation, but to defend his department and attack his critics, who included murdered children's parents and Soviet Union officials. Soon after the murders made news, the Soviets' official newspaper, *Izvestia*, had condemned HPD for its "astounding inaction," "indifference," and "murderous bureaucracy" in statements distributed worldwide by United Press International. Short, who had an oversized nose, the build of a boxer, and a jaw like a brick, came out fighting. He knew his job was in jeopardy. His supporter, Mayor Welch, was leaving office at year's end; the likely successor, a progressive, had attacked Short's policies as backward.

Seated behind his oversized desk, Short delivered a self-serving six-page speech to a crowd of around fifty journalists. The chief began by declaring that the seemingly shocking number of kids who disappeared from the Heights and other neighborhoods from 1970 to 1973 simply didn't stand out. "No pattern was evident in the disappearances," he declared. Already considering his own run for mayor, Short sounded more like a politician than an investigator when he opined that "parents all over the Heights are pretty well misinformed concerning possible ties among missing youth and their accused killer." Glancing around the room with a gaze that department historians described as one that "could laser through a subordinate like a finely honed knife," the chief declared that any link between the various victims and the suspected killers was a myth "created by the media."

"It might make a better story but there just wasn't a link," he said, ignoring the fact that journalists in the room knew otherwise. One Houston newspaper had already published an oversized map showing that families of at least six victims lived within one to five blocks of the Henley house and that others lived near Corll's known addresses.

The no-nonsense chief, described by fans as a "coolly efficient professional," proceeded to blast the families of missing and murdered teens, declaring that runaways' parents "sometimes don't tell us the truth." By then, several murder victims' relatives had already told reporters that the department had done nothing to search for their missing boys.

"The recent tragedy involving murders of numerous juveniles has prompted some inferences that the Houston Police Department should have or could have proceeded with more intense investigations of those children reported to us as runaways and later found to be victims," the chief declared, dismissing those reports as a "disgusting attempt at scapegoating."

Short ducked some of the tougher questions, including ones about possible connections between Corll and so-called "boy porn rings," as he droned on for twenty minutes, claiming police could do little in cases involving runaways, because "running away" was not a crime. Responding to such reports was merely "a public service."

Reporters never laughed aloud, but some comments reflected their incredulity. Don Mason, an up-and-coming young journalist for *The Dallas Morning News*, challenged the chief by asking: "Would a boy in a bathing suit who gets into a car be called a runaway?"

Short never addressed Houston parents' allegations that none of their murdered children should have been classified as runaways or missing adults, but instead as victims of abductions and suspected homicides. So many of Corll's known victims had inexplicably left behind loving homes with no change of clothing and nothing in their pockets. Some older victims had abandoned steady jobs, cars, apartments, and serious girlfriends. Instead Short spouted statistics. At that point, the bodies of fourteen boys or young men killed by Corll had been preliminarily identified. Of those, thirteen had been reported missing to HPD, he said. Collectively, HPD officers had responded with 88 phone calls and 26 field interviews. That's all his department had time to do, Short implied, given the 5,228 runaway reports and 2,770 new missing persons cases in 1973 alone.

At one point, Short deviated from his script, referring to Corll as "a homosexual type" and describing the crimes as a homosexual killing spree, prompting a challenge from Arthur Bell, a New Yorker who was covering the case for *The Village Voice* and was perhaps the only openly gay journalist present that day.

"What do you mean by 'homosexual type'?" Bell asked in a resonant voice that filled the room. Bell could be charming and persuasive, but at that moment he sounded irritated.

"I thought everybody knew what a homosexual was," the chief sneered.

Bell's voice carried as he offered a counterview: "There is no 'homosexual type.'"

Chief Short had no real answer to that either. Dean Corll was clearly in a category all his own.

Finally, Short lowered his voice an octave, glanced at a clay model of Houston displayed near his semi-octagonal desk, and lobbed a parting shot: "Obviously parents could have done a better job of raising their children," he said, singling out Malley Winkle's widowed mother, Selma, for ridicule because her boy had gone missing with his buddy and she'd allowed her neighbors to report the disappearances instead of doing it herself. Understandably, the chief's statements further alienated families planning to bury their murdered sons or still waiting for news about the missing.

One of Corll's last victims was Homer Garcia, a student at the elite Bellaire High School, who met Wayne Henley at a summer driving school and may have accepted a ride home from Wayne, who main-

tained a friendly facade even as he performed his service of procuring boys for Corll to kill. Homer's father, Luis Garcia, clipped
newspaper accounts of Short's news conference and related his response in a memoir for family members:

> As you may have noticed, Chief Short by his statement has branded
> all victims as runaways. That is false; our son Homer was not a run-
> away and the record shows that most of the other victims were not
> runaways either. I can only conclude that Chief Short was trying to
> hide under the umbrella of the laws [on] runaway children. On the
> other hand, he possibly wanted to protect his police department
> and conceal his incompetence. Whatever his motive, Chief Short
> and his department never gave us any assistance in locating our son
> when we reported him missing. He was never around when needed.

One of Randy Harvey's friends, a student at the University of
Houston who worked part time as a bartender at a club in Montrose,
phoned the Pasadena police in 1973 to suggest they look into Randy's disappearance, but the tip was apparently ignored. At some
point, investigators apparently did try to determine whether Randy's mother had dental records, but it's unclear whether she ever got
that message. Understandably, some parents preferred to believe
their missing boys were still out there somewhere and had not been
tortured, raped, and murdered by a madman. There was, of course,
the perceived risk of stigma attached to being related to the Lost
Boys, all of whom had been described on network news and in the
international press as the rape, torture, and murder victims of a prolific killer and "sex fiend."

But it seemed strange that one particular missing Houston teen's
father never seemed to attempt to claim any murder victim's remains:
Willard K. Branch, Sr., a Houston police officer. Perhaps Officer
Branch figured that making an ID would only generate adverse publicity and bring shame on himself, his family, and his department,
though he never explained his reasons either in public statements or
privately to his other children. (Yet another missing boy, Jim Glass,
the son of a Harris County sheriff's deputy, was quickly identified.)

In fact, Officer Branch made misleading statements to the press about his missing son, Willard K. "Rusty" Branch, Jr. The elder Branch claimed in an interview that he had used "every police trick I know on my own" to find his son "and came up with a complete zero. It was like he dropped off the face of the earth." Yet records show that his father did not officially report Rusty Branch as a missing person when the seventeen-year-old vanished in February 1972, apparently while hitchhiking home to Houston. He did so approximately nine months later. Rusty Branch's name appeared in an August 1973 missing persons list published by newspapers when news of the mass graves broke, and yet Rusty's father seemed oddly reluctant to provide crucial records to ME investigators working on identifications. Officer Branch (or another relative) supplied only one badly outdated photo—a picture that depicted seventeen-year-old Rusty, a compact football player at a Houston high school, as a round-faced little boy. He provided no dental or medical records, though he knew such information was critical to making an ID.

Instead of advocating for his lost son, Officer Branch curried favor with Chief Short by going on the offensive to defend his department in an August 1973 interview with the *Houston Chronicle*. He insisted that finding teenagers was more challenging than finding adults, who might have fingerprints on file or use credit cards that could be traced. The HPD missing persons bureau "does everything they can to locate a child," he said. "If you just give them any little lead, they will check it out." Officer Branch earned a laudatory letter in his personnel file from Chief Short, who personally requested FBI assistance in Rusty's disappearance. Branch went on to receive several promotions, eventually retiring as a captain. He told his other children, Rusty's little brother and two sisters, that he never stopped looking for Rusty. He claimed to still be doing so in 1980, the year he died of a heart attack at forty-nine.

His children did not think he was telling them the truth. His eldest daughter believed Officer Branch knew more about Dean Corll than he ever admitted.

IN THE HEIGHTS, OWNERS of a neighborhood grocery store and other boosters formed a civic association and set out to rid their community of its reputation as a serial killer's hunting grounds. They planted rosebushes around Hamilton Junior High, where so many murdered boys had attended school, and launched a public relations campaign. Over the years, new families moved in, attracted to the neighborhood's linear parks, Victorian homes, and clapboard bungalows. Residents fixed up abandoned mansions, renovated rundown houses, and established historic districts. Shabbier blocks were razed and replaced by upscale condos and strip malls. The places where Randy Harvey, Malley Winkle, and other Lost Boys once lived were erased.

A handful of families of the teenaged killers and of the murder victims lingered in their Heights homes. For a dozen years, David Hilligiest's relatives remained neighbors with the Henleys and attempted to be cordial when they met in shops or on the street. Other grieving parents and siblings left Houston or passed away never knowing what became of their Lost Boys. As time passed, the threads of the lives of so many missing and murdered teenagers grew tangled. Those who remembered rarely spoke of them; it was simply too painful. Yet many memories of the last troubling encounters with boys who simply vanished lingered and altered lives.

Few knew that some remains recovered in August 1973 remained unidentified for decades after Corll's demise and that other missing persons and bodies were still out there, waiting to be rediscovered. Scattered clues were left behind in Harris County archives—in hand-typed missing persons reports, in Polaroid autopsy photos, in investigators' handwritten memos, and in detectives' crude diagrams.

Some victims' remains had been boxed up and stored in the Harris County ME's vault. Three cardboard boxes of bones sat on a shelf for decades, their contents slowly deteriorating and largely unattended. Then one day, Sharon Derrick began to open those boxes, one by one.

CHAPTER 6

THE FIRST MYSTERIOUS BOX
OF BONES

HARRIS COUNTY MORGUE, 2007

SHARON DERRICK HAD ALWAYS had lofty goals, though she'd put her dreams on hold after she and Al married in 1976 when both were in their teens. As husband and wife, both initially continued their studies as undergraduates at the University of Texas, where Sharon initially majored in broadcast journalism and film and had even been offered a job after completing an internship at a TV station, before becoming fascinated by anthropology. Her early career inspirations came from a charismatic professor and from Dian Fossey's studies of gorilla groups in the misty mountains of Rwanda. Fossey had undertaken that risky work in 1966, which led her to fame, groundbreaking revelations, threats, and eventually to being murdered in 1985. Sharon Derrick chose to study ancient human civilizations closer to home.

Then before she could finish her degree, she got pregnant. Still struggling to pay bills, Sharon dropped out and got a job to help cover Al's schooling. She figured the pause on her studies would be temporary, but could not find the time for classes when they relocated to Pullman, Washington, or even when they moved back to Texas in 1983 after Al won a spot at the competitive Texas A&M veterinary school. Their return was tough. By then they had three kids, and she'd become the primary caregiver for their two daughters and young son, while Al immersed himself in studies. Sharon feared the intellectual companionship and partnership they had enjoyed was becoming lopsided. "Al was starting to look down on me as a housewife with only a high school diploma," she recalls (though Al protests). "He was getting so far ahead of me in education, it felt like I might lose him. We almost divorced. Maybe it was the seven-year itch."

Derrick returned to classes, and by studying late at night and in between school pickups and chores, she finished her undergraduate degree in 1988. Then she kept going, choosing a bridge program that launched her immediately into a doctorate. Her hardworking parents had never attended college; her father had been too busy working and helping his widowed mother even to finish high school. Two of Sharon's siblings earned bachelor's degrees; one brother became the director of music at a community college. But no one else was crazy enough to try for a Ph.D. Soon Sharon Derrick had dived so deep into anthropology that she rarely had time for long conversations about anything else.

In 1991, Sharon and Al moved to Cypress, a Houston suburb, where Al founded his veterinary practice and Sharon continued to commute to College Station, where she conducted research under a prominent anthropologist. At that point, she aimed to become a bioarchaeologist, an expert in the excavation and analysis of archaeological human remains. She traveled around the state exploring prehistoric and historic sites and studying remains, including a Caddoan Indian skull someone abandoned in a dilapidated farmhouse. Sharon juggled fieldwork and coursework with her teenaged daughters' activities, as well as soccer games and auditions for her youngest, James, a budding actor who won roles in plays and commercials. It took her nearly a decade to finish her doctorate.

She and Al had trouble catching up even at night—she stayed up late studying while he responded to emergencies. They continued to bond over their interests in science and in making discoveries. But Sharon found it easier to examine dead people than to discuss dying animals; neither quite understood their partner's predilections.

Sharon's dissertation temporarily stalled in 1998 when she was diagnosed with Stage 3 breast cancer. She maintained her super-mom facade between rounds of chemotherapy and radiation, hiding the dire prognosis from her children. Her progress stopped as Derrick descended into self-pity and depression. Then one day Al said: "If you don't have much time left, you don't want to waste it." His words resonated, and their partnership resolidified. She finished her treatment and her dissertation, and earned her Ph.D. in 2001.

Five years later, she pivoted to yet another demanding specialty: forensic anthropology. All of her life and academic experience prepared Derrick for the challenge she chose next: identifying the Lost Boys. Derrick knew how to focus and persist even if reaching her goals took years. And she had already survived and succeeded—against long odds.

HARRIS COUNTY MEDICAL EXAMINER Dr. Luis Sanchez's decision to hire Derrick in 2006 and later to establish a team of forensic anthropologists put Harris County ahead of other medical examiners' offices. Few other U.S. counties employed any forensic anthropologists in the 2000s, though the 9/11 terrorist attacks in New York City had raised awareness of the need for experts able to identify the dead even from small specks of bones and DNA.

But the specialty of forensic anthropology that Derrick chose was far older. It initially began in America as a shadowy side project for a few illustrious academics in the 1930s, when FBI agents began quietly sending bones associated with criminal cases to the anthropology laboratories at the Smithsonian's National Museum of Natural History. One Smithsonian luminary, J. Lawrence Angel, a dapper English anthropologist who was partial to bow ties, cigars, and Agatha Christie mysteries, began to moonlight so regularly for the bureau in the 1970s and 1980s that he ended up with the moniker Sherlock Bones. Angel relished even the most odiferous and perplexing of cases. "He sang around the office, quietly and unobtrusively, and those of us who got to know him usually could tell from the melody what type of work he was doing, particularly when he was collecting data from a skeleton," wrote Dr. Douglas Ubelaker, another pioneer in the field and one of Angel's early students. Many eminent scientists who dabbled in death got dubbed "bone detectives" by the press, but preferred the term they invented: "forensic anthropologists."

Pioneers like Angel relied on reference data from the Smithsonian's vast skeletal research collection, including remains from prehistoric archaeological sites worldwide, to calculate modern American murder victims' height, age, and sex. Over time, though, forensic anthropologists began to realize that evolutionary differences meant that estimates for modern cases based on data from far older bone collections could be way off. In the 1980s, forensic anthropologist William "Bill" Bass dreamed up a way to modernize those comparisons by creating the Anthropology Research Facility at the University of Tennessee, dubbed the "Body Farm." His program solicited people to donate their corpses to his facility in Knoxville, where forensic researchers could conduct unusual experiments to simulate murder scenes and record observations of variations in the decomposition process. Donors' bodies were buried in shallow graves, left out in the sun, stored in derelict or burning vehicles or crude shelters, and submerged in water in efforts to re-create conditions from real crime scenes.

By the time Derrick began her first Lost Boy case, forensic anthropologists had been conducting experiments and running body recovery exercises on the Body Farm, near the University of Tennessee's football stadium, for two decades. Forensic entomologists had conducted endless experiments into the pace of development of wormlike blowfly larvae in bodies. Others examined decomposition questions, such as: How long does it take for an arm to fall off? Or for a skull to start showing through a face, given the passage of time and daily average temperatures? "Not many people have our kind of experience watching bodies as they decay and timing the rate at which maggots drop off of them," Bass has observed. All that information could help restore lost identities and solve crimes. As Bass wrote: "Every one of these lessons would serve me well in the years ahead as I began applying the secrets I learned from the long-dead to understanding the stories of the recently murdered." The Body Farm gained fame through a bestselling novel, nonfiction books, and serial televised adventures. Six more facilities were subsequently developed to allow researchers to determine how differences in climate and geography affected the dead and decomposition, including sites in Florida, Michigan, and two in Texas.

IN HER FOUR YEARS at the county health department, Sharon Derrick had managed to keep an emotional distance when she reviewed bodies and bones of babies and small children, some of whom perished from extreme forms of abuse. But it sometimes troubled her to examine the remains of the Lost Boys, these long-dead teenagers. By 2006, when she began working on those cases, James, her youngest child and only son, was about the same age Corll's victims had been. He was finishing high school and still dreaming of becoming a professional actor. Sometimes he went out and didn't say where he was going or came home late. "You know how you would feel if one of your sons was missing," she says. "I worried about him when I worked at the morgue, especially if he didn't get home in a particular period of time." Some weekends or late nights, she'd get called to an accident scene involving a vehicle fire that rendered bodies difficult to identify. Occasionally, she'd hang around and ask more questions, "because I was thinking could it possibly be my son."

In January 2007, Derrick obtained permission from her direct supervisor, Dr. Dwayne Wolf, M.D., an experienced forensic pathologist, to examine the contents of the box labeled ML 73-3349, containing the bones of the boy and his boots. Wolf, the office's imposing second-in-command, seemed stern, but his name tag bore a tiny Martin guitar, betraying the musical habit that consumed much of his free time. Occasionally, without changing expression, he would deliver a dry joke or warm praise. His intense commitment to high ethical and professional standards commanded respect. Before Derrick's arrival, Wolf had already begun to arrange to collect DNA samples needed to identify some bodies inside the long-term storage vault, but he was busy as a senior pathologist in one of the nation's largest counties. Without saying so, he seemed to appreciate that she was taking over that task.

When Derrick checked out that first 1973 box, an inventory control specialist stationed at a central desk scrawled the case number, ML 73-3349, on a whiteboard with a dry-erase marker in accordance with office security protocols. The box containing the physical evidence of this teenager's last day on earth was relatively light. Derrick toted it down the hallway to the "decomp room," a compact space set apart from other autopsy suites, which was normally used by pathologists tackling more odiferous cases, as well as to store saws and other tools. Though these bones had little smell, Derrick sometimes worked with bone remains containing scraps of spoiled soft tissue (colloquially known as "cheese") or with fresher bodies that sometimes arrived rotting and infested with maggots. This small room would later become a hub for skeletal examinations conducted by the county's forensic anthropology section.

Still relatively new to the office in January 2007, Derrick wasn't sure she'd be allowed to wheel a shiny stainless steel autopsy table into the decomp room for a bone case. Pathologists needed those tables, which were almost too big for this room anyway. Instead, she obtained a plastic-backed sterile sheet used to protect ambulance gurneys from bodily fluids and carefully laid it on a smaller table already in the room. Derrick set down this box, opened the lid, and with gloved hands began to carefully examine the artifacts and bones inside. She had already pulled related files and learned the cause of death from 1973 autopsy reports and photos: This teenager had been shot in the face at close range. Forensic pathologists had originally found a .22-caliber bullet in his sinus cavity and a nylon cord tied around his neck; the bullet and the rope had long ago been removed as evidence.

With gloved hands, Derrick examined what remained of his clothing. Weight was impossible to determine from bones alone, but this boy had been slender, with only a thirty-inch waistline, judging by the length of the belt recovered next to scraps of his deteriorated blue jeans.

All of this boy's bones but one bore a rich caramel color—a sign they'd been buried in Houston's notoriously heavy soil often called clay gumbo. In clandestine graves, bones tended to assume the tint of the earth. The autopsy report confirmed his skeleton had been found in Corll's boatshed. Only the skull was bright white, suggesting it had likely been cleaned with bleach or boiled prior to a previous forensic exam. Well into the 2000s, a morgue tech was regularly using a hot plate and oversized pot to boil and clean bones—a process that Derrick opposed, arguing that boiling bones could damage and alter their appearance and destroy DNA. (Her efforts would eventually end the office's bone boiling and bleaching in favor of more careful alternatives.)

The boy's skull immediately interested her. The 1973 reports showed that Stimson, the forensic dentist, had already noticed a telling feature: "The jaw relationship is undershot, as there is a protrusion of the maxilla." Derrick later reached out to Stimson, who, in his early seventies, continued to consult on a part-time basis, and he came to the office to assist her. His white hair had receded, forming a ring around a large bald spot and revealing a scar from brain surgery, but he still got visibly excited reviewing photos and records on the Lost Boys. From her own examination, Derrick agreed that this boy, in life, had a long face and an undershot square chin with a divot. In colloquial terms, she imagined him as a younger and more attractive version of the classic Canadian Mountie cartoon character Dudley Do-Right.

She lifted each bone and placed it individually on a small table, recording its measurements. Most of his skeleton was present, save for a few vertebrae and two lower arm bones (the radius and the ulna) on what would have been the left side. Derrick wondered if she might be able to find those missing bones inside another box associated with the "Houston Mass Murders." She used calipers, tools she'd acquired in her days as a graduate student at Texas A&M, to precisely measure curved bones, like the ribs and pelvis. It could be difficult to determine the sex of a child or adolescent based on bones, though this skeleton definitely appeared male. The pelvis was very narrow; typically, even an adolescent girl had more room in that region to facilitate childbirth. Derrick used measuring tape and a long bone board, also from her Aggie days, to precisely measure the leg and arm bones. She paid close attention to the epiphyses—

the expanded ends on each of his long bones. In humans, those os- sify separately from the main bone and become permanently fixed to the shaft of an arm or leg bone only after full growth is attained. Because they generally ossify, or turn from cartilage to bone, at age ranges that are similar for all humans, the epiphyses provide impor- tant clues for estimating the approximate age of an unidentified child or adolescent.

Derrick measuring bones
PHOTO TEXAS A&M UNIVERSITY–CORPUS CHRISTI

Based on measurements she fed into a computer program, Der- rick determined that this boy had likely been quite tall—perhaps six feet or even six two. Yet it was clear that he had not yet reached his full height, since most of his epiphyses had not yet fused. (Nonsci- entists refer to the epiphyseal plate as the "growth plate.") In other words, he still had room to grow, and if he'd lived, he would have gotten even taller.

Next, Derrick carefully moved the skull into another room so that a technician could take X-rays on equipment that was old in 2006, but better than the machine used in 1973. The results confirmed this boy's wisdom teeth had not yet erupted, another sign that he'd likely died before turning eighteen. Derrick recorded her observations of his teeth and skull, along with the bone measurements, and used them to consult modern statistical databases built and validated by other anthropologists to establish estimates of his likely age and other characteristics.

Long bones have been used for more than a century to estimate the height of a decedent from skeletal remains. But procedures and the amount of reference data had vastly improved since the 1970s, when many pathologists refined their estimates by using comparison data from thirty thousand archaeological remains at the Smithsonian Institution and repositories maintained by the U.S. Army. Those collections included statistics about the skeletons of people who'd died in the 1800s or before, but nineteenth-century Americans were generally shorter and smaller than their modern counterparts. The Smithsonian's collection included far older remains of people who perished after periods of famine, plague, war, deadly childhood diseases, and struggles related to subsistence hunting and gathering. It reflected human history, but not modern microevolution.

Derrick could take advantage of the Forensic Anthropology Data Bank, which contained more than three thousand modern cases. The archive, begun in 1986, included four hundred cases analyzed by Angel, the Smithsonian's own dapper "bone detective," and other data from forensic anthropologists nationwide. All that new data enabled forensic anthropologists to improve estimates of gender at birth, age, and height for unknown U.S. decedents, and to reduce mistakes, such as misidentifying a man as a woman or a teenager as an older adult. Precision was important, since major miscalculations could doom the chance of making a match between an unknown decedent and a missing person. Using those tools, Derrick estimated that her first Lost Boy might be as young as fifteen and was likely between five feet eight inches and six feet one and a half inches tall. In 1973, pathologists had postulated that this boy had been older and shorter, estimating his age at eighteen to twenty and his height at five nine to five eleven and a half.

To Derrick, it seemed possible that this teen *had* been reported missing, but mistakenly eliminated as too young (or too tall) to match these remains. Perhaps his name was somewhere in the ME's tall stack of 1970s missing persons. Every day as Derrick commuted through the Heights to work, she thought of him. *Who was he? And is his family still searching for him?*

CHAPTER 7

THE PARADE OF BODIES

HARRIS COUNTY ME'S OFFICE, 1973

Pat Paul in the 1970s Harris County morgue

OR TWO FULL DAYS, a parade of private mortuary workers cruised in their "body cars" from the boatshed to the morgue on August 8 and 9. Houston morticians competed for county business in those days by monitoring police radios and rushing to death scenes. If jobs were particularly messy, like this one, some picked up day laborers to use as haulers. Those crews systematically zipped the murdered teens' putrefied bodies or skeletal remains into body bags, then loaded them into the cargo bays of black stretch sedans for the 6.7-mile journey to an obscure side entrance of Ben Taub Hospital.

Unfortunately, the Harris County Medical Examiner's Office, located in the hospital's basement, was too small in 1973 to accommodate even its usual caseload: By the 1970s, Houston had more than four hundred homicides annually, plus victims of suicides, accidental deaths, or "unattended deaths" at home that all had to be autopsied or at least investigated. The overload meant that for a while, more than a dozen remains of Corll's murder victims were deposited on carts topped with metal trays and left in a row inside the morgue's rear entrance. Arriving employees faced an obstacle course of untimely death. They had to get used to it. "You just walked by death every day," remembers Pat Paul, still a morgue rookie then.

All investigations and autopsies were overseen by Dr. Joe, the colorful figure who'd been Chief Medical Examiner since 1960 and the county's lead forensic pathologist even longer. Back in 1956 the Texas Legislature had created the office of County Medical Examiner and required the largest urban counties to hire a qualified professional to fill that role. Harris County officials recruited Jachimczyk, then an assistant professor of legal medicine at Harvard School of Medicine. He accepted a pay cut to take the $20,000-a-year position with an outdated morgue and massive caseload. When asked to explain his odd choice, Jachimczyk said he'd felt discriminated against at Harvard as the son of an ice deliveryman and Polish emigrant. Ivy League institutions, "whether they like to admit it or not, are bound by musty tradition which does not ignore wealth and prestige," he wrote. Waxing nostalgic about his dad one day, he asked Pat Paul if her family icehouse still had ice tongs—she retrieved a pair and presented them as a gift.

Jachimczyk was a World War II veteran with an iron will, a colorful and sometimes comedic personality, and a relentless work ethic. He recruited talented staff members, but constantly felt forced to lobby county commissioners for adequate funding and space to carry out his mission. Sometimes, to juice his budget and to argue for improvements, he'd invite politicians on tours of his busy basement and lead them through the daily throng of bodies.

Under Texas law, even now, only the largest counties employ specially trained medical examiners to perform autopsies and to determine the manner (suicide, accident, homicide, or unknown) and specific cause of death. Death investigations in the rest of the state are overseen by justices of the peace, elected officials who often lack medical or legal training.

Despite his space crunch, Dr. Joe insisted in August 1973 that all of Corll's victims be sent to Harris County. Seventeen sets of remains soon arrived from the boatshed. He repeated that edict after ten more victims' graves were discovered in the forest near Corll's family cabin in Angelina and San Augustine counties in East Texas and on the beach near High Island in Chambers and Jefferson counties, jurisdictions that lacked MEs. "Some places are still pretty primitive," Jachimczyk told a *Texas Monthly* reporter who visited his operation in 1975: "The sheriff or a JP or somebody'll come in, take a quick peek at the body and say 'Oh-ho, there's a hole there, musta been shot.' It's ridiculous."

Most elected JPs with authority over death investigations outside Harris County agreed to cooperate, though the autopsy for fifteen-year-old Billy Lawrence, whose body had been found in the woods, was initially conducted in a shed in Lufkin by a freelance physician hired on contract by an East Texas JP. That physician didn't follow Harris County protocols; Billy Lawrence's bones were initially identified after a rapid viewing of what the father believed to be his son's decaying face. (Later, Dr. Joe insisted on reexamining the remains. In an X-ray, he discovered a bullet that had been missed and updated the cause of death to include shooting, thereby addressing an error that otherwise could have upended prosecutors' efforts to convict David Brooks of Billy Lawrence's murder.)

Five days after Corll's death, the corpses of Dean Corll and the remains of twenty-six of the twenty-seven murder victims ended up in Dr. Joe's morgue. Lab workers quickly affixed tags with handwritten case numbers to the toes of intact bodies, and skeletal remains were tagged on a long bone. Each was labeled with ML—for medical legal case—and then the year and a case number indicating the order received. Thus, the seventeen sets of remains from the boatshed were labeled ML 73-3332 to 73-3357 (not in consecutive order, since unrelated cases arrived simultaneously).

Property and clothing were also inventoried and labeled with case numbers. Photos of partial and complete articles of clothing, scraps of twine, bones, and other evidence were captured with a ubiquitous 1970s tool: a Polaroid Instamatic. Then each body—or pile of bones—was weighed, measured, and placed on a table for autopsy. The hope was that the remains of all of these boys and young men would soon be matched with the names of missing persons and restored to their grieving parents.

An idealistic and brilliant workaholic, Dr. Joe stayed in the morgue from dawn until after midnight on many days that August. He performed one autopsy after another, using a foot pedal to activate a tape recorder beneath the table, and dictated his findings aloud, recordings later typed up by the department's transcription team. He once told Matt Wingo, a longtime chief investigator's son who later joined the staff, that the job was never about money for him. "If you want to get rich, you're not going to be a public servant. But this job offers ample spiritual rewards. I'm rich in spiritual awards." Dr. Joe was serious about that spiritual side. Somehow, he found time to study theology and become an ordained minister.

Dr. Joe, like others in Houston, had never dealt with such a complex body recovery site before. The task of determining IDs from the intermingled remains of teenaged boys in mass graves left by a serial killer was supremely difficult in 1973. (And it remained difficult in 2006 when Derrick began to reexamine some of the same evidence.)

Working in a crowded office apart from the autopsy suites, Pat Paul, still a receptionist, grappled with investigating leads on missing male adolescents or young adults. Paul focused primarily on unresolved cases involving boys from the Heights and other Houston neighborhoods from 1970 to 1973. She pressed police for typewritten reports and information from incoming calls about other teens, not all of whom had previously been reported missing. Eventually, the office assembled a list of fifty likely candidates—nearly twice the number of remains recovered.

Paul wasn't a real investigator yet, but as a mother, she could relate to the grieving parents she encountered. The official ME investigators were mostly macho former police officers, though colorful colleague J. L. "Tooter" Turner had started out as an undertaker, and retained a charming manner with the bereaved (and his license, since it sometimes proved useful). Short and squat, Turner had only one functional arm, but he could nonetheless lift a corpse of any size alone and wrangle it into a hearse. Turner was cordial; the rest weren't particularly welcoming. One old-school officer liked to crow about the good ol' days when legal disputes had been resolved on the hanging tree and when juvenile delinquents were returned to parents for whuppings with belts. *Perhaps such attitudes helped explain why so many disappearances of Houston adolescents had initially gotten ignored,* Paul thought. Some missing kids had obvious reasons to distrust police: They wore long hair, smoked pot, or were experimenting with sex. A handful had minor juvenile arrest records. Many were the children of divorced parents living with busy single moms and, as she well knew, women tended to get less attention from authorities than men.

Some parents pressed hard for access to unidentified remains, insisting they could identify their children just by viewing decomposed bodies or bones. Paul typically shared only photos of a deceased teen's clothing or teeth, as well as descriptions of potentially identifying characteristics, like scars, tattoos, hair color, and estimated height. She often had to repeat office policy: The Harris County Medical Examiner's Office did not allow prospective relatives to view decomposed bodies or skeletal remains, though they could choose to do so in a mortuary after the remains had been identified. Paul warned against that option: "Once you look, you can never unsee that."

She knew that lesson from experience. As a morgue employee, she opted to view the body of a pilot sent for an autopsy after he and her father had perished together in a plane crash in 1969. She deeply regretted her decision. Afterward, she could never forget the pilot's crumpled corpse or stop imagining the agony her father must have suffered.

The first IDs of boys whose parents could supply dental records came quickly, only hours or days after the discoveries of the graves. As time passed, other Lost Boys' family members were invited to view hair samples and items found with bodies as part of the ID process. "It was so sad for these families. A lot of them were poor," she remembers.

Everett Waldrop, the father of one of two sets of missing brothers, had been horrified after newspapers published David Brooks's August 9, 1973, statement, which said Corll "killed some boys" in 1971 while living at Place One apartments, a complex on Mangum Road next to the construction site where Waldrop had been assigned that year. "Maybe he had them in the apartment when I went to work," Waldrop told a reporter for the *Houston Chronicle.* "Maybe they were being tortured right next door and I didn't know it." Waldrop insisted on being given two sets of remains after learning that wallets and insurance cards bearing his sons' last names had been found inside a grave labeled Boatshed Hole No. 8. Donald, fifteen, had been carrying his own insurance card; Jerry, thirteen, had the card of an older brother, Waldrop told investigators. But Waldrop could supply no dental records.

Jachimczyk warned his staff not to make assumptions based on paperwork collected at the chaotic boatshed site, where graves overlapped or contained multiple remains. His motto was: "Nothing is ever obvious. Always be suspicious." Waldrop, who by 1973 had moved back to Atlanta with his wife and surviving children, kept clamoring for the bodies found beside his boys' IDs. Eventually, Dr. Joe caved and shipped them off.

Within days, the ME uncovered a terrible mistake: Charts of teeth from the bodies sent to Georgia subsequently matched records obtained from the dentists of a different pair of murdered boys. It turned out the Waldrop brothers' IDs and wallets had been buried beside other boys who were similar in age. After reviewing records, Jachimczyk announced that the Waldrops had been given the bodies of David Hilligiest and Malley Winkle by mistake. The Waldrop boys had been buried in a different hole beside a more cryptic memento—a page torn from an HPD report.

An embarrassing exchange ensued in the press, with Everett Waldrop blaming Dr. Joe and Dr. Joe blaming Waldrop. Parents and Harris County officials argued over who would pay to ship two sets of remains back to Texas and two from Houston to Atlanta. Eventually, "Tooter" Turner drove off to assist with arrangements, his undertaker's license coming in handy.

Dr. Joe was furious. Though he sometimes made jokes, he saw no humor in errors. Publicly and in private communications with staff, the ME declared that he was committed to ensuring all other Lost Boys were properly identified, no matter how long it took. No one else would be authorized to announce any ID. By the end of September 1973, nineteen of the twenty-seven known victims' remains were deemed to be properly identified and restored to families.

The ME worried over the victims whose identities stayed cloaked in anonymity: five from the boatshed, two from the beach, and one from the forest. Those bodies remained in the cold storage vault, labeled only with case numbers. At times, he despaired. "It's overwhelmed us. It has really put a strain on our facilities," he said.

"In twenty years, this is the first time I have been having nightmares about my work."

CHAPTER 8

THE BOY AND HIS BOOTS

HARRIS COUNTY ME'S OFFICE, 2006–2008

AFTER MUCH OF HER initial examination was complete, Sharon Derrick learned that the case of the Lost Boy with the boots had already been reviewed by another forensic anthropologist— a Texas State University professor hired as a consultant prior to her arrival. He'd already submitted a sample for DNA testing to the University of North Texas's Center for Human Identification, but the lab found no match to any family members of missing persons who'd provided DNA samples included in government databases. Her excitement faded: This case seemed like a lost cause.

Police investigators and medical examiner's offices had long relied on the National Crime Information Center (NCIC) to search for matches between the unidentified dead and the case descriptions or dental records of missing persons. They also used the FBI's Combined DNA Index System, or CODIS, to search for potential matches to the DNA of unknown decedents. But NCIC searches were clunky and DNA samples from most of America's army of forty thousand unidentified dead rarely matched entries in CODIS, which in the early 2000s contained relatively few DNA reference samples from missing persons' relatives. Far more CODIS entries contained suspects' DNA samples extracted from blood or semen left behind after murders or rapes or collected from people convicted of felonies.

DNA samples from inmates and crime scenes in CODIS rarely matched the unidentified dead—though such a search generated an astonishing ID for a Houston murder victim whose remains had been hidden inside a barrel in a backyard. That match initially seemed like a computer glitch: Somehow, the DNA of an anonymous murder victim found in 2010 perfectly matched the victim of an unrelated 1990 homicide. But it turned out to be a true breakthrough. The identification of Stacie Lee Ann Lutz Anderson came through a tragic coincidence: Anderson's identical twin, Tracie De Ann Lutz, was the 1990 murder victim. Tracie Lutz's murder remains unsolved, but her twin's killer seemed clear from her ID: "Stacie vanished in late 1999 at age 30, two years after she had married a man 23 years older than her. Her husband, Dennis Ray Anderson— a convicted murderer already paroled from a Texas prison—never reported his wife missing," the *Houston Chronicle* reported. Anderson had committed suicide shortly after his missing wife's remains had been recovered from the barrel in his yard.

By the late 2000s, Derrick had another powerful search tool to use. In 2007, the NamUs database of Unidentified Persons was launched by federal government agencies to help tackle the nation's "Silent Mass Disaster." Later, NamUs added a parallel missing persons database, an effort that encouraged police and members of the public to supply data on older unsolved missing persons cases. The NamUs databases included a section available only to investigators, including links to DNA test results of the relatives of missing persons, which were still securely stored in CODIS. But its basic data on the missing and unidentified was public—opening a path for family members, internet sleuths, and crime bloggers to search for matches and to provide tips. For years, the Center for Human Identification at the University of North Texas Health Science Center served as a government contractor to support NamUs, which meant Derrick and other researchers could use that lab to process DNA samples from unknown dead people or from the relatives of missing persons and upload case data to NamUs (and contribute related DNA test results to CODIS) without fees. Almost immediately, there were backlogs for testing. But the new system galvanized the public and quickly became a success: By 2023, NamUs had been used to make more than 6,700 identifications, many in cold cases.

Even in new searches of NamUs and CODIS, Derrick initially received no matches for the DNA samples she'd submitted for the boy in the boots. She refused to give up, opting to submit additional samples from his teeth on the chance that newer tests might provide better DNA profiles. In the meantime, she'd located stray arm bones inside another of the 1973 boxes that might belong to this boy and submitted them for testing too. She knew that DNA tests on those bones could take nine months or longer given the demands on the busy UNT lab. In the meantime, she pursued other clues.

Over the years, Houston forensic artists had helped make IDs by sketching portraits of the unidentified deceased, reanimating faces from autopsy photos or reimagining them from bones. Though drawings of faces from fresh corpses could be particularly accurate, Derrick worried that too many sketches based on skulls resembled mannequins or masks. After conferring with colleagues, Derrick decided in April 2007 that it would be worth the risk to ship all three of the Lost Boys' unidentified skulls to a Louisiana lab—the Forensic Anthropology and Computer Enhancement Services, FACES, in order to obtain modern 3-D portraits.

In the 1990s, Mary Manhein, a pioneering forensic anthropologist at Louisiana State University, had launched FACES to assist coroners and MEs in parishes statewide with identifications, body recovery, and murder cases. That work intensified after Hurricane Katrina struck in August 2005, claiming the lives of at least eighteen hundred people, many of whom had been lost in floodwaters and remained unidentified even years later.

The FACES lab employed a skilled artist named Eileen Barrow, already nationally known for her innovative facial reconstruction skills. Derrick hoped that Barrow could create more accurate likenesses for these teens by taking advantage of databases filled with measurements of the thickness of layers of skin from the faces of dead people studied at body farms. Barrow created three-dimensional clay models atop all three skulls. Then she uploaded images of those models into a computer and enhanced them to produce updated images.

Barrow's facial reconstructions had already generated new leads for identifications in supremely challenging Katrina ID cases and for other unknown murder victims. Her work later played a key role in shedding light on the identity of a seaman who had drowned in 1862 when the USS *Monitor* sank just off Cape Hatteras, North Carolina, during the Civil War.

The *Monitor*, the nation's first ironclad vessel, was famous for winning a celebrated battle with a Confederate ship called the *Merrimack* only nine months before it foundered in a gale and sank 240 feet below the Atlantic. When a team of underwater archaeologists from Derrick's alma mater, Texas A&M, raised its armored gun turret in 2002, they recovered two of the sixteen mariners' remains. Those men had been dead 150 years when Barrow was asked to reimagine their visages in 2012. The younger seaman's identity remains difficult to discern. But the bearded man whose 3-D portrait Barrow re-created resembled Robert Williams, a burly Welsh crewman with a horseshoe-shaped mustache who went down with his ship. Lisa Stansbury, a project genealogist for the National Oceanic and Atmospheric Administration, dug up Williams's name and photo and verified his age and height as part of ID efforts between NOAA, FACES, and the Joint Prisoners of War / Missing in Action Accounting Command. There was strong circumstantial evidence for Williams's ID, though a definitive match with his descendants through DNA tests remained elusive. Both men were reburied in Arlington National Cemetery.

DERRICK HOPED THAT UPDATED images might generate new leads for these three Lost Boys. She liked knowing that the 3-D computerized portraits were highly adaptable so that Barrow could easily superimpose alternate hairdos or add facial hair to facilitate comparisons to prospective missing persons. Derrick planned to post all three on the ME's unidentified cases webpage. Maybe someone would spot a familiar face or web sleuths would uncover a connection.

While Derrick waited, she had an unexpected stroke of luck.

In the summer of 2006, a forensic anthropologist named Jason Wiersema joined Derrick as part of the lab's growing team. Wier-

FACES reconstruction for case No. ML-73-3349, one of the Lost Boys

sema, a vigorous, compact man who favors a full beard, specialized in mass fatality events like the plant explosions and hurricanes that often struck Houston and other Gulf Coast communities. Wiersema had worked on the 9/11 recovery process in New York, and he later set up a rapid death investigations response team that the Texas Medical Center magazine nicknamed Forensics on Call. Wiersema could come off as arrogant, but had a decent sense of humor and a cool head, enviable characteristics for a disaster specialist.

In his first few days on the job, Wiersema walked into Derrick's office with an unexpected air of excitement: He was clutching a few musty folders stuffed with random papers and handwritten notes that he'd found while cleaning out a filing cabinet. "I think you'll want to look at this," he said, handing over a fat file.

Right as he left, Derrick began shuffling through the documents and discovered several missing persons reports she'd never seen before. Her eyes fixed on two intriguing handwritten notes. One memo showed that a teenager named Lenore Harvey had visited the morgue in 1973 to ask about her brother Randy, who vanished in 1971. Another indicated Lenore had called back again in 1974 but left no home address or phone number.

Derrick felt a surge of excitement: If she could find this sister and collect DNA samples, perhaps this girl's question could be answered at last: *Was Randy Harvey among the murder victims buried in the boatshed?*

Fortunately, Derrick was one of the ME's office's biggest computer nerds. She knew how to create elaborate spreadsheets and query databases for clues. Derrick put on her investigator's hat and began to dig for public records to help locate Lenore Harvey. She already knew that Lenore, like her brother Randy, would have been a teenager in 1973. She'd been looking since she first found these boxes of bones in 2006 for a woman with a similar name who would likely be a Texan in her midfifties. *Simple, right?* Derrick began with Accurint, a subscription service that enables national searches of birth and death certificates, drivers' licenses, court records, and other public data. She also tried Ancestry.com, a consumer genealogy website filled with family trees, yearbooks, and other archives. She hoped to find a current Texas address and phone number for "Lenore Harvey," but her first searches came up with no Texas women of the right age associated with that name.

Searching by surname alone was worse: Harvey was slightly less common than Smith or Garcia, but Ancestry.com alone had more than a million birth certificates for Harveys.

Derrick felt an intense wave of frustration: She finally had a name, but couldn't find a sister. In some desperation, she returned to the familiar 1973 paper case files and her own extensive notes. At first Derrick found nothing about Randy Harvey in a folder of missing persons files assembled by the ME's office. But then she spotted his name on a dot matrix printout of fifty missing Houston teenagers. Eventually, Derrick dug up a scant one-page police report that showed that Randy Harvey, of 1324 Shepherd Drive in Houston Heights, had been reported missing by his mother on March 11, 1971. The HPD officer wrote only two lines in his narrative, and there seemed to have been no real follow-up. Still, the report contained telling details: Randy was just fifteen. He already stood six feet tall but weighed only 125 pounds—around the same height and age she would later estimate for her boy in the boots.

Deep inside her well-read copy of HPD's homicide report, Derrick discovered another intriguing clue: Randy Harvey had never been named as a murder victim by Corll's accomplices, but a handwritten note indicated he'd been their classmate at Hamilton Junior High. The reports confirmed a connection between Randy Harvey and David Brooks: Prior to the murders, David had called police, accusing Randy of stealing his stereo.

There was one person who could tell her more, Derrick thought—David Brooks himself.

She knew exactly where he was. David Brooks had been locked up in prison since 1973. The trouble was, he never granted interviews.

CHAPTER 9

CLUES FROM AN ACCOMPLICE

TEXAS STATE PRISON, ROSHARON, 2006–2007

David Brooks's booking photo, 1973

Brooks after decades in prison

BEHIND BARS FOR THIRTY years, David Brooks kept a low pro-file. He had continued to deny killing anyone and had been con-victed of only one murder, that of Billy Lawrence. At age eighteen, Brooks had provided only three brief statements to police—and had never publicly spoken again. His long silence stood in contrast with the talkative Elmer Wayne Henley, Jr. Henley still liked the limelight and had given many interviews in which he spoke seemingly with-out shame of his role in Corll's murders. "Elmer Wayne Henley feels many things, remorse not among them," the headline of a *Texas Monthly* article declared in 1976.

In a rare unpublished interview, David Brooks's former wife, Bridget, was blunt: "Wayne is a media whore and is more than happy to tell you what he thinks. But David Brooks is not someone who's interested in all that. Even if it were to help him." For decades after his incarceration, she had remained in touch with her ex. She made it clear that neither of them trusted journalists or investigators. "Because everything so far has been turned around."

Perhaps Wayne Henley would have been more eager to help, but Derrick felt repelled by his gory admissions and publicity seeking. She figured he might already have shared all he knew. Maybe David Brooks could better assist her. Derrick hoped that maybe "now that he had been incarcerated all his adult life, he might want to tell somebody that wasn't media his thoughts and feelings." Derrick wasn't sure her bosses would approve of her plan, even if Brooks agreed. Speaking to a convicted killer falls outside a forensic anthropologist's standard job description, but Sharon Derrick remained determined to make these IDs. To her surprise, she obtained permission from Sanchez, the chief medical examiner, and then contacted Brooks via an official at the Texas Department of Criminal Justice. Though Brooks had turned down other requests, he agreed to speak to her as a representative of the ME's office. She later learned that he'd quietly communicated in the past with Dr. Joe and remembered the legendary ME as discreet and fair.

Derrick felt both nervous and excited as she prepared to visit David Brooks in December 2006. She'd never before entered any prison, and Brooks was, in her mind, a shadowy and frightening figure. Though he seemed decidedly less dangerous than Wayne Henley, Brooks had admitted to helping lure victims to Corll and assisting with burials. Rattled about confronting a killer alone, Derrick reached out to David Crain, a sworn peace officer who agreed to accompany her. She later realized that had been a mistake: Brooks seemed ill-at-ease around a Harris County investigator. He hadn't said much. "Brooks seemed a little scary to me. His gaze was very cold—I don't know if that is a protective mechanism that he got over time or if he was always a little bit off," Derrick later recalled. "He had light grayish-blue eyes that had probably faded out over the years."

In December 2007, she decided to return to the prison alone. This time she brought along facial reconstructions of the three unknown victims that she'd recently received from the FACES lab—images that had not yet been released to the public.

At that time, Brooks was assigned to the Ramsey Unit, a prison with a capacity of 1,522 that sat alongside lonely Farm-To-Market Road 655 on fourteen thousand acres of land that once served as a plantation and remains a prison farm. The hulking complex seemed isolated on its patch of coastal prairie, though it was only a forty-minute drive from her office. Derrick checked in at the guardhouse, presented her Texas driver's license and Harris County credentials, and was ushered into the administration area. She left her phone in the car as instructed, but brought in records and the new facial reconstructions. She was ushered into an attorney room with a table where Derrick could speak face-to-face with Brooks, rather than being forced to communicate through a phone and a thick sheet of plate glass like most prison visitors.

Derrick greeted Brooks as he was escorted into the room by a guard. His hair had mostly gone gray and his former wire-rimmed glasses were now prison-issue plastic, but his face still seemed familiar. "I feel like I know you," she said, explaining she'd often gazed at 1973 newspaper photos in the *Houston Post* and the *Houston Chronicle* that showed Brooks as a slim, newly married eighteen-year-old on the day he had joined Henley in a search for the graves of teenagers buried on a beach. In those photos, Brooks seemed bewildered. His face appeared unlined, his blue eyes hidden behind his owl-like wire-rimmed glasses, and his white-blond hair cut into a perfectly straight pageboy.

Now Brooks, a taciturn convict in his fifties, was sitting directly across from Derrick at a table in an interrogation room enclosed in glass on two sides. He wore handcuffs affixed to a wide leather belt, leg irons, and his inmate's white jumpsuit. The prison guard had freed his hands, but his legs remained shackled and chained to the table. Her effort to break the ice with him flopped. "You don't know me," he said.

In his presence, Derrick felt a surge of adrenaline and a steadiness of purpose that calmed her. She concentrated on her mission of identifying Lost Boys. She took out the three FACES images, and slid the first across the table, and then held her breath as Brooks pondered it. He paused over the computer-generated image of the brown-haired boy with big eyes and a prominent jawline, the boy Derrick believed to be Randy Harvey.

Brooks said he recognized that boy as a murder victim. "I don't know who this is, but I think he was shot in the head," he told Derrick.

"Do you think that's Randy Harvey?"

"I don't know *who* that is," Brooks repeated. He claimed he wanted to be helpful, but he sure didn't want to admit much.

Brooks said he didn't know the murder victim in the second portrait, a boy who had been buried beside a striped swimming suit. Derrick wasn't sure he was telling the truth. He did not react to the face of the third victim, a reconstruction created from the skull of a Lost Boy whose unidentified remains, she'd learned, had been examined by another forensic anthropologist hired as a consultant before her arrival, and then reburied in the county cemetery.

"Corll killed on his own, but I don't know any of those boys," Brooks said. "I wasn't with him and I don't know who the boys were."

Perhaps even the FACES reconstructions weren't accurate enough for Brooks to recognize boys he knew, Derrick thought. Or perhaps Brooks didn't want to name teens as murder victims even thirty years later. She knew he was hoping to be paroled. Later rumors of the possibility that the Texas Board of Pardons and Paroles might grant his request prompted outrage and anger among the relatives of Corll's previously identified victims. Despite their opposition, Brooks, who'd been convicted of one murder, seemed to have a better chance at parole than Henley, who'd been convicted of six.

Brooks still seemed to rely on support from his ex-wife, Bridget. He clearly yearned for the life he'd lost. Derrick figured "he didn't want anything coming out in the press about him speaking with me, and the only reason he agreed the first time was because he said that Jachimczyk had been kind and honest and did not screw him around."

To her surprise, Derrick realized as she gazed at Brooks's tired face that she felt some sympathy for him. She knew that Brooks had first met Corll as an elementary school kid and had been groomed and assaulted by the sadistic and homicidal pedophile for several years. From her previous job examining the deaths and case histories of Houston's abused children, she knew about the devastating impact of early sexual trauma.

Brooks had met Corll when he was only ten or eleven and drifting between his divorced parents' homes, according to police reports and statements Derrick had read. At that time, Corll's candy store, a small warehouse with a loading dock, was near his grandmother's house and his grade school. After his parents' divorce, his mother, a nurse, had moved eighty miles away to Beaumont, initially taking her son along. But Brooks was only fifteen in 1970 when his mom sent him back to Houston, supposedly because he'd gotten into trouble for stealing a pot-bellied stove in a backwoods Louisiana parish. From that point on, Brooks never saw his mother again and clashed with his father, who saw him as "a sickly kid who wore those hippie glasses," his defense attorney Jim Skelton later explained. "And here came Dean, who didn't call him a sissy. David idolized him. He told me that Dean was the first adult male who didn't make fun of him."

Derrick had read everything Brooks told police in August 1973. When Brooks was thirteen or fourteen, Corll had persuaded him to drop his pants, and began performing what the Texas law branded "oral sodomy," then considered a crime even among consenting adults. "My first homosexual contact with Dean was during the time I was living in Beaumont in about 1969," Brooks said in one statement. "I had called Dean and told him that I was in town and he came and picked me up at my grandmother's house and took me to his house on 22nd street . . . he gave me a 4-foot black light at that time. . . . And sucked my dick." Corll first paid Brooks "$5 when he sucked me off and later, he raised that to $10 a time." From then on, Corll groomed Brooks as a sex partner and an accomplice to his illegal activities. In exchange, Brooks could use Corll's place to party, or to live whenever he wanted to escape his father.

A terrible transformation in their relationship came when Brooks went to visit Corll at a complex called Yorktown Townhouses in late 1970 or early 1971. "I just walked into the apartment without knocking and when I got inside, I saw that he had two boys strapped down on his bed. Their hands were tied to the bedstead. Both of the boys were nude," he told police.

Corll entered the room naked, and obviously surprised. He clearly hadn't heard Brooks use the key Corll had given him to enter the apartment. "What are you doing here?" Corll yelled,

Brooks responded that he'd just stopped by and wanted to know what was going on.

"I'm just having some fun," Corll said. He left the boys bound and gagged in the bedroom and accompanied Brooks to another room, where they sat on a sofa and talked. After a few minutes, Corll promised Brooks a car "if I wouldn't say anything about what I had seen."

Brooks left, hitchhiking home. Corll later told Brooks he was involved in a group that bought and sold boys and that he'd shipped the pair off to California. Brooks claimed that he eventually learned that Corll had killed them but that he never knew their names.

Derrick still wondered about the identities of those boys. Perhaps they were two of Corll's earliest known murder victims: Danny Yates and Jim Glass, fourteen-year-olds allegedly lured to Corll's place after attending that antidrug revival in the Heights in December 1970. Or maybe they were the Waldrop brothers, fifteen-year-old Donald and thirteen-year-old Jerry, who disappeared on January 30, 1971. They could also be, she knew, other boys whose bodies had never been found or identified.

David Brooks stayed with Corll regularly from age fifteen to seventeen, moving from apartment to apartment, allowing Corll to perform oral sex on him or otherwise sexually servicing Corll, and procuring others for Corll's parties and sexual torture schemes. Corll sometimes spoke of his crimes, once telling him "about killing a boy in a bathtub and mentioned that he [had] broken a piece off of the tub," Brooks told Houston detectives. "Sometime when we were talking, he would say how hard it was to strangle someone and the way they did it on TV wasn't realistic because it took quite a while to do it." Over time, Brooks had gotten the impression that Corll "had killed perhaps as many as twenty-five or thirty people."

Brooks had always insisted he "never killed anyone." He claimed in his initial August 9 statement that he'd left whenever things got ugly. Derrick thought Brooks's statements contained cryptic clues about other boys who likely remained unidentified. For example, Brooks said Corll mentioned a Hispanic boy he'd killed while living in an apartment on Bellefontaine Street, near Bray's Bayou, an address police never managed to locate. "He told me that this Mexican boy had been coming at him and he shot the boy one time in the head and [it] didn't seem to do anything so he shot him again and that killed the boy," Brooks told police. Derrick knew of only two Hispanic victims: Homer Garcia from Southwest Houston and Frank Aguirre from the Heights. Neither lived near Bellefontaine Street. Brooks also mentioned a Heights boy who'd been picked up at 11th and Rutland, held for four days, and killed in 1971. That boy didn't seem to match the characteristics of any known victim either.

Brooks introduced Henley to Corll in late 1971 or 1972. Perhaps Henley had been intended to be a murder victim too, but quickly turned into a willing accomplice, and the killing spree accelerated. "They became close friends and Wayne became involved with Dean sexually to some extent," Brooks had told police.

DERRICK WASN'T GETTING MUCH more information from Brooks in her own interviews. In their second meeting, Brooks seemed wooden and emotionless. He was very institutionalized after all those years in prison, she thought. At one point a fight broke out elsewhere in the unit and an alarm sounded. Brooks tensed, jumped up, and put his hands behind his back. The guard walked over and clamped on handcuffs, and then Brooks sat back down, like an automaton.

Very gradually, Brooks seemed to relax when he shared stories about the daughter born to his wife, Bridget, after he'd been locked up for life. He told Derrick he'd been very proud of her. Rachael

Lynn Brooks had been bright and beautiful; she had visited her father in prison up until 1992, the year she died in a car accident on her high school prom night. Brooks showed the most emotion when he spoke of his own lost child. His eyes shone, though no tears ever seemed to drip onto his cheeks.

Soft-spoken and at times monosyllabic, Brooks wasn't eager to discuss Dean Corll or the teenagers Corll killed with his help. "I don't remember. I don't remember," he repeated. Brooks eventually confirmed that he'd known Randy Harvey, but refused to identify him as the boy in the first FACES image. He told Derrick that police in 1973 had unfairly accused him of killing Randy Harvey because he'd accused Randy of stealing his stereo.

Brooks got angry when Derrick politely prodded him. At one point, he almost yelled: "I never killed anybody and I didn't kill Randy Harvey!" Dean Corll shot Randy in the head, Brooks said. But he swore that he was uninvolved in that murder or burial.

Brooks seemed to be telling the truth, Derrick thought. She knew Brooks had been prosecuted only for the murder of Billy Lawrence, a fifteen-year-old held for days in Corll's house in Pasadena in June 1973. Perhaps Brooks was wary because his own words had previously been used against him. On August 10, 1973, in his third and final statement to police, Brooks had admitted to seeing Billy Lawrence with Corll and doing nothing to help him escape. Though prosecutors could not prove Brooks shot or strangled Billy, Brooks admitted he'd seen the boy naked in Corll's bedroom and tied to the bed a day or two before the murder, and to being in the house when Corll killed that boy. Afterward, he and Henley helped haul the body, wrapped in plastic, to Corll's family cabin. "We left about 6 P.M. to go to the lake and I know he was dead and in a box when we left so I must have been there when he was killed." Texas law holds that an accomplice to murder can be subject to the same punishment as the mastermind; thus, some of Brooks's own admissions, combined with other evidence, had been key to his conviction.

There was no statute of limitations on murder, so perhaps Brooks was still worried about being tried for another crime if he said the wrong thing now. Since Randy Harvey had never been identified as a victim, no one had ever been charged with his murder.

Brooks asked that Derrick not disclose that he'd spoken to her. She made no promises.

Only as Derrick prepared to leave did Brooks share what seemed like a vital clue. He offered to sketch the location of the home where the Harveys had once lived. She handed him a piece of paper and a pen, and Brooks drew a small, crude map. He placed the house, which he labeled as pink, on the corner of 13th and Shepherd, wedged between two bars and a 7-Eleven convenience store.

After she left the lonely Ramsey Unit to drive home, Derrick felt more convinced than ever that Randy must be her boy in the boots. When Derrick later typed Randy Harvey's address from a 1971 missing persons report into a computerized mapping tool, the location came out as Brooks had drawn it from memory, though some 1970s bars and businesses he'd sketched on Shepherd Drive were long gone.

Maybe Brooks was trying to help after all. But unless she found Randy Harvey's family, all her work would remain only a theory.

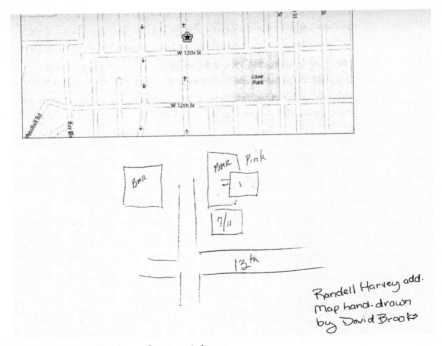

Map that Brooks drew for Derrick

CHAPTER 10

THE SEARCH

HOUSTON, 2007–2008

L ENORE HARVEY, THE BEREFT teenager who visited the morgue looking for her lost brother in 1973, could be dead herself, Derrick feared. Even if Lenore were still alive, she could have gotten married, divorced, or remarried and be using different names. Derrick searched for Texas birth certificates for Randy Harvey, hoping to find clues to locate Lenore or their mother. Finally, she found a 1955 Pennsylvania birth certificate for a Randell Harvey, which listed his mother's first name as LaFrances instead of Frances, the name on the missing persons report.

Derrick grew excited when she located a LaFrances Holt Lovrek in Trinity County, and an address only an hour's drive north of Houston. Then her hopes were dashed by another entry: LaFrances Lovrek had died in 1994. Randy's father, one LeRoy Harvey, rumored to be a former police officer, appeared to have passed away more recently in Lafayette, Louisiana.

Derrick kept busy working other cases, but in between and in the evenings, she kept scouring 1973 HPD incident reports. From the Harris County archives she obtained electronic versions of the 1971 to 1973 editions of Houston city directories, originally thick, hardbound books published annually by the R. L. Polk marketing company for large cities nationwide. Those books listed the names and professions of individuals and businesses associated with residential and commercial addresses—references she used to track Lost Boys and their families and their neighbors back through time. Derrick also began obsessively reading obituaries for anyone in Texas named Harvey, and scrawling names on a yellow legal pad of survivors or next of kin hoping to locate distant relatives, perhaps second or third cousins.

Based on her painstaking comparisons of far-flung Harvey family obituaries, Derrick deduced that Lenore Harvey had to be alive but might be using both a different first and last name, perhaps Rusty McNiel or Rusty Gutierrez. In November 1973, the Harris County Clerk's archives revealed that a teenaged Lenore Harvey had once applied for a marriage license with a boy named Gutierrez. Unfortunately, the surname Gutierrez was even more common than Harvey. (Ancestry.com alone held 3 million records.) At times, Derrick despaired. "It's really hard in Texas to find the right Gutierrez," she groused. Still, in between other cases, Derrick kept googling, and cold calling anyone who might know Lenore or Rusty. Most calls led to nothing. Busy signals. Messages that were never returned. Disconnected phone numbers. As the months passed, Derrick couldn't stop thinking about this Lost Boy.

Derrick became so involved with her search that she talked her husband, Al, into moving closer to Houston Heights. In 2008, they relocated to Oak Forest, initially renting a house and later buying a newly built house on a large lot that was smaller than their suburban home (and twice as expensive). Her husband knew that neighborhood offered a reasonable commute for his clinic in Cypress and for her work at the Texas Medical Center. But Derrick had another motive: She intended to spend as much time as possible driving the streets where Corll's victims had once walked and ridden bikes. She memorized the addresses of the places where they'd lived and where they'd likely been abducted or killed. It became a kind of ritual. Perhaps if she drove by their old haunts often enough, she might be better able to spot forgotten clues or locate allies to help her find missing persons, unravel secrets, and restore lost identities.

With no more children at home to watch after her workdays ended,

Derrick launched headlong into the Lost Boys project. She soon began to realize that she was becoming obsessed with making the identifications and understanding these boys' lost lives. In the coming years, she would spend unhealthy amounts of unpaid overtime chasing rumors and listening to theories offered up by strangers who called or emailed about disturbing memories. One Christmas dinner, she found herself discussing the doomed teens and reviewing 1970s yearbooks with her aunts and cousins, who had their own recollections to share: One of her cousins had attended high school with murder victim Frank Aguirre. Another had enjoyed a first kiss with David Brooks's half sister. In a way, the Lost Boys became part of her own DNA.

Finally, on an otherwise typical workday in 2008, her endless dialing of possible Harvey relatives paid off. She happened to reach a woman who said: "Oh yes, I know Rusty." It turned out that "Rusty" was indeed a nickname for Lenore Harvey, who had auburn hair in her younger years. Minutes later, the distant relative passed along an address and phone number. After searching for more than a year, Derrick had finally found Lenore.

Derrick took a breath and prepared to return a message that a teenaged girl had left her office back in 1974.

Lenore (Harvey) McNiel's initial response was unexpected and somewhat upsetting: a long pause and a barrage of suspicious questions. Derrick realized, to her chagrin, that her introductory story probably seemed whacko and smacked of a scam. Derrick struggled to find the words to convince Lenore that a Harris County ME's official had uncovered her antiquated phone messages and really wanted to meet.

Lenore's tone warmed as she realized that Derrick truly was offering a chance for answers. After so many years, the news of a possible ID came as a shock and seemed nothing less than a miracle. Then this Lost Boy's sister began crying, and in between sobs, repeated, "Thank you, thank you, thank you!"

Derrick felt elated, though Lenore told her that this call, while welcome, had in some ways come too late.

"Our mother is dead," she said. As Derrick had suspected from the obituary she'd found, Frances Conley had died in 1994 at age sixty-six without knowing what had happened to her only son. Her ashes had been scattered on Lake Livingston. Still, Lenore Harvey was eager to meet. "I'll bring along my sister," she promised.

It turned out that Randy Harvey still had two surviving siblings who cared about him. Lenore Harvey McNiel and Donna Harvey Lovrek, Randy's younger and older sister, respectively, shared a small trailer house in the woods in a settlement less than an hour north of the Harris County Medical Examiner's Office.

IN HONOR OF THE Harvey sisters' visit, Derrick prepared a special display in a meeting room that doubled as a classroom in the ME's office on May 24, 2008. On a tray on a small table, she arranged the personal effects she'd found for Case No. ML 73-3349: A thick navy-blue jacket with scarlet lining, which looked like an old mechanic's uniform. A pair of deteriorating bell-bottom blue jeans. A tattered brown shirt with a peace sign on the pocket. A belt for a thirty-inch waist. A pair of 1970s men's lace-up leather work boots. A bright orange plastic comb. All the clothes and keepsakes had been carefully cleaned and preserved in hope that such a viewing might one day be possible. In the middle of the table, she placed portraits that artists had created based on this Lost Boy's skull, one drawn by hand and another from the FACES lab. Both revealed different visions of a sandy-haired teen with a long face, a jutting square chin, and a generous mouth.

When Lenore (Harvey) McNiel and Donna Lovrek arrived, Derrick went out to the parking lot to greet them. Lenore's red hair had faded, though it was evident how she'd earned the nickname Rusty. She literally leaned on her older sister, who was clearly protective. But there was something striking about Lenore's appearance that made Derrick gasp in excitement: Lenore had the same face shape and jutting jawline as this Lost Boy.

Filled with a barely suppressed excitement, Derrick ushered the sisters into the reception area, where they presented IDs and checked in. Then she led them into a small interview room, the place she'd previously met relatives of missing persons to collect DNA samples. She warned, "This is going to be difficult," but neither wanted to back out. They followed her down the hall and into the classroom, where Derrick had displayed items associated with this unknown boy.

Lenore stood silently for a minute with her eyes fixed on the items before blurting out: "I can't say these are his specific clothes, but that looks a whole lot like his Fina jacket."

Donna said: "Are you sure?"

"Oh yeah," Lenore replied. She reminded her sister that she had waved goodbye to Randy when he rode off on his bike that last morning. "Those boots, those are his. I know those boots. And remember those combs we all had—isn't that his orange comb?"

"It sure looks like it to me," Donna agreed. The sisters told Derrick that all three siblings had owned identical plastic combs in three different colors. Randy's had been bright orange. They didn't recognize his tattered shirt—the tan material had darkened from contact with soil in the boatshed burial and the passage of time. But those were definitely the kind of bell-bottoms Randy wore, they said. The waist size on the belt—30"—was right too. Their brother had been tall and skinny. Both remembered his shoe size. The leather work boots Derrick had found would have fit Randy.

Lenore McNiel had cried when she first spoke to Derrick by phone, but neither sister wept during this long-awaited meeting about their brother. *They seem happy—not giddy happy but relieved that the belongings appear to be his,* Derrick thought.

The siblings voiced only one regret: "I wish Mama had been able to know this," one said. "She would have had some peace when she died."

As the sisters kept talking, Derrick felt increasingly optimistic—though a comb and clothing were hardly enough evidence to confirm an ID. "They also knew that he wore those boots for work and that the jacket was like one that his employers made people wear at the gas station," Derrick later reflected "My height estimate was pretty close. He was around six feet. My analysis was his height was six feet to six two."

Derrick tried to contain her own excitement: "Apparently we do need to take your DNA for comparisons," she told her visitors. Derrick knew she needed to assemble more evidence before Randy's remains could finally be released to his family. Together, they returned to the interview room and Derrick gave each sister a set of gloves and a swab to wipe inside of her own cheek. (Derrick had found that most people felt more comfortable taking their own sample.) The cheek swabs contained cells that could be used to develop a DNA profile to enable comparisons with her unknown person. She placed each swab in its own laboratory-approved plastic bag, obtained copies of Lenora and Donna's Texas driver's licenses, and later shipped the samples via a secure mailing system to UNT's Center for Human Identification.

Derrick hoped that by collecting samples from both siblings, she could confirm a family relationship. But she knew that one (or even two) sisters did not always share enough DNA to verify an ID. Every child inherits 50 percent of their DNA from each parent, but a very different 50 percent can be passed down to each child. Generally, siblings share around 25 percent of their DNA, though the percentage varies. For that reason, experts generally try to find more than one relative to test if no parent is available. "You can get a low kinship index and that's the reason when if you're going to use siblings [for an identification] you really want two," Derrick explained.

Right before they left, Donna Lovrek confided: "I'm not sure how this is going to work out because my mom always kidded with me that I had a different dad." Derrick's heart sank, though she kept smiling. She didn't mention aloud that half-siblings share even less DNA, only about the same amount as first cousins. Later when the test results arrived, she realized Donna's suspicion was probably right: Verifying a match between these three siblings would prove even more complicated.

Derrick urged both women to search for more photos of their brother. Snapshots taken closer to when he disappeared, she told them, also could be used to help verify his identity.

Unfortunately, the Harvey family had lost most of their photos in a house fire. The only image Derrick initially received was a blurry black-and-white snapshot of Randy, then around ten, holding a toy airplane and horsing around with two cousins. In the photo, Randy wore a boyish smile and a crew cut. Derrick examined his visage with dismay: She could not tell whether this child had developed a long face or distinctive jutting chin by age fifteen, features she needed to see in order to make a visual comparison with the skull.

A FEW MONTHS AFTER meeting Randy Harvey's sisters, Derrick and her husband moved into the house in Oak Forest, blocks from the Fina station where Randy had once worked. "The station site was just down the bayou about five minutes—on my way to the highway," Derrick remembers. Ella Boulevard was by then a busy four-lane thoroughfare. The Fina station no longer stood; the intersection held an empty lot full of weeds. "But I would drive by that location when we were trying to make the ID almost every day just because it meant so much to me."

Derrick had reasons to feel optimistic about this ID: In her first face-to-face encounter with Lenore, she'd immediately noticed characteristics she'd observed in her forensic examination of the boy in the boots. "The bone structure of the faces and the protruding anterior teeth of McNiel are similar to the bone structure and protruding anterior teeth of ML 73-3349," she later wrote in a report. "In particular, the shape of the face, placement of the orbits and zygomatic bones, and shape of the mental eminence of the mandible of ML 73-3349 are consistent with those characteristics of McNiel." But the Harris County ME's office had a strict protocol for confirming IDs. Unless the DNA test results were better than she anticipated, a committee would be convened to review her data and vote before verifying any ID.

Fortunately, two key photos arrived from Randy's sisters and cousins, some of whom still lived in the Houston area. "I got a real photo of Randy on his bike and a close-up of his face from Donna," Derrick recalls. That close-up of Randy, a long-faced fifteen-year-old boy with a prominent dimple, floored her. The focus was sharp, and she enlarged it for comparison purposes. The skull she'd examined seemed to fit Randy Harvey's facial structure perfectly "down to the cleft on his chin." He looked like the younger version of the Canadian Mountie cartoon character Dudley Do-Right that Derrick had imagined right after examining his remains.

The sisters visited the lab only about a year after Derrick first discovered those boxes. But obtaining DNA lab reports for a cold case could take another year due to backlogs—many other missing persons' families were waiting for the NamUs lab, and some tests involved active homicide investigations. Fortunately, at her request, officials at the UNT lab agreed to put a rush on these cases. These sisters, she thought, had already waited long enough.

THE RESULTS CAME BACK four months later, but as Derrick had feared, the DNA comparisons did not definitively establish that the three were siblings. Derrick had requested comparisons of two different types of genetic profiles—one of nuclear DNA used to tie individuals to close kin, like siblings, parents, and children, and one of mitochondrial DNA, which could be used to link people who share the same mother and far more distant maternal ancestors. Unfortunately, the statistical odds of the sisters' sibling relationships with this Lost Boy fell within a gray area—not strong enough by itself to confirm the ID. "Lenore had a little bit higher index [of matching] than Donna did, but she was still just one sibling against a sibling," Derrick recalls. The mitochondrial DNA results did show all three shared similar traits, but that mtDNA pattern was relatively common: found in about one out of every two hundred people. That was helpful data, but not enough evidence by itself to confirm the ID.

The Harris County ME's office convened a committee. A geneticist, two anthropologists, and the senior pathologist reviewed everything Derrick had collected over two years of hard work, including height and age estimates, the belt and shoe sizes, as well as the DNA test results. "So, we had a big meeting and looked at all the physical and anthropology evidence and at all the other unidentified boys in our case list," Derrick remembers. "We looked at personal effects, evidence, and facial reconstruction that we had from the lab in Louisiana." Derrick argued strongly in favor of the ID. "The sibling resemblance to the skull was amazing," she argued. "We showed slides of the sibling [Lenore McNiel]—and the family teeth and smile. Then I compared that to the front teeth, eyes and setting of the eyes, and the shape in the computer reconstruction of the skull."

Sanchez, the chief medical examiner, wasn't quite convinced. He wanted more time. Only after a second meeting and another round of discussion did all agree. Based on shared sibling characteristics, clothing and property recognized by the sisters, facial reconstruction data, and the DNA results, the boy in the boots was declared to be Randy Harvey in an amendment to his autopsy approved on October 16, 2008.

In November 2008, Donna Lovrek and Lenore McNiel organized a memorial service for Randy, and invited Derrick to his long-delayed celebration of life. That same black-and-white family photo she'd seen of ten-year-old Randy playing was propped up against the urn. It showed him holding aloft a wooden plane as younger cousins gazed up admiringly. Randy "was all boy," recalled Sherri DeAngelo, a shipping executive from Katy, Texas, who'd once been the small girl cousin beside Randy in that photo. Sometimes they had gotten into mischief together, Sherri told a *Houston Chronicle* reporter at the service. "We used to jump off my grandma's porch. We'd have to jump over the tomatoes." And if they missed, they got swatted on the back of the legs, though just enough to make them squeal.

As the mourners prepared to leave, they heard the lyrics of one of Randy Harvey's favorite Zombies songs from the soundtrack his family assembled for the service—"Time of the Season." It was now Randy's time. Derrick mourned with Randy's sisters but felt electrified by her discovery. After more than a year of efforts, one of Derrick's Lost Boys had a name: Randy Harvey. She was sure that more answers would soon follow. "I felt true excitement that I might be on to something. I thought I could make a difference in these cases."

The lab results she'd received from the UNT's Center for Human Identification turned up another surprise: The stray bones Derrick had discovered in another of the 1973 storage boxes and sent off for DNA testing did not belong to Randy Harvey; his arm bones remained missing.

Those extra bones belonged to yet another Lost Boy whose identity was still a mystery.

THE LOST BOYS

THE FIRST ID:

Randell Lee Harvey, 2008

Randy Harvey, 15, disappeared while
biking to work at a gas station in
March 1971. He lived with his mother
and little sister in a house on

Randy Harvey, portrait
by Nancy Rose

Shepherd Drive in the Heights. His bones were found mingled
with others in a hole in the boatshed in 1973 but were not
identified and were stored for years in a box labeled Case No.
ML 73-3349. Randy Harvey's ID helped generate national
attention and leads for Derrick's efforts to identify other Lost
Boys.

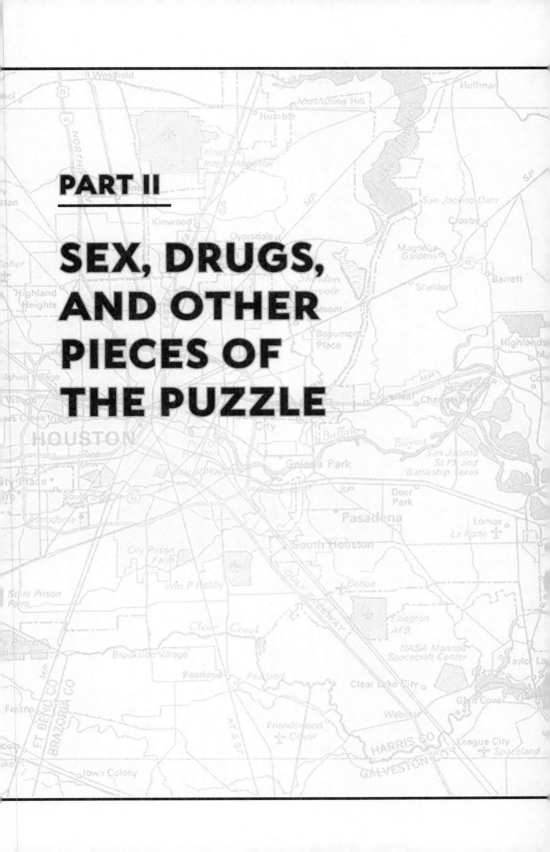

PART II

SEX, DRUGS, AND OTHER PIECES OF THE PUZZLE

CHAPTER 11

THE CANDY MAN

HOUSTON, 1973

DEAN CORLL'S FATHER AND stepmother delivered a huge stack of the dead man's photos to Pasadena police detective David Mullican days after Corll's violent death: a vast collection of school portraits and black-and-white candids of slim teenaged boys. There were boys wearing swimming trunks and toting surfboards on Gulf of Mexico beaches, laughing teens astride motorcycles, and long-haired adolescents ordering meals at a hot dog stand. Corll appeared in none of the snapshots, but his white van often served as a back-drop. Corll's mother, Mary West, lived in Manitou Springs, Colorado, where she ran yet another candy store but granted several interviews. She confided to one Houston reporter that her son filled his van with plush cushions and a black-and-white TV set to make it more appealing to teens. "He was always buying things that would make him feel important to these little kids," she said.

Corll's father, Arnold, an electrician like his deceased son, had a long and combative relationship with Corll's mother, Mary (Corll) West: The two had married and divorced each other twice, and she'd accused him of physical abuse before they parted for good. Arnold saw his son regularly; Corll stopped to visit, putter around with electronics, or do his laundry; his mother had not laid eyes on her eldest in at least four years. Yet in interviews, they formed a unified front:

From Corll's collection of teenaged boys' photos

Both claimed their son had been falsely accused by his killer, Wayne Henley, a juvenile delinquent with a record of thievery, assault, and drug abuse. Mary West swore to Corll's innocence. "My son didn't kill all of those boys," West insisted. She argued that he wasn't violent and that he'd been "used somehow" by Henley and other teens.

Officers expected to find more murder victims and missing persons in Corll's photo collection, given that the Polaroid they'd found in a frame on Corll's dresser depicted fifteen-year-old Billy Lawrence, a Houston boy who'd been killed that same summer. Other shots seemed to have been taken inside the house on Vince Bayou too. One showed a long-haired boy seated at Corll's Formica kitchen table blowing out birthday candles on a cake; another revealed a teen reclining on a mattress, his eyes closed and face contorted in what seemed like euphoria. But when detectives showed photos to Hamilton Junior High officials in the Heights and to others in the Houston Independent School District, they were surprised to discover that many of Corll's young friends were alive and well. Those teenagers' tales suggested that for years, Corll had photographed, partied, traveled, and lived with adolescents, seducing and attacking some but often concealing the violent impulses behind his friendly candy-man facade.

BEGINNING IN HIS EARLY twenties, when he was closer to a teenager himself, Corll cultivated a circle of adolescents—some of whose mothers were widows or divorcées—initially as friends through gifts of candy, money, parties, and trips to the beach or to his family's fishing cabin. Over time, Corll had used drugs, sex, and more sinister forms of persuasion to keep many of them under his control.

Indeed, Corll devolved into a dark Peter Pan figure—a narcissistic killer in the business of collecting or abducting children who had somehow gotten lost. Dean Corll grew up when Disney's *Peter Pan* was at the apex of its popularity; it was released in February 1953, the year he turned thirteen. As an adult, Corll created a world for his teenaged associates that in some ways resembled Neverland. In order to attend Dean Corll's parties or join his band, it seemed you had to be snatched up by Corll or one of his minions, receive an invitation, know where Corll lived (since he often moved), or somehow obtain his unlisted phone number.

Disney tells a lighter version of Peter Pan. In J. M. Barrie's original 1911 book, upon arriving at Neverland, Peter Pan immediately proposes murdering a man, a pirate who has fallen asleep in the pampas. "If you like we'll go down and kill him," he says. Corll often wielded a gun or a saber in his own Neverland, and his adventures also involved "savages and lonely lairs" and "murders [and] hangings," as Barrie wrote of Pan. Darker adventures occurred at night.

Then, as Barrie wrote: "When you wake in the morning, the naughtiness and evil passions with which you went to bed have been folded up small . . ." Indeed, some contemporary analysts have speculated whether Barrie, at the very least, fantasized about the boys whom he befriended in a local park and who were the basis of his stories (although no definitive evidence of sexual abuse has ever been published about his years-long association with them).

WITHIN TWENTY-FOUR HOURS OF Corll's killing, Billy Ridinger, the bright-eyed teen with tousled sun-bleached hair who appeared in Corll's beach snapshots, volunteered for an interview with the Pasadena police, along with his mother. Ridinger's parents had befriended Dean Corll in 1963 or 1964 when Corll lived in the Normandy Apartments, a complex along the bustling North Loop 610 highway. Corll was still operating a candy store when he first met Dorothy Ridinger and her husband, William; Billy was about ten at the time. Like others in the complex, the Ridingers knew Corll as the Candy Man. "He always had several pockets full of candy which he distributed to kids," Dorothy recalled. Over the years, Corll became like "almost one of the Ridinger family." The Ridingers kept in touch with Corll when they moved to Fort Worth and rekindled the relationship when they later returned to Houston and bought a red brick house shaded by live oak trees in a subdivision on the city's northwestern edge. The Ridingers remained on Autumn Forest Drive while Corll hopscotched from place to place, racking up dozens of addresses. (Ridinger family members sometimes vouched as references for Corll, at least twice helping him land apartments despite his record of skipping out on leases.)

On August 9, 1973, Dorothy Ridinger told Pasadena police that she certainly noticed Corll's tendency in his twenties and early thirties to befriend teens. It did seem "kind of strange that Corll should run with people that much younger," she admitted, but passed it off as him "just liking to be around young people." She didn't seem to question why Corll spent so much time with her son, Billy. Generally, fewer parents in the 1970s seemed aware of sexual predators or of the process some used of "grooming" underaged victims by providing gifts, favors, and trips, perhaps in part because there were no sex offender registries or strong laws against child sex abuse. The Ridingers seemed oblivious to what became a life-threatening friendship for their son.

Billy Ridinger came to see a Houston homicide detective alone around noon on August 10, 1973, in a follow-up interview held after David Brooks claimed to have saved him from Corll's torture board. This time Billy Ridinger shared jarring details about his relationship with Corll. The twenty-year-old high school graduate told the detective that since age twelve he'd visited Corll weekly, visiting his candy store, attending movies, and traveling with the killer. He'd visited and stayed overnight at places where Corll was known to have raped and tortured other teens. Billy described meeting at least two murder victims, both seventeen-year-old Heights boys, while partying at Corll's place. He mentioned Mark Scott, killed in April 1972, and the Haney brothers. (Ruben Haney was killed by Corll in August 1971; his brother, Tommy, died of a morphine overdose in July 1972.) But Billy didn't say whether he'd been present on the nights when Ruben and Mark were raped and killed.

Billy claimed that Corll "never made any advances toward me sexually," until Corll first offered to pay him $10 to have "homosexual relations" sometime in 1972. Billy said he refused, but continued to visit Corll. "About a month after he propositioned me, I talked to him on the telephone and I decided to spend the weekend at his house," Billy told police.

On that night, Corll picked Billy Ridinger up in his white van and drove to his apartment in a brick building on Schuler Street, where Corll lived from February to July 1972. David Brooks and Wayne Henley were already sprawled on a sofa watching TV. They preferred police crime dramas like *Mod Squad*, *Kojak*, and *Mannix*. Billy knew both boys and sat beside them. A few minutes later, Corll pulled out a pair of handcuffs, promising to show him how to slip out of them—a party trick Corll had previously used to trap other boys.

Suddenly, Corll snapped those cuffs on Billy Ridinger's wrists. Someone else stretched duct tape over his mouth and slipped a pillowcase over his head. Then he was wrestled to the floor. "I couldn't see anything, but I heard hammering," Billy recalled. The next thing he knew, his hands were suspended by a rope to metal hooks hung high on the wall. Another rope around his neck was affixed to the same hooks. Any escape attempt could have strangled him.

Around eleven o'clock, Ridinger was moved to a back room and strapped to the torture board. He remained there through the night as Corll repeatedly visited to sexually assault him, finally declaring, "I can't let you go."

He had one hope: During a break in this ordeal, David Brooks popped in, promising to try to help. Billy Ridinger had spent about sixteen hours on the board when Wayne Henley entered to deliver a verdict: "We're thinking about letting you go, but if you ever say anything it will be all over for you." Afterward, Corll took Billy home in his white van, as he'd done after other visits.

In August 1973, Houston officers asked Billy Ridinger why he never informed his parents or authorities about being attacked. Given the timing, his prompt action could possibly have saved a dozen lives, including a string of teens murdered in that same apartment.

"I didn't tell anyone what had happened because I was afraid they would kill me," he said. Incredibly, he visited Dean's house at least fifteen times after being assaulted, in order to "show them that I wasn't going to tell anyone what had happened."

Houston investigators believed Ridinger's story, partly because David Brooks had already told them, "I believe the only reason [Billy Ridinger] is alive now is because I begged them not to kill him." One officer called him "the sole survivor of Corll's sexual fetish," though Brooks had also claimed that Corll retaliated by tying him to the torture board overnight, repeatedly raping him and forcing him to beg for his life.

Billy Ridinger was never required to testify against Brooks or Henley in open court. He wore a bag over his head to keep journalists from photographing his face when officers led him in to testify privately before the Harris County grand jury.

WAYNE HENLEY LATER INSISTED Ridinger knew more than he told police and could have helped identify other victims. In May 2014, he wrote Derrick, urging her to interview him. "Billy had a long-term relationship with Dean Corll that pre-dated my own," he wrote. "Billy was a regular visitor at Dean's place and Billy was treated much the same as David was by Dean. It was always my feeling that Billy and Dean had some sort of under-the-table relationship."

That tip was not one that Derrick felt comfortable pursuing. She passed along the information and was told that a Houston police officer approached Ridinger, but obtained no more details.

IN AUGUST 1973, DETECTIVES separately tracked down Corll's former classmates from Vidor High School and friends who had attended his funeral, where the casket had been draped with an American flag in honor of his military service. Few admitted they knew Corll had been gay—he had not openly defined himself that way—and none described him as violent. "If Dean Corll had knocked on my door last Wednesday night before this story broke, I would have invited him in for a beer," one high school buddy said.

His mother, Mary West, described her son as basically asexual. West met up with a reporter for the *Colorado Springs Sun* for a long interview and drinks at a local café, telling him, "Dean never showed any sign he was a homosexual. He had more of a disinterested attitude toward sex." Two of her ex-husbands, though, had questioned Corll's behavior; one, a merchant seaman, had told her he disapproved of Corll's habit of inviting young boys to the candy factory after hours.

Texas, like most states, outlawed even consensual sex between adult members of the same sex in 1973. Not surprisingly most gay men were not "out"; many had girlfriends, or got married, and hid any signs of homosexual interests to avoid losing jobs, family, and church relationships. Those who came out could face dishonorable discharge from the military, criminal charges, or being shunned.

The Stonewall Riots had erupted in New York City in 1969, igniting the gay rights movement there. Progress was slower in Texas. Still, in the late 1960s and early 1970s, Houston offered a burgeoning gay bar scene in the area known then as the Montrose, and Corll had visited at least one gay club, according to interviews conducted by police and journalists. One man admitted to having consensual sex with him, describing Corll as a gentle partner.

Arthur Bell, a freelance writer who was a gay activist and also had covered the Stonewall Riots for *The Village Voice,* delved deeper into the response of Houston's gay community to Corll's crimes than other reporters did. "Checking out the local gay circuit, employees at the local steam bath claim no knowledge of Corll and Henley and no interest in the case. At a well-known hustler bar in the Montrose area (Montrose is the Greenwich Village of Houston), the bartender admits that Corll was seen in the place three months ago and had visited on a couple of other occasions. So had some of the kids," Bell wrote. He found it odd that this aspect of the murders appeared to be "totally ignored by the local scribes: not all the victims were straight neighborhood kids or runaways. Some did, in fact, play at homosexuality, and Corll was not completely a recluse. He was known by a certain segment of the gay world."

Openly gay, lesbian, trans, or bisexual people who visited Houston's gay bars in the 1970s did so at some risk to their own safety. A Houston ordinance, effective since 1861, targeted "cross-dressing." The ordinance, finally repealed in 1980, was used by HPD's Bar Squad to raid gay clubs and to target drag performers, transgender people, or anyone wearing clothing deemed inappropriate for their sex assigned at birth. Women could be hauled to jail simply for wearing jeans with a front zipper, men for wearing makeup. "Like I say, the cops did not harass us in trying to enforce any laws, it was a sport for them. It was their recreational activity," Houston activist Ray Hill said in an oral history about that time. Customers at Montrose clubs or walking neighborhood streets could also be targeted by carloads of men or boys bent on violent hate crimes they disguised as games and called "queer bashing." The Texas statute outlawing "sodomy" was rarely enforced, but it was not overturned until 2003 when the Supreme Court found all laws criminalizing sexual acts between consenting same sex adults to be unconstitutional in *Lawrence v. Texas,* a case that originated with HPD's arrests of two men who'd been having sex in a private apartment.

Some leaders of Houston's gay community were "out" and beginning to organize in 1973, and a newly launched community newspaper, *The Nuntius,* covered the Corll case. But Houstonians' gay liberation watershed moment came in 1977, when more than four thousand activists marched toward the Houston Hyatt, protesting the appearance of homophobic full-figured gal Anita Bryant at the Texas state bar convention. Bell found Houston's most prominent gay leaders reluctant to discuss Corll or his victims in August 1973; instead, activists were engaged in a fight to elect a more progressive mayor, improve the city's civil rights record, and oust police chief Short. "In all instances, the gay angle is way way way periphery to the fact that here was this madman killing innocent kids," Bell wrote.

Charles Berger, of the Houston Gay Political Coalition, told Bell that he did not think the Corll murders needed to be excused by the gay community because Corll was gay, "no more than the Manson Family murders need to be excused by the straight community because Manson was straight. Each was the work of a particular type." In an unsigned 1974 editorial, a writer for *The Nuntius* expressed concern about local newspaper coverage, some of which seemed to suggest that every homosexual in Houston was somehow responsible for the murders. "Does Dean Corell [*sic*] represent homosexuals or a mad man? Should all left handers, shadowless people and heterosexuals that [veer] from the norm be exterminated before they can lay their eggs and hatch a new generation of sex-thrill killers?"

The DA and other Houston boosters seemed eager to defend their city, and to declare that the whole disgraceful episode "could have happened anywhere." Bell wasn't so sure. After spending a day watching teenagers' graves being excavated and more time interviewing victims' families and friends, Bell concluded that Houston was a "hothouse of a helltown" and that the Heights, which he described as "a lower middle class redneck area where most of the killings took place," seemed to be "the logical stage for this macabre drama." Bell had been treated kindly when he'd visited the Hilli-giests' home, a comfortable family gathering place with a well-tended flower garden. But elsewhere in the Heights, he'd had "a gun stuck in my face by the parent of a boy I was interviewing. The parent didn't accept my credentials, didn't like my shoulder-length hair, labeled me a pill freak, a drug addict and faggot and ordered me out of the block at the count of ten or I'd have a bullet in my head."

Bell figured the same violent undercurrents had surely affected Dean Corll, a closeted gay Texan raised in a gun-loving state whose sexual identity had to be concealed perhaps under threat of death. "Despite the shining buildings and booming businesses, Houston is a repressive town and it's this atmosphere of repression that breeds hatred and occasionally a psychotic killer. If Corll couldn't accept what he was because it went against the grain of accepted lifestyles, he had to destroy the evidence of his guilt by killing." Bell also contemplated a sexual motive for the murders that circulated in the press. Henley described how Corll twitched and displayed other signs of withdrawal before ordering another kill. Perhaps Corll initially strangled sex partners to heighten orgasms, and after killing the first one became addicted to the terrible thrill that came from raping victims who became involuntarily aroused in the throes of death.

IN AUGUST, THE PASADENA police interviewed a woman who claimed to be Corll's girlfriend, Betty Hawkins, a single mother of two. Hawkins, a thirty-year-old Houston bookkeeper, came into the station where she told investigators she had dated Corll off and on for five years. Those "dates" were generally in the company of her children or Corll's teenaged friends, including Billy Baulch, who would be murdered in 1972, Billy Ridinger, or David Brooks. In all that time, Corll attempted sexual contact twice, once fondling her genitals and another time pursuing penetration before announcing that he "just didn't feel like it," Hawkins reluctantly told officers. Like Corll's other friends, she had never noticed anything odd in his home or van, but felt bewildered by Corll's frequent moves and his constantly changing cars and wardrobe. "Dean wore a lot of different clothes. I don't believe I ever saw him in the same shirt twice," she said.

For years, Dean Corll had been wearing masks. Like many other gay men, he had been hiding his sexual identity, and became adept at leading a double life. He'd also developed and hidden tendencies toward sadism, rape, and serial murder. Yet some of his oldest friends insisted he started out as a normal kid—a likable band nerd and hardworking mama's boy.

CORLL WAS BORN IN Fort Wayne, Indiana, on Christmas Eve 1939. His mother claimed he was only a toddler when his father, Arnold, punished him harshly for stepping inside a toilet bowl while potty training (and while wearing his shoes). Much later, Carol Vance, the elected Harris County DA from 1966 to 1978, claimed "Corll's father dished out macabre beatings to young Dean for the smallest of trespasses." His mother, Mary, was needy—a dark-haired, matronly romantic, seemingly always looking for love. She sometimes strutted around the house in full makeup, dresses, and heels, but her first husband abused her, she complained in phone calls to her sister and in divorce petitions. The couple had two small sons before Arnold was drafted for World War II: dark-haired Dean and fair-haired Stanley, whom their mother dressed in matching outfits for portraits.

When Arnold returned from the war, they squabbled, separated, and then divorced. In 1951, when Corll was eleven, Arnold and Mary reconciled and moved the family to Pasadena, where they bought a three-bedroom house along the murky waters of Vince Bayou, a tidal stream contaminated by heavy industry and under-regulated waste pits. His parents' second marriage lasted only two years, but Arnold Corll hung on to the Lamar house, even after his next wife died and he married a third woman, also named Mary. For twenty-two years, Dean Corll had lived with or visited his father, often tinkering with his van, fixing TV sets, or doing laundry in that Pasadena house—the same place where Corll would torture and kill his final victims before being gunned down himself.

Corll's quixotic mother moved more often. She next married a traveling salesman, Jake West, another troublesome husband whom she would also divorce and remarry, making him her third and her fourth spouse. She later declared her son had never found his own life partner, partly because of the hopeless examples he'd grown up with. (She ultimately married and divorced three different men; his father, Arnold, was married four times, to three different women.) Dean, she said, "was the kind of person who never wanted to get close enough to anyone [that] they could get ties on him. He had seen so many broken marriages."

Dean Corll was a teenager when Mary West and her second husband resettled their clan near Vidor, where Mary's sister, Virginia, and her husband had moved after selling their Indiana farm in favor of steady shipyard work on the Texas Gulf Coast. At that time, Vidor, along busy cross-country Highway 90, was a popular bedroom community for white families of workers at refineries and plants in Beaumont–Port Arthur, known as the Golden Triangle. But Vidor had a reputation as one of the state's most notorious sundown towns. Any Black people visiting the city were instructed to leave before nightfall, and some whites moved there because "there were no Blacks in their school district," one of Corll's classmates recalls. Its population was then (and remains) more than 97 percent white.

At fifteen, Dean Corll had nearly reached his full height of five feet eleven, but he showed no interest in sports when he arrived at Vidor High in 1954. (Physicians had recommended that he forgo athletics because of a heart murmur developed after suffering rheumatic fever as an infant.) His little brother went out for sports; Dean made his mark as a trombone player in the band. "He was just an average classmate. He wasn't real shy—he talked and carried on just like the rest of us," remembers Jerry Allen, who played trumpet and sat in the brass section too. Though other boys wore flattops, Corll slicked back his hair and kept it neatly combed, cultivating a James Dean look. Corll never had a girlfriend but seemed well liked. Everyone came when he hosted a party for bandmates at his mother and stepfather's place out in the country.

Dean Corll preferred stage band, which played jazz, big band, and pop tunes. Allen, like other strict Southern Baptists, sat out whenever they played for dances (since dancing was regarded as sinful). Corll, raised Methodist, rarely attended church and looked particularly pleased in a stage band photo at a Valentine's Day gig in the late 1950s. In that photo, he's surrounded by kids his own age against a backdrop of shiny hearts and cutout cupids. Looking back, the most obvious difference between Corll and his high school classmates was that he never stopped hanging out with teenagers.

Corll in the stage band at Vidor High School (second row center—under the E in Varieties)

In Vidor, his mother and stepfather began to pick up pecans and create homemade candies. Soon much of Corll's spare time was consumed by hauling and shelling pecans, inventing recipes, making and distributing candy, and disposing of waste for the family candy business. His cousin Judy thought his mother exploited him. "If a mother could have caused this type of behavior in a person," she later told police, then "Dean Corll's mother, my aunt, was a prime example." Dean was constantly harassed and treated unfairly, she said. "He had to work long hours in his mother's candy store . . . with hardly ever a day off." Corll planned to graduate in 1958, but failed English and does not appear in the yearbook with his senior classmates in their caps and gowns.

There wasn't much talk when Corll and his family left town. "Summing it up, he was a normal teenager. I don't recall anything that unusual he did or said and I was shocked when I heard that he killed all of those kids," recalls Jerry Allen, who moved to Austin after his own graduation in 1959, married Corll's cousin Judy, and became a police officer. "It's really surprising. . . . He had to have been really cruel and I never detected anything like that when I knew him. He tortured some of those kids and then murdered them. . . . When I knew him, I never would have figured that he had that kind of streak in him."

CORLL'S MOTHER AND HIS stepfather opened their first candy store, the Pecan Prince, on 12½ Street in Houston Heights in 1958, near bustling Reagan High School, then segregated and the neighborhood's only senior high school for whites. The candy-making couple feuded—partly over West's comments about Dean, who into his early twenties kept hanging out with younger male "friends." "Kids flocked around him there," his mother recalled. One juvenile customer at that shop complained that Corll hit on him, journalists later reported. Corll's mother rebutted the account: She claimed that a teenaged boy had propositioned Dean, who rebuffed him.

Around the time of that encounter and amid increasing tensions in her marriage, Mary (Corll) West, a bold woman who favored fur coats though it was rarely cold enough to comfortably wear them in Houston, sent her eldest away to live with his widowed grandmother on a farm near the unincorporated town of Yoder, Indiana. He spent 1960 to 1962 there, sometimes gazing at stars through a telescope until his mother summoned him home to Houston.

Leroy Lewandowski, another Heights boy, met Corll at the Pecan Prince after the store moved to 721 East 6½ Street near Denton Cooley Elementary School, named for one of the Heights' founders.

By then, Corll had returned to work and was bunking in a glorified shed on-site. Leroy later told police he was fifteen or sixteen years old when he joined other teens who regularly rode to the beach in Galveston or Freeport with Corll, who kept souvenir photos of them shirtless in wet swimsuits that police would later seize as evidence. Leroy said he broke off the friendship when Corll came by Reagan High School and "hit [me] up to have sex with him." After learning Corll "was queer," Leroy dropped him.

Into his twenties, Corll continued to act as his mother's right-hand man in the candy business. An undated photo of Dean and his mother side by side in one of their Heights shops shows them surrounded by paperwork and candy boxes piled atop tables and desks. Dean Corll, wearing a tight white shirt that shows off his muscles, towers over his boxy mother, who is clamping a hand atop one shoulder, seeming to draw him down. Behind them, time seems frozen on an oversized clock hanging on the shop wall.

Corll's mother soon dumped West and moved the business again. Her ex ended up running their old store while she incorporated a new venture, the Corll Candy Company.

Over his mother's objections, Corll enlisted in the U.S. Army in August 1964. He qualified for and received training as a radio technician—an elite program that typically required a high IQ—and was assigned to the radio repair school at Fort Hood, in Killeen, Texas. According to his mother, his military career lasted less than a year because she needed his help and begged for a hardship discharge. An Army spokesman told Houston newspapers that Corll had an exemplary record and was honorably discharged in June 1965. In contrast, Carol Vance, the Harris County DA, claimed Corll was administratively discharged because of "homosexual leanings." Certainly by his early twenties, Corll knew that if anyone suspected he was gay, he might be shunned, dismissed, or attacked. After Corll returned to Houston, he "engaged in some sadistic homosexual encounters with young men" in the late 1960s, Vance wrote.

Around that time, Corll had used his Army training and his father's connections to land a job at Houston Lighting & Power, checking relay systems while continuing to moonlight at the family candy store.

Meanwhile, Corll's mother had signed up for a mainframe computer dating service that paired her up with a merchant marine. This new husband clashed with Corll too, telling Mary her eldest hung out with too many younger boys. (He later told a reporter he suspected his stepson was a "queer," although "murdering never entered my mind.") This marriage didn't last either. By 1968, Mary had resumed using the surname West and begun operating the Corll Candy Company from a bungalow renamed Corll's Candy Kitchen on West 22nd Street in the Heights where the shop and its loading dock bordered the noisy playground of Helms Elementary School. Corll was working full time at Houston Lighting & Power but still helped at the store. He installed a stereo system and invited kids to hang out after hours. "He'd let them in nights to play penny-ante [poker] or pool on a table he had set up in a back room. He was always giving them rides on his motorcycle," his mother recalled in an interview.

Even his mother agreed that Dean, into his twenties, attracted youthful companions. He focused at first on boys he'd initially met as elementary school kids through his candy business and enticed them by sharing motorcycles, surfboards, rides, drugs, and alcohol. Then he began to pay teens for stolen goods, for sexy or lewd photos, for sex acts, or for other services. Still, it was hard to fathom why some teens returned to party even after getting glimpses of the frightening secrets he hid behind the closed curtains of his soul.

David Brooks met Corll at the Candy Kitchen in 1967 when he was in the sixth grade at Helms: "He would give candy to kids leaving school, which was across the street from the store. Also, he owned a motorcycle and would give kids rides [and] take kids to the movies." Among those who regularly hung out or worked there in the late 1960s and early 1970s were Malley Winkle and Billy Baulch, Corll's future murder victims.

At least twice, Malley took his younger neighbor David Hilligiest there to eat sweets and shoot pool, though David's mother didn't approve. Once, Mrs. Hilligiest was driving by and spotted the boys' bikes outside. She parked, went inside, and told Dean Corll she didn't want her child hanging out at a business and she'd appreciate it if he'd tell David to go home if he ever dropped by again. It was a cordial conversation: Before leaving, she bought a box of candy.

Corll worked hard at the candy stores, often laboring into the night devising new recipes or burying candy waste in the yard. But he was also exploring another life. Dean Corll was actively seeking male sex partners in the early 1970s, and occasionally visited gay bars.

One of Houston's most opulent gay venues, aptly named The Palace Club, reopened in 1970 after the previous location had been torched by arsonists. Located on the penthouse level of a high-rise on 3400 Montrose Boulevard, it featured two stages, three gleaming bars, an elaborate dance floor lit by circular chandeliers, and a sweeping view of the Houston skyline. Its owners had spent more than $100,000 to "give the Homophile Society the finest club of this type in the country," a writer for *The Nuntius* boasted. Live bands performed on the main stage outlined by carved Roman columns and draped in bunting, and the club attracted teens and adults—gay and straight—who went there to dance and to party. Wayne Henley was among its clients; so was at least one of Corll's murder victims.

Mary West divorced again in 1968 and, supposedly acting on the advice of psychic advisors, decamped to Colorado, with Corll's half sister, Joyce, in tow. She closed her Houston candy store and opened a new one in Manitou Springs. This time, her top assistant, Dean Corll, stayed behind, for a while sharing an apartment with his father and his younger brother.

For the first time in his life Dean Corll, pushing thirty, lived far from his mother and had an income totally independent of hers, though the two often talked by phone. Wayne Henley once claimed that Corll told his mother all about his clandestine activities, but if that was true, she never admitted it. Corll seemed to thrive at the utility company. He moved up to a supervisory position, though he frequently took sick leave and visited doctors, reporting illnesses that were real or imagined, perhaps as ways to explain odd absences.

SOME OF DEAN CORLL'S patterns of covert behavior seemed familiar to sociologists, like Laud Humphreys, who wrote a popular and controversial 1970 book based on his undercover study of patterns of homosexual sexual activities in public restrooms in the Midwest and later took an interest in Corll's crimes. Humphreys classified Corll as a "closet queen," one of the men who deeply hid their homosexuality, wore a "breastplate of righteousness," and generally avoided gay bars or openly gay relationships. Public bathrooms, often in parks, were venues in those days where many bisexual or gay men could find multiple willing partners for casual sex acts with little risk of exposure. Humphreys titled his book *Tearoom Trade: Impersonal Sex in Public Places,* since some called those secretive meeting places "tearooms," an adaptation of the British slang term "tea" for urine. Though Humphreys conducted his research elsewhere, similar hookup sites existed in Texas: One popular "tearoom" was inside a rest stop off busy Interstate 10 just east of the Houston city limits.

The "closet queens" Humphreys interviewed in "tearooms" superficially resembled Dean Corll: They had only a high school education, displayed furtive behavior, and preferred sex with teenaged boys—people they could control or pay for sex and for their silence. Humphreys described some as "chicken hawks," a pejorative term used in the 1970s for adult men who broke taboos by cruising for underaged boys, picking up and propositioning hitchhikers, or hiring teenaged hustlers who were "gay for pay." A few closet queens would "regularly cruise the streets where boys thumb rides each afternoon when school is over," Humphreys wrote. "One closet queen from my sample has been arrested for luring boys in their early teens to his home."

Those searches could grow desperate as men passed age thirty and struggled to attract younger willing partners, Humphreys observed, and some feared exposure, arrest, and stigmatization so much that they engaged in activities dangerous to themselves or others. One described his endless search for underaged partners: "I just want to love every one of these kids," he told Humphreys. That man was eventually murdered by a teenager he'd picked up cruising.

For years, Dean Corll too cruised for boys in his convertible, his Pontiac GTX, or one of the other flashy cars, motorcycles, and late-model vans he frequently bought and sold. He approached school kids in his car or on foot and offered rides, treats, and invitations. One kid who grew up in Houston's upscale Memorial area recalls seeing Corll and teen helpers being allowed to roam the halls of his elementary school, handing out stale candy. (He didn't accept any.) A Heights boy, Tommy Railsback, a tall, slender athlete who attended school with some murder victims and knew Wayne Henley, remembers being forcefully invited to a party by a man resembling Corll as he rode his bicycle home from baseball practice. "He stepped out in front of me and caught my handlebars and asked me if I 'wanted to have fun.' I had a baseball bat and I said, 'Get away from me, old man.' I never will forget it. It was so close that I could have been caught up in that business."

Initially, Corll could blend in with the teenagers whose company he preferred, but by 1969, his hair was thinning and his waistline was thickening. He dreaded his thirtieth birthday. "His eyes would flash when I joked about his age," Wayne Henley's mother, Mary, recalled. "He couldn't take being kidded about that."

Like Peter Pan, Corll never wanted to grow up, and it seemed forbidden for his favorites to do so. In Pan's Neverland, too, "the boys on the island vary, of course, in numbers, according as they get killed and so on; and when they seem to be growing up, which is against the rules, Peter thins them out. . . ." Over time Corll's murders became so numerous that some victims' names and faces would blur, just as Barrie wrote of Pan: "He might have forgotten it so completely that he said nothing about it; and then when you went out you found the body; on the other hand, he might say a great deal about it, and yet you could not find the body."

LAUD HUMPHREYS, WHO WAS married to a woman when he published *Tearoom Trade* in 1970 but later came out as gay, studied Corll's crimes as part of a larger review of 111 homicide cases involving homosexuals that had been covered by *The Advocate*, which was then a fairly new national gay newspaper. "Society's attitude toward homosexuals causes some people to feel they have the right to beat up gays, and people who fear they are homosexuals are sometimes filled with such self-hatred that they develop psychotic patterns that can lead them to murder," Humphreys said in a September 1975 interview about that research, which he presented at the International Academy of Sex Research at New York's Stony Brook University.

As Corll grew more violent, he relocated more often. Though some neighbors complained of raucous pot parties and at least two landlords found bullet holes in the doors or walls of the units he abandoned, he maintained a low profile. Indeed, neighbors remembered Corll as a "real nice quiet guy," and one landlord called him "as good a tenant as we've ever had." As for any surviving victims who might have escaped, Corll seems to have counted on the secrecy that prevailed in Texas's gay community in the 1970s—and the shame or other consequences teenaged boys feared if they dared to report being chased, abused, or raped by an older man.

Several teenaged boys who encountered Dean Corll never forgot his boldness or their fear. Some say Corll began his hunt much earlier than the first documented murder in September 1970. Others say they're sure Corll used other helpers besides Henley and Brooks and roamed far outside the Heights.

CHAPTER 12

THE HUNT

PASADENA, HOUSTON HEIGHTS, THE GALLERIA,
SPRING BRANCH, 1969–1970

IN 1969, THE YEAR Dean Corll turned thirty, he often parked his van outside the Skate Ranch on Broadway, a teen hangout blocks from the Pasadena High School. Paul Gale, a high school student, lived near the rink in a modest neighborhood called Pasadena Gardens. Paul was seventeen—"fixing to turn eighteen"—when he first ran into Corll, who never went inside to skate and simply lurked in the parking lot, where he or a teenaged companion would invite kids to go party.

"What he'd do is pull up with Brooks in the vehicle, and as people walked by he'd get flirty, and every once in a while, one or two would go off with them," Paul Gale remembers. Mostly guys went, but girls did too. Paul believes at least one of those girls disappeared, though he no longer remembers her name.

Paul was walking home one day when that same older man pulled alongside him in a Plymouth Gold Duster, an eye-catching car with sharp lines and mag wheels, and offered a ride. Paul ignored him. "I passed him up . . . and he pulled beside me and I kept walking and he pulled up beside me again." He had just a half mile left to walk, but the Duster was a muscle car—newly introduced to compete with the Chevy Nova and the Ford Maverick. *Well hell, I'll get a ride!* As he climbed inside, Paul spotted a toolbox in the backseat. It seemed like a sign that the driver was a normal guy, an electrician, a carpenter or something.

Paul told the driver to hang a right on Glenn Avenue. "But when he pulled onto my street—and I told him where I lived—he sped up." Paul pushed open the door of the Plymouth and half-jumped, half-rolled onto the pavement. He wasn't hurt, but was badly shaken. Later the same guy, who now knew Paul's home address, somehow obtained his phone number.

The man phoned many times asking Paul to party until finally Paul's father got on the line and yelled at him never to call back. His parents notified the Pasadena Police; the caller was never caught or questioned. At the time, Paul didn't know the caller's real name, since the man used an alias. But in August 1973, Paul spotted his photo on international news reports: Dean Corll. By then, Paul was serving in the U.S. Marines in Guam. He sent a letter home that his mother shared with police and provided a statement to military authorities, alleging that Corll had lured and attempted to abduct teens in Pasadena prior to 1970. He never got any further response.

IN SEPTEMBER 1969, BERNIE Milligan, fifteen, was working late one night at the Heap-o-Cream store on Yale Street in the Heights, cleaning up huge ice cream vats and metal mixers in preparation for a health department inspection. He began walking home around 11 P.M., exhausted after the sticky, stinking job. The late summer heat felt relentless and Bernie was sweating, though he'd stripped down to his T-shirt. He saw no cars when he stopped at a closed gas station on the corner of 11th and Yale streets, stepped into a darkened alcove, and put a dime into the slot of the soda machine.

The machine hummed, and Bernie bent down to grab the neck of the cold glass soda bottle before hearing footsteps behind him. By that summer, Bernie was nearly his full adult height of six feet three, his hands and legs were tanned and freckled, his feet clad in oversized sneakers. He instinctively jumped up, pivoted away from the machine, and raised the cold glass bottle in his right hand.

Bernie didn't recognize the man—he learned Corll's name later—

but registered odd details. The stranger's eyes were deep-set and focused only on him. His pupils were dilated like a cat's and he held his arms up, fingers curled as if ready to pounce. "He looked like he was on the hunt," Bernie recalled. Bernie was taller, and his muscles, honed from workouts, tensed for a fight. If necessary, he planned to smash the unopened Coke over the man's head. "It was one of them long bottles, and it was going to be a weapon," he recalls.

Face-to-face, Bernie was stunned at how quickly the man's menacing expression transformed into a smile. *Had he imagined that snarl? That hunter's stare?* Suddenly the stranger looked like an ordinary thirtysomething, with fashionably long sideburns and the bearing of a former military man.

"Hey, buddy, how does this machine work?" Corll asked, as if everybody in 1969 America didn't already know how to crank a dial to select a soda from the usual choices: RC Cola, Coke, Sprite, Grape Nehi.

Bernie blurted out an explanation. He always spoke fast and his tone was naturally guttural, his first language being Czech. Then he strode rapidly away, ready to run. Usually he felt safe in his neigh-

borhood, where teens like him regularly walked or rode bikes even late at night. Hardly any of his classmates could afford a car. But he sensed this man might be dangerous. Bernie had only recently begun his sophomore year at Reagan High School, where he was a member of the track team. Some teammates could beat him in sprints. His talent was for hurdles and distance: If necessary, he could run a long time.

Without selecting a soda, Corll jumped into his convertible, then tried to tempt Bernie

Bernie Milligan (left) as a Reagan High School track team co-captain

with a ride. The sports car was sleek and deep blue, a car many boys would covet.

"No thanks," Bernie said.

The stranger eased the convertible forward. "I'll take you wherever you want to go," he hollered. The man kept creeping along in the lane next to the sidewalk, with his headlights off. "C'mon, buddy. Be a guy," he said.

What did that mean? Bernie didn't want to know and began to run, his long legs stretching out on the sidewalk. The stranger kept following alongside and hollering out offers. Bernie paused just long enough to heave the longneck bottle at the car. He aimed for the triangular window that stuck out on the passenger side and heard it shatter with a loud crack. Shards of glass and sticky bubbling soda spewed everywhere.

The driver stopped pretending to be friendly. "I'm going to kill you, you son of a bitch," he said.

Bernie picked up the pace, his feet slapping hard on the concrete, and began zagging west toward home, avoiding the direct route down 11th Street. His breathing grew loud, his arms pumped, and his brain scanned for ways to seek help. Only a block away, a pay phone stood outside Laufman's Food & Home Center, which had closed hours before. But to use it, Bernie realized, *I would have to put myself right under a store light and would stick out like a sore thumb.* He detoured down darkened alleyways and crossed unfenced yards, prompting dogs he couldn't see to snarl and bark, but he still heard the roar of the convertible behind him. At one point, the driver shot around the block and reappeared in front of Bernie, trying to cut him off.

His pursuer clearly knew the Heights' neat grid of streets as well as he did. In a panic, Bernie kept switching directions. He feared leading this stranger to his home. Only after the sound of the engine finally faded did Bernie backtrack to the bungalow on Dorothy Street. He fumbled with the lock, shut the door, and stood panting in the darkened entryway, his chest heaving as he strained to listen for the rumble of that car.

His mother was waiting up and Bernie immediately told her about the chase. Frantically, they began turning off lights and peering out the front windows into darkness. No cars passed. They whispered about whether to call police. *But what had really happened?* Bernie had no license plate number, no crime to report. Like many other teens in the 1970s, he didn't really trust the cops. Even if an officer arrived in time to question the man in the convertible, Bernie realized *he'd* probably be arrested for hurling a bottle. *Who'd believe a fifteen-year-old?*

DEAN CORLL'S FIRST CONFIRMED kill came on September 28, 1970, about a year after he chased Bernie Milligan. At that time, Corll lived in a high-rise apartment near the rising palatial Houston Galleria, a luxury mall that would open that November with 600,000 square feet of air-conditioned indoor upscale shops wrapped around an ice-skating rink. Corll, likely driving his convertible or his Pontiac GTX, found Jeffrey Konen, an attractive and intelligent college freshman with thick blond hair, looking for a ride near that massive commercial construction site on Houston's well-heeled west side. Konen had been the salutatorian of Houston's St. Thomas High School prior to enrolling at the University of Texas at Austin.

Corll, well-groomed and soft-spoken, could easily persuade the eighteen-year-old to take a ride. Konen was almost home and eager to see his girlfriend.

Corll later bragged to Wayne Henley and David Brooks that he buried that handsome boy's body under a rock on the beach on the Bolivar Peninsula. But Corll, Brooks claimed, didn't talk much about the boys he'd killed and buried alone—or with other accomplices.

IN THE FALL OF 1970, a teen named David Gibson and a friend accepted a ride from a man driving a white van after their movie let out at the Oak Village Theatre, a movie house inside a strip shopping center on Long Point Road. The single-screen theater, later renamed the Long Point Cinema, was popular with teens and featured live bands, contests sponsored by a local radio station, and midnight movies, like that year's hot sequel, *Beneath the Planet of the Apes*.

"They asked us if we wanted to ride around so we got in," Gibson recalled years later in a Facebook message. "But we knew it was a very strange position we were in after a while." For about an hour, David and his buddy rode around with a dark-haired older man with sideburns and another teen he didn't know. The conversation was odd and getting odder. At some point, David, who was carrying a pocketknife, demanded to be dropped off.

Reluctantly, the driver complied. David Gibson and his friend were let out at the theater—and the others kept cruising. Years later, David recognized the driver when newspapers published photos of Dean Corll. He believes the boy helping Corll that day was neither Brooks nor Henley. Gibson says he later spotted that teen in some of Corll's photographs; he believes it was a boy from Channelview whom police questioned in 1973 but never named as a suspect.

Still, David Gibson, who attended a junior high in Spring Branch ISD, considers his encounter a narrow escape. Not long after, a fourteen-year-old in David's homeroom class disappeared. That boy, Jim Glass, was murdered by Corll, along with Danny Michael Yates, another fourteen-year-old schoolmate. Both boys vanished in December 1970. And their bodies were found in Corll's boatshed in 1973.

DANNY YATES'S BIG BROTHER Bradley says that police missed an important part of that story: Prior to his disappearance, Jim Glass had been cruising around with Corll near movie theaters and helping recruit other kids to party.

Danny and his older brother Bradley Yates were only a year and nine months apart, and they spent hours exploring together when the family moved into a new brick rancher built on land his parents bought in 1961 in the Rosemont Terrace neighborhood. Their three-bedroom place had a rec room, a spacious attic, and an oversized corner lot. The Yates boys were only blocks from where the West Houston suburbs touched the as-yet-undeveloped wilderness around Addicks Dam, one of two clay barriers erected on the Katy Prairie to create reservoirs, which normally were dry, but during big storms could protect the city from devastating floods that roared east along Buffalo Bayou toward downtown. In their teens, the grasslands of pothole prairie beside those dams regularly filled with shallow wetlands and migrating flocks of snow geese. The trails there offered an escape from the stresses of home. Their mother had admitted to an affair and their parents' marriage was crumbling. "We rode bikes around to Addicks Dam and slid down the side on cardboard—one time went down on a go-cart. We'd camp out in an abandoned field overnight," Bradley remembers.

If the brothers ventured into an open lot right behind their own house, they could quickly reach a companion Danny's age, Jim Glass, a wide-eyed risk-taker who slicked his dark brown bangs into a fashionable swoosh and wore a Hawaiian-style puka shell necklace and a leather jacket with fringe. Jim seemed cool when his family arrived in 1966, Bradley recalls. In their junior high days, he provided joints and introduced the brothers to a convenience store clerk who allowed them to illegally buy cigarettes. On Friday or Saturday nights, the three neighbors often gathered to play pranks: hurling rolls of toilet paper into trees or filling a five-gallon bucket full of water balloons to throw at drunken customers departing the neighborhood icehouse. "And then we'd run around and hide out in that field where they couldn't find us."

For a while, it all seemed like harmless fun, even to Bradley, who by age fifteen had nearly reached his full height of six feet three and also had grown more cautious than the others. One night the younger duo targeted a cop with their water balloons. "That guy wouldn't let up. They finally crawled into a culvert underneath a driveway to get away," Bradley remembers. They waited on their bellies inside that muddy metal tube until the officer eventually left.

By the fall of 1970, Bradley was rejecting such juvenile antics. He was a fifteen-year-old freshman at Spring Woods High School and had bought a drum set and was learning to play. Inspired by his idol Don Brewer of Grand Funk Railroad, he wanted to be in a band someday.

Sometimes he worried that Jim Glass dominated his trusting younger brother. Bradley once saw Jim hit his brother in the stomach with a rock propelled by a sling shot, prompting him to double over in pain. They had a weird relationship. "Right when he disappeared, Jim Glass was abusing my brother. I don't know if they were having sex with each other. They called it corn holing," Bradley Yates recalls. He knew his younger brother had done the same thing with another boy, though his brother was dating a girl too; Danny kissed that girl in the laundromat of an apartment complex. Perhaps his little brother was gay or bisexual, or straight and just experimenting. Bradley never got the time to find out.

The trio's last misadventure began December 11, 1970, as another of Jim Glass's wild ideas: All three would go to the Thunderbird Twin Drive-In, where they could watch movies or spy on couples making out in cars. None were old enough to drive—Bradley was fifteen, the others were only fourteen. But they could sit outside on a bench beside the concession stand if they bought tickets. Houston drive-ins were open year-round and that Friday ushered in a pre-Christmas holiday heat wave—the day's high hit 71 degrees. Jim Glass's mother drove them there in a station wagon, but when they reached the huge parking lot on Clay Road, the marquee under the enormous neon T-bird revealed the double feature films were R-rated. They couldn't enter without an adult, yet Jim Glass shooed his mother away. In Bradley's memory, Jim shouted at her: "Get out of here!"

They were stranded.

That's when things got weirder. Bradley Yates proposed decamping for the indoor theater on Long Point Road, at least three miles away. They hadn't walked far when a dark-haired man with sideburns, a guy in his thirties, pulled over and offered a ride in his muscle car. Bradley clambered into the backseat with Jim Glass beside him; Danny rode shotgun. The driver had a wheedling manner, and they had barely gotten in when he asked: "Hey, do you guys want some beers?"

Bradley said no, but Danny and Jim accepted, so the stranger stopped at a convenience store and emerged with a six-pack. Danny popped the top and began sucking down a brew, while Jim Glass cradled his can between his feet. Bradley abstained. He felt increasingly uncomfortable: He wondered why Jim Glass seemed to know this "stranger." He spotted Jim and the driver exchanging smirks via the rearview mirror. His anxiety increased when the driver nosed his car onto the feeder road along Interstate Highway 10 and headed west. The Long Point Theatre was in the other direction.

"When are you gonna take us to the theater?" Bradley asked. "We're trying to get to a theater to see a movie. . . ."

"Why don't you let your brother finish his beer?" the stranger said in a voice that never rose much above the roar of the engine.

"Why don't you let us out here?" Bradley prodded. He noticed that they had nearly reached a side road that slanted back toward the Yates home. Briefly, he considered whether to throw open the door and jump, but didn't want to abandon his brother.

Finally, the stranger turned the car around. When they finally arrived at the theater, only the Yates brothers got out. Bradley Yates has other vivid memories of the Long Point Theatre: enjoying his first kiss; watching all of the *Planet of the Apes* movies, as well as *A Hard Day's Night*. But he doesn't remember the last movie he ever saw with his brother. He does recall how the stranger handed Danny a slip of paper with a phone number, inviting him to call if he ever wanted more beer. And how Jim Glass rode away with that man.

Three days later, on Sunday, December 13, 1970, Jim Glass and Danny Yates went to an antidrug revival at the Evangelical Temple, on West 11th Street, just outside the Heights. Bradley Yates had heard that the preachers could be entertaining, railing against pot as they played rock and roll, but he woke up with a cough, felt sick, and didn't go along. At some point during the service, his brother Danny wandered off with Jim Glass and disappeared.

In August 1973, their bodies were among those discovered in Dean Corll's boatshed, which Corll had just started renting in December 1970.

When Bradley Yates saw the photo of his brother's killer in Houston newspapers, he recognized Corll as the driver who'd picked them up earlier in December 1970. But Bradley Yates doesn't believe Jim Glass died at the same time as his brother. In the spring of 1971, Bradley insists he saw Jim Glass astride a Yamaha 90 motorcycle at an intersection near a neighborhood store. He yelled out "Hey Jim!" The boy just glanced at him and rode away. Bradley admits that encounter was fleeting, yet he has more of what he considers proof. Danny Yates's tombstone bears the date of his disappearance, December 13, 1970. Jim Glass's lists only the year 1971. Bradley believes that Jim Glass may have survived longer because Dean Corll had been using him. "The whole thing at the theater was obviously a set-up," Bradley says. "Jim Glass was trying to set us both up for Dean Corll. But after my brother disappeared, Jim Glass couldn't come home alone. Corll had to kill him."

Jim Glass's older brother, who attended the revival, and his parents have since died and can no longer speak for Jim. Autopsy records show that both Danny Yates's and Jim Glass's remains had been wrapped in a striped sheet and bound in ropes prior to burial. The Harris County medical examiner opined that both died on or about December 13, 1970.

David Brooks told police about a boy named Glass who supposedly was still alive in 1971. In his second statement to police, Brooks said "Glass" got killed when Corll was renting a place "on Columbia." (Corll rented a garage apartment on Columbia Place in the Heights from September to December 1971.) "I had taken him home one time but he wouldn't get out because he wanted to go back to Dean," Brooks said. "I took him back and Dean ended up killing him. Now that I think about it, I'm not sure it was Glass but I believe it was."

On official lists, Danny Yates and Jim Glass appear as Corll's second and third known murder victims. Their bodies were found in Boatshed Hole No. 4. By then the shed had gotten so full of graves that two other boys, killed in October 1972, had been buried in that same spot.

CHAPTER 13

WHO KNEW?

HOUSTON, 1972–1973

ERNIE MILLIGAN RAN INTO his old buddy Frank Aguirre by chance at a party in early 1972. It was a blustery winter night and a cluster of teens crammed inside the dimly lit living room of a friend's house off Airline Drive to listen to records and dance. By then they were seniors at different high schools and hadn't seen each other for months. Bernie was already dancing when Frank, a friend from Hamilton Junior High days, grabbed the back pocket of his jeans. Bernie pivoted and spotted Frank on a sofa with his arm around a strikingly pretty girl.

"How are you doing, Bernie?" Frank said, smiling and friendly as ever.

Bernie leaned over to chat: Frank had big news. His girlfriend had just agreed to marry him.

Bernie was floored. At eighteen, he couldn't imagine marrying anyone, but his old friend seemed thrilled. Frank's girl was stunning, Bernie thought. Her face bore some resemblance to the French actress Brigitte Bardot, but she was younger and so petite that she looked like a child in a buxom woman's body. Her name was Rhonda Williams, Frank said.

They smiled and shouted a few words at each other, but it was too loud in that living room for real conversation. Bernie wondered if

Frank's mom, who depended on her eldest, approved of his wedding plans. He knew that Frank, a full-time student, worked nights and weekends as manager at the Long John Silver's fish and chips shop on Yale Street. Both he and Frank grew up in homes led by single mothers—Frank's mom was a widow and Bernie's was divorced. The two friends had worked all through school and were looking forward to graduation in May 1972.

But the Williams-Aguirre nuptials would never happen, and Frank would never graduate.

Frank disappeared on March 24, 1972, a few minutes after finishing a shift at the fish and chips shop. He vanished with his hair still stuffed into the plastic cap required under health department food safety rules. His prized Rambler Rebel was missing too. Frank, at seventeen, was too old to be investigated as a runaway by HPD. His mother, Josephine, went to the homicide division in person to speak to detectives. Officers made a few inquiries about her missing son but did not launch a full-fledged murder investigation, though Frank had, without warning, abandoned school (after having bought his class ring) and his job (without bothering to collect his last paycheck).

Frank's sudden disappearance rattled a lot of Heights teens. *He had no reason to leave,* Bernie thought. He never considered that Frank Aguirre, a dependable high school senior, would run away. Like other Heights teens who had attended Hamilton or Hogg Junior High, Bernie had heard of other neighborhood kids who had suddenly vanished. At least five hundred posters had been plastered in shop and restaurant windows after Malley Winkle and David Hilligiest disappeared in May 1971, but no one had ever found them either.

Maybe some teens did run away, kids told themselves. Maybe fifteen-year-old Randy Harvey got tired of pumping gas in March 1971 and took off. Bernie didn't know Randy very well. But Frank Aguirre? It made no sense. He had a girlfriend, a car, and a job, and a mother and little sister who loved him.

RIGHT AFTER FRANK DISAPPEARED, Bernie Milligan heard a rumor that his buddy had somehow gotten mixed up in organized crime. A mutual friend claimed that Frank was "dead and buried." Bernie found that declaration bizarre and never believed it, but Frank was definitely gone. Only two months later, another former Hamilton Junior High schoolmate, Mark Scott, also vanished. That was unsettling, though Mark was no runaway: He had dropped out and was already living on his own. Some Heights kids knew that Mark had recently been arrested or heard he'd sent a postcard to his parents saying he was going to Austin or Mexico. Maybe Mark *had* just taken off.

Frank Aguirre's girlfriend, Rhonda Williams, felt heartbroken, but helpless. "When children disappeared, we did believe that they ran away and we were always trying to figure out what happened to these kids, but we weren't the adults, we were the kids," she later explained. By 1973, even more Heights boys would disappear. One was her cousin, Charles Cobble.

AS A CHILD, BERNIE Milligan had considered the Heights a "magical place to grow up." Though no longer an independent city, the Heights still had stately parks, schools, pools, and an esplanade lined with mansions (even if some were in disrepair). He envisioned it as "a splendid picture-perfect movie-like Southern neighborhood," like those featured in 1950s movies. Famous Texans like the network newsman Dan Rather and Denton A. Cooley, the pioneering heart surgeon and son of a Heights founder, had grown up there. Patrick Swayze, the good-looking actor who later gained fame in the 1987 film *Dirty Dancing*, attended Waltrip High with Frank Aguirre. Swayze's mom ran a popular local dance studio, worked for the Houston Ballet, and later became a Hollywood choreographer.

But in the 1970s, several blocks of the Heights' older bungalows had been torn down and replaced by boxy apartments, seedy bars, and junk shops. Some Houston junior and senior high schools had riots over desegregation. A more transient and volatile mix of people started to call the Heights home; once, Bernie got shot at after he happened to witness a robbery (and tried to chase the thief). Another time, he heard gunfire and discovered a bleeding man who'd been shot and was lying near a pay phone at a convenience store at 10th and Shepherd. Bernie ran home and a neighbor called police but he had trouble getting help from the officers, who initially assumed the injured man, who happened to be Black, was merely drunk.

In junior high, Frank Aguirre was part of the Heights' minority of Mexican Americans, but hung out with white kids like Bernie, who regularly spoke Czech at home. Both belonged to a subgroup of poorer kids who worked side jobs and had no father around. "We were segregated by income, we were segregated by race, religion, you name it. We were segregated by that. And if you had a mom and dad and both had a great job, you didn't really hang around with the mom-only crowd, you know, that was going to be trouble," Bernie remembers.

Easygoing Frank didn't seem to worry about crossing boundaries of religion and ethnicity to bond with other kids, though Bernie knew those barriers were always there. Bernie had bumped up against them himself. Once in elementary school, an older kid learned that his first name was Burnet, after his father, and took a lighter to his arm to teach him what being "burnt" really meant. Later, Bernie wondered if that's what got Frank Aguirre killed: He dared cross lines to propose to a white girl.

During their Hamilton years, Bernie and Frank befriended brothers who were Southern Baptists, the anti-dancing, anti-drinking, anti-card-playing religious crowd that dominated so much of Texas. The brothers defied their parents by hanging out with non-Baptists who listened to rock and roll. Bernie sometimes attended youth group with the two, but was targeted by their preacher after admitting he knew his Bible verses from attending All Saints Catholic Church. At one point in the service, the pastor declared " 'SATAN is among us,' and pointed at me and said 'here is SATAN, leave this Church,'" Bernie recalls.

One afternoon, the four friends went to the Aguirres' to listen to a new album by Iron Butterfly, a group pushing the limits of psychedelic music to create a new genre called heavy metal. Bernie noticed

Frank's cool stereo system and wondered how he'd managed to afford it. Frank placed a shiny new LP on his turntable and cranked up the volume, and they all rocked out under a black light to Iron Butterfly's mesmerizing hit, "In-A-Gadda-Da-Vida."

Bernie Milligan was flabbergasted when he learned a few months after Frank disappeared that his friend's former fiancée was dating Wayne Henley, another former Hamilton Junior High schoolmate. Bernie didn't really remember Wayne from school; Wayne was younger and they moved in far different circles. Bernie deeply disliked him when their paths crossed later in the Heights. By then, Wayne Henley had a juvenile record for thievery, drugs, and assault and constantly appeared to be drunk or stoned.

If police had ever bothered to really investigate what happened to Frank, the trail would have led right to Wayne Henley, Bernie thought. Wayne had supposedly been Frank's friend—but Frank had things a loser like Wayne would covet: plans for the future, a cool car, and Rhonda Williams. And Wayne Henley was the last person seen with Frank on the night he disappeared.

Bernie Milligan sometimes felt guilty that he never contacted HPD about his own run-ins with Wayne Henley, David Brooks, and Dean Corll.

Bernie learned Dean Corll's name in July 1973, nearly four years after being chased by the stranger in the blue convertible. By that time, David Brooks was dating Bridget Clark, a Reagan High student who Bernie knew from All Saints Catholic Church. Bridget and Bernie had mutual friends—her best friend was the younger sister of his best friend. Those intertwined relationships meant that Bernie often saw David Brooks with his arm slung around Bridget inside the living room of Bernie's buddy's house near Milby Park. Bernie dropped by that house often, even after his best friend joined the U.S. Marine Corps and was deployed overseas. He felt like part of the family and stopped after work in 1972 and 1973 to check on his friend's widowed mother and younger sisters.

Bernie didn't remember David Brooks from the year they overlapped at Hamilton Junior High. By his early teens, Bernie was already working after school, and bonded more with athletes or kids into electronics like him. Unlike Brooks, he never used drugs. By the time the two met in 1973, David Brooks had transformed from a barely noticeable marginal student into a smooth operator. *He probably could have been a successful salesman or entrepreneur,* Bernie thought. Bernie had no idea how David Brooks made money, but he clearly had some: David drove a flashy Corvette and often picked up his girlfriend at Reagan High in a white van. By the summer of 1973, David Brooks and Bridget were serious—she was visibly pregnant with his child. Bernie heard they were planning to slip off to the courthouse and get married.

ON THE FOURTH OF July weekend, Bernie Milligan was hanging out at that same friend's house when David pulled up in a brown sedan. This time David was a passenger, and he leaned way out his window to get Bernie's attention. "We're going up to Lake Sam Rayburn to go fishing." David wanted to know if Bernie wanted to come along. His friend had a cabin, and they had already loaded extra gear and beer. "C'mon," he added with a big smile. "The fish are biting."

Bernie leaned against the side of the idling car to chat. He liked to fish but was way too busy working. He had graduated from Reagan High and already had a full-time job. And he became even less interested when he spotted that loser Wayne Henley slumped in the backseat.

The driver, an older man, had been facing the other way, apparently watching kids playing in Milby Park. At that moment, he glanced around, catching Bernie's eye.

Bernie Milligan had never forgotten the stranger with the dark-eyed gaze of a hunter. He could tell the other man recognized him too. "We have to go now," said the driver, gunning the engine and pulling away.

Disturbed by the encounter, Bernie Milligan retreated inside the house, where friends told him the driver's name: Dean Corll. Two former members of that household verify that they also remember troubling conversations and visits from Corll, Brooks, and Henley.

LIKE OTHER HEIGHTS TEENS, Bernie Milligan was horrified in August 1973 to see photos of Frank Aguirre in Houston newspapers as a murder victim. For him, and many others, that news was world-shattering. *How could so many boys, like his friend Frank, have been kidnapped and killed without the police knowing that any murders were happening?* Later, he couldn't stop wondering: *What did his friends and Bridget Clark know about David Brooks's involvement? Why did Rhonda Williams, who was supposedly so devastated over Frank Aguirre's disappearance, start seeing Wayne Henley? What did Henley's mother and Brooks's father know? And who else in the neighborhood knew or suspected Corll had been kidnapping and killing people?* "There was a hell of a lot of stuff going on in the Heights that I knew nothing about," he said. "People were protecting people."

Bernie Milligan continues to wonder who knew—and who could have stopped them. Over time, that curiosity led him to a undertake a long-running personal investigation into the motivations and methods behind Corll's crimes. Despite all he's learned, he's hardest on himself: *What if he'd gone to police in July 1973?* He couldn't help replaying the upsetting conversation he'd had with friends after seeing the man who'd chased him.

"That was the day I failed. . . . The day I failed was that day."

CHAPTER 14

MAPPING THE MURDERS

SERGEANT BEACH, 2019

BERNIE MILLIGAN HAD BEEN quietly collecting material about the Houston Mass Murder cases for years when he ran into Danny Furstenfeld, another Reagan High School alum, while walking along Sergeant Beach, a quiet cluster of fishing and beach houses near the Gulf of Mexico in the summer of 2019. The two men sat down at a patio table together in the sun and began talking about their careers and reminiscing about their teenaged days. Lean and muscular, Bernie still spoke as swiftly as he had when he and Danny ran track together at Reagan. Bernie had always admired Danny, who had also played varsity football and dated (and later married) one of the prettiest girls on the cheerleading squad. Danny, a year older, graduated in 1971 and later attended the Houston police academy, ultimately moving up from patrol to narcotics task forces before finally retiring in 2008 after a thirty-four-year career. Both men were in their sixties, their high school years decades behind them. But neither Bernie nor Danny had ever forgotten about Dean Corll or the other Heights teenagers Corll had killed.

They swapped stories, and Bernie explained how in his career as a telecommunications expert he'd become a different kind of investigator: probing communications leaks and ultimately obtaining top security clearance to track hackers as a federal government contractor. As old friends and professional sleuths, Bernie and Danny began to discuss the questions they'd pondered as teens: *How could that many kids disappear from their old neighborhood without anyone noticing?*

At some point, Danny Furstenfeld told Bernie that he had been approached to participate in a documentary series, *The Clown and the Candyman,* which was examining whether Dean Corll had connections to a multinational pornography ring that had been linked to another serial killer, John Wayne Gacy. Gacy, a construction worker who sometimes moonlighted as a clown, had targeted teenaged boys in Illinois, luring some victims to his home by performing magic tricks or promising jobs or other favors. Curiously, Corll and Gacy had each kidnapped, raped, and killed more than two dozen teens in the 1970s and their crime timelines, while in different states, overlapped. Gacy's first known killing came in 1972, and he continued until he was finally caught in December 1978.

Caroline Grist, a determined yet charming journalist who retained a charming accent from her native England, was a development producer for Cineflix, a company based in Toronto and New York City, and had been digging into the Gacy and Corll murder cases. She had a strong interest in telling meaningful crime stories and had been surprised to learn that the Corll case seemed largely untold on TV or film, perhaps because of the stigma that male victims of sex crimes faced in the 1970s and even decades later. Two books about the crimes had been published in 1974, but copies could be hard to find. Grist had met Danny Furstenfeld while researching another Texas project, but when she reached out, she was surprised to learn he'd grown up in the Heights.

Danny had immediately expressed interest in helping reinvestigate the Corll case. As a retired narcotics detective, he knew people from the underworld of 1970s Houston and understood the dynamics of drug dealers, fences, child pornographers, and male teen prostitutes. He believed Corll had dealings with those networks. But he was also aware that his old friend, Bernie Milligan, had known some murder victims far better than he did. He told Bernie he figured they could discover more by working together.

Bernie had almost no knowledge about the netherworld of sex workers and pimps that seemed so familiar to his friend. He'd never heard a term Danny threw around for men like Corll who targeted adolescent boys—"chicken hawk." He told Danny he'd always felt that there was more to Corll's crimes that remained undiscovered and figured he could contribute through the information he'd already been gathering and by tapping federal government training he'd received on how to profile hackers and other criminals.

Bernie suggested that they begin by creating detailed timelines—and by mapping the murders. "You start with the first kill. Then you begin to visualize how he is operating," he explained. Corll's murder spree had begun on December 13, 1970, and his last victim taken on July 25, 1973. Eleven had attended the same junior high as Milligan. He figured he could learn more by mapping the locations associated with the killers and those victims, including where they'd lived, where they'd been snatched, and where, if known, they'd died. Over the years, Bernie had become adept at criminal profiling, he told Danny. And now, he figured he could apply those skills to profile Dean Corll.

Profiling, a technique initially developed by the FBI, combined elements of psychology with crime statistics and data from interviews with convicted murderers that could be used to better understand killers' motives and even to develop potential portraits of unknown criminal suspects. Back in the 1980s, FBI agent Robert Ressler, a co-founder of the National Center for the Analysis of Violent Crime, had first begun interviewing prolific killers in prison and coined the term "serial killer" for those who'd confessed to multiple sexually sadistic slayings. By the center's later reckoning, 357 serial killers operated in the United States from 1960 to 1991, murdering more than three thousand people. Other experts figured that the death toll of those stealthy hunters of human beings had to be even higher. The development of the interstate highway system had speeded travel, given an advantage to truckers over trains—and inadvertently supplied faster getaway routes for murderers. Many killers, like Corll, were motivated by dark sexual desires, but, unlike Corll, most interviewed by FBI profilers exclusively targeted strangers.

Bernie Milligan had first learned how to apply similar techniques in his own work when he developed a subspecialty in security and investigated communications breaches. Over time, he'd gotten licensed as a private detective, founded his own company, and handled sensitive government assignments, including counterterrorism and intelligence contracts. Between 1982 and 1992, as a member of a counterterrorism support team, he'd received annual training in profiling, which he applied to investigations of cybercriminals and later taught to others.

From 1994 to 1996, Bernie Milligan worked with a team of psychiatrists and other experts to develop an operational profile of a group of hackers to understand how cybercriminals thought and functioned. Many were narcissists, motivated by their own egos to penetrate complex systems and steal information and funds, he learned. Some were fascinated with the seemingly innocuous 1985 comedy *Ferris Bueller's Day Off*, a film that, from Bernie's professional point of view, glorified breaking laws for pleasure seemingly without any consequences for a sufficiently intelligent smart-ass juvenile perpetrator.

He'd also read a lot of research done by other profilers on serial killers. At one point, Bernie had worked on another serial killer profile. He completed an early, accurate profile of the Unabomber, a reclusive domestic terrorist who killed by mailing bombs, as a side project for a California newspaper before any arrests were made. It later turned out that the suspect, as Bernie had predicted, was an egotistical narcissist with an extensive academic background who lived far off the grid.

Even before meeting up with Danny, Bernie had already been gathering news stories, police reports, and public information about the victims of Corll, Brooks, and Henley so he could analyze Corll's methods and try to answer questions that still troubled him. Through his training, Milligan had learned about organized and disorganized serial killers. Back in August 1985, the FBI Bulletin published an article in which a pair of agents described interviewing thirty-six serial killers and dividing them into two types. Organized offenders, they wrote, often had average or above-average intelligence, and their crime scenes showed "a semblance of order before, during, and after the offense"; disorganized killers tended to be more impulsive and messy.

Milligan considered Corll narcissistic and "highly organized." Organized serial killers often hid bodies and developed techniques and tools, including murder kits for abducting and killing their victims. Corll had often tricked victims into handcuffing themselves and forced captives to write letters or make phone calls to fool parents into thinking they were safe. His tools were elaborate: He toted a gray toolbox full of glass rods and dildos to force into victims' body cavities, carried a saber to cut off their clothes, and built a torture board with restraints to keep one or two boys tied down and away from phones or weapons. In the end, he and his henchmen loaded corpses into a specially built body box.

As they kept discussing the case, the friends became so engrossed that they barely noticed when the strong sun began sinking over the western horizon, though Bernie took regular breaks to take long drags from his Winston Light 100s. He told Danny that Corll seemed radically different from the sexually motivated sadists he'd learned about in workshops, textbooks, and serial killer databases. Few demonstrated Corll's knack for exerting control over teenaged accomplices. Perhaps cult leader Charles Manson came close, though Manson dispatched members of "The Family" to kill and seemingly did no dirty work himself. Corll paid Brooks and Henley, and perhaps others, for sex acts, stolen goods, and other boys—around $200 or more, at a time when minimum wage was $1.60 an hour. He provided drugs and alcohol. And he created drug-fueled party games for those teens that involved torture and murder.

After their initial meeting, the two friends "were on the phone an awful lot" discussing their theories, Danny's wife, Roki Furstenfeld, remembers. Like Danny, she had known Bernie since their Reagan High days. "Danny could not get over the burden that Bernie was carrying. He was concerned about it . . . I think he was very thankful that Bernie talked to him about it and they got together and this was something they could work on."

In one of their early follow-up phone calls, Danny told Bernie that members of drug rings often get addicted to the danger: the feeling of being a "player." That conversation resonated with Bernie, who told Danny that must have been part of what motivated Corll's accomplices. "They each wanted to be a player," Bernie figured. "Dean Corll understood enough about these people where he could create a game for them." In Bernie's assessment, Corll controlled those games and decided who lived or died. Corll provided plans and tools, but made others bring the boys, haul the bodies, and dig the graves. David Brooks, as a business owner's son, enjoyed a higher social status than Wayne Henley, and became Corll's roommate, driver, and the group's drug dealer. Henley was the foot soldier and the flunky.

BERNIE HAD NEVER FORGOTTEN his friend Frank and had no sympathy for Henley, even though he knew Henley's father had been a violent alcoholic. (Elmer Wayne Henley, Sr., had later been arrested in Louisiana for assault after allegedly attempting to shoot and kill his second wife's father, a Baptist minister.) But Bernie thought it was incredible how quickly Wayne Henley, Jr., had begun torturing and killing others to please Dean Corll, including kids he'd known all his life.

"Still, there were a lot of unanswered questions," Bernie told Danny. Many narcissistic and sexually sadistic serial killers like Corll had been abused as children and chose victims of an age when they themselves had suffered. Bernie figured something truly terrible likely happened when Dean Corll was in elementary school or junior high "that made it so important that he be around these young kids." Old police records, divorce files, and newspaper archives only hinted that Corll's father had abused Corll and that his mother had been "batshit crazy."

Over the next two years, Bernie and Danny collected more police reports and public records, tapping online sources and consulting informants and contacts they'd made throughout their careers. Danny, who'd been nicknamed Once Upon a Time for the meticulous case notes he kept as a police officer, scrawled observations on notebook paper and organized documents in binders. They met again and again, and together they created oversized timelines and maps on poster board. They pasted school photographs of the Lost Boys on one timeline and poked stick pins into oversized maps to indicate locations linked with Lost Boys' lives and body dump sites, and pins of another color to show Dean Corll's known addresses. Bernie would often tote those boards over to Danny's place in his tan Ford 250 pickup so they could go over them, Roki recalls. Soon those posters took up so much space in Bernie's house that his wife complained. They grew excited about their discoveries, though they never found any clear links between Dean Corll and John Wayne Gacy.

One of Milligan's timelines

Sometimes Bernie and Danny rode around in the oversized pickup to verify addresses that seemed inaccurate in old police reports. For Corll alone, they identified more than thirty possible addresses in Houston and Pasadena between 1967 and 1973, though they concentrated most on the places where Corll lived during the known murders. Many of the streets they drove were familiar, though only about half of Corll's victims lived inside the Heights' official boundaries, the friends noticed. While searching for perplexing locations or pondering connections, Milligan sometimes blurted out a Czech phrase, soliciting help from Jesus, Mary, and Joseph. Bernie and Danny both noticed during their drives that

Corll favored places near elementary schools, including Helms, Field, Cooley, and Love in the Heights.

Bernie attended Cooley Elementary School in the late 1960s, a period when Corll worked at one of his mother's candy stores across the street. He recalled playing baseball there one afternoon when a guy who other kids greeted as "the Candy Man" approached the fence. That must have been Dean Corll, he thought. Yet all of Corll's known victims were older than elementary school age. Bernie figured there had to be more: *How many elementary kids did he kill?*

One of Corll's old addresses gave Bernie a jolt. In 1969, the year Bernie had been chased through his neighborhood, Corll was renting a house on Dorothy Street only a block from his.

The duo were filmed driving by Corll's former homes and murder scenes for *The Clown and the Candyman* (Sharon Derrick appeared in the documentary's opening episode too, talking about her ongoing work on the Lost Boy cases). But the two friends thought that in the end the filmmakers seemed more interested in Gacy, "the Clown," than Corll, "the Candyman." Gacy had killed more known victims—thirty-three. And he'd had plenty of time to boast about his exploits before his execution in Illinois on May 10, 1994.

Danny and Bernie made discoveries about Corll that weren't in that show.

Danny was able to dig into records and confirm reports that Corll's one prior documented entanglement with the law had been a speeding ticket he'd gotten while riding a Harley-Davidson motorcycle in 1967. But he also discovered signs of Corll's side business selling stolen goods. Corll had stored a stolen car with bogus plates in the boatshed alongside the bodies in 1973. And Frank Aguirre's missing Rambler Rebel had been disassembled after his disappearance in 1972 and resold for parts in East Texas and Louisiana.

Inside his Pasadena house, Corll had kept a collection of murder victims' keys. The two men figured that Corll likely dispatched Henley and other teens to burglarize homes to reap additional profits. "Parents wouldn't change the locks because they were hoping the kids would come home," Milligan observed. One key stowed inside a cigar box at Corll's place opened the back door of the family home of Mark Scott, a junior high classmate of Henley's who was captured and killed in 1972. Another murdered boy's father, Horace J. "Jimmy" Lawrence, reported that a young man who identified himself as "Wayne" came by the house soon after his son Billy disappeared. Two days later, his house was burglarized, and cameras, guns, and the stereo he'd given Billy for his birthday had been stolen by someone who seemed familiar with the house layout. Danny suspected that Corll also used his knowledge as a supervisor at a utility company to identify when other employees went on vacation—and targeted their houses too.

Danny made notes on those finds, but even in retirement he was careful to protect his sources. (Shortly before Danny died of cancer in November 2020, he asked his family to shred his files.)

More discoveries came from the maps they created. Corll's first three known murders occurred in late 1970 and early 1971, a period when he'd lived at the Yorktown Apartments, a swanky high-rise complex on the west side of Houston. Corll carried out the last seven or eight during the summer he spent in his father's Pasadena home on 2020 Lamar. In between, Corll had lived at dozens of addresses for only weeks at a time.

At first, Corll apparently killed just one or two people while living at the same address and then moved on. Some places he shared with David Brooks. But Bernie noticed the pace quickened in 1972 after Wayne Henley began to supply victims. By then, Corll had moved to an apartment on the second floor of a commercial building on Schuler Street. In February 1972, Henley brought a long-haired boy he claimed not to know to party with Corll. (Based on police reports, that boy might have been Rusty Branch, a police officer's son.) The next to die there was Bernie's friend Frank Aguirre.

Bernie figured Frank and Rhonda's engagement triggered the attack. "Frank Aguirre died because he was dating Rhonda and because Henley wanted to date Rhonda," he said.

All of Corll's victims were raped and tortured. Details in an autopsy report showed that Frank Aguirre had been singled out for brutal treatment: He had been slowly smothered to death—his face entirely covered in adhesive tape, his mouth stuffed with a torn towel, and his neck wrapped in a hangman's noose. Milligan figured Frank had been targeted in part because he'd proposed to an Anglo girl. To Milligan, Henley's participation seemed evil: "Any human being is capable of murder. That's a fact. But to set up your friends, knowing full well what was going to happen to them . . . You're not talking about a normal thinking, feeling, conscious human being."

Bernie knew that Rhonda Williams claimed Henley didn't realize her boyfriend, Frank, would be murdered when he invited him to party at Corll's place. Bernie found that hard to believe since Henley already knew Corll had killed the previous teen he'd brought to party. Corll and Henley together killed at least three other Heights teens at the Schuler Street apartment in 1972, shooting, torturing, and strangling them, but generating surprisingly few complaints from neighbors. "It's getting easier. It's getting easier," Milligan observed, as he reviewed the data on the oversized foam presentation boards the two friends assembled.

Mark Scott was killed there in April. And the apartment on Schuler Street was also where, in May 1972, Corll tied up Billy Baulch next to his best friend, Johnny Delome, on the torture board, forcing Johnny to watch as Billy was raped and murdered. Henley parodied the banter used to introduce *The Tonight Show*'s popular host, Johnny Carson, by hollering "Heeere's Johnny!" before shooting that boy in the forehead. When Johnny somehow survived that first bullet, he, too, was strangled to death. Under Corll's tutelage, Henley had become a monster, Milligan thought. "Wayne was just out of control and he was doing whatever he could to put jingle in his pockets. He got into the trip of having the power of life or death."

By Bernie's count, at least five boys were killed at that location— and it was also where he figured Billy Ridinger and David Brooks had been tied to the torture board but survived.

Eventually, Bernie tracked down that "murder house," an apartment inside a commercial building that still stood on Schuler Street. The current owners seemed to know nothing about Corll; they denied connections Bernie had already confirmed. The building seemed familiar to Bernie: It was near the white bungalow where Milligan's gruff great-uncle, Frank Lasavica, lived in the 1970s. At one point, his uncle told Bernie that he'd discovered teenagers throwing reels of audio tape or 8 mm film in a grassy vacant lot that separated the Lasavicas' house from those apartments. His uncle Frank complained that teenaged tenants there threw wild parties and drilled holes and hung hooks on the walls. When the group broke their lease after only five months, Lasavica, a skilled carpenter, had been hired to replace all of the unit's wooden doors.

BY THE SUMMER OF 1972, Corll moved on to the modern high-rise Westcott Towers apartment complex. While living there, he kidnapped and killed two more young men, one seventeen and another nineteen. Those two, one from another neighborhood and one from the Heights, would not be identified until decades later, when Sharon Derrick began working on the Lost Boys cases. Then Corll moved into another unit in those towers, with David Brooks and a pet boa constrictor as roommates. In October 1972, Corll snatched up two more Hamilton Junior High boys who had cut school and had talked of going camping at Lake Conroe. Those boys, last seen in a white van outside a Heights grocery store, were fourteen-year-old Wally "Jay" Simoneaux and his pal Richard Hembree, thirteen. On the same day that Jay's mother reported his disappearance, the principal told her that "twenty other boys from Hamilton were also missing." When Corll left, the landlord there reported finding bullet holes in the door, though that wasn't uncommon in Texas.

THERE WAS AN ODD gap in the timeline of killings after that. Finally, in the summer of 1973, Corll rented his father's house on 2020 Lamar, and the pace of the murders increased. Prior to June 1973, Corll killed, on average, once every six or seven weeks: Nineteen known victims died in about thirty-three months, by Bernie's calculations. Then something sent Corll into a frenzy, Bernie thought.

"He became completely erratic. There were more killings. They were faster. It was like he was feeding some monster." Corll killed his last seven victims in a terrible spasm of violence that lasted seven weeks, from June 15 to August 3, 1973.

The first of four to die in June was Billy Lawrence. Then Ray Blackburn, a young man who'd been working temporarily in Houston and was trying to hitchhike home from the Heights to Louisiana to see his newborn son; Homer Garcia, who took driver's ed with Henley; and Michael Baulch, who had gone looking for his missing brother, Billy. In July, Corll and Henley tied two more Heights teens to the torture board, best friends Marty Jones and Charles Cobble, and urged them to fight by falsely claiming that only the victor would survive. After they were bloodied and weakened, Corll and Henley killed them both. The last victim lured to his death at 2020 Lamar was young Stanton Dreymala.

Officially, the death toll for that summer was eight, but ME officials debated whether to include Johnny Manning Sellars, a teenaged boy who disappeared from Orange, Texas, in July 1973 and whose body had been found on the beach, near other victims' graves. But Johnny had been buried fully clothed, wearing Levi's and a stylish patterned shirt covered with yellow mushrooms and toadstools, and he'd been killed by four blasts from a high-powered weapon, likely a rifle, rather than a .22, Corll's usual choice. The bullets passed all the way through his chest, shattering his heart.

Bernie thought Sellars, a teen from a small city near the Louisiana border, was definitely Corll's victim. Perhaps he knew something about Corll's auto theft ring, or had been gunned down on the beach after happening on a burial party. The murder weapon might have been a hunting rifle that belonged to Sellars, who'd recently been recruited by the U.S. Navy and carried eight rounds of ammunition for a .270 Winchester in his pockets. His corpse had been buried in a crouched fetal position that suggested time spent in Corll's body box, and his vehicle had been found abandoned and burned out in a wooded area in Louisiana, just over the Texas state line. In the end, Bernie suspected, Corll had been eliminating all potential witnesses.

IN THOSE LAST BLOODY weeks of his life, Corll had talked openly of fleeing Texas. Yellowed newspaper clippings of articles published in Colorado Springs and in Houston include his mother's accounts of a telephone conversation that she found alarming three weeks before his death. "How are you, Dean?" she asked.

"I'm in trouble, I'm going to leave town," Corll said. "I'm going to drop out of sight."

"You're not on dope?"

"No, but that would be one way of getting out of this."

"Dean, this is a big world," she replied. "You can go anyplace anytime, but come here first." In more than four years, Dean had never visited his mother or half sister in Colorado. This time he accepted her invitation but added that he'd be "hiding out."

Mary West tried repeatedly to reach her eldest again on Sunday, August 5, three days before his death. When her son finally answered, he repeated he was "having trouble" and "dodging somebody" but still swore he was coming to Colorado.

Based on their conversations, Corll's mother feared he was really planning suicide.

BERNIE READ THOSE STORIES and developed a different theory: Corll was gearing up to eliminate his accomplices and anyone else who knew anything about his operations before he left Houston—until Henley altered his master plan.

The timelines Bernie and Danny so carefully assembled revealed something else that troubled them, an unexplained seven-month break in the murders. Police had never found any victims who'd disappeared between November 1972 and June 1973. It seemed unlikely given the pace of his confirmed crimes that Corll went that long without killing anyone, they thought. During that period, talkative Henley had left town to work in Mount Pleasant, Texas, where he had relatives, and Corll and Brooks had been living outside the

Heights: first at the Princessa Apartments on Wirt Road in Spring Branch and then at a complex on South Post Oak Road in Southwest Houston, only two miles from the boatshed. None of the known victims lived near either of those early 1973 addresses.

Dean Corll had almost certainly killed more than twenty-seven people, Bernie thought.

CHAPTER 15

THE UNCOUNTED MURDER VICTIM

HOUSTON, 2008

AFTER RANDY HARVEY'S IDENTIFICATION became public in October 2008, Sharon Derrick did interviews with the *Houston Chronicle, USA Today,* NBC News, and other outlets about her efforts to restore the names of Dean Corll's victims. As word spread, Derrick increasingly felt pulled into the world of families whose grief remained fresh, seemingly frozen in time since the disappearance of beloved boys decades before. In one of her first presentations about the Lost Boys, she told a crowd of forensic scientists at a conference in 2006: "The mention of Dean Corll, Elmer Wayne Henley, and David Brooks still elicits strong reactions from the adult residents of Harris County and surrounding areas. It has been thirty-three years since the summer night their murder spree was exposed, but the violent nature of the crimes still resounds even in this age of graphic films and video games."

When her Harris County office phone rang, she often found herself talking to a relative whose desperate need for answers had never waned. Those conversations were draining and intense.

In 1974, a psychotherapist named Pauline Boss identified an enduring and particularly harmful form of what she called "frozen grief" after interviewing families of soldiers and pilots labeled missing in action in Cambodia and Vietnam. Caught between hope and hopelessness—never knowing whether loved ones were dead or alive—families of POWs and MIAs often seemed stuck, unable to process their feelings. "Most people need the concrete experience of seeing the body of a loved one who has died because it makes the loss real," Boss observed. Robbed of receiving remains to bury and of funeral rites, some mothers, wives, siblings, and children kept scanning the streets or gazing out open windows for a loved one years after logic dictated death was certain. "Even sure knowledge of death is more welcoming than a continuation of doubt," Boss wrote in a book about the phenomenon, which seemed unstudied, though similar themes often appeared in opera, literature, and theater. In her work, Boss identified patterns of frozen grief among the relatives of other missing persons, including the victims of genocide. She called this "ambiguous loss." It was "a loss that goes on and on," she wrote, and "those who experience it tell me they become physically and emotionally exhausted from the relentless uncertainty."

Many Houston families Sharon Derrick met seemed stuck in that same deep pit of uncertainty.

In the fall of 2008, Derrick received an unsettling email from another missing boy's sister that immediately captured her attention. Donna Taylor Robbins wrote about her brother, Joseph Allen Lyles, who disappeared on February 1, 1973. Allen had left behind all of his clothes and belongings in his bedroom of the home they shared in Spring Branch. Despite all of her research, Derrick had never before seen Allen's missing persons report or heard his name. Yet in his sister's story, she immediately recognized a possible connection: Dean Corll and David Brooks had lived together in an apartment near Allen's Spring Branch home in early 1973.

In their first phone call, Donna Taylor Robbins expressed what seemed like fresh anger and frustration over her conversations with Houston police. Decades later, she still felt stung by the indifference. Donna had immediately reported her brother missing in 1973, though she couldn't afford a home phone in those days and had to use a neighbor's. The officer told her they weren't going to investigate a missing "juvenile delinquent." She'd insisted on filing a report anyway, and never heard anything back.

After the bodies were found, she said she'd called the Houston police repeatedly until she received another dismissive message: "Miss Taylor—we have quit looking for bodies at this point because there's so many."

"They never gave me any hope whatsoever," Donna told Derrick.

Donna was disturbed when Derrick told her that her little brother's name, Joseph Allen Lyles, did not appear in 1973 police reports or in the ME's missing persons lists. Taylor, who lived near Huntsville at the time, was planning to apply for a job with the Texas Department of Corrections around the time they talked. She was so sure her little brother was a serial murder victim that she planned to disclose that a relative had been harmed (or killed) by an inmate, as prison rules required. When she eventually did apply, "I put down that my brother Allen was a victim of David Brooks and Wayne Henley," she recalls. Regulations dictated that she couldn't work in the same facility as either man. She ended up at the Polunsky Unit in Livingston, a bunker filled with isolation cells that include Texas's death row. Given the timing of their crimes, neither Wayne Henley nor David Brooks was eligible for the death penalty.

Other siblings Derrick interviewed in Allen's large family had always assumed Allen had been murdered by Dean Corll. His body had never been recovered. But they had good reasons for that belief. The story they shared was disturbing.

AT FIFTEEN, DONNA LYLES had run away to escape her troubled Pasadena home. She says she left in 1969 because her stepfather was sexually abusing her and neglecting her youngest brothers, Allen and Jack, the seventh and eighth siblings in their family of nine. At seventeen, Donna married an older man partly to establish an entirely independent household. For a while, Allen and Jack were sent away to live at the Harris County Boys' Home on NASA Route 1. Jack later struck out on his own.

Around the time Donna got married, her brother Allen returned home to attend Pasadena High for the 1971–72 school year. His siblings had high expectations: Allen was naturally bright and could beat even the eldest of his siblings in chess. But he was also basically raising himself. He was only sixteen when he got busted that year with a carload of boys who'd been smoking pot. "It was not Allen's car, but he was driving it. When they stopped him, he either had pot or paraphernalia in the car," Donna recalls. She doesn't remember what specific juvenile charges he faced, but he had no driver's license, and the Pasadena police told their mother he should leave town to get away from those friends. "They said if he didn't, he would have to go to a juvenile hall," she says.

Donna, only two years older, offered him a home in the Spring Branch apartment she shared with her new husband. In their fractured family, siblings often helped each other. Allen had always been a survivor. Before their mother left their father, a heavy drinker, they'd often been forced to move whenever he went on a binge or lost a job. As a small boy, Allen had been the one who had figured out how to jury-rig the lights when the electric company turned off power because of unpaid bills.

Donna believed her brother stood a better chance of finishing high school in Spring Branch, a prosperous Houston suburb that seemed a safe distance from Pasadena. She was already expecting her first child—a boy—when Allen came to live with her in the summer of 1972. About to become a mother, Donna worried about her brother, but knew she couldn't parent him. She felt she had no authority to do so—and she thought he was smarter than she was anyway. After her son was born, Allen sometimes helped with the baby. Allen was quiet and smart enough to qualify for "gifted" status, and as far as she knew, he did well in his Spring Branch High School classes. After a few months of living crowded together, Donna and her husband bought a house on Pitner Road, where Allen got his own room and a part-time job at the nearby Stop N Go. He often seemed busy studying or making elaborate pencil drawings of people or animals. Still, Donna worried. When she was younger, she'd suffered a vivid nightmare about Allen being chased down busy industrial Highway 225 and woke up certain he'd been killed. Her foreboding never faded.

Allen had turned seventeen in August 1972 but still lacked a driver's license, and his sister couldn't afford to help him get one. Once he took her 1972 Gremlin, which she'd bought new for $3,000, without permission and crashed it. After that, whenever he wanted to go see friends or skate at the nearby Rainbow Rink, Allen had to walk or thumb a ride. "Allen was a free-spirited person," recalls Jimmy Lyles, another brother, who lived with his wife in the same neighborhood then. "He was always thumbing."

The Rainbow Rink, a popular teen hangout, was where Allen met David Brooks, his siblings say.

Allen left his sister's home on February 1, 1973, after promising to return the next day: He knew Donna and her husband had tickets to see the Harlem Globetrotters and he'd agreed to watch his baby nephew. "OK, I'm going to go skating and I'm going to spend the night with this guy—but I'll be home," he told his sister.

Allen never came back. At first, Donna was angry about missing the game. Those tickets had been expensive and money was tight. Then she worried. She went into Allen's bedroom and found all of his clothing still tucked in drawers, along with his wallet, Social Security card, and all his drawings. When Allen disappeared, Donna despaired. She didn't know his friends' addresses or phone numbers, or his teachers' names, because she'd been busy with her baby and hadn't wanted to pry. She didn't know who he'd planned to spend the night with.

It was later, through her younger brother Jack, that Donna heard about David Brooks, the teen Allen befriended at the skating rink. David Brooks sold marijuana out of an apartment on Wirt Road, Jack told her. Before he wrecked the Gremlin, Allen had driven his sister's car, unbeknownst to her, to Brooks's place in the Princessa Apartments. The complex held funky three-story buildings with roofs that sloped down over the top floors. When they reached the parking lot, Allen ordered Jack to stay outside. "Don't come in. Don't come upstairs," he said.

Jack waited a while, then got bored and climbed the steps to rap on the apartment door.

Allen answered. Normally calm, he flipped out and shouted, "I thought I told you to stay in the car!" and threw a punch that bloodied his brother's nose. The two departed swiftly, and Allen warned

Jack to stay away: "These people are dangerous," Allen said, according to the story Jack later told. At the time of Lyles's visit, David Brooks and Dean Corll lived together in apartment 463. Three weeks after Allen disappeared, they left Spring Branch.

In August 1973, when Donna first heard about teenagers' bodies in the boatshed, she informed police that her missing brother had known Brooks. Again, she says that police failed to follow up. For years, Donna, Jack, and other siblings all assumed Allen had been tortured, killed, and buried by Corll, Brooks, and Henley. But they lacked proof beyond the knowledge that their brother knew Brooks and had visited that apartment. "For years I blamed myself for him being murdered," Donna said. She believed the nightmare she'd experienced about Allen's violent death had come true.

After hearing Donna's and Jack's stories, Derrick felt she might be close to identifying another Lost Boy. Donna, who was now living on family property in Onalaska, about ninety minutes north of Houston, agreed to join her older sister Cindi in a visit to the ME's office. Perhaps the DNA of two of Allen Lyles's sisters would be a match.

Derrick greeted them inside a building named for Dr. Joe, who had died in 2004, only two years before Derrick began carrying on his ID efforts in these cases. Both sisters provided samples. But after several agonizing months of waiting for results from the busy UNT lab, Derrick was forced to call with bad news: Their DNA samples did not match genetic profiles from any unidentified boy associated with the Corll case.

Donna Taylor Robbins felt devastated and profoundly confused. *Could she have been wrong for all these years about what had happened to Allen? If his bones weren't in the Houston morgue, where were they?*

Later, Derrick learned about yet another Spring Branch teenager who'd also gone missing in 1973. On February 21, 1973, Rodney Harris, age sixteen, had vanished from the same neighborhood not long after Allen Lyles. Harris, a student at Spring Woods High School, was a certified scuba diver who had sometimes hitchhiked from his home to the beach. His siblings had also called Derrick in hopes she might find answers.

Lance Harris, then a man in his forties who'd been a preschooler in 1973, still remembered seeing his big brother Rodney accept a ride from the driver of a tan sedan near the family's English Oaks apartment, about four miles west on Long Point Road from where Corll and Brooks lived that year. Mitzi Piersol, a thirty-nine-year-old mother from Cypress, had no memories to share: She had been only a year old when Rodney disappeared. Rodney's two half siblings and his mother all provided Derrick with DNA. There were no matches to them either.

Derrick felt flummoxed and frustrated. She too had noticed the same curious gap that Bernie Milligan had separately observed: No known Corll victim had been murdered between November 1972 and May 1973, the same period when Allen Lyles and Rodney Harris had vanished from Spring Branch. She knew Spring Branch as one of Corll's hunting grounds. His second and third murder victims, Danny Yates and James Glass, attended Spring Branch schools. The bodies of Allen, Rodney, and possibly other early 1973 murder victims must still be hidden away somewhere, Derrick thought.

DERRICK HAD STUDIED POLICE reports on the chaotic excavations inside the boatshed, and feared bodies had likely been left behind even in that confined space. The subsequent two-day search along a remote stretch of beach near High Island in August 1973 had turned into a circus that spanned three different counties, generated massive crowds, and involved bulldozers excavating holes seemingly at random along a five-mile strip of sand. Maps of the beach grave sites drawn by police artists showed the waterline and the location of a state highway that later washed away. There were no GPS coordinates or recognizable modern-day landmarks aside from the approximate locations of the Galveston, Chambers, and Jefferson County lines. The drawings included ovals that roughly represented the spots where six different bodies had been found buried.

From 1970 to 1973, that band of the beach was wide enough for the winds to form small knolls covered in grass or brush—sufficient cover for freshly dug graves. The first had been dug by Corll in 1970.

Primitive map of beach burials done by HPD

Later David Brooks, Wayne Henley, and sometimes Corll had set out for that beach in Corll's white van in the late afternoon or evening with a teenager's fresh corpse wrapped in industrial plastic and tucked into the "body box." Once they passed the High Island, a village with a cluster of shops and small homes perched atop a rise, the burial party would turn east on coastal State Highway 87. Before a series of violent hurricanes wrecked it, that lonely but scenic road, part of a 250-mile highway built in 1923, ran east along the Bolivar Peninsula, following the Gulf of Mexico all the way to Sabine Pass and the Louisiana line.

Derrick knew that visitors could still reach the lonely beaches Corll and his crew had used as burial grounds. But the highway they'd driven had turned into sand-covered chunks of rubble. By the time Derrick began looking for Lost Boys, those burial grounds could be reached only via a long walk or a four-wheel-drive vehicle needed to navigate rough sand that lined McFaddin National Wildlife Refuge, a 55,000-acre wilderness of beach and marshlands established in 1980. At one point, she and her husband, Al, discussed renting an ATV and organizing their own search. But it seemed futile. Hurricane Ike had once again sent a wall of water rushing over that low-lying peninsula in 2008, killing two dozen residents unable or unwilling to evacuate and sending rafts of wreckage from coastal homes spinning into the sea. If any graves had been missed, Derrick feared they'd be impossible to find.

CHAPTER 16

THE BODIES ON THE BEACH

HIGH ISLAND, 1970–1973

David Brooks and Wayne Henley assisting with the search for bodies in 1973
JERRY CLICK / *HOUSTON POST;*
© *HOUSTON CHRONICLE.* USED WITH PERMISSION.

WAYNE HENLEY ARRIVED WITH his Pasadena police escorts at the village of High Island around noon on Friday, August 10, two days after killing Dean Corll. By then, Henley already had led police to the boatshed, where seventeen mass burials had already been discovered, and then hiked through the woods in East Texas to four more graves. The rising body count meant Corll was closing in on twenty-seven kills—proclaimed by the Texas Rangers to be a record, as the highest number of modern murder victims linked by U.S. police to a single perpetrator or group. TV crews from as far away as

Sweden, Japan, and Pakistan had been dispatched to document the infamous historic moment.

Wayne and his handlers were hungry after their morning of digging for graves in the woods and stopped at the Bolivar Peninsula's best-known burger joint, Dot's Café. Wayne grumbled when he had to settle for grilled cheese. So many other beach-bound journalists, police, and tourists had already visited that the village café had run out of ground beef. The seventeen-year-old still seemed energized and undaunted even after two full days of searching for bodies and submitting to interrogations. Neither he nor David Brooks had yet been charged with any of those teenagers' murders, and he embraced his role as an instant celebrity. Soon he'd be fielding calls and letters from all over the world, plastering photos sent by girls on his cell walls, and requesting extra showers, since at his age, he still worried about pimples.

David Brooks, far more reserved, was already waiting a quarter of a mile down the beach road with an entourage of Houston police by the time Wayne arrived. David continued to deny killing anyone, but grudgingly admitted knowledge of the burial sites. One grave there had a "large rock on top of it," he had told Houston detectives. "I am willing to show officers where this location is and I will try to locate as many graves as possible." At eighteen, David was clearly hoping to avoid prosecution in exchange for his cooperation and to rejoin his pregnant wife and their soon-to-be-born baby daughter.

Wayne and David teamed up one last time to search for graves—starting with the one near that big rock. A caravan of one hundred cars filled with lawmen, journalists, and onlookers followed them. "We met up there with the biggest bunch of newsmen I've ever yet to see," Wayne Henley later said. Mullican, the savvy Pasadena detective, estimated they'd been surrounded by a constant throng of fifty to seventy-five reporters. During that first day, three helicopters hovered overhead and an airplane flew over with network TV crews taking aerial footage.

Crowds of onlookers flew into a frenzy when the duo finally found the rock. A construction worker operating a big digger motored over, and sweating officers and jail trusties, detainees again supplied from

Harris County, deployed hand shovels to expose a tangle of bones, bleached the same ochre as the sand. An unsuspecting family had parked near that rock for a weekend of beach camping, having no idea of the bizarre spectacle that would unfold around them. They packed up and left, though other gawkers quickly claimed their place.

The bones of this murder victim, buried nearly three years, lacked any clothing, but remained bound by rope. ME officials later connected the skull's teeth through dental records to Jeffrey Alan Konen, the missing twenty-year-old who'd been abducted by Corll near the Houston Galleria while hitchhiking home to Houston on September 28, 1970—Corll's first known murder victim.

The Pasadena Police Department's body-recovery scene photos, taken with natural light, are clearer than those taken inside the shed. One shot shows a pair of mysterious desiccated but intact feet with flesh beside Jeffrey's bleached and disarticulated bones. Years later, Derrick would examine those images and theorize that the feet likely belonged to another entirely different murder victim killed long after Jeffrey. But by then those feet were nowhere to be found amongst the other stored forensic evidence.

Wayne and David were unsure of the other beach burial locations. They spent four more hours strolling along in the sun with armed escorts, trying to spot subtle landmarks: odd divots in the sand, disturbed tufts of grass, or the faint smell of decomposition.

Finally, about 257 feet east of that rock, searchers located remains that belonged to Frank Aguirre, who had disappeared in February 1972 after leaving a lengthy shift at Long John Silver's. For eighteen months, the high school senior's body, though buried, had been exposed to the elements and scoured by sand. Only bones and strands of his long dark hair were readily apparent, as were signs of his ordeal: The rags of a gag remained in his mouth, and pieces of adhesive tape crisscrossed what had been his face.

Neither grave was more than three feet deep. A vigorous child digging in the sand with a plastic shovel might have uncovered some of these bones by accident.

Louis Otter, the sheriff of Chambers County, his stern face shaded by a cowboy hat, oversaw most of the excavations. Almost none of his constituents lived on this God-forsaken strip of sand about thirty-three miles from the county seat of Anahuac, yet Otter felt forced to temporarily divert most of his small department's resources here, where the heat, pressure, and publicity were intense. As the hours passed, Wayne Henley led the Pasadena officers further east on the beach and pointed out more spots where he believed bodies were buried. Scattered here and there, they spotted pieces of plastic and rope similar to those used to wrap and bind other corpses, but located no more bodies. Otter temporarily suspended the search citing high tides and crushing crowds.

Over the weekend, an astronaut at the Johnson Space Center persuaded NASA to dispatch a helicopter equipped with infrared scanners to hopefully pinpoint places where more graves might be hidden along the vast and dynamic beach. The high-tech method didn't turn up any clues. And neither David Brooks nor Wayne Henley ever returned to help guide diggers on the ground.

By the time Otter resumed operations on Monday, August 13, both teens had been charged with murder and had consulted defense attorneys. Their interest had vanished in helping find more remains that could be used as evidence against them. With the eyes of the international press trained on Texas, Otter brought in a crew with a trench digger and a backhoe to speed the search. "We're going to try to use a motor grader from the grass line . . . and we will have to make several cuts," Otter told the throng of reporters who'd gathered for another day of digging. He instructed one operator to use his machine's metal jaws to carve a ditch three feet deep along all 1.2 miles of beachfront inside Chambers County limits.

Adjacent Jefferson County, to the east, was another sheriff's problem.

At 10:15 A.M. Monday, only seventy-eight feet from Frank Aguirre's body, a construction worker atop a big digger uncovered another skull with dark hair. Those bones belonged to Richard Kepner, a nineteen-year-old Humble High School graduate who had encountered the killers in November 1972 when he stopped to use a pay phone in the Heights. Richard, a newcomer to the neighborhood and a stranger to his slayers, would not be identified until 1983.

In the gloaming of late afternoon, as Sheriff Otter was fixing to quit, the dozer's blade exposed a double grave containing remains that belonged to two more missing Heights boys: Billy Baulch and his best friend, Johnny Delome. Crowds pushing around police had thinned somewhat by then, but one spectator allowed an unleashed chihuahua to clamber into the hole and cavort among their bones.

"Why, Maggie, you come right out of there!" the tourist hollered down at the dog, who remained inside the pit until a state trooper jumped down and handed her back to the owner. At one point, Chambers County Justice of the Peace Betty Dugat, who'd spent two hot days surveying burial sites in her cowboy boots, became so irritated by the unruly crowd that she considered fining each person twenty dollars for interfering with her investigations.

Later that same day, a sixth body was unearthed 2.9 miles farther east, on the Jefferson County side of McFaddin Beach—near a deep cut in the sand where one High Island resident reported having spotted Wayne Henley walking away from a stranded car in late 1972 or early 1973. Away from the crowds, that same citizen quietly guided a Jefferson County sheriff's deputy to the area, where the officer located a grave by poking a long stick into a suspiciously soft spot. The hole he created vented a strong smell of decomposition.

The weathered sheriff assembled reporters to announce that last discovery. "This one was fresh, couldn't be no more than seven or eight months in there," he said in his East Texas twang. "No clue to name." This boy had been found crouched inside his grave, fully dressed, with a pair of surgical forceps dangling from his belt. Those scissors may have been a torture device, or a crude joint holder, the sheriff speculated. "We wrappin' 'em in Saran and we're shippin' 'em to Houston for an autopsy," the officer drawled, according to notes taken by Arthur Bell, who'd come to cover the quixotic search for *The Village Voice.* A national TV correspondent standing near Bell glanced at the gruesome find, turned aside, and vomited violently into the sand.

The eighteen-year-old boy found crouched inside that last grave was later identified as Johnny Manning Sellars, of Orange, Texas, who'd disappeared on July 12, 1973. That date was more than six months after the High Island resident recalled seeing Henley; left unexplored was whether older clandestine graves remained nearby. Sellars is counted by law enforcement as one of Corll's victims, though the debate remains unsettled. Had this fully clothed teen really been killed by Corll and his accomplices, or had he been buried by another killer who used the same beach as a burial ground?

By 5 P.M., Otter declared he was indefinitely suspending all searches.

The magic number of twenty-seven corpses had been recovered, based on the finds made on the beach, in the woods, and in the boatshed in the five days since Corll's own violent death. Why keep searching for more when Corll had already broken America's mass murder record? Still, the decision disturbed some investigators. At one point, they had been told they were looking for as many as nine bodies on the beach; they stopped digging after finding six.

"It always bothered me," said Larry Earls, then a young homicide detective who'd also helped search the boatshed. "Henley and Brooks told us that they thought there were more bodies, and there were other places where we wanted to dig, but we were told no."

Bones found in beach graves in 1973, from PPD files

IN OCTOBER 1973, HARRIS County assistant district attorney Don Lambright announced that forensic examinations of remains gathered by the diggers' steely jaws had already yielded evidence of bodies left behind. Harris County pathologists had discovered extra bones mixed with those of the murdered, including unexplained arm and pelvic bones. "There is a unique possibility that one of the graders working the beach could have graded up the bones from another grave site and carried them over to this one," Lambright said.

The conclusion seemed clear: More murdered teens likely remained buried on the beach.

CHAPTER 17

AN UNEXPECTED BREAKTHROUGH

HARRIS COUNTY INSTITUTE OF FORENSIC
SCIENCES, 2006–2010

S HARON DERRICK FACED AN uphill battle to prove herself when
she embarked on her brand-new career as a forensic anthropologist in 2006. Forensic science fields and ME's offices nationwide had
long been dominated by men. The physical anthropology section of
the American Academy of Forensic Sciences had been formed in 1972
by fourteen charter members, all men. By 1992, 80 percent of the forty
members were male. As more women entered the field, some pioneers
in the profession (a group some jokingly called the "Silverbacks")
seemed to be making it even harder to join the American Board of
Forensic Anthropology's list of Diplomates. All members were required to pass tests devised by their peers in order to become internationally recognized as leaders, which was Derrick's goal.

Derrick knew when she started that some colleagues her age had
already racked up twenty years of forensic experience, working in
autopsy suites, labs, and crime scenes. Her own progress toward this
calling had taken longer. So she felt dismayed at first when in mid-
2006, ME Luis Sanchez recruited a rising star from out of state as the
director of the new forensic anthropology team. Derrick was upset
that she hadn't been considered: After all, she'd helped write the job
description.

Dr. Jennifer Love had an impressive résumé and was more than a decade younger than Derrick. Both women had Ph.D.s. But Love had a degree in forensic anthropology from the University of Tennessee, home of the well-known "Body Farm," while Derrick had trained as a bioarchaeologist at Texas A&M and was learning forensics on the job. At first their relationship was rocky. Love was only thirty-two and had minimal experience as a boss. To her dismay, Derrick ended up feeling like a junior member of the team. "I was being a jerk and she was trying to feel her strength," Derrick recalled, "and I felt like I was being impinged on."

Derrick thought that Love and another new employee, a man who also had more formal training in forensic anthropology, looked down on her since she was excluded from some initial meetings. But Love soon began to reach out to Derrick and praise her contributions. Her new boss never interfered in Derrick's work on the Lost Boys. She left those IDs to Derrick, seeming to understand the connection she'd formed with those cases and encouraging her to explore new methods, including using the FACES lab to develop updated likenesses.

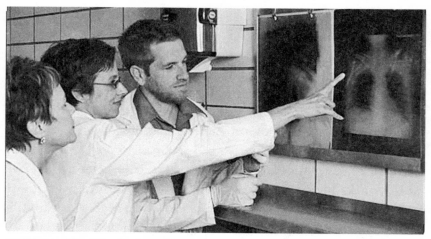

Dr. Sharon Derrick, Dr. Jennifer Love, and Dr. Jason Wiersema, forensic anthropologists, in the Harris County ME's office

Over time, the initial awkwardness between Derrick and Love faded and the two women formed a strong professional and personal alliance. They often tackled cold cases together, either as a team or peer reviewing each other's findings. Each woman, first Love in 2009 and then Derrick in 2013, earned her place in the male-dominated ranks of the American Board of Forensic Anthropology's elite Diplomates—and they celebrated each other's success. That designation gave both women national recognition as certified experts who had demonstrated "the maximum level of professional qualifications in forensic anthropology." Derrick became the hundredth member in its history. And Love went on to join national committees and fought to make the group's test for inclusion on the list fairer and less subjective.

Love was no show-off, but she made discoveries and possessed a confident magnetism that attracted press attention. One 2011 Facebook post about her Houston accomplishments read: "Every day at work, Harris County's Dr. Jennifer Love lives the life of a prime-time TV star as a forensic anthropologist with the Harris County Medical Examiner's Office. Her skill in the lab and at potential crime scenes helps unravel mysteries that have baffled authorities for years." Her colleagues teased her endlessly about being a "prime-time TV star." Though anthropologists like Love and Derrick did crack unsolved mysteries, a lot of their work involved tedious hours in autopsy suites or labs examining bones or odiferous decaying remains, recording precise measurements, consulting databases, and writing detailed scientific reports with loads of footnotes. The rise of True Crime and so-called CSI (Crime Scene Investigation) shows had greatly increased the perceived glamor of their profession. Yet at the end of long workdays, Love confessed that she preferred watching TV shows that had nothing to do with crime. "When you live it, you don't need to watch it at night."

Under Love's leadership, Derrick felt she had finally found her place and began to think of their new forensic anthropology division as a real team. Together, they were tackling a huge project. Their bosses wanted them to finish reexamining and collecting DNA from the remaining cases in cold storage, as well as to exhume and reexamine bodies of all unidentified juveniles from the county cemetery.

Since the 1990s, Washington's King County had been using forensic anthropologist Kathy Taylor to provide professional assistance to help identify victims from what was America's biggest unsolved serial murder case—at least four dozen homicides of women attributed to the "Green River Killer," named for the fast-running river where some victims' bodies were discovered. Beginning in 1982, the unidentified killer had culled young women from the streets, raped and strangled them, and then hid some bodies underwater, weighing them down with rocks. The county's longtime investment eventually paid off. Suspect Gary Leon Ridgway, a married factory worker and truck painter, was arrested in 2001 after technological advances enabled Washington officials to recover and replicate DNA from a small amount of sperm still clinging to the pubic hair of a single victim. Ridgway remains the U.S. serial killer with the most murder convictions: He pleaded guilty in 2003 to killing forty-eight women and was later linked to as many as eighty deaths. Taylor's work was key to his arrest and to the identification of several victims, including fourteen-year-old Wendy Stephens, a runaway from Colorado whose remains were first examined in 1996 and finally identified in January 2021. "We got word that it was a positive match. Literally that brought tears to my eyes," Taylor told her hometown newspaper, the *Mercer Island Reporter*. "Green River is what got me interested in the field. I got to work on the case and we solved the one that was really on my bucket list."

In the 2000s, very few other county ME's offices in the United States were employing full-time forensic anthropologists, despite the national backlog of forty thousand unidentified persons. "You did see some—but you still didn't see a lot," recalls Love. Only two Texas counties had them: Tarrant County (around Fort Worth) and Harris County. National forensic experts and political leaders, including President George W. Bush, a former Texas governor, continued expressing concern that too many murder victims remained unidentified. As a result, the University of North Texas's Center for Human Identification had been launched in Fort Worth, turning the Old West stockyard and cattle drive town into a nationally known hub for forensic anthropology research. That lab regularly provided help on Texas missing persons and unidentified cases. And by 2011,

UNT won a national government contract and for the next decade managed NamUs, the database of missing and unidentified persons, for the federal Office of Justice Programs.

Separately, the National Institute of Justice began regularly awarding grants to help local agencies reexamine cold cases, generally from the 1970s, 1980s, and 1990s, before DNA tests had been available. The NIJ later established a task force to study the backlogs and estimated that the "cold case crisis" had allowed an estimated two thousand serial killers and their accomplices to remain unpunished and possibly free to kill again.

Love figured that Harris County's best chance to obtain federal grant funding would be to focus on cold murder cases involving the youngest unidentified victims. On that list was a teen's torso clad in a purple surf shirt recovered in 1971 in a muddy lake near the NASA Manned Spacecraft Center, and a fresher corpse of a red-haired girl with freckles wearing a fringed cowgirl outfit whose body had been dumped in a field in 1982. The Harris County Cemetery also contained graves of an unidentified young man and teenaged woman, presumed to be a couple, whose scattered remains had been discovered near a boggy stand of palmetto trees after a dog brought home an obviously human bone in January 1981. The man, who had been shot, might have died defending the woman, who had apparently been strangled. Derrick thought of them as Romeo and Juliet. (Indeed, DNA evidence and some genetic genealogy sleuthing would ultimately prove their romantic connection: Dean and Tina Clouse were married and full of hope when they were murdered; astonishingly, their toddler, too young to remember that horror, had been spirited away and somehow survived.)

First Love and then Derrick wrote applications to obtain federal grants to tackle cold cases involving the unidentified, including unnamed victims of Dean Corll. Love initially applied for a $180,000 grant to help pay to exhume twenty-five unidentified bodies from the county's pauper cemetery. That first NIJ grant enabled them to add another forensic anthropologist–in–training to the team: Deborrah Pinto, another Ph.D., who bonded with Love over their shared addiction to all forms of chocolate. Later, Derrick got another grant to help support more exhumations and other expenses she used to reexamine Corll murder victims and other cold cases.

In Illinois, another investigator obtained NIJ grant money to help identify the as yet unknown victims of John Wayne Gacy, the so-called Killer Clown. Of his thirty-three known victims, twenty-six had been buried in the crawl space under his suburban house. Some were identified immediately; more IDs were made in the 2000s and 2010s with grant funds. Yet even in 2024, Cook County sheriff's officials were still seeking tips about five Gacy victims whose DNA had been analyzed but who remained unidentified.

While working on her first NIJ grant, Love decided to examine a particularly unusual box of bones that, according to records, had been discovered on a beach in Jefferson County in 1983 by a man who'd gone fishing and taken his dog. Love disliked entering the long-term storage vault. "Oh my gosh, we're going to have to deal with those bodies that have cauliflowers growing out of them?" she'd say. She hated the creepy atmosphere and its chilly temperatures (the room had to be kept at 37 to 40 degrees Fahrenheit) so much that she asked inventory control personnel to retrieve that box from one of the uppermost shelves. "It had the word 'Antiquities' on it and it also had 'Do not try to ID,'" Love later recalled. "I thought maybe it was an archaeological case."

Even for skilled forensic anthropologists, it remains difficult to determine accurate dates of death for unidentified skeletal remains collected at a body dump site. Although research conducted on donated corpses at U.S. body farms has helped clarify rates and forms of decomposition in many unusual settings, experts still struggle with estimating the "postmortem interval" or "time since death." Indeed, leading experts have been fooled—and publicly embarrassed by mistakes.

In one well-publicized blunder, Bill Bass, the founder of the University of Tennessee's Body Farm, had in 1977 mistakenly declared a headless corpse found seated atop a coffin in a tomb plundered by robbers to be a recent homicide victim—the man's fatal head wounds had still looked fresh, perhaps he'd been dead as little as two months, Bass told the press. To his astonishment, Bass later determined that this corpse belonged to Colonel William Shy, the Civil War soldier whose name was carved in the marker on that grave, and whose body had been partially pulled out of its tomb. Shy's remains had been extraordinarily well preserved by embalming fluid and his hermetically sealed cast-iron coffin. Those unusual factors help explain why the remains of a soldier killed in battle in 1864 and then dressed in a black tuxedo for burial had decomposed far less than Bass would have expected more than a century later.

Douglas Ubelaker, an eminent anthropologist and curator at the Smithsonian Institution, remembered what Bass had written about that blooper when he examined a headless torso found by a family hunting for arrowheads in an Idaho cave in 1979. He said it was "strictly his guess" that the man had died "between six months and five years earlier." Decades later those mummified remains were identified through DNA tests and genetic genealogical research as belonging to John Henry Loveless, an outlaw and ax murderer who vanished in 1916 after a jail break. The cave's cold, dry atmosphere had radically slowed his rate of decomposition.

WHEN LOVE OPENED THE box labeled "Antiquities," she found no relics or artifacts typically associated either with the graves of Native Americans or early settlers. "I was going into the box expecting to see something that felt archaeological. But it wasn't. The bone was in good condition," she remembers. The label "antiquities" simply didn't fit these contents. She saw no scraps of wood or metal from a casket, nor pieces of period clothing that often accompanied burials from pioneer days. "It was a teenager," Love recalls. "I remember his skeleton. There was some deterioration of the end of some bones, but it was in pretty good shape for being in that environment— a beach with sand. There was no clothing at the time I got the skeleton, no pair of jeans that would have said it was modern."

It appeared this boy had been buried in the nude, yet his bones were not as dark or yellowed as they would be if they had lingered a century in sand. A few remained fairly white. Later, Love dug up a Jefferson County sheriff's office report with a telling detail: This skeleton had been wrapped in pieces of plastic. These remains were anything but antique.

In February 2008, Love shipped a few bones from the Jefferson County case to UNT's Center for Human Identification hoping that improved DNA techniques would produce a complete genetic profile. That was the goal for all unidentified remains in the Harris County vault—to submit samples and generate new profiles in hopes of finding matches to DNA profiles from samples supplied by the families of missing persons. Labs had gotten much better at extracting and duplicating DNA even from older bones, but even in the late 2000s it could be difficult to obtain enough genetic information to allow for comparisons with DNA from prospective parents, children, or siblings. An incomplete profile with fewer markers was not nearly as useful. Love got lucky. A sequence of DNA often used by forensic laboratories to assess family relationships was successfully extracted from this long-dead boy's bone sample, forming a useful DNA profile.

In November 2009, her long hours of labor paid off with a match. At first, Love stared in amazement at the UNT lab report: The computer-generated analysis of this boy's DNA profile showed he had a brother-sister relationship with two women whose saliva swabs had been submitted by her colleague Sharon Derrick: the sisters of Joseph Allen Lyles, a seventeen-year-old missing since 1973. Love had already heard some of Allen's story and knew that Derrick was going to be thrilled.

She nearly ran down the hall to poke her head into Derrick's office: "What do you know about this?" she said, smiling as she handed over the report.

Derrick started to get goosebumps. "We've been looking for him!" she exclaimed.

The match came as a complete surprise. She'd had no idea Love was working on the "Antiquities" box; Love hadn't mentioned it, since nothing in her initial review suggested any connection between those bones and the Corll cases.

Derrick and Love were so electrified by the news of another ID that they briefly hugged and danced around the room in their white coats. Then together, they visited other offices to share the break-through. "I remember we were so excited when we got that ID," Derrick recalls. "So, we told Dr. Wolf—and we went and told the chief of staff."

After making the rounds, Derrick still felt giddy and short of breath. But she had another urgent task ahead: calling Allen Lyles's siblings. Although Derrick had more work to do before this match could be announced, this DNA link seemed extremely solid based on the lab report alone. The facts added up. Derrick could see from the Jefferson County reports that Lyles's remains, found ten years after his disappearance, had been discovered on the same stretch of beach as six other murder victims.

BY NOVEMBER 2009, SHARON Derrick had read about that rapid beach search many times and always worried that other graves had been missed. Now, she and Love had confirmed just that. Allen Lyles had been buried near other Corll victims, but his skeleton had been discovered only after waves, tidal action, and a passing dog uncov-ered his bones ten years later. Love and Derrick eventually obtained crime scene photos and Jefferson County archives that revealed "original investigators might have thought that it was one of the Corll cases, too," Love said. Love never figured out how the case was mislabeled as an "antiquity." As Derrick later observed, 1983 investi-gators had recovered plastic sheeting and two types of cord with these bones, a wrapping consistent with Corll's crimes. "The plastic and the types of cord were viewed as 'signatures' of the 1973 victims in all locations," Derrick wrote in her report.

Their finding verified that Corll had killed more than twenty-seven victims—Lyles was number twenty-eight.

With help from Love, Derrick had now identified two Lost Boys. But more unsolved mysteries remained, including two of the three mysterious boxes of bones she'd discovered in 2006. So far, DNA from those other boxes of remains didn't match relatives of any missing persons she'd located. She now worried that more unidenti-fied decedents buried under small markers with hard-to-read case numbers in the county cemetery might be Lost Boys. Derrick's commitment to these unidentified murder victims would take her deeper into Corll's labyrinth. Soon, she would prove again that Corll had more victims than those counted in 1973. But each revelation would exact a price.

THE LOST BOYS

THE SECOND ID:

Joseph Allen Lyles, 2009

Allen Lyles, 17, disappeared from his sister's house in Spring Branch in February 1973. He was a gifted artist who ran into David Brooks at a

Allen Lyles, portrait by Nancy Rose

skating rink. His bones were found on a beach in Jefferson County in 1983 and stored under Case No. ML 83-6849. To date, Lyles is the only murder victim of Dean Corll confirmed to have been killed between November 1972 and June 1973.

   With his identification, the number of known victims climbed to twenty-eight.

PART III

MISTAKEN IDENTITIES

CHAPTER 18

THE LOST BROTHERS—MICHAEL AND BILLY BAULCH

HOUSTON HEIGHTS, 1972–1973

Michael and Billy Baulch

MICHAEL BAULCH WAS BORN in 1957, smack-dab in the middle of a family of what would eventually be seven children. He and his two older brothers, and later the younger siblings, shared a two-bedroom bungalow with a single bath on West 16th Street, a sweet house on a large lot shaded by century-old live oaks. His father, Billy Gene Baulch, Sr., a native Texan and long-haul trucker, was often away. His mother, Maggie Jane, called Janey, stayed home to mind the younger kids. The eldest three boys were largely allowed to roam—the Baulches, like other parents in the

Heights, didn't worry about older children doing odd jobs or visiting neighborhood friends, cafés, barbers, stores, or parks alone and on foot. In some ways, the setting seemed idyllic: Their home was across the street from a rambling greenhouse, and their block overflowed with colorful flower beds. The Baulch brothers lived only blocks from Helms Elementary School, where Dean Corll and his mother sold homemade pralines and handed out free samples. Billy, Michael's older brother, befriended Corll and later got a job delivering candy.

Then the Baulch family started to shrink. The oldest boy, Marvin, was riding in the back of a convertible with friends and was ejected when the car crossed a bumpy railroad track. He was only fifteen when he died from his injuries on May 3, 1969.

By May 1972, Billy Baulch, Jr., had been the eldest surviving Baulch brother for three years. The good-natured and stylish seventeen-year-old with wavy brown hair cultivated a slick look that featured skintight jeans and polished cowboy boots with pointed toes. He was talkative and social and often in the company of his best friend, Johnny Delome, a long-haired sixteen-year-old who was younger yet considered the tougher of the two.

A pair of fourteen-year-olds were playing on the grounds of Cooley Elementary one afternoon when Billy stopped to chat. The younger boys, Steve Torres and another buddy, admired his signature jeans and boots. Billy told them he'd dressed up to party with friends. Wayne Henley and David Brooks pulled up in a white van minutes later.

Billy was already walking toward the van when someone inside hollered to the younger boys, "Hey, y'all want to go party? Man, we've got some good weed and some beer and we're going to get loaded."

It was tempting, but Billy shot down the invitation: "What's the matter with y'all? These are young kids!" As he climbed into that van, he called out a warning: "If you ever see these guys don't ever try to go with them."

Not long after that, Billy Baulch vanished, along with his friend Johnny. Johnny Delome had a reputation as a rebel. A family snapshot shows him in the driver's seat of a convertible, wearing a broad smile and a black cowboy hat jauntily tipped back on his head. By 1972, he'd quit school and gone to live with another relative after heated arguments with his stepfather, who demanded he cut his hair and didn't approve of his friendship with Billy. When the two headed to a neighborhood store to buy a Coke one day and didn't return, some friends assumed Johnny had talked his buddy into running away, though that theory didn't make any sense to the Baulches.

Both boys had left their bicycles at the house and had seemed excited about Baulch family plans to attend a double feature at the drive-in that night. Billy Baulch was particularly close to his truck-driving father, who sometimes took his son and namesake fishing or boating on a lake when he returned from long trucking trips. Their bond made it hard for Billy Gene Baulch, Sr., to believe that his son,

Billy Baulch's note home

whom he called Little Bill, would just take off. His concern deep-ened after the family got a note written in what they recognized as Billy's careful cursive. "Dear Mom and Dad," it said, "I am sorry to do this, but Johnny and I found a better Job working for a trucker loading and unloading from Houston to Washington and will be back in three to four Weeks." Billy Gene Baulch, Sr., found that story far-fetched. He knew of no such jobs for young teens and feared both boys were in trouble.

Despite the Baulch parents' pleas, their missing persons report to HPD generated scant attention. Billy Baulch and Johnny Delome were dismissed as runaways. Billy and Johnny were part of a string of disappearances in 1971 and 1972 involving teenagers with ties to Corll's candy store, a pattern police and parents didn't identify until it was too late. Malley Winkle, who also had worked at Corll's shop, had been reported missing with David Hilligiest in May 1971. Billy, who'd also worked for Corll, vanished with his friend Johnny nearly a year later. Those boys likely all knew each other, but their parents didn't. Malley and David lived north of Helms Elementary near the busy 610 Loop; the Baulches lived south of the school and didn't meet the Winkles or the Hilligiests until 1973 when the discovery of the murders united them.

Still, Billy Baulch had spent so much time with Corll in his teen years that his parents, as part of their search, decided to try to find the Candy Man. Eventually Janey obtained his unlisted number from the woman Billy had met as Corll's girlfriend. He spoke po-litely to both parents, who asked if he'd seen their son.

Of course Dean Corll said no.

MICHAEL BAULCH, THE THIRD brother in line, had always been the wildest—as a younger teen he'd run off alone and talked his way into a job aboard a shrimp boat. He didn't get any more cautious after one big brother died and another disappeared. At fifteen, Michael Baulch had strikingly dark hair and eyes that girls noticed. His face reflected more of his family's Native American heritage and he fa-vored a hippie look over his brother's cowboy style. His eyes were oversized and soulful, his face heart-shaped. He wore his dark hair parted in the middle and, for a portrait, donned a T-shirt promoting the funk band Slave.

During the 1971–72 school year at Hamilton Junior High School, Michael met Nita Bodiford, a fourteen-year-old romantic who had watched Franco Zeffirelli's 1968 movie version of *Romeo and Juliet* more than a dozen times and was beginning to pay more attention to boys. From the outside, Hamilton resembled a fortress that loomed over the Heights esplanade. Seating assignments first brought Nita and Michael together, since their last names both began with the letter *B*. They were too young to really date (and neither had money), so they lingered in the halls near their lockers and sometimes he walked her to class. "In those days, we didn't say 'dating.' We'd say: 'I'm messing around with Michael.' I'm sure we held hands and we kissed. He was a sweet boy," Nita recalls. She was a Heights girl, though as a teen bounced between her parents' and grandparents' homes on different sides of that neighborhood and in different school zones. By the ninth grade, she had left Hamilton for its rival, Hogg Junior High, and lost track of Michael.

They saw each other again in July 1973 when Michael walked into the Colonial House Snack Bar, a café just off the brightly lit 19th Street strip that serves as the Heights' central business district. Now sixteen and wearing her dark hair down to her waist, Nita was already ensconced in a booth full of friends. The snack bar, part of a local chain, had an affordable menu, long hours, and cool tabletop jukeboxes, where you could turn a dial to flip through and select songs to play as you ate. Her favorite that summer was the Eagles' "Witchy Woman." Nita's friend was a waitress, and managers didn't seem to mind if teens lingered for hours sipping a single Coke. She noticed that her ex-beau was as cute as ever—he'd grown his hair longer and still had those soulful eyes. Unfortunately, Nita wasn't available: She was dating an older guy with a car, though her parents did not approve.

Michael Baulch sidled over to talk. "My big brother—he's gone," Michael said. By then, Billy Baulch had been missing more than a year, which Nita and some other kids already knew. But what Michael said next surprised them all: "I know what happened to Billy, and I'm going to find him."

She and her tablemates cheered him on. None of them knew then that Heights boys were facing real danger. Nita frequently criss-crossed the neighborhood alone, often walking more than a mile to her favorite record store on Shepherd, to friends' and relatives' houses, or to this same snack bar, even at night. "It was all pretty safe—we thought," she recalls. Nita liked in those days to create and trade jewelry from beads she bought at a Heights department store called Kaplan's Ben-Hur. "We all made necklaces out of those little bitty glass beads. We'd make circles and flowers." Everyone she hung out with wore beads, woven surfer bracelets, or peace signs. No one seemed violent or dangerous. But looking back, Nita sees that con-versation as a sign that Michael Baulch—and maybe others—did suspect who (or what) was behind the unexplained disappearances of Heights teens. She still wonders when Michael said "I'm going to find him," whether he was talking about his missing brother or about Dean Corll.

MICHAEL BAULCH NEVER TOLD his parents about those plans. He was three weeks shy of his sixteenth birthday when he left home on July 19, 1973, saying he was headed to the barbershop for a trim. Janey and Billy Gene Baulch, Sr., initially hoped their middle son might simply have gone off on another adventure. Knowing what little Houston police had done to look for Billy, they did not imme-diately report Michael as missing. Instead, Baulch Sr. embarked on his own search: He contacted the Coast Guard, thinking Michael might have hired on to another shrimp boat, but found no record of him. And he wrote to the Social Security Administration to see if his sons were contributing to employment accounts. "Nothing worked," he later said. "Nothing helped a tiny bit. Everywhere I looked, noth-ing. I was losing my oldest sons one by one. . . . Lucky we had two more, and I told my wife, I said 'Janey, I can't seem to get one raised up. Now you'll have to take special care.' Janey gave her promise."

Michael Baulch had been missing only three weeks when the

bodies of Corll's murder victims were uncovered in the boatshed. When the news arrived on August 8, 1973, a week shy of Nita Bodiford's sixteenth birthday, it struck her like a storm. "I remember I was standing at 18th and Harvard. I was hanging out on the sidewalk with other teens when my friend Ada came up and told me about all the murders. . . . I don't know that I really remember the rest of the summer to tell you the truth. . . . The constant news and us just being unable to believe that so many boys had disappeared and no one had done anything about it." Like other Heights kids her age, Nita knew several of the murder victims—and both of the teens who had admitted to helping Corll kill them. One of her friends had dated David Brooks; another dated Wayne Henley's little brother. These were people that she thought she *knew*. Henley, in particular, she describes as "what we thought was a good Heights boy."

She'd repeatedly visited the Henley house with her girlfriend, since her parents' rule was that boys' homes could be visited only in groups. The Henleys' cluttered bungalow, a typical boxy affair whose front door opened onto the living room, served as a gathering place for the Henley boys and their friends. Kids tended to jumble up on the sofa or sprawl out on the floor to watch TV there, though Wayne's father, before he left home for good, had seemed hostile, and his mother sometimes appeared to be drunk.

Nita had been at the Henleys' on nights when Wayne trudged in covered in dirt, spouting some story about working construction. She now believed he'd been out burying bodies. She'd sometimes heard him ask, somewhat frantically, about the whereabouts of his little brothers. Maybe, she thought, Wayne had expected Dean Corll to snatch and kill them too.

For a long time, it wasn't clear what had happened to Michael Baulch. Wayne Henley and David Brooks, it turned out, told very different stories.

CHAPTER 19

GRAVES IN THE WOODS

PASADENA TO SAN AUGUSTINE, 1973

O N THE MORNING HE shot and killed Dean Corll, Wayne Henley had been reluctant to confess any crimes to Pasadena Detective Sergeant David Mullican. He felt sick to his stomach, out of breath, and likely still high from hours of swigging moonshine, sniffing paint fumes, and smoking pot. But Wayne had sobered up by the next day, August 9, when Det. Mullican called him back into that interrogation booth.

Det. Mullican supplied fresh coffee, and Wayne began to sob and shake as he lifted the cup to his lips. Mullican assured the seventeen-year-old he'd feel relief if he talked. "He was telling me that I ought to just go ahead and tell him about it. I would feel a lot better, otherwise I was going to have a nervous breakdown on him and I might have a heart attack and die, you never can tell," Wayne later testified in a January 1974 hearing during which his defense attorney tried—and failed—to get his damning confessions suppressed.

If Wayne didn't want to talk, Det. Mullican offered to arrange for Houston homicide detectives to interrogate him and administer a lie detector test. That didn't seem like a better option. "I didn't particularly want to go to the HPD," Wayne later explained. HPD homicide detective Karl Siebeneicher, Jr., a participant in the ongoing shed excavations, had already told Henley he "was kin to one of those boys."

(The detective's cousin was Marty Jones. Some thought the officer never really recovered from that loss; he committed suicide in 1977.)

Det. Mullican kept listening as Wayne began to babble, incriminating himself in a litany of horror: For two years, he had helped lure boys to Corll's place in exchange for cash rewards. Wayne said he picked up the first long-haired victim at 11th Street and Studewood in the Heights while cruising with Corll in a Pontiac GTX in early 1971. He talked that boy, supposedly a stranger, into accepting an invitation to party at Corll's place. They smoked pot together before Wayne left. That boy, and other teens Wayne knew well, had been overpowered or tricked into handcuffing themselves, and tied to that torture board that Mullican had already seen.

"Dean would screw all of them and sometimes suck them and make them suck him. Then he would kill them," Wayne Henley said.

Slowly, the seventeen-year-old admitted that he'd gotten caught up in Corll's torture games too. "I killed several of them myself with Dean's gun and helped him choke some others. Then we would take them and bury them in different places. I shot and killed Johnny Delome and we buried him at High Island. Then me and Dean and David Brooks killed two brothers. I think we choked them anyway."

Corll killed two sets of brothers. But Donald and Jerry Lynn Waldrop, newcomers to Houston, were abducted and slain in 1971, before Wayne admitted to joining forces with Corll. Perhaps Wayne was talking about the Baulch brothers, Heights kids he knew. Still, his breathless summary never made sense: It suggested that Billy and Michael Baulch had been "choked" and buried together, though Billy Baulch and Johnny Delome had been killed in May 1972, fourteen months before Michael disappeared in July 1973.

The details were horrific. Corll used his knife to cut off boys' clothes and used tools to torture them, plucking out their pubic hair and poking a two-headed rubber dildo into their rectums. Wayne Henley's stories spooled out and tangled as he talked. He told Mullican there were more bodies buried near Corll's cabin on Lake Sam Rayburn, but he again provided conflicting clues about who was buried where. "We buried Billy Baulch at High Island and Mike Baulch at Rayburn," Wayne said at one point.

David Brooks, questioned separately, gave another account of what happened to Michael Baulch. David, who knew both brothers well, told HPD officers he thought Mike Baulch's body had been buried in the boatshed, contradicting Wayne Henley.

A group of police officials transporting Elmer Wayne Henley, who is hiding his face, in August 1973.
POLICE FILE PHOTO

On the afternoon of August 9, as interrogations continued, John Hoyt, the elected sheriff in far-off San Augustine County, heard rumors about burials near Lake Sam Rayburn. The footprint of Texas's largest man-made lake was in his jurisdiction and Sheriff Hoyt phoned to request that the seventeen-year-old be transported immediately to East Texas to search before sundown.

Detective Mullican, always one step ahead of the defense attorney Henley's mother had hired, loaded Henley into his squad car for the 160-mile journey. Upon arrival around 5:30 P.M., Henley spotted several hundred people gathered around the San Augustine lockup. They didn't look friendly. "They were what I call rednecks. Hicks wearing straw hats and chewing on a piece of straw," Henley later testified. "There was just a passel of people everywhere. I didn't particularly care to be let loose amongst all of them."

Soon after meeting Hoyt and his men, Henley directed Pasadena officers down a winding dirt road to park on a lonely bridge in the

Angelina National Forest with a convoy of sheriff's deputies, another county sheriff, a Texas Ranger, DPS troopers, and camera-toting reporters behind them. He wore jail inmate coveralls provided by Pasadena PD but remained barefoot. To induce the teen to lead his deputies deeper into a trailless stretch of underbrush and brambles to forest grave sites, Sheriff Hoyt offered up a pair of white leather golf shoes he kept in the trunk of his own cruiser. Hoyt hesitated to hand over the fancy footwear but seemed eager to avoid delays. Hoyt, Mullican, deputies clad in cowboy hats and carrying shovels and sidearms, and reporters toting cameras with oversized handheld flashes then followed Wayne Henley through uneven sandy ground and spindly pines. There was no path, but somehow he located landmarks.

These woods and the nearby lake had been a playground for Henley and Brooks. On one occasion, they had left a dead boy's body in the van for several hours to go fishing before a burial that summer.

Before sunset, Wayne pointed out two shallow graves where deputies and others with shovels exposed corpses interred without any clothing at all. Wayne admitted that he'd helped bury his fifteen-year-old friend Billy Lawrence in one grave. Another held a hitchhiker from Baton Rouge they'd picked up near a Heights trailer park; Wayne didn't know his name. Two more graves were hidden deeper in the woods, but by then it was too dark to continue.

None too pleased, Wayne spent that night of Thursday, August 9, in a cell in the San Augustine County jail, where the crowd outside swelled to about three thousand. He never managed to speak to the defense lawyer his anxious mother had hired; so many cranks and reporters were phoning the rural sheriff's department that it took a long time for the attorney to get through to Sheriff Hoyt. By then, Henley was already asleep. Hoyt told the lawyer, "I couldn't let him come down just to use the telephone."

Wayne Henley didn't recall sleeping much that night. He was afraid—and with reason. The days of lynching were mostly over by the 1970s, but vigilantism was not dead in Texas. "Any time you've got a big crowd in East Texas, you better be concerned," said Hoyt, in his own recollection of that scene. That crowd was "milling around out there all night, some knocking on the door, some kicking on the door wanting in." Wayne Henley was left to wonder: *Were these hicks mad about the Houston boys' murders? Or were these vigilantes angry over the killing of Dean Corll, a U.S. Army veteran whose family still owned a fishing cabin in these parts?*

Dean Corll's mother, Mary West, remained in Colorado, but granted inflammatory interviews and wrote an open letter to newspapers claiming that her eldest son had been framed and defamed for atrocities committed by Henley, the juvenile delinquent who had gunned him down. She claimed the "torture boards" and evidence found in Corll's house must have been "planted."

Wayne declined a TV dinner and ended up in a solitary cell with a bare mattress stripped of its sheets. He disliked the close quarters, which exacerbated his asthma. Once the small window on the cell door was shut, he managed to rest only after receiving a tranquilizer.

WAYNE HENLEY AND HIS handlers set out again down the same country roads early on Friday, August 10. This time, Wayne hiked deeper into the woods, pausing to consider the way a small creek flowed through the trees. Showing no emotion, he led the way to two more spots in the sandy soil where unmarked graves were hidden. Inside one, searchers found remains later identified as Homer Garcia, the fifteen-year-old who'd been taking driver's ed class when he disappeared that same summer.

At 9 A.M., the last woodland grave was discovered—this one so shallow that at one point, part of this body had poked back up through the forest floor, and Wayne said he had been forced to return once before to conceal the corpse under a piece of concrete. That block still marked the spot, but Wayne did not say who was buried beneath it.

Sheriff Hoyt seemed pleased with the results, which gave him bragging rights to four of these instantly infamous murder cases. He took time to pose for photos that showed off his badge, gun, and oversized white cowboy hat. Before the others left his county, Hoyt asked Wayne to stand between Pasadena detectives Mullican and Smith so he could get a group portrait as a souvenir. "He wanted me to grin," Wayne Henley later testified during the 1974 hearing in which his attorney also tried to suppress his graveside admissions. But Hoyt wasn't so pleased when he saw his prized golf shoes, stained, scuffed, and filthy after the tramps through the woods. "I done ruined his golf shoes," Wayne recalled. "He didn't like it. And he's not the friendly outgoing type I guess you'd say. He's not that."

AFTER COMPLETING THE FOREST search, Wayne Henley joined David Brooks on Friday, August 10, to scour the beach for graves. When dusk fell, he rode back to the Pasadena jail with Det. Mullican and another officer inside a squad car. For more than an hour, the detectives again quizzed the seventeen-year-old, who was spent from two sleepless nights in cells and long days in the sun. The officers were only curious, they said, though one took notes. Wayne Henley mentioned a few victims by name, including "Mike Baulch." But he did not say where Mike had been buried. There were so many dead; maybe he no longer remembered.

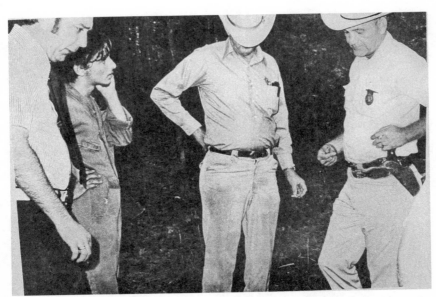

The search for forest graves, Det. Mullican conferring with Henley and local law officers.
PPD PHOTO

Michael Baulch was one of the eight boys killed in the nine weeks between June 7 and August 8, 1973, including Johnny Manning Sellars, of Orange, Texas, the only victim taken outside the Houston area. Three of the four victims buried in the forest near Lake Sam Rayburn had been killed that summer: Homer Garcia, Billy Lawrence, and Ray Blackburn, a twenty-year-old hitchhiker who'd been working in Houston and hoped to make it to Baton Rouge, Louisiana, to see his wife and meet his first baby when he accepted a ride from Corll's murderous crew.

For more than three decades, the fourth body from the woods remained nameless.

CHAPTER 20

"BONES THAT'S ALL THEY WERE"

HARRIS COUNTY MORGUE, OCTOBER 1973

THE CROWDED COLD STORAGE vault in the Harris County morgue still held eight unclaimed bodies from graves linked to Corll's killing spree when Janey Baulch arrived in the hospital basement with her niece on October 8, 1973, to try to identify her lost sons. The remains of Johnny Delome, her eldest Billy's close friend, had proven easier for his kin to claim: Johnny had recently visited the dentist and records of his teeth matched those in the skull found in a grave on High Island beach. His remains had already been reburied. Two months later, the Baulch parents were still waiting to hold their funerals.

Even with so many Houston parents grieving, the Baulch family's situation stood out. They had previously lost their eldest son in an accident. Now two more of their boys had been tortured and killed, according to the accomplices' confessions. Unfortunately, the Baulch boys had never visited a dentist and their parents had no dental records to provide.

Janey Baulch leaned on her niece for comfort as she reviewed Polaroid photographs of discolored clothing found alongside the boatshed bodies. Nothing seemed familiar. Then, workers showed her a "hair board" prepared with samples of locks cut from the graves of the twenty-seven deceased boys, which ranged in shades from a strawberry blond to a raven brunette. She thought maybe a sample from Unknown 26 had hair similar to Billy's, whose light brown locks had a hint of curl. She struggled to answer investigators' questions about her sons' teeth. The family supplied a photo of Billy in which he was smiling broadly. But Michael had clearly aimed for cool in his moody school portrait; his teeth weren't visible. Desperate investigators produced the upper part of a jawbone—the maxilla for Unknown 26—and rotated it back and forth in front of the stricken mother.

"That's Billy's teeth," she exclaimed, and burst into tears. For the next twenty minutes she was inconsolable. Somehow she managed to say she needed her husband's help to decide which bones might be Billy's—or Michael's.

On October 9, 1973, the Baulches returned to the morgue together to review more gruesome photos, hair samples, and pieces of skulls. Billy Gene Baulch agreed the remains of Unknown 26 seemed to share his beloved Little Bill's grin and hair. The body they chose had been found in a grave on High Island near Johnny's with a cord still lashed around its neck. "It's hard, you know," Billy Gene Baulch, Sr., told a *Houston Chronicle* reporter. "I had to do it. My wife had to do it." But how could the ME's office give the Baulches back only one of their two murdered boys? It wasn't clear where Michael had been buried since Brooks and Henley had given conflicting statements. His parents were forced to gaze at more teeth inside the maws of skeletal teenagers, with only memories of a lost son's smile to guide them.

Janey recalled that Michael once fell hard, chipping a tooth, and had another tooth that was cracked. Billy Gene Baulch, Sr., declared that he'd recognized a silver belt buckle found in Hole No. 2 in the boatshed as one he'd given Michael. He was handed the buckle and belt and examined both carefully. "I knew it right off," he later said. "I didn't give it to him for his birthday or anything. I just gave it to him." Based mainly on that memory, they selected a dark-haired boy whose remains had been recovered in the boatshed, even though his teeth and hair didn't seem quite right. That body was discovered on

August 8, 1973, the day that would have been Michael's sixteenth birthday.

"You don't know what it's like," Billy Gene Baulch, Sr., later told a journalist who visited their home, where the dead boys' school pictures were prominently displayed. "You don't know what they meant to me."

Janey Baulch could barely speak of the ordeal. She hid her face in her hands and wept. "Bones," she finally said. "That's all they were." On October 12, 1973, they buried their sons together in a single coffin in a plot beside their big brother Marvin's.

WITH THE BAULCH BROTHERS' IDs, the ME's official number of unknown Corll victims dropped to six. Behind the scenes, Pat Paul and other Harris County officials felt uneasy about placing so much stock in the slimmest of clues: a belt buckle from the boatshed. Most of Corll's teenaged victims had been buried nude. Nooks and crannies in that shed held jumbled sacks of discarded clothing, random items linked to thefts, to Corll's family, and to myriad murdered boys. The fact that Michael Baulch's identification contradicted Wayne Henley's statement about his forest burial bothered Pat Paul less than the lack of solid forensic evidence. Over time, Paul had become convinced that Corll's accomplices had forgotten or lied about some murdered boys' identities or burials. "You had to take what Wayne said with a grain of salt," she said. "He was such an asshole, but he thought he was a hero because he's the one who killed Corll."

It's unclear whether the Baulch parents reviewed or rejected photos of the only unidentified boy left from the woodland graves. He'd been found without any possessions: Only a winding strand of twine was buried beside him. His body had partially mummified under the shady forest floor strewn with pine straw. Pathos shone through that corpse. His eyes were gone and his mouth remained agape, assuming the shape of a death mask. Though his face seemed to have melted away through decomposition, he was a teenager with wavy brown hair parted down the middle.

THE LOST BOYS—1973 ME'S CASE LIST

ORIGINAL DEATH TOLL: 27 MURDERED; 7 UNIDENTIFIED AS OF OCTOBER 1973, IN ORDER OF ESTIMATED DATE OF DEATH.

	THE LOST BOYS
1	Jeffrey Alan Konen, 18, September 28, 1970
2	Danny Michael Yates, 14, December 13, 1970
3	James "Jimmy" Glass, 14, 1970
4	Donald Waldrop, 15 (brothers), January 30, 1971
5	Jerry Lynn Waldrop, 13 (brothers), January 30, 1971
6	**Unidentified boy with boots (boatshed) Case No. ML 73-3349**
7	Gregory "Malley" Winkle, 16, May 29, 1971
8	David William Hilligiest, 13, May 29, 1971
9	Ruben W. Watson (Haney), 17, August 17, 1971
10	**Unidentified boy with striped swimming suit (boatshed) Case No. ML 73-3356**
11	**Unidentified boy with leather wristband (boatshed) Case No. ML 73-3350**
12	Frank Anthony Aguirre, 17, March 24, 1972
13	Billy Gene Baulch, Jr., 17, May 21, 1972
14	Johnny Ray Delome, 16, May 21, 1972
15	**Unidentified tall boy (boatshed) Case No. ML 73-3355**
16	**Identified as Michael Baulch, 15 (boatshed) Case No. ML 73-3333**
17	Wally Jay Simoneaux, 14, October 4, 1972
18	Richard Edward Hembree, 13, October 4, 1972
19	**Unidentified boy (found on the beach) 1983 ID Richard Kepner**
20	William "Billy" Lawrence, 15, June 4, 1973
21	Raymond Stanley "Ray" Blackburn, 20, June 15, 1973
22	Homer Louis Garcia, 15, July 7, 1973
23	**Unidentified body (found in the woods) Case No. ML 73-3378**
24	John "Johnny" Manning Sellars, 18, July 12, 1973
25	Marty Ray Jones, 18, July 25, 1973
26	Charles Cary Cobble, 17, July 25, 1973
27	James Stanton Dreymala, 13, August 3, 1973

CHAPTER 21

A MOTION TO SUPPRESS

HARRIS COUNTY COURTHOUSE, 1974

PLENTY OF PEOPLE WERE threatening to shoot Wayne Henley or David Brooks on sight by January 1974 when Henley's lawyer requested that pretrial hearing in Harris County District Court seeking to have all his incriminating statements thrown out. Even though he'd been read his rights no more than an hour or two after Corll's homicide, Henley had been too young, too naïve, and too impaired by partying to knowingly waive his rights to remain silent or to consult legal counsel, the argument went.

Many Houstonians were already angry that Henley and Brooks had escaped the possibility of the death penalty through the Supreme Court moratorium. In a landmark case, *Furman v. Georgia*, the court had ruled in June 1972 that the death penalty violated the constitutional protections against "cruel and unusual punishment" because it had been applied in a manner that disproportionately harmed minorities convicted of rape or murder. This decision suspended all death penalty statutes in the United States and commuted the death sentences of 629 people. Since Texas generally supported capital punishment, particularly in Harris County, the ruling also almost certainly spared the lives of Henley and Brooks. In August 1973, local prosecutors announced they had "serious reservations" that the two would be eligible for the death penalty even under the language of Texas's hastily passed new capital punishment statute.

Whenever word got out that the accused teen killers were being transported from jail to a court hearing, armed would-be vigilantes tended to line up along public roadways seeking to impose their own punishment. At one point, Walter Scott, the father of a murder victim whose body remained unidentified, reported he'd been cold-called by a self-described hitman offering to kill either boy for a flat rate of $1,700. The man claimed he had "connections" and could bypass courthouse security. Scott said the caller pressed him twice to pay, promising, "You'll change your mind." Instead, Scott alerted police, though no arrests were reported.

Barely five months had passed since all those bones and bodies had been uncovered, yet Henley seemed headed to a rapid trial for six of the twenty-seven murders in January 1974. In support of his motion to suppress evidence supplied by Henley, Houston attorney Will Gray was arguing that the seventeen-year-old had never been properly advised of his rights and had been unable to make in-formed decisions anyway before signing two sworn statements and then leading police to nearly all of the remains they'd recovered.

Fifty reporters requested credentials to attend the hearing that January. One was famous—Truman Capote, the celebrity author with the debonair demeanor, high-society connections, and squeaky voice. Capote had signed a six-figure deal to file installments on the case for *The Washington Post*. (He requested a fee of $10,000 a week, plus expenses, a contract worth as much as $200,000 total, a whop-ping $1.8 million in 2023 dollars, according to handwritten notes on the negotiations.) Some figured Capote, who had interviewed dozens of killers while researching his classic *In Cold Blood*, might write a book on Henley, Brooks, and Corll. Gray, Henley's attorney, later let slip that his client was eager to collaborate on a book or movie deal.

Capote, who described himself as "one of America's most distin-guished writers and authorities on the homicidal mind," proposed a series called "Houston Diary." In a typewritten memo, Capote pitched a narrative on Henley's trial that would "incorporate a wider landscape to deal with the climate, the city, the fantastic cast of pe-

ripheral characters, the sideroads as well as the main streets surrounding this historic case." Capote described his idea as nothing
less than a late-twentieth-century version of Theodore Dreiser's
massive classic novel, *An American Tragedy*, about the 1906 murder
of Grace Brown at the hands of her lover.

"Perhaps it could have happened anywhere," Capote wrote in his
December 16, 1973, proposal, repeating a claim made by the Harris
County DA and other Houston boosters, "but the fact that twenty-
seven youngsters, and very possibly more, could disappear without
the merest ripple seems to be peculiar to this country at this particular time." Capote planned to take the mystery out of the Corll case
and simultaneously explore why a recent poll had shown that half of
the U.S. population felt uneasy about America and feared it to be
"affected by some serious and spreading, undefinable malaise," he
wrote. "Perhaps this is true; and if so, then the Houston case is possibly a strong symptom of it." Capote also wanted to learn why so
many boys had gone missing without the police, journalists, or the
community raising a general alarm. Capote told an interviewer he
saw the trial as a "jumping off point, to really tell about this whole
extraordinary culture—in Texas and the Southwest, all the way to
California—of aimless wandering, this mobile, uprooted life: the
seven-mile-long trailer parks, the motorcycles, the campers, the
people who have no addresses or even last names."

CAPOTE ARRIVED AT HARRIS County's 176th District Court for the
hearing on January 14, 1974, accompanied by John O'Shea, a married banker who doubled as his lover and business manager. Despite
his celebrity status, Capote was among the reporters and spectators
forced by court security guards to stop at a makeshift security check-
point with a metal detector hastily erected in the hallway outside the
fifth-floor courtroom. The place "looked more like an airport corridor than a hall of justice when the hearing began," wrote Kathy
Lewis of the *Houston Post*, who noted that some courthouse regulars
took a back stairway, bypassing the screeners. Reporters occupied
half of the wooden pews; few victims' family members attended.

Capote and O'Shea had traveled more than sixteen hundred miles on their journey to Houston, stopping overnight in Washington, D.C., with *The Washington Post*'s owner, Katherine Graham, who had been the guest of honor at Capote's Black and White Ball in 1966, and then in Monroeville, Alabama, where Capote's aunt Mary Ida Faulk Carter served up an old-fashioned Southern supper. In Houston, they stayed with Truman's friends Lynn and Oscar Wyatt, whose mansion was near the exclusive River Oaks Country Club.

But Truman Capote didn't remain long at the hearing. After watching seventeen-year-old Elmer Wayne Henley being led in, he stormed out, declaring, "I've seen this before." Apparently, the experience reminded him too much of watching Perry Smith and Dick Hickock enter a Kansas court fourteen years prior while writing *In Cold Blood*. Capote had a well-known aversion to anything that seemed unoriginal or smacked of a sequel.

They traveled on to Palm Springs, where Capote was hospitalized with a respiratory ailment he called pneumonia (though O'Shea described it as a way to wriggle out of the *Post* contract). Random House editor Joe Fox was tapped to inform the newspaper. Truman, he cabled, was hospitalized at an undisclosed location and would not be reporting on the Houston murders.

Capote recovered and journeyed from Palm Springs on to other preferred haunts like his native New Orleans and his New York apartment. But Capote was already struggling with a party-fueled addiction to tranquilizers and alcohol that would lead to a breakdown and later a dramatic break with his high-society friends, the Swans, over threads of gossip he managed to spin into fiction and publish in *Esquire*. He seemed to have forgotten all about the Houston murders, and yet he quietly accumulated a hundred pages' worth of newspaper clippings for his Houston Diary, all neatly pasted into a nutmeg-brown scrapbook. He read those articles, underlining details in red pen, and tapped his considerable connections to obtain three intimate black-and-white photos of Dean Corll. A family portrait from the 1940s shows Dean as a smiling cherub of about eight dressed identically to his kid brother, and two late 1960s snapshots reveal Corll as a muscular man in his twenties working at the family candy store, wearing a tight white T-shirt, jeans, and a smile.

Capote never published any of the impressions about the case that he recorded in pencil in his distinctive cursive script.

Truman Capote continued to visit Houston in the 1970s and early 1980s, often as a house guest in the Wyatts' River Oaks mansion. To the end of his life, Lynn Wyatt remained one of his favorite high-society friends. (She sometimes mused aloud that Truman liked her better than his New York Swans, which is why *she* was never skewered in his stories.) He exchanged information about Corll with Lynn's husband, Oscar, a wealthy Texas wildcatter, who sent a thick packet of Houston press clippings off to Truman's apartment in the United Nations Plaza in New York City. But decades later, Lynn, an heiress to a department store fortune and a trend-setting socialite, told a friend she had no memory at all of Capote's interest in the killer. Like so many other Houstonians, she'd forgotten all about Dean Corll.

Wyatt, a fashion icon who into her eighties still wears stiletto heels, long kept a gift that reflected her old friend's fascination with murder: a découpaged box covered with photos that Truman Capote had cut out and pasted as part of what he dubbed his "snake bite kits." Capote created twenty-five "snake bite kits" as a limited art collection in the late 1970s. Her own black-and-white box features the faces of convicted killers, including men he'd interviewed on death row in San Quentin for a network TV special that never aired. "It's gruesome, but it's so Truman," she said, showing off her bizarre keepsake to a journalist who came to tour her home for *Town & Country* magazine.

WAYNE HENLEY'S TRIAL NEVER happened in Houston anyway—a Harris County judge denied the defense motion to suppress his confessions and then in April granted another motion and ordered the matter moved two hundred miles west to the towering rose-tinted Bexar County courthouse in downtown San Antonio. After a trial in July 1974, Wayne Henley, looking solemn in a prison haircut and a stiff new suit, was convicted of six murders—including the slayings of Homer Garcia, Billy Lawrence, and Ray Blackburn, whose bodies he'd helped recover in the woods; of Frank Aguirre, the former friend whose body he'd helped find on the beach; and of Charles Cobble and Marty Jones, former classmates whose bodies had been buried in the boatshed. With the exception of Frank Aguirre, all had been killed in the summer of 1973.

On August 8, 1974, on the first anniversary of the discovery of the murders, Henley was slapped with prison sentences totaling 594 years.

A few months later, Brooks was convicted of one murder in Harris County: that of fifteen-year-old Billy Lawrence, who had been held in Corll's house for at least three days prior to being shot and strangled to death in the summer of 1973. Though Brooks denied killing Lawrence, he was sentenced to life for murder by omission, after a jury found he "willfully, intentionally and culpably" contributed to the death as Corll's accomplice. Brooks kept a lower profile in prison, continuing to hope for eventual release. For years, Dean Corll's "torture board" remained in a storage closet in the Harris County courthouse on the chance that evidence might one day be needed again.

Some victims' families felt they had gotten justice. Others felt forgotten. The Baulch brothers were never mentioned in any indictments, though Wayne Henley and David Brooks had named both as murder victims. Harris County officials had too much trouble identifying their bodies. Without solid IDs, prosecutors knew any murder conviction would be difficult—if not impossible—to obtain and to defend.

CHAPTER 22

THE BOY IN THE SILVER CASKET

HARRIS COUNTY MEDICAL EXAMINER'S
OFFICE, 2009–2011

SHARON DERRICK HAD BEEN working on the Lost Boys cases for nearly three years when she spotted photos in 2009 of a gleaming silver metal casket that had been donated to the morgue by an anonymous benefactor. She later confirmed that a teenaged boy whose remains had been examined for DNA prior to her arrival and then buried inside that elaborate casket in the county cemetery was yet another unidentified Corll murder victim. Derrick had begun her quest with three unidentified Lost Boys. She'd identified Randy Harvey, and then found a fourth victim, wrongly labeled an antiquity: Joseph Allen Lyles. Now she added a fifth unknown to her list: "the Boy in the Silver Casket."

The mysteries in this case only seemed to multiply. Derrick wondered: *Were there more mix-ups? How many boys did Corll really kill?* Then, almost by chance, she discovered another misplaced puzzle piece. Nearly always, bones used for training in the ME's office came from bodies donated for science. Somehow over the years, a cranium labeled as belonging to one of the Houston Mass Murder victims, Billy Lawrence, had ended up in the lab's teaching collection. When Derrick ordered DNA tests, the results confirmed the cranium actually belonged to the Boy in the Silver Casket. That

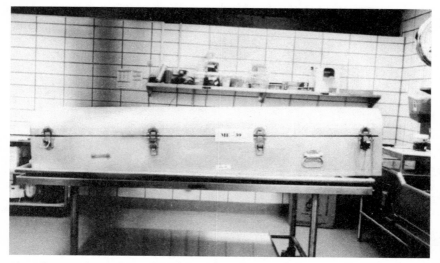

The silver casket

anonymous boy's DNA had been collected prior to his reburial, but apparently, he had been interred without this piece of his skull.

Derrick had received many tips about the Lost Boys over the years—and returning all of those emails, messages, and calls could be overwhelming. In 2010, a particularly intriguing tip came from Barbara Gibson, a Houston journalist who had interviewed Derrick about her search for the Lost Boys for a May 2010 article in *The Police News,* a Galveston-based newspaper run by editor Breck Porter. Porter's father and namesake had been the homicide lieutenant over the Corll cases.

After that interview, Gibson, who had previously investigated missing persons for a nonprofit and had a particular interest in cold cases, began digging into the murders and eventually amassed thousands of pages of records, which she meticulously analyzed. Over time, she and Debera Phinney, a true crime buff who assisted Gibson with research, became so involved in the mysteries of the Lost Boys that they established an online archive called the "Houston Mass Murders." At one point, Gibson interviewed Wayne Henley in prison, but suffered from agoraphobia and tended to focus more on research rather than face-to-face conversations.

Over a period of years, Derrick received several messages from

Gibson, but says they never met. At one point, Gibson told Derrick that she had uncovered what seemed like an error in the identification of Case No. ML 73-3333, the remains that the Baulch parents had claimed as their son Michael's based mainly on a belt buckle found near that grave. By carefully reviewing autopsy reports, Gibson noticed that those remains, found wrapped in a shroud of blue plastic, had already been so decomposed in August 1973 that nearly all internal organs had disappeared and only bones and a few scraps of "parchment like" thin skin remained. Yet Michael Baulch had disappeared on July 18, only three weeks before.

Derrick knew that human decomposition doesn't happen that quickly—not even in Texas's intense summer heat will insects invade and break down a buried corpse that fast. After three weeks, all of Michael Baulch's skin and organs should still have been present, especially since scavengers and larger predators that consume bodies faster had no known access to the boatshed.

Even donated bodies left out in the open air for research purposes inside the twenty-six-acre Body Ranch near San Marcos, Texas, retain their skin for months, or sometimes years. The Body Ranch, formally known as the Forensic Anthropology Research Facility, or FARF, is the largest such facility in the world in terms of acreage. (Everything is bigger in Texas.) The gated space, part of a larger spread that sprawls along a ridge on the Balcones Escarpment, is used both for research by Texas State University professors and graduate students and to teach visiting law enforcement officials and other investigators how to recover bones or find hidden graves. At any given time, more than fifty donated corpses occupy its rolling acres. Though many donated bodies and bones are buried for recovery exercises and experiments, others are left aboveground. One forensic anthropology student studying the decomposition process learned by using surveillance cameras that even deer will lick human bones, spawning posts about "Carnivorous Bambi."

Another forensic anthropology student studying bodies left out in the open found that even Texas's resident black vultures, with their wrinkled bald heads and hooked beaks, don't eat human skin, though they break down flesh and organs far more rapidly than previously believed. After leaving one donated woman's body in an area accessible to those birds for just five weeks, the remains swiftly decayed to the point that it appeared, even to expert eyes, as if she had been dead at least six months, based on the absence of flesh and condition of her bones. The findings of that grad student's 2012 study upended previous assumptions and helped Harris County's Jennifer Love identify a body that had previously been considered far too decomposed to belong to a recently missing person.

Yet it takes a very long time for human skin to disappear—far longer than a few weeks, whether or not vultures have access to a body.

On one small rise near a grove of huisache and mesquite trees, a series of screened cages is deployed at the Body Ranch to protect neat rows of donated cadavers from birds of prey and other large predators so that the rest of the decomposition process can be carefully charted. Only hours after the arrival of donors' bodies, blowflies and other insects crawl and fly through spaces between the wires to enter the nostrils and mouths of the dead. Flies and their offspring maggots arrive quickly, but "buzzing bees, grasshoppers, and butterflies will come and get a protein meal too," notes Danny Westcott, a forensic anthropologist who is the unique facility's director. Insects, like vultures, prefer muscle and organs to skin.

In January 2023, one metal cage on this grassy hill held the remains of one of the youngest donors: a slim twenty-two-year-old whose body had been provided by grieving relatives after he died by suicide in mid-2022. More than six months after arrival, the corpse retained its protective covering: His skin had simply blackened in the sun and shrunk around his bones to form a shell.

Long ago, Westcott heard about the Corll cases during his growing-up years in Wichita, Kansas, a city terrorized by its own serial killer, BTK, whose first murder came in 1974. Westcott points out that the decomposition process would be even slower for a young murder victim's body wrapped in plastic and buried inside a shed.

Soon after receiving Barbara Gibson's email, Derrick pulled autopsy photos for the remains identified in October 1973 as Michael Baulch. Photos showed a skeleton entirely draped in plastic with a cord tightly tied around what had once been a boy's neck. But much of his lower half looked like rubble. "It was hard to tell where the dirt ended and the bones began," she observed. The advanced decomposition suggested that body had likely been buried a year or more, far longer than three weeks. Gibson could be right: Michael Baulch had probably been misidentified. But Derrick needed more evidence to be sure.

Derrick knew that Michael and Billy Baulch were one of the two sets of brothers killed by Corll. (Remains of the others, Jerry and Donald Waldrop, had long ago been shipped home to Georgia for burial, also without the benefit of dental records or DNA to confirm IDs.) Derrick had previously focused on unidentified victims, but now she rooted around for autopsy reports and dental records for Michael Baulch's brother, Billy. Those reports revealed that Billy Baulch had distinctive molars and incisors that suggested a mixed heritage of European and Native American origins—a pattern of teeth that she had not noticed in other Lost Boys cases. Upon examining them, she also realized that the photos and charts of Billy's teeth looked nothing like those of the boy identified as his sibling.

Forensic anthropologists aren't fans of racial labels. They consider the concept of race to be a cultural or social construct rather than a biological distinction. Few differences are detectable after death between the skeletons of people who in life might be labeled as white, Black, Hispanic, Asian, or Native American. Still, certain traits sometimes appear in those whose ancestors evolved on different continents. Variations in the size and shape of ridges, cusps, grooves, and roots of teeth can provide subtle clues to ethnicity. One characteristic of the peoples who arrived in North America in prehistory and evolved here as hunters, fishers, or farmers can show up in shovel-shaped incisors. Billy Baulch had those shovel-shaped incisors—teeth with prominent ridges and deep oval dents that really look like "miniature shovels," which are often associated with Asian or American Indian roots and rarer in people of purely European or African descent. But his molars seemed similar to most European Americans'. Those combinations of teeth were not uncommon. To Derrick, they indicated that members of the Baulch family, like many Texans, likely had some Native American ancestry.

Yet the boy identified in 1973 as Billy's younger brother lacked that combination of distinctive teeth, though these siblings shared the same parents. The size and shape of the boy's palate from Case No. ML 73-3333 also differed from Billy Baulch's. Derrick thought the dissimilarities seemed significant enough to establish that there was "no familial relationship" at all between Billy Baulch and the boy identified as his sibling.

There had to be a mistake. Unfortunately, the teen identified as Michael—who Derrick now believed to be a Lost Boy unrelated to Billy—had been long ago buried in a shared casket with Billy in the Baulch family plot. Their parents, Janey and Billy Gene Baulch, Sr., were dead too. In order to fix this error, Derrick would need to find surviving siblings, seek reference DNA samples, and obtain permission to exhume the body beside Billy's, a costly and complex procedure in a private cemetery. She quietly delivered a presentation to Harris County colleagues based on her findings, and they supported her conclusions.

By tapping public records and Ancestry.com, Derrick found a possible address for Michael's little sister Debra Baulch Hernandez. Debra was only seven years old in August 1973 when her brothers' bodies had been found. She was now a grandmother whose apartment in Southwest Houston was well stocked with boxes of breakfast cereal and children's toys. Dark-haired like her brothers, Debra was both dismayed and intrigued when Derrick visited her home in 2010. She said her siblings shared Cajun and Cherokee roots and immediately agreed to provide a DNA sample. Derrick later tracked down the youngest Baulch brother in Austin—the baby conceived in the aftermath of their parents' terrible grief. Months later, characteristics in the DNA provided by Michael Baulch's siblings matched a sample from the Boy in the Silver Casket, the Corll victim buried anonymously under a square stone bearing only a case number.

Debra Baulch Hernandez told Derrick that everyone in the family had been forever affected by her brothers' murders. Upon their deaths, her mother and father had both been buried in the same cemetery near the graves of three boys they had always assumed to be their sons. She and other relatives ultimately chose to leave Michael Baulch undisturbed in his silver casket, but they asked that his name be carved on a new stone marker. The act of placing a name on the grave where Michael had lain so long as an unknown brought his surviving siblings some semblance of peace.

Like Derrick, Debra hoped that the difficult decision to disturb her brother Billy Baulch's grave and have another boy's body exhumed would bring answers to another family. With Debra's and her younger brother's approval, county officials obtained a state permit and a court order signed by a district judge to authorize the exhumation.

Michael Baulch became Derrick's third identification. But this answer, she already knew, had simultaneously raised new questions. Derrick hoped the Lost Boy buried in Michael's grave might be one of the missing persons whose desperate relatives she'd already met.

THE LOST BOYS

THE THIRD ID:

Michael Baulch, 2010

Michael Baulch, 15, disappeared in July 1973 after telling friends he was going to look for his missing brother,

Michael Baulch, portrait by Nancy Rose

Billy. He and his brother lived in the Heights, and both were murdered by Dean Corll. But in October 1973, another boy's bones were misidentified as his. His real remains, labeled only as Case No. ML 73-3378, had for years been buried in the Harris County Cemetery under that case number. His name now appears on that grave.

CHAPTER 23

THE MISSING MISSING

HARRIS COUNTY MEDICAL EXAMINER'S OFFICE, 2010

I N September 2010, Derrick made a public plea via the *Houston Chronicle,* urging more people to submit names of 1970s missing persons. "I believe if we persevere, we will get these boys identified," Derrick said. "It's very frustrating because I so want to provide these last boys with names. What will really help us is if families of boys who went missing at the time or who thought their loved ones might be one of Corll's victims would contact us or submit DNA samples for the missing persons database." She had ruled out many promising candidates and needed new leads to solve the mystery of the boy whose bones had been stored in a box with that faded striped swimsuit. And in 2011 she added the Lost Boy exhumed from the Baulch family plot to her list of riddles.

On February 8, 2011, Sharon Derrick and Dr. Deborrah Pinto arrived early at the Woodlawn Cemetery on Antoine Drive in Houston to avoid alarming other visitors with the startling sight of a coffin emerging out of the earth. The Baulch brothers' plot sat near the heart of the cemetery, under a cluster of pines. Pinto, a forensic anthropologist–in–training, had been hired under the county's new federal grant specifically to help with unidentified juvenile cases. Sensitive to the cold, Pinto shivered in her padded winter coat that morning. But Derrick felt so excited that she did not bother to throw a jacket over her short-sleeved T-shirt. In the 1970s, this cemetery had been near the quiet western edge of Houston, but by the 2010s, the two women were forced to talk over the drone of commuters' cars, SUVs, and semitrucks on the adjacent twenty-six-lane Katy Freeway, a section of Interstate 10 described as one of the world's widest highways.

Sharon Derrick (right) and Deborrah Pinto at the exhumation

When they parked near a stand of loblolly pines, the two women saw that the cemetery crew had already set up a backhoe and winch next to the headstone of Marvin Baulch, the eldest Baulch boy, and had dug five feet down to expose a coffin shared by Billy Baulch and another 1973 murder victim. "It's a myth that most people are buried six feet under," Derrick says. Especially in places with high water tables, like Houston, bodies tend to be buried in shallower graves and the caskets tend to have drainage holes. "They want the water to continue to flow through the burials because otherwise it builds up inside and the caskets float out," Derrick explains. More than once, she and other Houston anthropologists have been deployed to help retrieve and identify bodies cast adrift from cemeteries after the Bayou City's many floods.

Three workmen wearing skullcaps, heavy boots, and rubber

gloves jumped into the hole to position the winch and hoist the wooden casket with a metal bottom into a pickup truck. Then they hauled the casket to a storage area where Derrick and Pinto could privately examine its contents. This casket had no drainage holes and appeared so full of water that it bulged. In that quiet corner, workers pried opened the lid. Wearing two sets of gloves, goggles, and N95 masks, Derrick and Pinto carefully siphoned out murky liquid. Then they removed shreds of sheer dark fabric from the coffin's satin lining that shrouded body bags.

These two boys had been buried for nearly thirty-eight years, and yet the forensic anthropologists were pleased to discover that the bags containing their bones remained intact. Derrick and Pinto carefully opened those outer protective bags and discovered yet another layer of body bags beneath. The thick black outer bags had filled with water that leached through zippers, but the internal bags were surprisingly light. Incredibly, each bag was still marked with the original case number. Derrick and Pinto, working together, carefully removed and examined the wet but undamaged remains inside. After consulting photos, labels, and measurements, they retrieved the taller boy, Case No. ML 73-3333, and left behind bones identified as Billy's. Billy Baulch would be reburied alone.

Just then Derrick spotted something inside the casket that she'd read about but never before seen. Calcium from the boys' bones had leached into the water to form delicate shiny flakes of calcium carbonate. Those crystals floated atop the water and glittered in the sun.

DERRICK HAD TWO STRONG candidates for this Lost Boy. She had already contacted the sisters of a sixteen-year-old Dallas boy named Norman Prater, missing since the 1970s and described as a likely victim: He'd been last seen getting into a white van with teenagers who looked like Brooks and Henley in January 1973 near the all-night Dallas café where his mother worked. From 1970 to 1971, Prater had attended a Houston junior high school, and regularly visited his father there, *Dallas Morning News* stories said. By the time

Derrick followed up, Prater's mother was no longer alive, but she found his siblings and collected DNA samples. So far, the patterns identified in their DNA had not matched other Lost Boys. But perhaps this time they would.

She had also heard from the sister of a missing Houston teen: Roy "Ikie" Bunton, a Heights boy with long legs and arms who disappeared in the summer of 1972.

When she later examined this Lost Boy's skeleton, Derrick estimated that the missing boy she was looking for had been older than Michael Baulch, sixteen to twenty rather than only fifteen, and taller—perhaps five feet ten to six feet four. She generated those estimates from his long bones measurements and statistical calculations that she performed in FORDISC, a software program that incorporates reference data from thousands of modern forensic anthropology cases nationwide.

Both Norman Prater and Ikie Bunton remained strong candidates. Each had been missing longer than Michael Baulch, consistent with evidence of decomposition gleaned from the remains she'd exhumed and examined. But Ikie was the taller and elder of the two—and Derrick began to suspect the missing nineteen-year-old might be a match. Ikie had been six feet one. And tellingly, the advanced state of decomposition of this body was similar to the appearance of remains recovered in the boatshed of other boys who'd been killed in mid-1971 to mid-1972, the time frame in which his sister said he'd disappeared.

AFTER READING ABOUT DERRICK'S discoveries, Mildred Hataway had called in 2009 to talk about her brother Ikie, who had worked at a Houston shoe store. Ikie lived near Reagan High, and the location of the Corlls' first Heights candy shop, and he'd vanished in mid-1972, at a time when Corll and his teenaged henchmen had been actively trolling the neighborhood. Yet Mildred Hataway seemed to be the only one of her siblings who wondered whether her missing brother had been murdered.

Ikie Bunton's name never appeared in Houston newspapers as a possible murder victim in August 1973. Though he grew up in the Heights and was only a few years older than Wayne Henley and David Brooks, they never mentioned him in their statements, though each separately described picking up a Heights teen whose name they did not know. Nineteen-year-old Ikie had never been reported missing by his family. After he vanished on his way to the Thom McAn store at Houston's new Northwest Mall, his mother and some siblings apparently assumed he'd taken off to pursue another life. For years at Bunton gatherings, his name was never mentioned. "I never heard the family speak about him. I only heard my husband speak about him," remembers Caryl Coronis, who married Gerald Bunton, Ikie's older brother, years after Ikie vanished.

IKIE WAS WHAT SOME people call a "*missing* missing person." His name did not appear in the ME's collection of 1970s missing persons reports or in national databases, which is not uncommon. There are multiple reasons for such omissions. Often relatives or investigators assume that an adult—even an older teen like Ikie—voluntarily disappeared and chose to stay out of touch. Police can refuse (or forget) to create a missing persons report or decline to enter anyone over eighteen into NCIC or NamUs unless there's evidence of foul play. When an adult—or even a child—is formally reported missing, police reports can get lost, purged, or be left out of national databases by mistake.

Estrangement remains prevalent in U.S. families, and in the 1970s, relatives who moved away often lost touch given the expense of long-distance phone calls. Then, as now, families fell out or fell apart over arguments, drug and alcohol use, physical and emotional abuse, dysfunctional relationships, politics, and sexual orientation. Even in the 2020s, an era of global cell service and ubiquitous internet, a Cornell University professor's study of fractured American families indicated that at least 27 percent of adults had deliberately cut off contact with at least one close relative. Estrangement most frequently occurs between an adult child and one or more parents—"a cut usually initiated by the child," as *The New York Times* wrote of research into the troubling trend. But if a missing family member has actually met with foul play, the lack of any police report (or entry in missing persons databases) makes it harder for authorities to identify someone like Ikie Bunton if remains are ever recovered.

When she first heard from his sister Mildred, Derrick didn't have any unidentified remains that seemed to match Ikie, who at six feet one had been taller than most of the Lost Boys and who had straight, light-brown hair and no fillings in his teeth. That changed when Derrick learned of the mix-up with Michael Baulch's ID.

The remains she'd exhumed in February 2011 had been recovered from Hole No. 2 in Corll's boatshed. This boy had died with a gag in his mouth and his facial features were unrecognizable, but the cause of death was clear: a gunshot wound in the center of his forehead and another behind one ear. (During the autopsy, two .22-caliber bullets were found still lodged in his brain cavity.) In the 1973 excavations, this boy's bones had been hoisted with such force from his makeshift grave that only 90 percent of them were still present: Several ribs and the bones of both hands and feet were missing, likely left behind in the clay soil beneath the boatshed. Even lacking those bones, Derrick could tell this boy had been tall, with correspondingly long arms and legs.

Hataway made an appointment to see Derrick and provide her DNA. During their brief meeting in 2009, she told Derrick she'd always kept a scrapbook that her brother had made as a kid with a montage of images cut out of magazines and some of his favorite postage stamps.

Derrick asked if she would be willing to lend her that scrapbook. "There's a chance," Derrick said, "that Ikie's DNA might still be on the back of one of those stamps." A few days later, Hataway returned with the keepsake. "It was a treasure to her and it was very hard to let it go, but we all thought it might provide a clue," Derrick recalls. Hataway made Derrick promise to return it as soon as possible.

When Sharon Derrick examined the scrapbook, she felt deeply moved. The cardboard pages had been stapled together by a young boy's hand and offered glimpses of his fascinations and dreams. The "young-boy-bound" book, about a half inch thick, held stamps, pictures, stickers of cars, and notes in a childlike scrawl. As a teen, Derrick had also enjoyed cutting out images of people and items she liked from glossy magazines. She once created a collage that she'd given her mother as a gift. Sharon clipped out an oversized eye with long lashes and pasted it in the upper right corner above a horse, a dog, a girl dancing in boots, and other images as a message: No matter what she did, she always felt her mom watching over her. Years later, she hung that early 1970s art as a framed decoration in the guest bathroom of her own home. But for Ikie's sister, the scrapbook was the only remaining souvenir of a beloved sibling. As soon as she'd collected samples, Derrick returned the book with its stamps restored to their original spots.

Unfortunately, DNA tests from the scrapbook yielded nothing. Perhaps in this case, Derrick hoped, the sample from just one sibling's DNA would be enough to match mitochondrial or nuclear DNA extracted from this boy's bones. No other relatives came forward.

BORN ON NEW YEAR'S Eve in 1952, Roy "Ikie" Bunton had been the fourth of six children, the younger of two brothers in a houseful of girls. Bunton's grandmother dubbed the tot "Ikie" after newly elected President Dwight D. Eisenhower as a way to tease Bunton's father, who did not like "Ike," the nickname of the former general who took office only days after the birth. Somehow "Ikie" stuck. The Buntons prospered while the family patriarch was alive; Gilbert Bunton held a steady job as a carpenter with Houston Lighting & Power. (His tenure didn't overlap with Corll's.) But Ikie was only ten when his father passed away suddenly at age sixty on December 10, 1963. "The family was kind of put into a tailspin," recalled Caryl Coronis, who heard the story from her husband, Ikie's big brother, Gerald. The Buntons moved away from 1718 Crockett Street in a historic neighborhood near downtown and bought a Heights house so close to Reagan High that the din from the Bulldogs' football games and marching band practice sometimes intruded on family conversations. Within two years, the eldest Bunton brother, Gerald, enlisted and went off to Vietnam. The reluctant man of the house, Ikie, was left at home with his sisters and mother. He rebelled, started smoking pot, and once got into trouble for breaking into the school next door.

But by 1972, Ikie had turned nineteen and steadied himself. He'd landed a shoe store assistant manager's job inside the Northwest Mall, a gleaming modern mecca that attracted many teens. The Bulldogs band played for the grand opening. The mayor and other dignitaries celebrated Houston's first real mall, anchored by Foley's department store, along with its identical twin, Almeda Mall, on the city's south side. In addition to well-lit and air-conditioned shops, the Northwest Mall featured one of Houston's first multiplex movie theaters. The only downside: The mall was four miles from Ikie's home, a long walk that involved crossing bridges and busy highways or a complicated bus ride with transfers. Sometimes he got rides.

When Ikie failed to return home on August 21, 1972, his mother did not report him missing. He was so independent by then that she apparently assumed he'd gone for good. There's no record of whether Ikie's mother, a receptionist at Ben Taub Hospital, checked if her son's body was at the county morgue in the hospital basement then or in August 1973. His brother, Gerald, still serving in the military in 1972, assumed Ikie had gone away to make his own life, he told Coronis after they married in 1989. He never discussed Dean Corll or the possibility of murder. By the time Gerald died in 2009, Ikie had not yet been identified as Corll's victim.

By 2011, none of Ikie's dental records were available, but Derrick was encouraged by the photo his sister supplied. The as-yet-unidentified boy had fine light-brown hair and one of his front teeth had a prominent chip. A similar hairstyle and chipped tooth showed up in a black-and-white school portrait in which Ikie grinned broadly. By October 2011, comparisons of mitochondrial and nuclear DNA from this Lost Boy's rib bone to samples from Mildred Hataway helped confirm that the boy buried as a Baulch was really a Bunton. When his remains were released for burial in December, Derrick attended a private memorial service.

Derrick felt touched by Ikie's story—yet another boy, like Randy

Harvey, who'd been snatched off the streets en route to work, though Ikie had a job in a sparkling new mall, that seemingly safe haven of the 1970s. Derrick had been lucky to obtain a grant to pay for the exhumation, since an inactive murder case didn't fit the parameters of forensic investigations the county was compelled to prioritize given its limited budget. Required permits, exhumation and reburial fees, and court costs could run $10,000 or more. Grant funding and the Baulch siblings' cooperation had allowed Derrick to correct the error and provide answers to two families.

Derrick had momentum: She'd restored four victims' names in just five years. Already she suspected yet another Lost Boy had been misidentified—and once again a key clue came from his teeth.

THE LOST BOYS

THE FOURTH ID:

Roy "Ikie" Bunton, 2010

Roy "Ikie" Bunton,
portrait by Nancy Rose

Ikie Bunton, 19, disappeared after leaving for work at a shoe store. He lived in the Heights, but he was never reported missing. In October 1973, his remains, labeled Case No. ML 73-3333, were misidentified as Michael Baulch and buried with Michael's murdered brother, Billy. The mistake was corrected only after his sister came forward and an exhumation and DNA tests revealed his true identity.

CHAPTER 24

A DEVASTATING DNA MISTAKE

HOUSTON, 2009–2010

I N HER SPARE TIME, Sharon Derrick found herself contemplating
autopsy photos of a large gap between yet another murdered boy's
two front teeth. Technically this case was closed: The Lost Boy with
that gap-toothed smile had long ago been identified as Mark Scott.
The elder of two brothers, Mark Scott was a gangly seventeen-year-
old with big blue eyes when he disappeared from the Heights in
April 1972. Derrick knew from police reports that Wayne Henley
had named Mark, his schoolmate and neighbor, as a murder victim
in 1973. But morgue records showed he had been identified more
than twenty years later. *Why the delay?*

Mark Scott's bones had remained unidentified so long that his
outspoken father, Walter, had become a familiar public figure—
a loud voice for all of the Lost Boys. For years, he had given interviews and gone to the beach on solo expeditions to dig for his son's
supposedly missing remains. It made front-page news when Harris
County officials announced in January 1994 that Mark Scott's bones
had been sitting in the morgue's cold storage all along. That long-
awaited announcement arrived shortly after a blitz of publicity com-
memorating the twentieth anniversary of the discovery of the
murders.

Initially, the ID seemed unshakable, based on the documents

Derrick reviewed. She found an amended autopsy report and read through news clippings from the *Houston Post* that showed this identification had been confirmed partly through mitochondrial DNA (mtDNA) tests. The mtDNA analysis had been conducted by an outside lab and then reviewed by Elizabeth Johnson, a genetics expert hired in the 1990s to lead the county's then new DNA operation. Johnson no longer worked in Houston, but Derrick knew her by reputation. In the 2000s, Johnson had become nationally known for watchdog forensic work that had helped expose problematic DNA testing and flawed testimony by scientists at the Houston Police Department's crime lab. Johnson's work on those cases, coupled with efforts by defense attorneys, had helped exonerate a teenager falsely accused of rape and expose dozens of wrongful or flawed convictions. The resulting scandals had forced the closure of HPD's lab, subsequently replaced by an independent city lab.

In preparation for launching Harris County's separate DNA lab in the 1990s, Johnson had traveled to Washington, D.C., to learn about mtDNA protocols from experts at the U.S. Department of Defense POW/MIA Accounting Agency. That agency's enormous mission was to retrieve and identify remains of an estimated thirty-nine thousand servicemen and servicewomen deemed missing in action (but not lost at sea) from World War II, Korea, Vietnam, and the Cold War. Through their work, the POW/MIA Accounting Agency's teams had established the critical importance of mtDNA for identifications. It was far easier to extract mtDNA even from minute fragments of old bones and teeth, in part because every human cell contains from 1,000 to 2,500 mitochondria; and patterns in mtDNA data could be compared to mothers, siblings, or anyone whose maternal lines intersected.

Military leaders had launched their ambitious efforts in the aftermath of the Vietnam War. By that time, the Johnson Space Center in Houston had already sent men to the moon. No longer did servicemen—or grieving military families—find it acceptable to abandon loved ones' bodies on remote battlefields or crash sites, forever labeled "missing in action." Those forensics operations were initially based at the Central Identification Laboratory Hawaii (CILH) and included only one self-taught forensic anthropologist.

That operation had quickly expanded, adding dozens of forensics experts who developed cutting-edge search and recovery techniques for missions carried out in challenging terrain, everything from remote islands controlled by tribal peoples of Papua New Guinea to helicopter and plane crash sites in roadless Laotian jungles laced with land mines. "They perform forensic detective work under the microscope and in the wildest of the wilds, all aimed at bringing home those lost in America's wars," author Earl Swift wrote in a book describing the far-flung and dangerous efforts. Once remains were located, they often used mtDNA tests to distinguish between crewmen known to have perished in the same crash or soldiers lost in the same battle. Over the years, more than three quarters of their IDs involved mtDNA.

By the time Johnson visited Washington, D.C., forensic scientists in military labs had become the leading experts in developing and refining tricky identification protocols, even as the understanding of mtDNA itself was rapidly evolving through worldwide research.

IN 1994, THE *HOUSTON POST* heralded the identification of Mark Scott as a remarkable example of the power of those mtDNA tests. MtDNA is passed along only on the maternal line, so Mark Scott had been identified through similarities between the mtDNA from the unknown boatshed body and his mother, Mary. The *Post* decreed that those results meant that after two decades, Walter Scott could stop searching and finally put away his shovel, though the normally outspoken father had surprisingly little to say: "The family's pretty well torn up. We're grieving." On January 29, 1994, Walter, Mary, and Mark's little brother, Jeffrey, then in his early thirties, placed an urn with those cremated remains inside a columbarium of the Chapel of the Chimes at Brookside Memorial Park. The search for Mark Scott seemed over.

SHARON DERRICK NOW FEARED that this heralded breakthrough had instead been a major mistake. Everyone still working on these cases in 1994 wanted to provide answers for the Scotts and for the community. Over the years, researchers like Itiel Dror have established the role of cognitive bias in ME's offices, demonstrating how forensic pathologists' decisions have been influenced by "irrevelant non-medical information" even in the important determination of whether a young child's death was accidental or a homicide. Based on additional forensic evidence Derrick reviewed, it seemed to her that normally careful ME officials, perhaps swayed by emotions surrounding the notorious crimes' twentieth anniversary, had announced the ID despite clear conflicts with Mark Scott's known physical characteristics. Autopsy photos and reports on the remains identified as Mark's in 1994 revealed a teen with two crooked front teeth separated by a wide gap. In life, this boy would have had a space big enough to whistle through. Yet Mark's school portraits stored in those same files showed a photogenic boy with remarkably square front teeth, and no gap at all between them. *His teeth looked like a pair of those Chiclet chewing gum squares.*

Quietly, Derrick began investigating whether these remains belonged to another boy: Steven Ferdig-Sickman, a seventeen-year-old who also disappeared in 1972. Steven, like Mark Scott, was six feet tall and fairly skinny. Steven had been reported missing after attending a party in July 1972; Mark vanished two months prior. In life, Steven had much darker hair than Mark, but hair color changes after death and burial. Still, Derrick couldn't understand why such major differences in teeth might have been ignored during the ID process— though she felt certain the publicity surrounding the twentieth anniversary played some role.

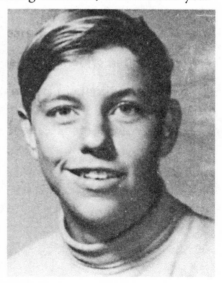

Mark Scott
PHOTO FROM HARRIS COUNTY ME FILES

She had more unanswered questions about the strength of the mtDNA evidence that only new genetic tests could answer. Derrick was no DNA expert, but she knew that using mitochondrial DNA testing for identification purposes was relatively new in 1993 and 1994. Over the years, testing protocols and scientists' understanding of the frequency of patterns of mutations in mitochondrial DNA had radically changed after additional rounds of research.

In 1987, American researchers announced they had traced our origins to a common hypothetical female ancestor: a "Mitochondrial Eve" who lived 140,000 to 280,000 years ago. Further worldwide efforts in the 1990s and 2000s uncovered astounding similarities in populations as widely scattered as the ancient peoples who'd left their homes in canoes to explore and colonize islands across the Pacific Ocean. Given recent findings, Derrick theorized that the sample used for this mtDNA match could have somehow been contaminated or the odds of a match with Scott's mother misinterpreted or miscalculated.

MTDNA IS BOTH ANCIENT and mysterious. It is found within the cells of plant and animal life and is thought to have evolved in ancient times from bacteria, which converted into mitochondria over eons. More than one thousand mitochondria are found inside each human cell, which makes mitochondrial DNA easier to recover from fragments of bone or flesh even long after death. Scientists have successfully extracted and examined mtDNA from Egyptian mummies and from a 5,300-year-old Iceman discovered in the Alps in 1991. Over decades of research in different corners of the world, geneticists learned that mitochondrial DNA evolves so slowly that patterns in its mutations can be used to trace the maternal ancestral history of all humankind. In 2001, Bryan Sykes of Oxford University explained the implications in a bestseller titled *The Seven Daughters of Eve*. "These genes tell a story, which begins over a hundred thousand years ago and whose latest chapters are hidden within the cells of every one of us," he wrote.

Sykes began his own mtDNA journey by connecting genes from that Iceman buried for millennia on a snow-capped mountain to those of a friend, Marie Moseley, a native of Ireland, who had donated strands of her red hair to the study and shared the same mtDNA. "I have found DNA in skeletons thousands of years old and seen exactly the same genes in my own friends. And I have discovered that, to my astonishment, we are all connected through our mothers to only a handful of women living tens of thousands of years ago." In fact, Sykes wrote, most Europeans could connect their mtDNA to seven maternal lines. Research worldwide has continued to establish additional hypothetical common ancestors. Those results were astonishing, but a bit discouraging for researchers who sought to use mitochondrial DNA alone to verify individual mother-child relationships. It turned out that many Americans with Western European origins had similar mtDNA. It was therefore not quite as useful for identifications as once hoped.

When Derrick finally located the DNA report, she realized that Elizabeth Johnson, who reviewed the comparison of mtDNA extracted from the unidentified boy's femur with a sample from Scott's mother, had not found the match as definitive as the celebratory news stories suggested. "On the basis of mitochondrial DNA analysis, the unknown bone sample from ML 73-3355 cannot be excluded as originating from the biological offspring of Mary Scott," her report said. In 1973, Houston had more than a million residents and was already America's fifth-largest city. At that time, Johnson estimated that about 1.5 percent of all Caucasians would share that same mtDNA. That might have seemed convincing in the early 1990s, but those statistics or the tests themselves might have been flawed, Derrick feared.

There were human factors at play in the decision to identify Mark Scott. Pat Paul, who had retired by the time Derrick arrived in 2006, wasn't involved in that ID. But she remembers the tremendous pressure the lab faced from Walter Scott to identify his son and from the general public whenever a big anniversary of the Corll murders rolled around. At the time, the office likely put more weight on mtDNA evidence, since the technology was exciting and new. And another source of pressure to find answers in the Lost Boys cases was building: Dr. Joe was planning to retire in 1995, after thirty-five years as chief medical examiner, and he badly wanted to solve these mysteries before he left.

FOR UNKNOWN REASONS, STEVEN Ferdig-Sickman, another tall teen missing since 1972, had never been considered as a candidate for those same bones, according to Derrick's review of the ME's case files. Perhaps his missing persons case had been overlooked because he lived outside the Heights with his mother, stepfather, and little sister in a house near busy Highway 290. Superficially, Derrick could tell both from the ME's records and HPD missing persons reports that Mark Scott and Steven Ferdig-Sickman had been alike. Both were seventeen, nearly the same height, and disappeared the same year—Mark in April 1972 and Steven that July. Such similarities helped explain why ME officials could have made a mistake. And both Steven and Mark were big, strong teens likely to defend themselves—as this boy seemed to have done. At least three of his ribs had been broken before he'd been strangled to death, the autopsy showed. To determine the truth, Derrick needed to find Sickman's family and conduct more DNA tests.

Working quietly, Derrick managed to locate Steven Ferdig-Sickman's stepsister, Sandy Sickman Henrichs, who still lived in the Houston suburbs; Henrichs connected Derrick with Steven's mother, Erma, who had, years after her son's disappearance, returned to her home state of Missouri. Through police in the city of Springfield, Derrick arranged for the mother's DNA sample to be collected, knowing she'd eventually have to visit the Scotts too. On December 14, 2009, a sample from Steven's mother arrived at UNT's Center for Human Identification via UPS. But Derrick waited several months before reaching out to the Scott family. This time she wasn't going to be a heroine, calling about a long-awaited breakthrough. Instead, she feared the Scotts had been given the wrong body, held a funeral, and stored the remains of another family's son in a memorial garden under a false name for more than a decade.

Fortunately, Derrick had already discovered that a bone sample had been retained at the ME's DNA lab from the remains given to the Scotts for reburial in 1994. She shipped a fragment off to the UNT lab in October 2010 for testing.

That same month, Derrick, who practiced the art of diplomacy in all of her dealings and especially in identifications, reached out by phone to Jeff Scott, Mark's younger brother. She gently told him that she was reinvestigating the identities of all of Corll's victims. "We want to make sure there has NOT been a mistake," Derrick said. "There have been some questions raised and we just want to confirm that's Mark." Derrick avoided mentioning her concerns about the front teeth. She didn't want to alarm the Scotts—not until she had additional evidence and DNA to back up her hunch.

Jeff Scott told Derrick that he'd always looked up to his big brother, "a really great guy." He confided that the tragedy had ruined his father's life, altered family dynamics forever, and destroyed the previously interconnected network of neighborhood kids. The Scott brothers grew up in the northern part of the Heights near other victims' families: the Hilligiests, the Winkles, and the Aguirres. "My brother knew many of the murder victims," Jeff Scott said. His big brother knew Wayne Henley and David Brooks too, but fell out with them before he disappeared, Jeff told Derrick. "He was afraid of them."

In the fall of 2010, Derrick drove down a shady residential road and parked in front of the gray Heights bungalow on 25th Street where Mark Scott grew up—a five-minute drive from the home where Derrick's aunt and cousins still held noisy family reunions and holiday parties. As part of her research, she'd already driven by this house as well as other addresses associated with victims—and their killers—in order to better understand their relationships in terms of geography. Some families' homes had been torn down in the ongoing regentrification of the Heights; a generic row of condos had erased the entire block where Malley Winkle had once lived with his mother, Selma, and little brother, though the Baulches' former home still stands, well loved by another large family. So do the Henleys' and the Hilligiests' former bungalows. In her years of work on these cases, she'd never visited any house where the family of a Lost Boy still lived.

THE SCOTTS' PLACE SEEMED unchanged since the 1970s, from the outside at least. But construction crews and bulldozers were busy elsewhere on 25th Street, which, like other neighborhood streets near the busy 610 Loop, was being rapidly redeveloped. Austere contemporary condos had risen elsewhere on the block, giving the impression that the family was living in the shadows of the past, penned in by towering modern walls.

Mark's father, Walter, had been dead more than a decade, but his brother, Jeff, and his mother, Mary, a long-retired switchboard operator, still lived there. Mary Scott kept her yard full of flower beds and retained her dead husband's habit of scattering seeds on the sidewalk to feed pigeons. She'd named some birds that gathered there, including a particular favorite she called "Miss Whitey." She sometimes spoke to the birds, seeming to see them as symbols of hope.

Derrick had read an August 1973 news story about Mary Scott, who recalled Wayne Henley as her son's school chum. "Wayne came over for a junior high school party we had," she told a *Houston Post* reporter. "He was quite talkative . . . Wayne was the first to arrive and the last to leave." She had been horrified to hear he'd participated in Mark's murder.

Long after Henley went to prison, the Scotts, like other murdered Heights boys' relatives, would run into Henley's mother or his little brothers, who stayed in their house on West 27th Street for thirteen years. Those encounters weren't easy for relatives on either side. In 1975, one of Henley's brothers died in a motorcycle accident, though some friends thought it might have been suicide. An investigator's report states that Ronnie Henley, sixteen, was driving at a high rate of speed on the wrong side of the road on December 5, 1975, when he crashed into an oncoming car. He died of a broken neck with only a dime in his wallet.

DERRICK WALKED UP THE stoop of the weathered wood-frame bungalow and pushed the doorbell. Jeff Scott greeted her at the front door. A skinny fifteen-year-old when his big brother vanished, Jeff was now a thickset middle-aged man consumed with extreme couponing and entering contests (he'd won several). In the outline of his face, she spotted a vague resemblance to photos of his forever young brother, Mark. On the phone, Jeff had seemed pleasant enough, but very protective of his mom, who was fragile in her early eighties, and Derrick had figured she would not get to meet her.

Jeff ushered Derrick into a living room filled with overstuffed chairs, side tables topped with wood veneer, and lamps that looked worn, perhaps decades old. Derrick's eyes stopped on a gold-framed school portrait of Mark displayed on a credenza. That photo, the same one she'd studied, showed a slightly younger version of Mark with his short hair neatly swept to one side and wearing a turtleneck and a toothy grin. His front teeth seemed straight and square, with no gap between them. Derrick suppressed the urge to ask to see Mark's bedroom, wondering if it still looked the same as it had in 1972, the year he disappeared.

She felt taken aback to find eighty-one-year-old Mary Alice Scott waiting on the flowered upholstered divan. Displayed on the wall above the widow's head, an abstract painting with elaborate swirls of brown looked like a cloud hovering over the vintage décor. Derrick was in that moment surrounded in the Scotts' cluttered living room by mementos and snapshots of a 1970s family that basically no longer existed: Mark had disappeared long ago and Walter Scott was also dead.

This was the first mother of her Lost Boys that Derrick had ever met in person. Initially, all she could think of to say was: "I want to help you and Jeff."

Mary Scott didn't reply right away. More than once, she put one hand over her face during their visit, possibly so that Derrick could not see her tears.

In August 1973, Mary Scott, a genteel though obviously grieving mother, wore a long dark mane of hair piled above her head in an elaborate beehive. By 2010, her hair was thin, short, and snow white, though still carefully coiffed. Her memory was pockmarked by time. Years before, she'd lost her husband, Walter, a tall, hulking man who had once been an ambitious if eclectic entrepreneur; he had owned a pair of full-service gas stations and a nursery, and for a while he'd imported seashells from the Philippines, bleaching them and offering them for sale at a local flea market. But the loss of their eldest had consumed him, and he'd become hunched and diminished. In his final years, he'd worked only sporadically as a carpenter and developed heart problems. Mary Scott had paid most of their bills with her steady income as a switchboard operator at Dresser Industries.

Derrick wore her ID badge and a navy-blue shirt with oversized white lettering that identified her as an ME Investigator, and had come here on official business. Yet she hated to upset Mary Scott. Moved by the encounter with Mark's mother, Derrick paused, and then attempted a softer version of what she'd told Jeff by phone. "Other people are still waiting for news about their lost sons and brothers," she said gently. "I want to be sure no mistakes were made."

Mary Scott was gracious, telling Derrick that she didn't want any other family devastated by Dean Corll to be prevented from learning the truth. At one point, Derrick slipped Jeff a swab to brush the inside of his cheek for the updated DNA comparison she needed. On this first visit, she couldn't bring herself to ask his mother for a sample.

AS DERRICK WALKED BACK to her parked car, she felt shaken. She had a strong hunch that she would have to return with bad news. Derrick was grateful that she would never have to seek the Scotts' permission to exhume a body. She'd confirm the error if Jeff Scott's DNA failed to match DNA already extracted from the femur the office had retained.

Derrick didn't tell the Scotts she'd already collected DNA samples from another boy's mother (indeed, she expected the results soon). Nor did she mention the photos she'd found from Steven's 1972 missing persons case. One showed him as a bored-looking seventeen-year-old with sleepy eyes and oversized lips. He had let his mouth drop open as the photographer snapped the shot, revealing a large gap between his front teeth.

CHAPTER 25

PARTY TIME

OUTSIDE THE LOOP, HOUSTON, 1969–1972

STEVEN FERDIG-SICKMAN FACED A challenge in March 1969 when his mother and stepfather moved into a relatively new house, a seven-room brick rancher in a fast-growing section of Houston near the Northwest Freeway. At thirteen, months after his classmates had made friends and formed cliques, he became the new kid at his junior high, and he stuck out. He was one of the oldest in his seventh-grade class, taller than many classmates, and had a set of protruding front teeth. Though a more athletic and extroverted teen might have used his superior size to an advantage, Steven struggled.

Luckily, he befriended Daniel Vancura, who lived across the street. Both were born in August 1954, only days apart, though Daniel was a grade ahead and attended a different school. Together, the two perfected the art of doing nothing—hanging out and looking for girls, mostly. Sometimes they drove out to Vancura's parents' place in the country. "I would invite him to come with us," Daniel recalls. "We went to Lake Sommerville and we went fishing . . . but mainly we were looking for girls. That's what everybody was doing."

But by high school, the two boys spent less time together. The Vancuras opted to shell out tuition for Catholic high school. Daniel attended St. Pius X High, founded in 1956 by the Dominican Sisters, which offered small classes and tough academic standards. Steven went to Scarborough High School, which had been hastily converted from a junior high in response to the rapid growth of suburban homes built for the families of returning World War II veterans beyond the 610 Loop. In his high school years, Steven found new buddies at Langwood Park, a mixture of woods and playing fields along one of the Bayou City's many slow-flowing streams that served as a congregation point for teens. Ronnie Kettler befriended Steven Ferdig-Sickman there. "Everything's kind of blurry" from the 1970s, he says. "We just met through mutual friends. There'd be groups of us and we'd just hang out." The Kettlers lived north of the park on Granite Street, the Sickmans a few blocks south on Jim Street. Their relatively new and semirural neighborhoods were broken up, like much of Houston, by bayous and busy highways.

Steven didn't much like Scarborough High and sometimes cut classes to hang out or to work a construction gig. Somehow he managed to evade detection by Houston ISD's notorious anti-truancy program. Even at sixteen and seventeen, he remained close to his mother, Erma, a caring and generous parent. Erma, the oldest of eight siblings, watched over her only son. She slipped him cash and helped him get his first car: a Ford Mustang. Most of the time, he got along well with Sandy, his stepsister. "We were a typical brother and sister," she later recalled. "We picked on each other and we aggravated each other." His mother had married her father in 1959, when Steven was five and Sandy too young to recall life without him. But in his teen years, Steven clashed with his stepfather, Eugene. Even after Steve was six feet tall, whenever he dared try to grow out his thick dark-brown hair, his stepfather would grab him, hold him down, and lop it off again. The resulting haircuts were humiliating. Even after going to the barber, Steven ended up sporting what his friends considered "old man cuts."

His buddies were growing their hair long—even Daniel Vancura, who had gotten too busy with homework to hang out as often. Daniel became more reluctant to stop by the Sickmans' after he discovered that even visitors risked being subjected to one of those rough homespun head shearings. By the summer of 1972, Daniel Vancura, the Kettlers, and some of Steven's other friends had graduated and landed full-time employment. Steven dropped out and was working odd jobs. "He got some construction-type jobs that would last a few weeks—or his mom gave him money and he would be gone all day," Daniel Vancura remembers. As conflicts with his stepfather escalated, Steven talked of moving out and making a new life elsewhere. At night, the childhood friends sometimes still got together, but Steven seemed more interested in partying and could stay out later. "I always had a curfew—and he really didn't," Daniel Vancura remembers. "I never missed a curfew. When it got close to twelve midnight, and we didn't have anything to do, I would go home."

On Thursday, July 20, 1972, Steven made plans with the Kettler brothers, and he drove his Mustang over to their place on Granite Street. The expansion of Highway 290 had sliced their section of affordable Houston suburbia off from schoolmates in larger neighborhoods east of that highway. That summer, area teens were congregating at Normandy Apartments, on Ella Boulevard near the 610 Loop. The complex gained popularity because of a couple who hosted parties there: a former Pius X cheerleader who had married a boy old enough to provide alcohol to other teens. Steven left his Mustang parked on Granite and took off with the Kettlers.

What happened that night became fuzzy over time. According to Ronnie Kettler's recollection, Steven wanted to leave before the others were ready. According to another version, the party was wilder than expected and when his friends decided to leave, Steven opted to stay. At some point, he called Daniel Vancura for a ride, but it was after curfew. Friends believe Steven eventually left the party alone and on foot. Somewhere between Normandy Apartments and his home on Jim Street, a distance of about four miles, Steven disappeared. That was very early on a Friday morning—and only two weeks before he and Daniel Vancura would have celebrated their eighteenth birthdays. Friends worried, but recalled how Steven had talked of taking off.

Ronnie Kettler always assumed his friend was out there somewhere. Maybe he'd hitched a ride—and just kept going. "He always said he was going to leave . . . and make something of himself and then come on back." Ronnie hoped that was true.

FROM THE FIRST MORNING without him, Steven's mother, Erma, felt frantic. She never believed her son would leave without his Mustang, which remained parked on Granite Street. She called to report him missing to Houston police, who showed little interest. Her son was so close to his eighteenth birthday that they considered him an adult. She got no help or answers for many years. "At least in those days, they didn't care," Daniel Vancura remembers. "If somebody filed a missing persons report, they said they 'just ran off.' She went up there I don't know how many times. She went up there a lot."

Erma Sickman called so often that "over time, they would just hang up on her," Sandy Sickman recalled.

DANIEL VANCURA FIGURES THAT if someone at HPD had analyzed missing persons reports in 1971 or 1972, they would have spotted patterns in disappearances long before bodies were found in August 1973: Some murder victims, like his friend, had inexplicably abandoned cars or jobs. (Steven had left his Mustang parked at his friend's house, Mark Scott had abandoned his Honda C70 motorcycle, Frank Aguirre his Rambler and his job at Long John Silver's.) "But this was pre computers. If they had a computer back in them days, and someone took a little time, most of these guys would have popped up as *not* runaways," Daniel Vancura says. When the bodies of those twenty-seven missing teenagers were finally unearthed, Daniel still wondered why his friend's remains were not quickly identified even though there were so many others. Steve Sickman, he thought, would stand out, even in death, as a tall boy with protruding crooked front teeth.

Houston police seem to have overlooked another clue: The last place Steven Sickman visited, Normandy Apartments, was an address investigators linked to Dean Corll. In fact, Corll had met another teenaged victim at that complex: Billy Ridinger, one of the only boys known to have survived Corll's torture board. Steven Ferdig-Sickman lived only a few miles west of the Ridinger and Brooks families. But if David Brooks attended the party where Steven Sickman disappeared, Ronnie Kettler doesn't remember meeting him there.

Possibly, Corll was out cruising that night and Steven accepted a ride home or a party invitation. It's hard for Daniel Vancura to consider how his friend's decision to walk home alone had such terrible consequences, especially when so many teens survive much bigger mistakes.

Daniel Vancura began to date Sandy Sickman, who turned to him for comfort after her brother disappeared. In 1975, Sandy and Daniel Vancura married and later had three children. Although he and Sandy eventually divorced, Daniel Vancura remained in touch with his former mother-in-law, Erma. He witnessed how she never forgot her son: She always took Christmas and birthday presents into his bedroom, which was never remodeled. She and her husband, Eugene, stayed in that same three-bedroom house on Jim Street until 1986, hoping that Steven might come home.

For years, when July 20 rolled around, Sandy Sickman commemorated her brother's disappearance by making pilgrimages to see the Kettlers. When she read in the late 2000s of new efforts to identify Corll's victims, she reached out to Derrick, fearing that her brother's remains might be among the unidentified. In March 2011, new DNA test results proved her right. Tests from the femur the lab had retained from remains given to the Scott family matched DNA supplied by Steven Ferdig-Sickman's mother instead. The match was one of the strongest of any of the DNA test results in Derrick's work on the Lost Boys cases.

That news brought both relief, and profound grief. "My journey since I was fourteen years old was to bring him home, but not in this fashion," Sandy Sickman Henrichs told a *Houston Chronicle* reporter who visited her suburban home. She mourned her brother and pitied the Scott family.

Sharon Derrick's brief final conversation with Mark Scott's family on a Saturday morning in March 2011 was one of the most difficult of her career. Derrick felt compelled to return to deliver the bad news in person. She revisited their small house in the Heights, where she told Jeff Scott and Mary Scott that DNA from the bones identified as Mark's had matched another murder victim. This time the UNT lab results left little doubt that these remains they'd been given really belonged to Steven Ferdig-Sickman. The remains had been identified based on both mitochondrial DNA tests and another genetic test, which taken together showed that it was "35 million times more likely" that these remains originated from the biological child of Erma Sickman than from an unrelated individual. And Erma Sickman had only one son: Steven.

Derrick said she was sorry. What else *could* she say?

Both seemed stunned, though Jeff appeared to have already guessed this result. Mary Scott made no reply at first. Nearly forty years after Mark's murder, her grief remained intense and unending and her health seemed to have deteriorated. Jeff attempted to reassure her: Perhaps, one day, a storm or high tide would at last reveal the location of his brother's bones, he said.

Derrick had trouble going on. She feared Mark's remains had likely been left behind in the search of the beaches on the Bolivar Peninsula, a low-lying, often-flooded coastal area that had recently been hit again by another hurricane and storm surge. Slowly, she explained that she needed their permission in order to return the remains, which had been cremated, to Steven's family.

"If we've got someone else's son, I want his real family to have him," Mary Scott replied. Together, the Scotts signed the paperwork necessary to remove ashes stored under Mark's name and provide them to the Sickmans. Both Jeff and Mary Scott provided new DNA samples in the hopes that Mark's real remains might someday be located.

"All I'd like to know, before I die, is where that man put my son," Mary Scott told Derrick in a stern tone she might have once used with an errant child. "I want to know where my Mark has gone."

ERMA SICKMAN HAD BEEN thirty-nine when her son disappeared and had waited thirty-nine more years for his return. Back in her hometown of Springfield, Missouri, she organized a church service in August 2011, mourning her boy at last. "He needs a memorial service. He was a very good son," she told a reporter for the *Springfield News-Leader*. Upon her death six years later, she left instructions to keep him close. "Erma will be buried with the ashes of her son, Steven, as she wished. They are now complete," her obituary said.

SHARON DERRICK'S QUEST HAD changed Houston history. The names Steve Sickman and Roy "Ikie" Bunton were now part of the official list of confirmed murder victims of Dean Corll. But the unexpected news of Steven Sickman's identification did not replace Mark Scott as a recognized victim. Instead, Corll's known death toll increased to twenty-nine. Based on the number of confirmed victims in Texas, he remained the state's most prolific serial killer.

Derrick was beginning to realize that it wasn't "closure" she was providing to families of the Lost Boys. In a way, it was the opposite: She was providing an opening for each relative—a passageway from the limbo of perpetual uncertainty into learning the true fate of a beloved brother or a beloved son, though it meant giving up whatever spark of hope for life might still shimmer. Even as she restored Lost Boys to their families, Derrick still thought of them as "her boys." Perhaps for some, it might have been easier to forget, but Derrick believed these boys and their families deserved to be remembered.

THE LOST BOYS

THE FIFTH ID:

Steven Ferdig-Sickman, 2011

Steven Ferdig-Sickman, 17, disappeared while walking home

Steven Ferdig-Sickman, portrait by Nancy Rose

from a party in July 1972. Steven left behind his prized Mustang parked on a residential street; his mother and little sister always suspected foul play. His remains, found in August 1973, were labeled as Case No. ML 73-3355. In 1994, those remains were misidentified as belonging to another murder victim, Mark Scott, 17, and cremated by the Scott family. The mistake was discovered by Sharon Derrick, and his identity was confirmed through new DNA tests.

The count of Corll's known murder victims rose to 29 with this ID.

Mark Scott

Mark Scott, 17, was named by both of Corll's accomplices as a murder victim in 1973 and is recognized as one of the original 27 known victims. In 1994, the remains of another murdered teen, Steven Ferdig-Sickman, were mistakenly identified

Mark Scott, portrait by Nancy Rose

as his. The error was discovered years later by Sharon Derrick and verified through forensic tests. Mark Scott's real remains have never been recovered.

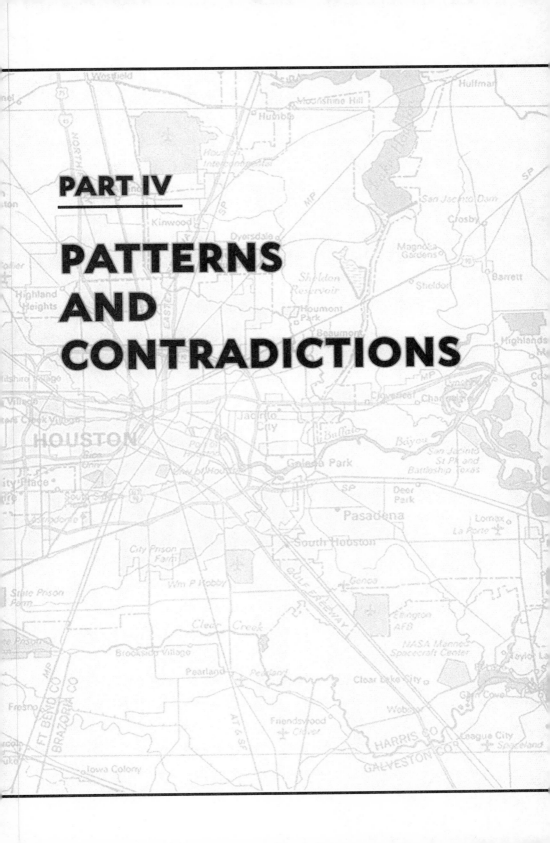

PART IV

PATTERNS AND CONTRADICTIONS

CHAPTER 26

A KILLER'S REVELATIONS

HOUSTON AND HUNTSVILLE, 2010–2011

Elmer Wayne Henley, Jr., in 1973; Henley as a prisoner more than forty years later

S HARON DERRICK COULDN'T STOP thinking about Mark Scott and the troubling fact that his body had never been found. There were unusual elements to his April 1972 disappearance. More than any other victim she knew, Mark Scott had spent time with Wayne Henley and David Brooks, partied with them, and doubtless knew they were stealing and dealing drugs. Sometimes Derrick wondered if Mark Scott had been killed because he knew too much.

Mark had belonged to a tight circle of Heights teens that included other murder victims like Malley Winkle and Frank Aguirre. Some neighborhood kids saw Mark as a charming jokester; others considered him a bully and a juvenile delinquent. Even before Frank disappeared on March 24, 1972, Mark purchased a knife and carried it constantly, though its blade was larger than Houston law allowed. *What if he'd been carrying that knife because he feared for his life?*

Mark had been stopped by Houston police and charged with possession of an illegal knife, an old police report showed. That arrest, not his first brush with the law, had alarmed his parents. Though he was not yet eighteen, prosecutors were threatening to charge him as an adult, which meant the conviction would go on his permanent record. Walter and Mary Scott met with a Harris County prosecutor to plead in person for their boy. When Mark subsequently disappeared in April 1972, his parents didn't call police for eight months, in part because they'd received a postcard in Mark's handwriting that said: "How are you doing? I am in Austin for a couple of days. I found a good job. I am making $3 an hour. I'll be home when I get enough money to pay my lawyer."

Sharon Derrick suspected that Mark never made it to Austin. This postcard was one of many missives that Corll forced his victims to write to fool their parents. Wayne Henley had never been charged with Mark's murder: Without a body, no charges had been filed against anyone. But Henley had admitted in interviews to abducting Mark, his former friend. *So where was the body? Maybe the killer knew.*

DERRICK HAD TWICE VISITED inmate David Brooks in prison, first in December 2006 and again in December 2007. On the first visit she'd obtained valuable clues, but Brooks had been more helpful in a second conversation when she went alone—without a police officer. Then after Randy Harvey's ID was announced in 2008, he'd cut off communication. Brooks seemed incensed that she'd told the press about the map he'd drawn in response to her questions—and appeared to blame her for scotching his hopes for parole. Derrick felt repelled by Wayne Henley's ongoing publicity seeking, including his art shows and media interviews, and hesitated to seek permission to visit him at all. But she wanted answers for Mark Scott's family. Wayne might know more about Mark's burial and perhaps provide clues about the identities of other Lost Boys—if he could untangle hazy memories of his school days and of drug-fueled killing sprees. She once again obtained permission from her supervisors, wrote to the warden, and set a date. Again, Derrick would go to interview a killer alone.

Sharon Derrick drove an hour north on Interstate 45 through the Houston suburban sprawl and the piney woods of Sam Houston National Forest to a prison in a rural county north of Huntsville. On the way, she found herself tuning her audio system to a 1970s channel on Sirius XM. In 1972, the year when Mark Scott was abducted and murdered, Roberta Flack had climbed the charts with the love song "The First Time Ever I Saw Your Face," America was singing about a trip through the desert on "A Horse with No Name," and Neil Young was searching for a "Heart of Gold." Derrick let her thoughts drift back with those familiar songs as she followed Interstate 45 toward the enormous prison complex in rural Anderson County, where Henley was serving time.

Derrick had prepared for her upcoming interview by rereading 1973 statements Henley gave police, his pretrial hearing testimony, and media interviews he'd granted. She'd even reviewed the cryptic notes from audio tapes in which Henley, in the mid-1980s, had agreed to undergo hypnosis and record mumbled recollections in a prior effort to identify these victims under Dr. Joe, the legendary former chief medical examiner. She also watched an odd ninety-minute 2000 documentary on YouTube called *The Collectors*, which featured people who enjoy obtaining "Murderabilia," including art and souvenirs associated with notorious criminals like Henley. Wayne Henley appeared in the film, talking animatedly about a hobby he'd acquired as a convict. He was color-blind, unable to tell red from green, but had taken up watercolor painting and created realistic depictions of bright yellow sunflowers and landscapes he'd never see again, as well as elaborate pencil sketches and portraits. She'd read about how Houston's Hyde Park art gallery owner had hosted two sold-out Wayne Henley exhibitions in 1997 and 1999, one of which was featured in *The Collectors*. The shows drew protests from victims' families and friends. One of their signs read HANG HENLEY! NOT HIS ART.

The film includes footage of Bernie Milligan, who attended the exhibit as a protester. Soon after entering the gallery, Milligan purchased an oversized sketch of an androgenous youth, which the gallery owner loudly praised as Henley's best work. Immediately after finalizing the sale, Milligan snatched the drawing from the wall, over the owner's objections. As cameras were rolling, he declared it a "worthless piece of trash," removed the paper from the frame, and went outside to dump it on the street. Then he doused it with lighter fluid he'd brought for this purpose, ignited the paper with his cigarette lighter, and watched the flames rise. When one of the film's so-called "collectors" scrambled for a scrap of paper as a souvenir, Milligan rushed to grab the smoldering shreds and reignited them until only ashes remained.

Henley's gallery sales and later his media interviews were shut down after victims' family members lodged complaints with the Texas Department of Criminal Justice. In 2001, Texas adopted a law that prohibited inmates from profiteering from murderabilia and called for confiscation of any proceeds deemed to derive from the notoriety of any crime. Henley kept on painting and sketching in prison craft rooms, but his art was peddled more quietly, mostly via shadowy online dealers. Later, relatives shut down Henley's media interviews too.

DERRICK HAD A FAR different mission from any filmmaker. She wanted to know everything that Wayne Henley recalled about the Lost Boys, no matter how small. She planned to compare his recollections to information she'd gathered from other sources and recorded in a spreadsheet. She needed to uncover whatever he knew about Mark Scott, but her focus was broader. "I wanted to see if we had other mistaken IDs," she said. "And I wanted to know what else he had to tell me so I could try to track people."

Derrick parked her BMW in the lot outside the prison, leaving her cellphone inside her car as required. She went through the prison ID check and X-ray machine, passed through two sets of autolocking electronic doors topped with razor wire, and then was greeted by an official who ushered her into a windowless office stripped of any adornment. She'd been allowed to bring in blank pieces of paper, a pen, and her files, but no tape recorder. She'd barely taken a seat at a swivel chair behind the desk when a guard brought in Wayne Henley. Once Henley was inside, the guard departed, leaving Derrick alone in a locked room with a convicted killer serving six life sentences.

Henley attempted to break the ice with a joke. "When I first got here, other prisoners kept dumping boxes of cereal on my chair in the mess hall," he said, grinning. "Since I was a serial killer."

Derrick smiled but didn't laugh. In preparation for this meeting, she had donned the same kind of mental armor she used to stomach particularly troubling cases in an autopsy suite. Yet she didn't feel threatened. For her, meeting Henley was thrilling, like watching those 1973 police reports come alive. She had seen photos of him as a seventeen-year-old with cheeks pocked with pimples and a sad adolescent attempt at a mustache. He was smaller than expected— only five feet five, just two inches taller than she was. Under the fluorescent light of the prison office, Henley looked like a geezer, a Texas good ol' boy gone gray. His bare scalp was visible on his shorn head, and his skin was clear. He was fifty-four, nearly the age some people retire in the free world, and wore thick black glasses. Henley had spent all of his adulthood behind bars. Over the years, he stayed in close touch with his mother, at least one brother, and a handful of friends. He'd even exchanged letters with Rhonda Williams, the teenaged girl whose boyfriend—Frank Aguirre—he'd murdered in 1972 and whose life he had saved in 1973 by killing Corll. Williams had undergone years of therapy after her ordeal and decided to reestablish contact with Henley. She had more or less forgiven him, though her decision to contact him—and grant media interviews about it—made some victims' family members angry. In contrast, Henley said he never corresponded with David Brooks. *What did they really have to say to each other?*

Derrick had sparred with Brooks in interviews and struggled to get him to reveal clues, but Henley spoke freely. In some ways, he seemed delusional. "He still thought he was going to get paroled," Derrick figured. "He was training as an office manager for a job when he got out." By mail, he told her he'd been courting a French-woman; sometimes prisoners were allowed to marry by proxy.

Henley's voice took on the folksy tone of a practiced Texas story-teller as he launched into the gory tale of how he'd murdered teens he'd known, including childhood playmates and junior high friends. Derrick figured he'd often retold that story to inmates and reporters. As Henley spoke, she scribbled facts in longhand on blank sheets of paper and tried to maintain eye contact. "I wanted to show him that I was interested in him, because that's part of the game. He wants people to be interested in him," she recalls. She grew nervous hear-ing about the homicides, but tried to keep a clinical approach. "It was just cut and dried, this is a killer I'm talking to, I just need to know what he could vomit out at me that could help me with my work," she later said. On her yellow legal pad, Derrick assembled a list of how Henley claimed each boy had been killed: "One was drowned, Mark Scott strangled and shot, Billy Baulch strangled; Johnny Delome shot in forehead," it began.

As he talked, Derrick scribbled down the victims' names, forms of violence, and burial sites. She would later compare his statements to autopsy reports and other records in her growing collections and look for inconsistencies that could be clues. She listened closely when Henley mentioned finding Corll with two boys he didn't know, both tied up in the bedroom of a rental house in October 1972. Der-rick figured that Henley was describing Jay Simoneaux, fourteen, and Richard Hembree, thirteen, a pair of Hamilton Junior High boys who disappeared on October 2, 1972, and who had been iden-tified in 1973. But one of her most baffling unidentified cases, Case No. ML 73-3356, the boy whose bones had been found near those striped swimming suit trunks, had likely been killed in 1971 or 1972. *Could that unidentified boy have been abducted with a friend? Or was Henley describing other teens whose bodies she didn't have?*

Henley also mentioned a boy he'd picked up at 11th and Stude-wood streets in the Heights sometime in 1972. That date and location didn't match any known victim in the spreadsheet she'd assembled. *Who was he?* Perhaps Ikie Bunton, who had lived four blocks from that address and whom she'd recently identified? Or someone else? She was pretty sure the unnamed teenager found with the striped swimming suit had been abducted and murdered in late 1971 or early 1972, based on the condition of his remains.

Henley confided that as a junior high school dropout he'd been completely in thrall to Dean Corll, whom he simultaneously admired and feared. He ultimately worried Corll might harm his little brothers, whom Corll liked "a little too much." But Henley admitted he came to enjoy torturing other people. "I'm not going to lie to you, there was a thrill."

Derrick's take was that Henley had been nothing but a punk "with acne and a bad mustache" until Corll boosted his sense of self-importance. "He was part of something—part of something secret, and part of him embraced that," she later observed. The violent, highly charged atmosphere Henley described loosely resembled that of *Lord of the Flies,* William Golding's classic 1954 novel. Henley had probably read that book, required by so many junior high English teachers, about adolescents stranded in a world without adults who begin to turn on each other, convinced they must kill or be killed. He'd been a relatively good student before he began swilling beer, sniffing spray-paint fumes, and following Corll's orders.

Henley admitted he knew Mark Scott better than most other murder victims. Mark had attended plenty of parties at Corll's ever-changing addresses, he said. Corll really liked Mark, but he turned against him in April 1972 for reasons Henley did not explain. "Dean wanted him out of the way," Henley told Derrick. On command, Henley went to pick up Mark, who went willingly to a place Corll was renting that year.

Horrible things happened in the apartment on Schuler Street, Henley said.

DERRICK HAD DRIVEN BY the Schuler Street location where she believed Corll and Henley tortured and killed teens like Frank Aguirre and Mark Scott in 1972, though she didn't realize at the time that Corll apparently used two different addresses on that street—a house that had been razed and an apartment that still stood. Derrick wondered if Mark knew—or suspected—when Henley came for him that his missing neighbor Frank Aguirre had already been murdered. Or perhaps Corll worried that Mark might squeal to prosecutors about Corll's role as a drug supplier and fence for teens. Around that time, the Scotts had been attempting to negotiate a plea deal related to their son's knife possession charge.

For whatever reason, Corll thought Mark had been "talking too much," Henley said.

Inside the apartment, Mark was quickly overpowered and handcuffed. Then Corll took Mark to a bedroom and bound his feet and wrists to the torture board. Corll kept the seventeen-year-old captive for two nights and one long day, to torment and repeatedly rape him, Henley said. On Corll's command, Henley and Brooks both got high and participated in the sessions. "Mark Scott was messed with. He was beaten and burned with cigarettes. All three of us did it. Dean hated him," Henley said. Henley, knowing that Mark was particularly proud of his long blond hair, decided to shave his head, letting the locks slowly drift to the floor.

Derrick thought she finally spotted a smidgeon of regret when Henley spoke about this murder. "You could tell it really bothered him," Derrick remembered. The story was "gut-wrenching."

ON THE LAST NIGHT of his life, when the rest were sleeping, Mark Scott somehow managed to contort his long muscular frame, gradually loosen the ropes that bound him to the plywood, and free one hand. In this moment of mortal peril, he managed to reach the rotary phone to dial a friend, but he mumbled into the receiver, possibly with a gag still in his mouth, and couldn't make himself understood. Later, he pocketed a small knife that his captors had used to cut him. Mark hid the weapon and made one last desperate attempt at self-defense when the rest returned.

"I grabbed it and then he kind of gave up," Henley said.

After that, all three took turns shooting Scott with a pellet gun, and Corll raped Scott again. It may have seemed like a crazy dream to Wayne Henley, who'd been high on paint fumes and pot, until Corll decreed that Henley needed to "pop his cherry" and make the kill.

At that point in their prison conversation, Wayne Henley fidgeted in his bench seat and looked pained. By then he had already lured two other boys to Corll's lair. But he claimed Mark Scott was the first person he killed. He told Derrick he'd always liked Mark, a friend since childhood. At some point, Mark begged Henley to shoot him. Instead, at Corll's urging, Henley tied a noose around Mark's neck and pulled as hard as he could. "It's much harder than you think to kill someone," Henley told Derrick.

Corll ordered Henley to stand on Mark's back and use his leverage to tighten the cord, still Mark didn't die. Finally, Henley left the bedroom to retrieve Corll's .22 and shot his junior high classmate twice in the head at close range. Afterward, perhaps as a kind of reward for Henley, Dean Corll cleaned up the blood and wrapped the body in sheets of plastic bound by another rope. Then Henley folded Mark's corpse into Corll's "body box" and drove to the beach.

Wayne Henley remembered traveling east along Interstate 10 late that night. He crossed the long bridge over the San Jacinto River, took the exit at the village of Winnie, and followed a lonely road that crossed marshes and passed darkened homes and shops in High Island. Finally he rumbled a few more miles east along the isolated Gulf highway, got out a shovel, and dug a grave in the heavy sand near the surf line. He buried Mark there, leaving his former friend's nude body crouched in a fetal position and wrapped in a shroud of plastic.

After Mark Scott's murder, Wayne came to like killing. "I killed them because Dean said to. I guess I enjoyed it or just didn't care anymore or I was just trying to please Dean. It was not something I was forced to do."

Derrick had observed many horrible souvenirs of human suffering in autopsy suites and in graves, but the dead didn't speak of their pain. Her rare encounters with killers typically involved only a fleeting glance at a defendant in a courtroom whenever she testified as an impartial expert witness. As Henley retold the intimate and horrifying story of Mark Scott's murder, she'd felt flashes of terror, anger, and disgust.

Then Wayne Henley repeated another story Derrick had read about. Two days after killing Corll, he spent hours roaming around sand dunes with David Brooks, shouting out suggestions to search teams and chatting with sweating police. Henley stripped off his shirt and posed triumphantly bare-chested for news cameras when they found the first grave, near a large rock. But spotting other landmarks in the shifting sands had proven difficult. Back in 1973, Henley had insisted that officials called off the search before all the bodies were recovered. He told Derrick the same thing. Mark Scott's body had never been found.

"You don't have him," he said.

CHAPTER 27

THE EDGE OF THE KNIFE

HOUSTON HEIGHTS, 1969–1972

AROUND THE TIME HE turned sixteen, Mark Scott left his parents' home. Exactly how he paid his bills was not something he shared with the hippie friends who clustered on sidewalks and circulated from porch to porch between the Heights' teen-friendly households often long after night fell. They were smoking cigarettes or joints, listening to Wolfman Jack on AM radio, flirting, or just killing time. In those sidewalk and street encounters, teens didn't often talk about their troubles, but Mark had his share. "He was a really sweet person," recalls Cindy Bazar Holton, who counted herself as his friend. "When I met him, he was renting a bare room with a light bulb hanging from the ceiling."

Many Heights kids out roaming the streets were looking for a party, a date, or a cheap meal (the taco deal and the parking lot at Jack in the Box were particularly popular), or just a way to avoid stifling unair-conditioned bungalows stuffed with noisy siblings and nosy parents who criticized their hair, their friends, or their habits. Others, like Mark, roamed for more complicated reasons. Some teens' parents drank heavily; harsh physical abuse was common. "You were lucky if you had neutral parents," Cindy says. "Most of us had crappy parents and crappy lives at home, and it wasn't unusual for people to leave." Cindy left home for good not long after her stepfather beat her up in front of a Houston police officer, who then arrested *her*.

Teens living on their own often defended each other. Cindy managed to survive partly through the support and protection of friends, squatting or sharing others' homes, and somehow managed to keep attending classes at Waltrip High from 1969 to 1973. For a while Mark Scott was part of her circle. "All of us that were out on the street knew each other. We all felt safe," she said. "Most teens would have odd jobs or they would do petty thievery or they were selling drugs." Accepting invitations to crash or attend parties from people you did not know well or from strangers—friends of friends of friends—was part of that life.

Houston was booming in the 1970s, home to some of the world's largest refineries and chemical plants and NASA's Johnson Space Center. Teens had their pick of menial jobs, mostly working at fast food restaurants, delivering newspapers, or pumping gas at full-service stations. Upstart construction companies often hired adolescents without experience, even for dangerous tasks like helping erect the high-rise apartment complexes that were cropping up on arterials. But plenty of teens who were desperate—or eager for quick cash—paid their bills in other ways. Some resold pills or pot. Cindy scrounged for odd jobs but knew others who sold their bodies. If you were a boy, that usually meant going to Montrose to cruise the streets or the clubs.

Mark Scott preferred jokes over deep conversations, friends remember. By 1971, he'd grown lank and muscular, with a physique resembling his oversized father's, but their physical likeness didn't mirror their relationship, which had clearly cracked. Some friends described Mark Scott as goofy, but there was something overtly daring about him. He sometimes carried a knife or a gun, he wore his dirty-blond hair long, and one of his front teeth had a permanent rust-colored stain. By the time he turned seventeen, he rode around on a Honda C70 motorcycle and had the broad, rugged face of a man. That year, he often hung out on the block of 16th Steet where a pair of popular sisters lived, and blended into their tribe of hippie teens.

That's where he met Robert Rose. Robert, like his friend Mark, had dropped out of school after junior high. But the two were fundamentally different. Robert married young, didn't drink, and held steady jobs; sometimes he roofed houses, hot, stinking work that made his clothes fill with the sweet muddled scent of tar and sweat. Once he invited Mark Scott to help on a roofing job, but Mark never showed. Looking back, Robert can't explain how they got close. In those days, many boys were adrift in Houston, and they drifted together.

Robert played rhythm guitar and sang, and he formed a band called Tarpon with two other teens. He liked to write songs, and his band also played popular covers, like "Nobody," a hit single from the Doobie Brothers' first album, and Creedence Clearwater Revival classics. Tarpon never had paying gigs, but its members amused themselves playing for friends in the backroom of a house. Mark hung out to listen, but he never mentioned knowing how to play guitar. Maybe he figured he wasn't good enough even to jam with friends.

Although Mark was independent and living alone, he sometimes stopped by his family bungalow on West 25th Street to see his little brother, Jeff, a teenager who had gotten a job flipping burgers at the local McDonald's, and his mother, who sometimes provided cash. He avoided his father. Robert visited the Scotts' place with Mark only once. At that point the entire yard around the bungalow had been cultivated and was filled with strawberry plants. Inside the house, the freezer was chock-full of frozen shortcakes. Robert found that odd. *Was this the family's favorite dessert? Or was it yet another of Mark's dad's weird entrepreneurial ideas?* During their visit, Mark mentioned that the backyard shed had a purpose besides gardening: His father had used it as "a jail" to lock him up.

With other teens, Mark could be pugnacious—rarely backing away from a fight. Robert remembers how he once jumped another friend for no real reason. So, Robert was surprised to see Mark panic when his father arrived unexpectedly. He remembers Mark saying, with what seemed like alarm: "We've got to get out of here now." He ordered Robert to sneak out the back and put his VW in neutral.

The two pushed the Beetle down the narrow gravel drive and into the street without the motor running so his father wouldn't hear. Once they pulled onto 25th Street, Mark urged Robert to gun the engine and get away fast.

At some point, Mark began to reveal to close friends that he was stealing on a regular basis. These weren't the usual schoolboy antics of pilfering from parents or swiping bikes; he was breaking into commercial businesses. At one point, Mark bragged about burglarizing the same rinky-dink Heights gas station where he'd once worked, pocketing piles of coupons that could be traded for free glasses with the classic cursive Coca-Cola logo. Later he went back to that same store during the day to redeem the stolen coupons. "Mark sometimes made crazy decisions," Robert remembers. Another time, Mark bragged about electric guitars he'd somehow acquired. They were nice instruments, and Robert and a friend each bought one, but then police appeared, declaring the guitars had been stolen from a music store. Robert and his other buddy returned them and fibbed about buying them on the street.

Even Mark Scott's little brother, Jeff, knew that by 1972, Mark was regularly getting into trouble—though by then Mark was living on his own and Jeff might not have known the whole story. (Jeff had his own troubles: He ran away several times and ended up in juvenile detention.)

By age seventeen, Mark Scott was making money as what people called a hustler. He'd go to the gay-friendly neighborhood to get picked up by men. Legions of teenaged boys in the 1970s in Houston, Los Angeles, and other cities regularly roamed gay neighborhoods looking for older men who paid them to give or receive oral or anal sex, or sometimes just to watch them strip or masturbate. Some boys were homeless or runaways; others were locals. The Montrose had a swanky feel: A 1973 *Texas Monthly* article touted it as "Houston's Left Bank" with "European-style restaurants and sidewalk cafés," rebuilt Victorian homes, and "bistros with an international barrage of foods and wines." Urban professionals and academics, gay and straight, chose the neighborhood for its nightlife and its oversized historic homes. At some point, Mark began "rolling queers" he met in the Montrose, he told his friend Robert.

Mark Scott, striking and well built, found it easy to attract gay men. The men Mark met often owned expensive electronics and other valuables. Mark didn't discuss services he provided, but once his clients fell asleep, he'd told his friend, he'd case their apartments. Before leaving their places, he'd figure out how to leave a window unlatched. Later he'd return to swipe stereos, TVs, jewelry, guns, or other items he resold. "He would go back to the house and take what he wanted," Robert Rose recalls. "Basically, he told me he was using the guys for what he got out of their houses."

Robert found it odd when he learned that his friend's fence for stolen electronics—a slick dark-haired guy with sideburns—was another older gay guy. The man was at least thirty, but hung out with boys who were ten to fifteen years younger. Mark Scott considered the dude to be some kind of "technological genius" who had learned about radios and electronics in the U.S. Army and could fix or take apart anything. That man's name was Dean Corll.

Dean Corll was, to the outside world, a hardworking electrician, his candy-selling days now behind him. He moved often and visited his father's place in Pasadena once a week to do laundry. But for boys like Mark Scott, he was a fence—someone who buys and resells stolen goods—and a ready source of drugs and cash. In the early 1970s, Corll regularly loaded a coffee table with pills, pot, and drinks for parties and kept hundred-dollar bills in his wallet to lure teens in the same way he'd once attracted younger kids with candy.

At least twice, Mark Scott asked his friend Robert to drive him to Corll's place, where he'd disappear inside to dump stolen goods. At some point Mark became afraid of Dean Corll, avoiding him as much as possible, his little brother, Jeff, later said. But if Mark feared Corll, he never revealed that to Robert Rose. "He wouldn't have told me that because Mark was macho—he would have thought that was a weakness," Robert says. In those days, Mark bolstered his bravado by taking speed, and masked his emotions by popping pills he called "mini bennies."

They visited Corll once at an apartment on Schuler Street. (The same address where Corll and his accomplices later tortured and killed Mark.) Another day in early 1972, Mark asked Robert to drive him to a house somewhere on Cortlandt Street in the Heights, to meet Corll again. He's unsure whether Corll or someone else lived there. (HPD officers verified that Corll rented a place on that street.)

"Mark wanted to show me a big fancy stereo," Robert recalls. When they arrived, a slim teen with straight white-blond hair was already parked in the driveway in a Corvette. That teen didn't greet them or say anything—he just kept staring at Robert through a pair of dark sunglasses.

Dean Corll reached out, telling Robert he was a musician too. Robert stood outside talking to Mark and Corll, who wanted to know about his band.

The whole time that blond kid in the Corvette kept staring. "What he's looking at?" Robert finally asked.

Mark answered: "That's David Brooks. He's just weird like that." They all went inside briefly to see the stereo, but Robert wasn't interested. He felt uneasy and left.

MARK SCOTT HAD BEEN walking around with his brother on the day a Houston police officer stopped and searched him and found that oversized knife. Locked up in the Harris County Jail, the seventeen-year-old used his free call to reach Robert Rose, who drove his VW downtown, paid $100, and sprung his friend from the crowded lockup along Buffalo Bayou. For some reason, Robert kept the handwritten receipt he got from the jail that day. He holds on to memories too. Decades later, Robert Rose cannot stop thinking about the maybes. Maybe Mark Scott could have defended himself if police hadn't seized that knife. Or maybe he should have left Mark in jail. Maybe then his friend would still be alive. "All this stuff happened within two weeks of when he was murdered," he said. "I was always upset that I got him out. I had no idea he was in any danger."

The memory of their last meeting is painful. Mark showed up in the Heights again with a gun—possibly one he'd stolen. Perhaps Mark planned to sell that gun to Dean Corll or perhaps he planned to use it on Corll. Robert doesn't know. He does know his friend disappeared days later, and the police did nothing to find him.

He remains angry that no one thoroughly investigated the disappearance of Mark Scott and of so many other teens. He thinks the case was closed too quickly and whitewashed. Authorities weren't open about how some victims had been involved in selling stolen goods, or were paid for sex by Corll and other adults. They didn't try hard enough to find the bodies. If investigators had done more, maybe Mark Scott's body would have been recovered long ago, Robert thought.

Sometimes Robert wonders if he too was supposed to be killed on the day they visited Dean Corll in that house on Cortlandt Street. "I wonder if I was supposed to be jumped that day." He cannot shake this dread. "It's possible he may have been supplying some of the other boys—that's the horrible part . . ."

CHAPTER 28

WHO IS SWIMSUIT BOY?

HARRIS COUNTY MEDICAL EXAMINER'S
OFFICE, 2011–2018

BY 2011, SHARON DERRICK had identified another vexing problem in her work on the Lost Boys. At that point, she had only one complete skeleton left to identify from those original 1973 Houston Mass Murder boxes: remains labeled ML 73-3356 from the boatshed that included the bones of a boy buried beside a gold, red-and-white-striped Catalina brand swimming suit, nicknamed by the press Swimsuit Boy. She also had just a few pieces of another unidentified adolescent: those troubling extra bones—bones from someone's right and left forearm—that she'd found while working on Randy Harvey's identification.

Yet in her quest to identify the murder victims, she'd heard from at least a dozen people with sad and credible stories of missing teenaged relatives who had a documented link to the Heights or to the killers. "The calls and letters kind of just kept coming," she recalls. "People with a missing person that sort of fit the scenario and the age of the known boys were the ones I keyed in on." Most were Texans, but people called or emailed about missing boys from Arizona, Louisiana, and Missouri too. She couldn't bring herself to dismiss the idea that Corll could have killed hitchhikers from other states—after all, one of his confirmed victims was originally from Baton Rouge, Louisiana. All were boys or young men last seen in the 1970s.

Given the slow pace of scientific tests and DNA labs, Sharon Derrick had made tremendous progress on these cases in a short time. In 2008 and 2009, she and her colleagues at Harris County had identified Randy Harvey and Joseph Allen Lyles. In 2010 and 2011, Derrick had helped restore the names of Michael Baulch, Roy Bunton, and Steven Sickman. A glowing portrait of the five IDs she'd made in the Corll serial killer victims' cases appeared as the cover story of *Texas Monthly* in April 2011. In his article "The Lost Boys," Skip Hollandsworth, a masterful true crime writer, lauded Derrick as a determined academic who made astounding discoveries, though he also painted a stark portrait of the heartbreak Mary Scott suffered after Derrick informed her that she'd received the wrong boy's remains.

Derrick felt frustrated by her inability to identify the boy whose bones had been stored with his faded swimming suit inside one of the boxes she'd found in 2006. Despite not knowing his name, she'd already attended his funeral.

ON A SUNNY NOVEMBER day back in 2009, Derrick stood under a green canvas awning next to an open grave at the Harris County Cemetery, a patch of green dotted with small square gravestones that is near a regional landfill and noisy industrial sites on Oates Road. Derrick, her light-brown hair now going white and her eyes sometimes misty with tears, had traveled here to give a speech and say a prayer over the remains of a Lost Boy she had never been able to identify, the one known only as Case No. ML 73-3356. "It breaks my heart not being able to put a name to his face," Derrick said. She had no real choice; office policy called for older unidentified remains to be buried after DNA tests were collected, new exams were conducted, and all leads were exhausted. Instead of her usual white lab coat, Derrick donned a dark-gray pantsuit for the service. She vowed to keep pushing for this Lost Boy's ID, but instead of remaining in the morgue's cold storage vault, he would occupy his own space in the Babyland section of the county cemetery. His unidentified bones had been placed in an infant-sized casket—a one-by-three-foot white box adorned with golden swirls and metal handles. Around the tent stood four wreaths of flowers, one with white carnations in the shape of a heart. On an easel at the graveside was an oversized artist's rendering of the boy's face, revealing a button nose and prominent brows over blazing brown eyes. Of course, the artist had no way of knowing his true eye color, but extrapolated based on the dark locks found on and beside the skull in his boatshed grave.

Dan Davies, a Houston funeral home chaplain, delivered a brief eulogy. "We don't know the name of this person, but the Creator does," he said. "This is a soul gone to the undiscovered country from which no one returns."

The boy Derrick had come to bury had no known family, though she knew he belonged to someone.

Her hopes had been lifted by an incredible development only a week before this scheduled burial service in November 2009. Derrick and Love had collaborated in the identification of the previously unknown murder victim of Dean Corll: Joseph Allen Lyles. By sheer coincidence, Lyles's identification had been announced the previous day. The metal chairs under the green canvas shading the grave site were occupied by two of Lyles's sisters, who elected to attend this service to mourn their own loss and to encourage others to contact the ME's office about this unknown boy. Soon, the name of Allen Lyles, an artistic dark-haired seventeen-year-old, would be carved in a square stone over another grave here that had previously been marked with only a case number. "We are at peace—now we know where he is," said his sister Cindi Michalk, who wore dark sunglasses and cupped her hand over her mouth, holding back tears. She clutched a framed copy of her brother's photograph close to her heart.

Derrick hoped this boy, buried as Case No. ML 73-3356, would soon be restored to his family too. "We had plenty of DNA—and I felt like if we kept looking for missing persons that somebody would turn out to be him," she later reflected. She never called him Swimsuit Boy and tried to get the press to stop using that moniker. She wanted to give him back his true name.

In late 2011, Derrick attended reunions at high schools in the neighborhoods where other Lost Boys had lived, still seeking clues about that unnamed teenager. She lingered for hours in the cavernous cafeteria of Waltrip High, wearing her white lab coat and name tag and sitting beside a poster with two portraits of this Lost Boy, one done by the FACES lab and one by a Houston artist. She smiled and tried to buttonhole people about their 1970s memories, feeling like the weirdest wallflower at the high school dance. Most people were far more interested in hanging out with old friends and reliving their Waltrip Ram glory days than reminiscing about how teenaged boys and young men their own age had been raped, tortured, and then strangled or shot to death by a serial killer and his minions. "It wasn't all that helpful," Derrick recalled ruefully. "Possibly the people who showed up aren't the people who hung out with those folks. I sat there all night and tried to talk to people. I had a couple of bites, but then when I talked to them it wasn't anything substantive."

One woman who reached out around that time had worked as a lifeguard and thought she recognized this boy's face, but had no idea of his name and had worked at several busy pools. Another local who'd lived near a murder victim from Garden Oaks said that as a teen he'd found the body of another dead teenager in the grass near railroad tracks that bordered his neighborhood, but the corpse had disappeared by the time Houston police arrived. Derrick never found any police report.

Derrick had been contacted by the relatives of other missing dark-haired boys or men who had disappeared mysteriously, collected their DNA, and then eliminated them as a match for this boy, including Norman Prater, the Dallas teen who had previously lived in Houston; David Waggoner, a dark-haired motorcycle-riding Marine whose parents owned a house near Dean Corll's Pasadena place; and Rodney Harris, the still-missing Spring Branch teen who'd lived near Corll's apartment and who'd vanished in February 1973.

Unfortunately, other boys' names listed in the ME's collection of potentially related missing persons were so common that Derrick had never found any kin. Houston police had reported that a fifteen-year-old named John Harmon, or Harman, had disappeared from

Westcott Towers, where, from July 1972 to January 1973, Corll shared an apartment with David Brooks and a boa constrictor. But if that boy ever existed, Derrick unearthed no trace. The same was true of John Green, who supposedly disappeared in December 1972, and of Fred Holmes, missing since March 1972. Derrick could find no missing persons reports, addresses, or relatives for them. She later learned that some detailed handwritten investigators' logs on the Corll cases, compiled by Pat Paul and others, had been tossed when office files were computerized. Derrick slowly added more potential names.

Each additional lead meant cold-calling strangers, tracking down kin, interviewing distraught friends and family, and attempting to collect DNA samples. Still, the identity of the last remaining Lost Boy (whose complete remains she had) eluded her. She'd once theorized that he might have been fooled by Corll's gang into going to swim at the beach or to Corll's father's cabin on Lake Sam Rayburn. Derrick hated the nickname Swimsuit Boy; it seemed inappropriate to reduce a boy's life to a pair of swim trunks. She knew that while he'd been buried near that once fashionable swimsuit, nothing guaranteed it was really his.

Essentially, Derrick was confronting the same problem Pat Paul had faced in the ME's office in 1973: There were too many missing persons. Though now she could use DNA, none of the samples from families she'd already found matched these remains. She'd already confirmed the existence of twenty-nine victims—more than the original estimate of twenty-seven. But what if Corll had really killed thirty-five or forty teens? Through a painstaking review of her research, Derrick became convinced that other missing boys had likely been killed by Corll. She knew that Elmer Wayne Henley, Jr., had insisted in interviews that more victims' bodies remained undiscovered. If that was true, where were they?

CHAPTER 29

AN UNEXPECTED OFFER

NUECES COUNTY COURTHOUSE, 1979

IN 1979, WAYNE HENLEY won a surprising legal victory—a judge ordered all of his murder convictions and his six life sentences to be tossed out. In response to an appeal, a judge ruled that Bexar County jurors had been compromised after being contacted and interviewed by reporters during Henley's original 1974 trial. A new trial was scheduled, though fewer journalists showed up for round two. Henley was still exempt from the death penalty, but no one doubted that Henley, now one of the nation's most notorious convicted killers, would quickly be resentenced to that same 594-year prison term.

The unexpected order for a retrial prompted a behind-the-scenes scramble to find dental records for the six murder victims, recalls Lewis Dickson, an attorney who was part of the Harris County DA's prosecution team. "Without those, we wouldn't have been able to prove even their identity at the retrial," he remembers. At the last minute, the chief clerk of the Texas Court of Criminal Appeals in Austin came through. "They . . . found the dental records down in the basement of the Court of Criminal Appeals. So, fortunately, we were good to go again."

This time, Henley's trial would take place at the gleaming white high-rise Nueces County Courthouse in downtown Corpus Christi, a setting that seemed ultramodern in the 1970s, like something straight out of *The Jetsons* cartoon. Many Texas counties still have tidy town squares with towering brick courthouses topped with cupolas, dating from the late 1800s or early 1900s and featuring statuary and stained glass. Corpus Christi leaders had erected their own palace of justice in 1914 to address local conflicts and those along the Texas-Mexico border and to provide emergency shelter at a time when many remembered the 1900 Galveston hurricane, the nation's deadliest coastal storm. Then in 1977, county leaders replaced that neoclassical courthouse with a boxy white concrete tower that featured a shopping mall–like central atrium with trees and plants. The trendy new building lacked security entrances with X-ray machines that would later become ubiquitous.

Doug Shaver, a skilled Harris County assistant district attorney who later became a judge, traveled to Corpus to lead the retrial team with Carol Vance, the elected district attorney, and Dickson, a younger prosecutor. As DA, Vance rarely handled trials, but politically he felt compelled to assist in this high-profile case. Vance had not yet made any announcements, but this would be his last trial as a prosecutor—after two decades, he'd decided to take a better-paying job in private practice.

Shaver remembers the atmosphere at the Nueces County Courthouse as fraught; it was the first case he tried where portable metal detectors had been brought in to screen all participants because of threats still being made on Henley's life. Henley was by then twenty-three years old. He'd been in custody six years, and seemed unremarkable compared to the volatile and violent defendants Shaver had previously encountered. "He was just a quiet young man as far as I saw him in the courtroom every day for weeks," Shaver recalls.

Henley sat beside his lawyer at the defense table. Shaver, Vance, and Dickson were stationed only a few feet away at the prosecutor's table, and Shaver sometimes wondered whether assassins might burst inside. "I hoped they were a good shot because I was sitting right next to him most of the time."

Normally, prosecutors don't confer one on one with accused killers during a trial. But at one point, Shaver stepped outside to use the men's room and met Henley in the hall. "We were having a recess and I walked by Elmer Wayne and he said: 'If you can give me a deal in this case, I can tell you where some more victims are.'"

Shaver was unflappable, but Henley's seemingly reckless claim startled him. Shaver had always believed "there were considerably more victims" than had ever been discovered. "We knew he killed twenty-seven—we were going to try him for the six [murders] and we'd been trying to find out for parents who were calling all the time who the rest were. We had some bodies in the refrigerators that we hadn't identified," he remembers.

"Why didn't you bring this up before?" Shaver asked. Henley's response floored him.

"I was reading in the paper about a fellow named Gacy," Henley began.

John Wayne Gacy had been arrested in Illinois in December 1978 and news of teenaged boys' bodies found in the crawl space beneath Gacy's suburban home was everywhere. Gacy was eventually charged (and later convicted) of killing thirty-three young boys from 1970 to 1978, at least five more than Corll and Henley. Henley seemed upset that he'd "lost his world record" in terms of total known murder victims and offered to say "where another five or six were," Shaver remembers. In exchange for a plea deal, Henley claimed he could supply details on those victims' identities and burials.

Shaver was incredulous and unwilling to negotiate. Henley, looking at life in prison, had a strong motive to lie. And there was, Shaver knew, no guarantee that any more bodies could be found even if Henley actually recalled burial locations. At one point, authorities had already tried to search a stretch of East Beach on Galveston Island based on a tip from a local who claimed she'd seen teenagers digging there late at night. Houston police had dug around one of Corll's former candy shops too and found absolutely nothing.

Shaver jokingly offered to arrange for Henley's release on parole. "But one of the demands would be that you stand at Heights and 8th every Friday night"—the idea being that Henley would not last long at that intersection with so many people determined to kill him.

Henley didn't find that response funny, and their conversation ended there.

"We never got any farther than that," Shaver recalls. "I wasn't going to give him a deal." Henley was convicted again in 1979 of all six counts of murder, resentenced, and shipped back to prison for life.

In celebration, Lewis Dickson, the youngest prosecutor on the team and already something of a wine connoisseur, treated Shaver and Vance to a bottle of 1970 Mouton Rothschild, an excellent French vintage, and a stretch for his public employee salary. (Vance, more of a beer guy, didn't fully appreciate the gesture.) If Shaver ever mentioned that Henley had offered information about more victims in exchange for a plea deal, Dickson no longer remembers it.

In subsequent interviews with journalists, with the leader of a nonprofit search team, and with Sharon Derrick, Wayne Henley never offered solid leads about where any other bodies might still lie buried.

CHAPTER 30

TOO MANY MISSING PERSONS

HOUSTON, 2011–2013

IN 2011, SHARON DERRICK, by chance, uncovered surprising evidence about Corll's additional victims by digging deeper into the forensic samples stored in the archives of another department in the fast-growing Harris County Medical Examiner's Office: the county genetics lab. For two decades, that lab had been a distinct part of the office with its own director, and separate filing and storage systems. Over the years, the genetics lab had become more prominent and sophisticated, a crucial part of the operation recently renamed the Harris County Institute of Forensic Sciences.

From her previous research, Derrick already knew pathologists had retained bone and tissue samples from the 1973 cases in genetics lab archives. She'd been able to use one of those bones for DNA tests that had helped identify Steven Sickman. But after making additional inquiries, she learned the lab was also storing plastic bags containing individual bones that pathologists had deemed to be extras or nonmatching during the 1973 autopsies. Derrick checked out the DNA lab's entire 1973 bone collection and began examining the contents of those plastic sacks, which resembled Ziploc freezer bags. Derrick laid out each of the stray bones on white sheets on tables and carefully measured and sorted them. Her standard procedure involved placing bones "in anatomical position so that you can see if you have part of one person, a whole person, or two or three people. And then at that point, you do an inventory."

All of the extra bones were labeled, but Derrick could immediately tell which came from Corll's boatshed and which from the beach based on color and texture. Beach bones tended to be sun-bleached and worn, an effect of exposure to abrasive sand and salt-water. Some felt rough to the touch. Conversely, boatshed bones had absorbed the brownish orange-clay tint of Houston soil and bore white stripes of lime. The killers had used lime to hide the stench of decomposition and perhaps because they believed lime would speed up that process. In 1898, Oscar Wilde immortalized the practice of using quicklime to consume the corpses of condemned men dumped in piles by jailers in his grisly poem, "The Ballad of Reading Gaol": "And all the while the burning lime / Eats flesh and bone away, / It eats the brittle bone by night, / And the soft flesh by day." But Derrick knew from modern research that these killers and Oscar Wilde were mistaken about lime. Although lime has been used for hundreds of years to prevent the spread of disease from cholera and plague victims, and does help mask odors at burials, it tends to slow decomposition and can act as a preservative.

Even with advances in forensics that enabled DNA testing of ancient bone fragments and teeth, Derrick knew it might be impossible to solve the mysteries posed by those extra bones. She was able to determine that some belonged to victims whose remains had long ago been identified. No Corll victim's remains had been returned to a family without a skull, but many had been lacking ribs, vertebrae, foot bones, hand bones, or other small bits. One of the bags of extra bones she examined that had been found near Frank Aguirre's grave on High Island belonged to another Heights boy, Johnny Delome. The DNA from a stray vertebra matched Delome's close friend, Billy Baulch.

Ultimately, the lab analysis of three extra bones from the beach produced DNA profiles that failed to match DNA she'd previously gathered from Corll's known murder victims or from families of missing persons. That was disappointing; she'd hoped that one beach bone sample might match DNA from Mark Scott's family. It might have been comforting if she'd been able to provide something—even if it was only a single bone—to Mark's grieving mother and brother. She'd also hoped to find proof that Rodney Harris, the Spring Branch boy who had disappeared in 1973 right after Allen Lyles, had been buried on the beach just as Allen had been. His family still needed answers too.

She already knew that Allen's grave—and the grave of Mark Scott—had been overlooked in those hasty August 1973 searches of the beach. Her latest findings meant that more murder victims' burial sites had likely been missed. Based on DNA test results, Derrick concluded that those extra bones belonged to three different individuals and created entries for them as likely 1973 murder victims in NamUs, the database of missing persons and unknown individuals that shared basic data with the public. Long ago, those cases had been labeled PA 29/30/31, the PA designation confirming they'd been recovered outside Harris County.

Her review of DNA results from the extra bones associated with the boatshed burials turned up more surprises. She found part of a child's cranium, a frontal bone that shared that same caramel coloring and striping of lime as other boatshed bones. Further examination revealed that the partial skull likely belonged to a boy of only nine or ten—three or four years younger than any of Corll's known victims.

Derrick also had those mysterious four stray arm bones she'd found in a 1973 box that had failed to match Randy Harvey's DNA. Based on the bone evidence, Derrick concluded that remains from two more unknown individuals could still be buried in the boatshed. Autopsy records from 1973 indicated that the extra bones of the much younger child and of yet another unidentified teenager had been buried in or near the same hole where the killers had buried Randy Harvey in 1971.

These stray bone cases had all seemed hopeless in the 1970s. But Derrick could tap DNA testing to reveal another of Dean Corll's secrets: Counting the three sets of bones from different individuals from the beach and two more from the boatshed, Derrick had rediscovered evidence of as many as five additional victims.

Unfortunately, limited DNA test results failed to generate any leads about the youngest potential murder victim's identity. Tests conducted at UNT identified barely enough DNA information to confirm he'd been male and not enough to make an ID.

But the lab did extract enough DNA for the four other victims to generate usable profiles for DNA comparisons to the relatives of missing persons. Perhaps someday there would be a match.

CHAPTER 31

A FORGOTTEN CALL FOR HELP ON 9/11

HARRIS COUNTY MEDICAL EXAMINER'S
OFFICE, 2001–2017

IN HER SEARCHES OF genetics lab archives, Derrick stumbled upon a memo filed away for a decade that led her to another electrifying discovery. On September 11, 2001, a woman named Dana Falcon Jones had phoned about her missing brother, Donnie Falcon, a seventeen-year-old who'd been living in Houston when he disappeared in 1971. Falcon, who lived in Corpus Christi, hoped the lab could help her arrange to provide a DNA sample as part of her long search for him. But not long after that call arrived, news broke about terrorists hijacking four planes and the attacks on the Pentagon and the Twin Towers. Suddenly, all government offices' regular operations basically ceased. With so many delays created by the national emergency, other work piled up, and the 2001 request to analyze a sister's DNA for a potential match to one of Dean Corll's victims was filed away and forgotten.

Derrick had never seen the name Donnie Falcon in any 1973 missing persons or police reports. His sister's phone number from 2001 was disconnected, but Derrick found what seemed like a current address and fired off an old-fashioned letter.

Dana Falcon Jones still lived in the cozy Corpus Christi home where she and her brother had grown up. A native willow shaded her sandy front yard and she kept a carved wooden welcome sign and potted plants on her eyelash front porch. Naturally outgoing and warm, Falcon Jones phoned immediately after receiving Derrick's note. From their first contact, the mother of two daughters treated Derrick like another member of the family. By phone, she told Derrick that Donnie Falcon was her cherished baby brother, the youngest of her parents' four children. She was the third child and the only girl; Donnie had arrived six years later.

HIS BIG SISTER EAGERLY told stories about Donnie, whom she remembered as a sweet, fun-loving child and teenager. She often laughed when she talked about him, though his long absence had broken her heart. No one had ever believed he'd run away.

Dana was twenty-three and living in Corpus Christi with her husband and two small daughters in July 1971 when Donnie disappeared from their mother and stepfather's Houston home. But by the time she spoke to Derrick in 2011, her mother and stepfather were both dead and Dana wasn't sure where Donnie attended high school. She had trouble finding school photos and sent older snapshots that showed him as a dark-haired little boy. In the latest one, he looked ten or eleven and wore an engaging grin. But when Derrick shared the portrait that the FACES lab had produced for Case No. ML 73-3356, Dana told Derrick that her brother had become a handsome teen whose face resembled that reconstruction. Donnie, who grew up near the beach, loved to surf and might have been trusting enough to accept a ride from a stranger to get there.

Sharon Derrick got more excited as she listened to Dana talk about her brother. The dark-haired boy found buried beside a striped swimming suit had been about seventeen years old—the same age as Donnie. Their heights seemed similar too. And Derrick believed the boy found beside the swimsuit had been killed in 1971 or 1972, the time period in which Donnie had disappeared. *Could this surfer from Corpus Christi be her Lost Boy?*

Donnie Falcon seemed like one of the best leads on the Lost Boy with the striped swimming suit that Derrick had ever received. She made a few calls and found a Corpus Christi investigator who agreed to visit Dana Falcon Jones at home and collect DNA samples from her and from a brother. As they waited for the DNA results, Dana Falcon Jones shared so many stories that scenes from Donnie's life came into sharp focus. Dana, a grandmother by then, still remembered how she felt when Donnie first arrived at their house as a newborn. She wasn't happy to give up her status as the youngest at age six. "I had two older brothers, and when Donnie was born, I wanted a sister, and Daddy came to me and said, 'You have another brother,' and I started crying.

"'You want me to send him back?' my daddy said.

"And I said, 'No. That's okay.'"

She remembered riding her bike on their home's steep narrow driveway when Donnie ran up. He was four. She was ten. "You want me to give you a ride?" she said. "I put him on the handlebars. He fell and bumped his head on the cement. My mom was so mad because next day was school picture day so he had a school picture with a big old bump." She laughed again at that memory. "The only time I ever got in trouble was defending Donnie—a friend said something about Donnie. It was kid stuff; I don't even remember what she said." But she recalled her response: "'Don't mess with my little brother.' . . . I think I pushed her."

As a twelve-year-old, Donnie Falcon got a pony for his birthday and rode it until the animal either wandered away or was stolen from its urban pasture. As a teen, he played drums and surfed the waves alongside the Padre Island pier. In the 1960s, Dana married and moved to New Jersey with her husband, a Marine, and had her first baby. Donnie, only thirteen, rode the bus alone to visit them in 1967. He held her eldest daughter, then two and a half. He braided a leather strap and wrapped the band around the toddler's forehead, "like a hippie." Remembering Donnie, Dana smiled and laughed. Over and over again. Until she got to the year 1971.

Dana Falcon Jones's parents had divorced by then, and their mother, Minnie, remarried. Harley Brown, her stepfather, was kind and well liked by the Falcon siblings. In 1971, Donnie moved to Houston, where his mother and Brown had found better-paying jobs—Harley as a drug counselor for veterans and Minnie in the business office of one of Houston's high-rise hotels. The family rented unit 16 in a brand-new complex on Drake Street, sharing a two-bedroom place equipped with ceiling fans to cut through Houston's thick heat. The apartment was tucked inside a white concrete cube in a quiet neighborhood with live oaks and manicured lawns minutes from the Rice University campus. That year, 2,414 Americans died in Vietnam, a devastating number, though down from the record high of 16,592 in 1968. Donnie Falcon's two older brothers and Dana's husband all served in the military, but Donnie was still too young to be drafted and seemed footloose and carefree. He attended school, grew his hair long, and played the drums. He'd grown up riding the waves and tried to surf when he could, though the beach was farther away.

Dana Falcon Jones vastly preferred Corpus; she found the booming Bayou City overwhelming in its endless sprawl. Jimi Hendrix had played a wailing guitar in a sold-out show at the downtown coliseum; weed, LSD, and heroin were part of the city's drumbeat. Early 1970s desegregation and busing efforts had spawned riots at some high schools. But she figured that her little brother was safe, watched over by her savvy stepfather and by their mama, Minnie.

Donnie Falcon returned to Corpus to visit his sister in the summer of 1971. By then, Dana Falcon Jones had two little girls and had moved back to the family bungalow to raise them. She liked to repaint it in bright colors: sunny yellow or sky blue. Her brother took time to cuddle with his nieces—he loved being an uncle—and to make another trip to the beach. Dana Falcon Jones noticed how her good-looking little brother turned heads. As a teen, some of her friends thought he looked like "an Indian prince."

Donnie turned seventeen in July 1971. Then in August, he disappeared. There was no message. He was just gone. That seemed strange to Dana. Even as a teen, her baby brother remained sweet and deeply attached to his family. "Mama went to the police, but they said they couldn't do anything because he was seventeen," she remembers. Her mama kept calling, but police kept saying Donnie was essentially an adult. "Then again they had so many missing boys at that time," she says. Once, Dana traveled to California, chasing a rumor that Donnie might have joined a band or a cult. They never found any sign of him. She despaired after she called Harris County in September 2001 and never got any response. She and Donnie had been forgotten again.

DERRICK BELIEVED DANA FALCON Jones deserved answers and again urged the UNT Center for Human Identification to prioritize DNA tests. But Derrick's hopes were dashed by the results. The DNA from Donnie Falcon's siblings did not match the genetic profile of her last Lost Boy. Derrick felt devastated. She'd formed a connection with Dana and had felt sure this time that she'd found a name for the boy who'd proved hardest of all to identify. She'd begun to fear that her failure to find his family might mean there'd been another mistake in the 1973 IDs: *What if this missing boy, like Steven Sickman and Ikie Bunton, had been long ago buried under the wrong name?* Unwinding tangled webs of intertwined identifications and misidentifications had taken a toll on Derrick, though she'd ultimately identified two missing boys and reconnected Michael Baulch with his real remains.

Derrick knew from police and autopsy reports that several older IDs seemed pinned to slim evidence: No DNA or dental records, for example, had been provided to identify Ray Blackburn. His father, a minister from Baton Rouge, had helped identify his remains by tracing a line in teeth thought to be related to Ray's habit of using a toothpick. And then there was Billy Lawrence—whose ID had been made after an autopsy conducted in a shed.

AND NOW HER TIME seemed to be running out. Derrick was eligible for the county retirement and she'd begun to seriously consider that option. The pace in the Harris County lab was grueling, her children were grown. She was not willing to give up on her last Lost Boy, but worried she might never find his family. "The more time I spent with the science, the more I got involved mentally and you could say emotionally," she told a *Houston Chronicle* reporter. "I don't work on the case to the point that I can't get my other work done. But I come back to it when I can. Now it has become this trek that I'm on, and I have to finish it."

She knew that identifying any of the five missing boys whose stray bones had been recovered from the beach and the boatshed was a real long shot. Despite her discouragement, Derrick remained so committed to her search that she found it difficult to unplug, even when her eldest daughter, Jaye, gave birth to her first grandchild in 2013. She almost had to force herself to take a few days off to visit them out of state. She'd hit a wall, but sensed more discoveries ahead.

Finally, in 2014, Derrick received another DNA report from UNT's Center for Human Identification with a huge surprise—another Lost Boy had been found. The DNA sample from the arm bones that she had sent away for testing in 2008, initially believing they belonged to Randy Harvey, had matched someone else: the siblings of Donnie Falcon.

In Donnie Falcon's case, the DNA match with Dana and a brother proved very strong. There was no internal debate in the Harris County ME's office about the ID. But pathologists raised another issue: Since only four bones had been recovered, there wasn't enough evidence to declare Donnie Falcon to be a murder victim. Wolf, the office's by-the-book deputy director, and Sanchez, the chief medical examiner, agreed that Donnie Falcon's cause and manner of death should be listed as "unknown."

Sharon Derrick understood their argument. In theory, Donnie Falcon could even be alive and just missing parts of both arms. But she felt sure Donnie was among Dean Corll's victims. *Why else would any of his bones have been found buried inside Corll's boatshed?* Derrick knew that the old photo she had of Donnie as a small boy probably didn't resemble him as a seventeen-year-old but attempted to contact David Brooks about Donnie anyway. In August 1973, Brooks had told police about a Mexican American boy who dared to fight Corll. That boy had been fatally shot when Corll lived somewhere on Bellefontaine—a street near Brays Bayou that was near the apartment where Donnie lived in 1971. Perhaps Brooks, reticent as he was, might remember Donnie's face as someone he'd seen with Dean Corll. Texas prison officials soon sent back a message: Brooks did not recognize Donnie.

THE NEWS OF THE DNA match thrilled Dana Falcon Jones. It gave her an answer and it meant she could bring some of her little brother home. At her request, his bones were turned over to an undertaker for cremation and then shipped to Corpus in a small box. She brought his ashes inside their family house, lately painted a brilliant blue. This time the remains were shipped through official channels, which meant Derrick didn't immediately get to meet Dana—though much later they found a way to celebrate together in Corpus Christi, sharing sandwiches, iced tea, and a long hug.

Derrick meeting with Dana Falcon Jones and Dana's daughter Debra Christy in Corpus Christi

Dana Falcon Jones was a storyteller, though her smooth voice had been roughened by time and by the long hours she worked at the betting window of the Corpus Christi Greyhound Track. Even after the dogs stopped racing, she kept charming customers as they picked their favorites, placed bets, and prepared to watch simulcasts on big screens. Sometimes she told regulars about her beloved baby brother, who'd been abducted and killed by Dean Corll during a dark chapter in Texas history. Dana knew the ashes she received represented only pieces of her brother. Part of the same arms that had toted a surfboard and hugged her babies. For her, that was enough. She kept the box with her in the house they'd shared. To her, his homecoming seemed like a miracle.

Unofficially, Derrick counts Donnie Falcon as one of Corll's murder victims. *But where were the rest of his bones?*

Derrick had studied Houston police reports about the boatshed search and knew some officers feared two bodies had been left behind even in 1973. She had practically memorized the crude hand-drawn diagrams created by Houston and Pasadena police. From crime scene photos, she could tell that police and prisoners digging with shovels had sometimes gotten so impatient that they had forcefully hauled bodies out of the clay gumbo, leaving smaller bones behind. Some remains recovered from the eleven different "holes," like Donnie's, were in graves that seemed to overlap.

A 1973 autopsy report showed the bones of Randy Harvey had been mingled with the unidentified bones of a much younger boy— perhaps the one whose cranium she had examined. Based on her interpretation of those diagrams, Donnie's four bones had been buried near the remains of two other boys: ML 73-3350, the body identified in 1985 as Rusty Branch, a Houston police officer's son, and ML 73-3356, the teen with the swimming suit who remained unidentified. It seemed the killers might have buried some victims in shallower graves on top of older graves as the shed filled with bodies.

The original search had not gone deep enough, Derrick thought, nor had the shed footprint been thoroughly excavated. Officers had focused on places where the earth was humped or had clearly been disturbed. The rest of Donnie's bones were probably still there.

The search of Corll's boatshed had ended in twenty-four hours. No one ever set up a formal search grid, though even back in the 1800s, archaeologists were already beginning to suspend precisely measured strings across a dig area in order to systematically excavate mass burial sites and accurately map finds. By the 1970s, some military and law enforcement agencies had begun to use those same methods to systematically investigate complex outdoor death scenes, but that didn't happen at the boatshed in Houston. Nor did the diggers use hand trowels or screens to sift through clay from graves to find smaller bones or pieces of property, as is routine for modern body recovery sites. "Bone can look like rock. It might not be really recognizable. . . . Every piece goes through a sieve—that might be teeth, that might be bullets, that might be pieces of clothing or other evidence that's very important to the case," explains Dr. Dawnie Wolfe Steadman, director of the Anthropology Research Facility, in a training video about the body recovery exercises regularly conducted at the University of Tennessee and other body farms.

The shed where Corll once rented space remains on dead-end Silver Bell Drive in Houston. For years, the metal stall that once held hidden graves has housed mowers, tractors, and rakes or other equipment and supplies belonging to landscaping businesses. *That shed should be searched again,* Derrick thought. This time, she or others trained in forensic anthropology could thoroughly map the area, sift and sort through dirt, and record the exact locations of any finds, whether that be only scraps of clothing, tiny bones, or entire skeletons. Every item could be photographed and bones or teeth sent away for DNA testing. Maybe they'd be able to recover more of Donnie's bones—or those belonging to that little boy.

But that was a dream, Derrick knew. She would need other allies even to gain access to that shed. The only way a search could happen is if the owners of the private property agreed—or if Pasadena or Houston police reopened these murder cases and a judge issued a warrant or perhaps an exhumation permit.

Dana Falcon Jones hoped that a new search could happen someday—though she already felt sure she knew what had happened to her brother and where his killers had buried him. But under Texas laws, it appeared that she had no legal standing to insist on an excavation of his presumed burial site even as his next of kin.

Even Sharon Derrick had only so much authority over the Lost Boys cases. In the time she had left at the Harris County ME's office, she refocused on the other remaining unknown victim linked to the Corll cases. She still badly wanted to know his name.

THE LOST BOYS

THE SIXTH ID:

Donnie Falcon, 2014 (unannounced)

Donnie Falcon disappeared from his home in Houston in July 1971.

Donnie, a gifted drummer and surfer,

Donnie Falcon, portrait by Nancy Rose

had recently relocated to Houston from his hometown of Corpus Christi. His murder has never been officially counted with Corll's other victims, mainly because so few of his bones were recovered from the boatshed in August 1973. For years, four of his bones were commingled with other remains and forgotten. Those bones, found near another body labeled Case No. ML 73-3350, were given the case number ML 73-3350 A. His sister came forward in 2001, and more than a decade later, through new DNA tests, his bones were linked to his siblings. The rest of his remains are missing.

With this identification, Corll's confirmed death toll rose to 30.

CHAPTER 32

AN ANONYMOUS TIP

HARRIS COUNTY MEDICAL EXAMINER'S OFFICE, 2012

I N 2012, SHARON DERRICK began getting odd emails from a controversial independent film director named Josh Vargas, who was developing a fictionalized biopic about Dean Corll, Wayne Henley, and David Brooks called *In a Madman's World*. Vargas, who had got his start acting as a monster in Houston haunted houses and graduated to filming zombie shorts, had big ideas for this pseudo docudrama that Derrick found disturbing. Vargas began their first phone conversation by "bragging about how Henley was working with him," Derrick recalls. To her, the young director came off as arrogant, boasting about how he'd interviewed Henley at least a hundred times in prison and by phone. He'd begun writing a script based largely on Henley's version of events. Though Vargas claimed his film would not depict graphic violence, he planned to hire actors and film re-creations of abductions and attacks, including scenes with the torture board, inside some of the same Houston houses or apartments where Corll had actually lived. His actors would be using clothing supplied by Henley's mother that had supposedly been stored away since 1973, Vargas told Derrick. And that was part of why he was calling her.

Some items still had blood on them, Vargas said.

"He thought the old blood might help us identify a boy," Derrick recalls. To her, the entire project sounded horrifying. She worried about the film's effect on the victims' many aging parents, siblings, and friends who still lived in Houston.

BACK IN AUGUST 1973, Houston lacked any services for crime victims or support groups for the families of murdered or missing persons, like the ones Texans later formed to provide mutual support and to lobby for victim-centered reforms. Many grief-stricken relatives of the murdered and missing boys killed by Dean Corll never got any counseling at all.

Decades after her son's murder, Elaine Zorman Dreymala still displays Stanton's last smiling junior high portrait, along with a group shot of his soccer team and other favorite photos in a hallway gallery beside many more images of Michelle, her living daughter. She treasures the memories of her son and their rituals: His favorite song was "Loves Me Like a Rock" by Paul Simon, and they sang it together every morning on the way to school. "Our family bike rides in the evening were a special time for us. We all rode together in a group." Still, she was sometimes tempted to tell people who casually asked that she had only one child. Only rarely did she confide that she'd lost a baby soon after his birth. She loved talking about her other son, Stanton, but dreaded retelling how he had become Dean Corll's last murder victim. Those memories were so painful. Stanton had called from Corll's place to say he'd been invited to a party; his father had sternly warned him to come home. Later both parents wished their boy had mentioned an address or hinted he was in trouble in that call or in another he made to a friend. They figured, from what they read later, that Corll compelled Stanton to make those calls, as he'd done with other victims.

Stanton's death had been so hard to accept that for a long time after his disappearance, she'd kept setting an extra plate at the family dinner table. After reading about Derrick's discovery of ID errors in other cases, the family requested DNA tests, even though their son's ID had been confirmed in 1973 through dental records. Fortunately, genetic tests verified the match.

The Dreymalas, who live in Pasadena, and many other families of Corll's twenty-seven known victims from 1973 never met, except perhaps briefly at one of the court hearings or murder trials. And certainly, the sisters and mothers of the Lost Boys who'd been identified after 2006, largely through the efforts of Sharon Derrick, generally did not know other victims' families. Then, in the 2010s, some Lost Boys' relatives began swapping experiences on a private Facebook group launched by Michelle Dreymala Wilson, Stanton's grown-up baby sister. She initially made the page public, but realized that oddballs and murderabilia fans were trying to post, so she locked it down and tried to screen members to provide a safe space for victims' friends and family to exchange information. In large part, relatives began using the page to organize and boost opposition to seemingly endless rounds of parole hearings that came up for Wayne Henley and David Brooks every year or two under state laws in place since the 1970s.

Michelle's big brother had been abducted on August 3, 1973, only five days before Henley killed Corll. At thirteen, he'd been one of the youngest known victims. By the 2010s, Elaine and James Dreymala, Stanton and Michelle's mother and father, were among the few surviving parents who continued to be healthy enough to drive north to Palestine or south to Angleton (100 to 350 miles round trip depending on the location) to protest in person at parole hearings for Brooks and Henley, adding their voices to those of other victims' siblings. But those trips had become a struggle. Once, their Cadillac broke down on busy Interstate 45, forcing them to seek parts and emergency repairs along a rural stretch of the busy highway. They had to phone for a ride, though they ultimately made the meeting.

Over time, the Dreymalas and other victims' relatives collaborated with the crime victim advocate Andy Kahan, who later became the executive director of the nonprofit Crime Stoppers of Houston, to lobby the Texas legislature to increase the interval between parole reviews for Henley and Brooks, and others convicted of particularly violent crimes. Eventually they were successful, limiting the reviews to once a decade. In yet another effort, Randy Harvey's two sisters and Kahan pushed for a law in 2009 that enabled family members of murder victims killed years (or decades) before their bodies were identified to qualify for the same financial assistance provided to more recent crime victims' families. In April 2009, Derrick wrote to a legislator in support of the reform:

> Upon the unexpected notification that Randy had been identified after 35 years, Randy's family grieved for him all over again. Then they began the process of arranging his funeral [and] applied for Crime Victim's Compensation. Unfortunately, the current law does not provide for disbursement of funds to families whose loved one was murdered prior to January 1, 1980, so Randy's family was left on their own. . . . This scenario, while relatively rare, will continue to occur throughout our state as scientific methods for identification advance.

The bill passed—and was dubbed the Randy Harvey Law—a victory victims' relatives celebrated in their Facebook group.

The prospect of an independent film centered on Henley's version of their loved ones' murders angered the Dreymalas and others, who reacted strongly to statements Vargas made about his project to the *Houston Press*. In the 2013 interview, he admitted that his film would hurt people and make them sick, but argued it would have *a historical meaning*. "I knew that there was a worthwhile story to tell buried under the gruesome details of that case, and I wanted to be the one to tell it," Vargas said. He'd spoken mostly to Henley, but said he'd gotten hooked on the story because one of his best friend's uncles had been killed by Corll and claimed to have communicated with other victims' families. He certainly spoke with Rhonda Williams, who agreed to cooperate and had begun doing her own interviews with the *Houston Press*, *Texas Monthly*, and KTRK TV about how she'd survived Corll's torture board.

By the 2010s, Williams had come to see herself as a heroine. She repeatedly professed the belief that she alone had persuaded Wayne to kill Dean Corll and that otherwise she and Tim Kerley would have ended up dead, and Corll's killing spree would have remained undetected. In 2011, she told Skip Hollandsworth of *Texas Monthly*:

"Whatever evil was in Wayne, there was still some good in him, and finally the good won. Wayne saved my life, and he saved Tim's life too. Wayne killed the devil." Rhonda Williams had left Houston soon after testifying against Henley in 1974. A juvenile judge intervened, arranging for her to live in foster care far away from her abusive father and under an assumed name. Although she suffered from PTSD, Williams had slowly reassembled her life. She became a social worker, determined, she said, to help neglected and abused kids like the girl she'd once been. (Williams also wanted to write her story, but didn't finish before her death in 2019.)

Many murder victims' family members were angry with Vargas— and with Williams. Some questioned why Williams hadn't told police more about Wayne Henley when her boyfriend, Frank, disappeared in 1972—and why in the world she'd dated Henley and, after all these years, contacted him in prison. Everyone feared Vargas would depict Henley, a convicted serial killer, as a hero.

Elaine Zorman Dreymala, Stanton's mother, vastly preferred to recall her towheaded son Stanton's happy first thirteen years, playing with the tight-knit block of neighbor kids, riding his bike, playing cornet in the junior high band, and meeting his very first girlfriend at church camp. His mother wanted to be left to dream about what his adult life might have been, rather than confront actors' grisly reenactments of murders. As part of a thread of angry responses to Vargas in their Facebook group, she wrote: "He did not meet with us. However, I don't want to talk to him or have anything to do with this piece of sensational trash. I had nightmares last night just reading the post. . . . Vargas is obviously just as twisted as the people he is writing about." She later posted again, after watching an excerpt of the film. "I am so full of anger and rage this morning that I don't even have the words to say all I am feeling," she wrote. "I feel sorry for all of the family members that may have watched last night because I know they must be feeling just like I do today. So many things came flooding back in a moment and it was torture. As for Henley, most of you know how I feel about him so I won't go into that again. I just pray for everyone that is hurting this morning may find the strength to go on."

BEHIND THE SCENES, JOSH Vargas kept reaching out to Derrick. "He emailed a few times and then sent a photo that he claimed was of a living boy who had been locked inside the body box," she recalls. She discarded his emails but remembers Vargas saying, "Henley said not to give this to you but I thought you should have it." The blurred photo, supposedly a copy of the Polaroid original found in a stash of Henley's castoffs in an abandoned school bus, showed a dark-haired adolescent with an unidentifiable face crouched in a confined space. Later that boy's identity—and the photo's authenticity—became the subject of online debates after Vargas and others shared it with un-solved mystery bloggers, online forums, Reddit, and true crime pod-casts. Some declared the boy to be a terrified Corll victim, obviously being stuffed into the infamous "body box." Others argued the image was an obvious fake.

Derrick didn't know what to think. Her impression was that the boy seemed to be crouching at the bottom of a stairwell, not inside the wooden crate Corll and the others used to transport corpses. (She had seen a photo of the body box, used as an exhibit in Henley's trials.) She and Wolf, the deputy director, reviewed an enlargement and concluded they could not determine anything about the teen's identity or even whether the photo was authentic. Wolf said, "I can't tell if it's a boy or a girl. We're not going to follow up on this." Later Derrick wondered if Vargas deliberately leaked the image to pro-mote his film, which was released in 2017. She never watched it.

RICK STATON, A FORMER Baton Rouge, Louisiana, licensed under-taker and well-known dealer of items he peddled as murderabilia, circulated his own copy of that Polaroid. For years, Staton adver-tised and sold paintings Wayne Henley had created, along with copies of a photo of Corll at the Henleys' dinner table, via Facebook. Staton also peddled art and miscellanea associated with other kill-ers, including primitive clowns painted by John Wayne Gacy, his longtime pen pal. In an interview for the Florida-based *Criminal*

Perspective podcast, Staton described the Polaroid as depicting "a victim of serial killer Dean Corll" whose photo was found in the "belongings of Elmer Wayne Henley, Jr."

Back in 1973, authorities had apparently never obtained a warrant to search Henley's mother's house for bloodied clothing, weapons, or photos that could have been used as evidence. Apparently into the 2010s, she (or someone else) was still selling or renting candids of Corll, along with her son's castoff possessions and paintings. (A Texas law banning prisoners from profiting from selling items linked to their notoriety does not apply to family members.)

As buzz about "the Boy in the Box" increased, Derrick received a call from Bradley Yates, whose brother Danny is considered Corll's second known murder victim. Bradley believed the photo depicted Jim Glass, the neighbor teen who disappeared with his brother in December 1970. He told her he recognized the boy's unusual gray-and-white-patterned shirt as one he'd owned but that his little brother had borrowed and given to Jim. Maybe Bradley Yates was right. If so, the Boy in the Box was a murder victim who'd been identified in August 1973.

DERRICK HAD OTHER PHOTOS of a boy described as a Corll murder victim that she took more seriously. In July 2010, in her office mailbox, Derrick had received an oversized manila envelope postmarked New Orleans, Louisiana. It had no return address. Inside were five clear color Polaroids of another dark-haired teenager posing shirtless on a bed, some in profile, some with his gaze cast down, and some staring at the camera. The boy, who looked fifteen to seventeen, had thick bangs, flushed cheeks, and prominent eyebrows. On the back of the manila envelope someone had printed in pen in all caps, PHOTOGRAPHS OF BOBBY FRENCH, DEAN CORLL'S ELEVENTH VICTIM, TAKEN BY DAVID BROOKS APPROXIMATELY FIFTEEN MINUTES BEFORE THE MURDER.

Derrick was startled by those images: This youthful stranger's face somewhat resembled the skull reconstruction she'd gotten from FACES for the boy with the striped swimsuit, but this dark-haired

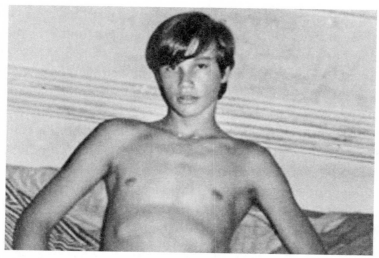

One of the photos of "Bobby French" that Derrick received anonymously

teen was alive, tanned, bare-chested, and animated. In some photos, he appeared to be gazing seductively into the lens. *Was the anonymous sender a friend of Brooks's or of Henley's who wanted to help? Or were these from the murderabilia dealer?* If Rick Staton was the source, as far as she could tell, he'd never posted them for sale or publicized their existence on his Facebook page or in podcasts. She could think of no easy way to verify the tip, but her gut told her that it seemed worth pursuing.

Off and on, for years, Derrick quietly searched missing persons reports and other databases for adolescents named Robert French or Bobby French. In her free time, she used her Ancestry.com account to run searches of yearbooks and of Texas birth certificates for males with variations on those names born in Houston between 1950 and 1960—since Corll's victims had all been between thirteen and twenty years old. A few seemed like possibilities. An Aldine High School yearbook showed a student named Robert French, who seemed to resemble "Bobby." But records and conversations with classmates proved that boy lived to adulthood and died in East Texas. Corll's maternal aunt and uncle were Frenches, but they had only one adopted daughter. A man named French worked with Corll at Houston Lighting & Power, but had no son named Bobby. In desperation, Derrick published the name and a photo. Still, no one seemed to know about any missing boy named French.

She felt haunted by the steady gaze of the adolescent dubbed Bobby French by an anonymous tipster. Perhaps this boy had moved to Houston from Louisiana. It was harder to do research in Louisiana, since parish marriage, birth, and death records weren't generally searchable online. Or maybe Bobby French was not this murder victim's real name. More than anything else, the provocative photos Derrick had received suggested that this winsome dark-haired boy with flashing eyes might have been one of the teenagers photographed by Dean Corll. Derrick knew about Corll's collection of photos of adolescent boys—she'd reviewed copies of them from police files, looking for clues. And Corll had bragged to Brooks and Henley that he was part of a ring that produced pornography and traded boys for sex. Someone out there knew this boy. And someone had taken these photos—but who and why?

PART V

PLAYERS IN A PORN RING

CHAPTER 33

THE ACCOMPLICES IN THE SHADOWS

HOUSTON, 1973–1976

IN AUGUST 1973, WAYNE Henley and David Brooks, interviewed separately in different cities, each told police that Dean Corll was part of what would later be called a sex trafficking ring. "Dean told me that he belonged to an organization out of Dallas that bought and sold boys, ran whores, and stuff like that. Dean told me that he would pay me $200 for every boy I could get for him and maybe more if they were real good-looking boys," Henley told the Pasadena police. David Brooks, questioned separately in Houston, said that Corll belonged to a group that actively moved boys to California for paid liaisons with older male customers. "During one of our conversations Dean mentioned that there was a group of people in Dallas which had similar activities to his. He mentioned a man by the name of Art who he said had also killed some boys."

Shortly before he ended up killing Corll, Wayne Henley told several people he was fixing to leave the state with Corll and with his girlfriend, Rhonda Williams. On the day of Corll's murder, Rhonda told police that Henley already had visited "Dallas several times with Dean and that a warehouse was in Dallas where [I] could make $1,500 a week doing something illegal." Wayne supposedly never told her exactly what that was.

The father of two brothers killed by Corll in 1971, Everett Waldrop, repeatedly named Roy Ames, a Houston-based record producer and a friend of Corll's, first as a kidnapping suspect and later as a likely accomplice in their murders. Waldrop and his wife both told police in 1971 that their missing children, Donald and Jerry, had been hanging out with Ames and other homosexual men who had been photographing them before they vanished, according to HPD reports. Houston officers followed up on one of the Waldrops' tips and discovered that Ames had active warrants and a history of complaints involving lewd photos and photographing nude boys. But they made only one documented attempt to question him and gave up after a man at a commercial photography studio, an address Ames used, claimed he "did not know Ames but is always getting [his] bills and mail." Everett Waldrop tried to investigate on his own, and said he informed police that they should search Corll's boatshed before Henley did. After his boys' bodies were found there, he again urged police to question Ames, but reports do not indicate that happened. Waldrop complained that everything he'd dug up had been ignored. "I don't expect justice," Waldrop told the *Houston Chronicle* in August 1973. "There's just no justice in Houston."

In the days and weeks after the murders were discovered, tipsters and detectives from Dallas, San Diego, and Los Angeles reached out to Pasadena and Houston officers with more information about Corll's alleged involvement in a boy porn ring. One California police informant claimed he'd been sent to Houston, where he'd attended a party with Corll and been photographed by Ames. The tipster told police that "Roy Ames knew Dean Corll and used him to exploit young boys."

Even Selma Winkle, who'd once worked at Corll's candy shop and knew him better than other murdered children's parents, believed more players were involved. She'd known Corll as an exceptionally hard worker, and recalled how Malley on weekends and after school had cleaned steel vats for Corll, scraping off the floor and sweeping up broken pieces of pecans and candy. "My personal belief is there's a big ring behind this whole thing. A ring from no telling where. I don't believe that one man could take all these children and do this and live without his conscience killing him."

PASADENA AND HOUSTON POLICE essentially closed the Corll/Henley homicide cases in September 1973—after about a month. A Harris County grand jury quickly indicted Brooks and Henley. No other accomplice was ever charged, though other teens who knew Corll or Henley were asked to give statements or to testify before the grand jury. By law, grand jury testimony is secret. Then in a startling departure from typical court procedure, the foreman, a Houston optometrist named Don Cherry, and other grand jurors prepared a blistering report on the investigation that they delivered to District Court Judge Miron Love in October 1973. The grand jurors' report was never made public, but some findings leaked. The *Houston Post* and *Houston Chronicle* both published excerpts in November, including allegations that the police and DA's investigations "lacked professional imagination, thoroughness and professional coordination." Among other complaints, grand jurors alleged that authorities abandoned the investigation too soon, leaving unexplored "the possible involvement of others and related criminal activities." The report blamed the Harris County DA for failing to follow up. "There appeared to us to be a lack of inquiry into a number of important details." The DA's office did not properly communicate with police on whether its personnel had investigated a "wealth of leads," grand jurors concluded. "There was no feedback to the police on this case whatsoever."

Officials quickly counterattacked: Chief Short dismissed the grand jurors as "silly." DA Vance said: "We will continue our investigation and continue to run down leads whether they turn out to be wild-goose chases or productive." Vance noted he'd assigned an assistant district attorney to the murders full-time, something he'd never done before. But behind the scenes, some investigators were grumbling that they lacked manpower and resources.

ON APRIL 5, 1975, Roy Clifton Ames, the same man who multiple tipsters had named years before as Corll's associate, was arrested at the Travelodge Motel on Heights Boulevard, a few blocks from Hamilton Junior High, and charged with distributing child pornography based on literally tons of evidence uncovered by Houston Police and by federal postal inspectors. In searches of a warehouse, office, and other locations, officials seized more than a hundred thousand pornographic publications, films, and other more personal items that Ames's attorney later tried to recover, including Ames's collection of toupees and sound recordings. Ames was charged with distributing pornography across state lines in the federal court for the Southern District of Texas. He was separately charged with related state felonies in Harris County, including sexually assaulting at least three minor boys and colluding with a group of local men to distribute child pornography internationally.

But there was an even bigger bombshell hidden inside Ames's immense cache. A small group of officers assigned to review those images revealed to reporters that at least eleven of Corll's murder victims were pictured in that porn collection. Incredibly, neither Roy Clifton Ames nor police ever commented on why or how so many of Corll's murder victims appeared in the pornographer's stash. Officers never publicly identified those eleven boys or specified whether their photos had been taken on the same days or weeks that they'd been kidnapped, tortured, raped, and murdered. What little they did say was that the porn ring had been operating in Houston for a long time. Many boys in those photos were alive, including adults who had been photographed years before.

In a pretrial motion filed in Harris County court related to the state sex crime charges, Ames's lawyer, Hugh Lowe, argued that prosecutors should not be allowed to make remarks linking Ames to "the so-called homosexual mass murders or the Coryll [sic]-Henley affair in which a number of youths were apparently killed in the Houston area." In his motion, Lowe did not bother to spell Corll's surname correctly. Ames was swiftly convicted of federal mail-order pornography charges and shipped off to a prison in Missouri to serve what was supposed to be a fifteen-year sentence. Once Ames was locked away, Harris County prosecutors dropped the state charges, including allegations that Ames sexually assaulted teens who were still alive, including a Heights boy who had known at least two of Corll's murder victims and been invited by Brooks and Henley to attend a party.

In a 1976 news story, Lt. H. A. Contreras, then one of the few Latino officers in HPD's senior ranks, admitted that police knew Ames was involved with more than collecting and distributing pornography of underaged boys. Ames participated in a "shuttle service" to supply boys to customers, an arrangement that seemed similar to the kind of schemes that decades later billionaire Jeffrey Epstein would be accused of involving teenaged girls. "We knew that they were shipping kids—boy prostitutes—boys back and forth to the west coast in the Ames's deal," Contreras said. "But they just never got time to work that . . . Ames and some of his people were engaged in this. They would send California kids here and Houston kids to California." Indeed, FBI agents caught Ames mass-mailing child pornography in 1968, though he avoided arrest.

In September 1976, J. P. "Jigsaw John" St. John, a Los Angeles homicide detective, traveled to Texas with his partner, Kent McDonald, to explore similarities between the Houston cases and the murders of eleven teenagers in California. St. John, who later became nationally known as an expert in serial slayings after working on the Hillside Strangler and the Night Stalker cases, told Texas police that the California homicides he was investigating "bore strong similarities" to the methods by which Corll's victims were "tortured and killed." Those cases involved a homosexual killer who also used accomplices to kidnap, rape, and kill teenaged boys and then dump their bodies on roadsides. (St. John eventually solved the California cases, but if he found links to Corll he never revealed them before his death in 1995.)

Pasadena's Detective Mullican and two HPD detectives accompanied the Californians to two prisons in Brazoria County, south of Houston. They visited Henley at the Ramsey II Unit but found him "very hostile," Mullican wrote in a report. Then they traveled thirty miles south to see Brooks, who was brought into the Warden's office at the Clemens Unit for an interview. Brooks previously told HPD that Corll had Dallas contacts whose activities were similar to his.

This time, Brooks added that Corll was "super secretive about his mail, picking it up at a Post Office Box, reading it and then destroying it." Curiously, case files don't indicate whether Henley or Brooks were questioned about Ames or about the pornographer's photos featuring eleven murder victims.

During their last conversation in 2007, Brooks told Sharon Derrick that Corll participated in a "gay pornography ring" that included "sending doped up kids to California" to work for porn flicks. Some Texas boys told him they were going out of state for high-paying jobs—and were never heard from again. "All that was true," Brooks said. "And no one fully investigated at the time . . . there are things that no one is going to know." (He never revealed more before dying in 2020 of COVID-19.)

Only one of Corll's murder victims whose image was found in searches of the items seized from pornographers was identified in police reports: fifteen-year-old Billy Lawrence.

The story of Billy's disappearance and murder show that by the terrible summer of 1973, Corll and Henley and their allies were increasingly operating in the open, and their killing spree was spiraling out of control.

CHAPTER 34

AN ATTEMPTED ESCAPE

HOUSTON AND PASADENA, TEXAS, SPRING 1973

BILLY LAWRENCE, AT FIFTEEN, had oversized eyes framed by long dark hair, and even a glance from him would thrill his nine-year-old neighbor, Michele Boudreaux. In an era when Donny Osmond's "Puppy Love" looks and long dark locks regularly made the cover of *Tiger Beat,* her neighbor Billy was handsome enough to appear in magazines too, she thought. "I had a crush on him. He used to make fun of my hair being shorter than his. I went and got my hair cut into a pixie, and his was long, starting to grow past his shoulders."

Billy Lawrence's photo, found on Corll's dresser circa 1973 and later used as a murder trial exhibit

Billy was a bit of a rebel. He hung beaded curtains across the door of his bedroom and spray-painted his name on the back wall of his garage. Often he tucked that sweet face deep inside the hood of a Baja poncho, the signature cotton garb of California surfers and Houston's aspiring hippies. (Michele kept one of his ponchos and, decades later, sometimes still slips it on.)

Her dad, L. N. Boudreaux, Jr., a state trooper with the Texas Department of Public Safety, grew up with Horace "Jimmy" Lawrence, Billy's father, in the industrialized Denver Harbor neighborhood, near the Port of Houston. Both men later bought comfortable homes for their families on large lots in Garden Oaks, a peaceful neighborhood that seemed a world apart from the heavily polluted area where they'd met as children. But Trooper Boudreaux, strict with his own kids, told them he didn't approve of how Billy had begun hanging out at the neighborhood pool hall, the Cue Club, or of the friends he'd made there.

In the spring of 1973, Billy stood five feet eleven and had grown brawny from training to play football at Booker T. Washington High School, a formerly all-Black school where he'd been assigned as part of Houston ISD's integration efforts. Michele knew, vaguely, that her idol sometimes got in trouble. That year, he and other teens regularly roamed their neighborhood, a suburb outside Houston's core city where homes sat on landscaped quarter- or half-acre lots, far more space than what separated the Heights' chockablock bungalows. She liked to watch Billy play football with the older boys in those shady yards. Billy was almost unfailingly amiable, but some of his new friends seemed rough or even dangerous. One was Wayne Henley.

Billy Lawrence often stopped by the Boudreauxs' place. He'd cut through lawns with towering pines along a path only neighborhood kids knew in order to avoid looping around the block. Michele's stay-at-home mom often made meals for him even if it wasn't suppertime. Sometimes Michele's mom fixed breaded cube steak for dinner as a special treat and then let Billy pick off the crust—something she would never allow her own children to do. For some unexplained reason, her mother seemed to think Billy needed help and protection. She had even suggested they adopt Billy, whose father was a widower. Michele's busy trooper father scoffed at that. If Billy had troubles, he didn't share them. Michele knew his father drank, because Billy sometimes showed up when his dad was on a bender. She was unaware that Mr. Lawrence, although loving while sober, tended to pummel Billy when he was not.

ANOTHER HOUSTON TEEN REMEMBERS that in the spring of 1973 Billy Lawrence arrived unannounced one day at the Henley house on West 27th Street in the Heights—a hot seven-block walk from his Garden Oaks home down Yale Street that required ducking across the traffic milling around the elevated 610 Loop. Billy's nose was bloody; he'd been beaten. He told the other boys, who had gathered there to smoke pot, that his father hit him and he couldn't go back.

Gary Gibson was hanging out at the Henleys' that afternoon. He remembers seeing Billy sitting on the edge of Wayne's twin bed with a bloody nose and crying. "Billy was an adorable sweet kid," Gary recalls. Gary, about five years older than Billy, wanted to help and offered advice: "Go back to your dad. Just try to avoid him. The streets are much worse than your dad could ever be." That time, Billy Lawrence listened.

AS THE 1972–73 SCHOOL year ended, Billy Lawrence seemed to be running around with increasingly large groups of teens in Garden Oaks, Michele recalls. He and Wayne Henley and the others seemed to be using the yards and a nearby park as a staging ground for outings and activities she didn't understand. Some nights, those older boys stayed out late in the park, drinking or smoking weed (she knew what it smelled like, even then) and spray-painting graffiti on bathroom walls and picnic shelters. One morning, her father woke to find his police cruiser vandalized in their driveway. Someone had scratched the word PIG in huge letters and spray-painted DUKIE— childish 1970s slang for crap—on the side of the sedan. Sometimes, those same boys appeared to be playing a rougher version of hide-and-go-seek. Once, Michele saw a teen she didn't know crouching in the ditch in front of their house—so scared he looked pale and was literally shaking. For a while, on her mother's invitation, he left his hiding place and came to sit on the porch. A few minutes later, when

326 | THE SCIENTIST AND THE SERIAL KILLER

Wayne Henley pulled up in a beige sedan, the other boy seemed reluctant to leave. Henley was persuasive, obviously a leader, but she
wondered why someone who seemed so frightened would follow
him. "To me it seemed dumb," she recalls. "Now I wonder if he was
afraid that boy would hurt him or one of the moms if he didn't go."

Sometimes Michele saw big groups of teens piling into a white
van or the boxy sedan that Wayne Henley drove. Billy didn't say
where they went, though a tipster later told police that Houston
boys were being hauled to a ranch near the town of Brenham and to
private homes where they were photographed and filmed for magazines and movies featuring nude boys and sex acts.

Investigators in Houston and Pasadena eventually discovered
that some local boys were featured in a porn film shot on Padre Island; others appeared in magazines with names like *7 Up, Bonanza,
Gay Boy,* and *Hot Rods.* In one issue, *Hot Rods #3,* police found a
photo that looked just like Billy Lawrence—though his father didn't
want to believe it, the officers concluded "there is a good possibility
that it is the dead victim's photo." In December 1973, after the Corll/
Henley murder cases were officially "closed," police received a tip
that someone from California had visited a large warehouse in
Houston that held pornographic photos of some of the murdered
boys. At the time, police determined that the informant didn't have
"enough information to be of any further help to us."

The world of pornography—not just child pornography or pornography featuring homosexual acts—was largely hidden in the 1970s.
There was no internet and only limited venues showed sexually explicit films. The Harris County District Attorney's Office had tried
(and failed) to halt distribution of a 1972 film called *Deep Throat,*
which featured Linda Lovelace, an adult actress performing oral sex
on adult male actors. In the 1970s, that film had been banned as obscene in twenty-three states. Later, some participants were criminally
charged and the U.S. Supreme Court refused to review their convictions. It wasn't until 2002 when the Supreme Court reversed itself,
ruling in *Ashcroft v. Free Speech Coalition* that pornography between
consenting adults is a protected form of expression under the First
Amendment, even if some participants might appear to be juveniles.

In the 1970s, photographs, magazines, and videos of teens in the nude or performing sex acts were traded by networks of shadowy dealers who tracked their clandestine customers on note cards and developed huge mailing lists. It was against federal law to send sexually explicit images involving juveniles across state lines or abroad. Yet the forty-five-year-old leader of the porn group busted in Dallas in August 1973—only a week after Dean Corll's violent death—had amassed a hundred thousand customers' names and addresses. The ringleader, John Paul Norman, was accused of operating a "procurement" ring known as the Odyssey Foundation that offered dues-paying members a catalog of photos of young boys seeking "sponsors." Norman, a former schoolteacher, had been arrested in Houston for sexual assault in the 1950s and was subsequently linked to male teen pornography and prostitution cells in Illinois and in California.

Though Dean Corll claimed to have connections in Dallas, police in 1973 said they'd found no evidence that linked Corll to Norman. After posting bond in Dallas on multiple felony charges, Norman fled to the Chicago suburbs where he was arrested for indecent behavior with ten other teens and still managed to carry on his mail-order boy porn operation, according to a 1977 investigation by the *Chicago Tribune*. Over the years, Dallas and Houston police officials have continued to deny any ties between Corll and Norman. And yet in the 1970s, Chicago police sergeant Ron Kelley, head of the youth division, told the *Tribune* just the opposite: Dallas police had uncovered evidence connecting Norman's ring to Corll and to his murder victims.

Reporters also discovered that a lot of evidence that might have connected Norman to Corll was missing, lost, or locked away. Index cards with at least thirty thousand of the hundred thousand of Norman's customer names that the Dallas police confiscated in 1973 had been turned over to the U.S. State Department, and a State Department spokesman told the *Tribune* those cards had been destroyed because they were "not relevant to any fraud case concerning a passport." Why the cards had been sent to State, and not to the FBI, was never explained.

HARRIS COUNTY'S OWN COURT and police records show that Dean Corll was directly linked to another notorious child pornographer: Roy Clifton Ames, who, by the late 1970s, federal investigators and lawmakers alike had identified as a "major commercial dealer" of child pornography and one of the world's largest "boy porn" distributors.

Ames's federal prosecution prompted hearings in 1977 by members of the U.S. House of Representative's Judiciary Committee and by a Texas legislative committee formed to study the sexual exploitation of juveniles. Both groups reviewed evidence on Ames and others who promoted child pornography and prostitution and heard testimony on how existing federal and state laws failed to protect teenagers against predators. "This case probably earned the City of Houston the title of 'Kid Porn Capital of the World,'" the Texas legislature's special committee declared of Ames's operation. "Four and one quarter tons of porn and equipment were initially confiscated. Later two additional tons were seized by HPD."

Bizarrely, even after he'd become infamous as a convicted child porn distributor, Ames was never publicly investigated as a murder suspect or as Corll's alleged accomplice, according to the 1970s police, court, and prosecutors' files. At least once, Houston police officers did approach Ames after his arrest to see if he would be willing to offer up "information about other producers" as part of plea negotiations, according to Robin Lloyd, a journalist and author who researched the murders and the pornography case and testified to members of Congress about his findings. "In spite of the fact that Ames was facing a ten-year sentence, he laughed at the police and told them his operation would run just as well while he was in jail as it would if he were out," Lloyd said during the 1977 hearings on the "Sexual Exploitation of Children," held by the Subcommittee on Crime of the Committee on the Judiciary, House of Representatives. Lloyd also told lawmakers that Houston police had quietly estimated that Corll's "unholy trio had actually had sexual contact with possibly three hundred young boys, exclusive of the twenty-seven they murdered," findings he'd published in a related 1976 book about sexual exploitation of underaged boys, *For Money or Love: Boy Prostitution in America*. And the numbers of male teen hustlers in Houston didn't seem to decline even after Corll's murders were exposed. In fact, one thirteen-year-old told Lloyd that business "doubled overnight."

During those same 1977 federal hearings, Lloyd H. Martin, a veteran Los Angeles police officer and one of the founders of the city's unit to fight the sexual exploitation of children, testified that an estimated thirty thousand children in L.A. were being targeted by pedophiles and pornographers, including older men who preyed on teenaged boys. Nationwide, many more victims remained uncounted and largely invisible, Martin said. "To my knowledge, there is no other police department other than the Los Angeles Police Department dealing with this problem specifically. How extensive it is, no one knows, but I will tell you from my experience that it is gigantic," he said. Martin urged members of Congress to pass stronger laws to help exploited kids. The Mann Act had existed for years to cover the trafficking of women and girls across state lines, he said, but no federal law protected boys. "I will tell you that this problem is not only just in the state and city of Los Angeles, it goes all over the [nation] and I definitely think that we need something federally [so] that the Federal agencies can assist local law enforcement."

Even busts of major players like Roy Clifton Ames made little difference, witnesses lamented. Too often images produced and distributed of exploited kids—and even images of Dean Corll's murder victims—were copied, reused, and recycled forever. Separate public hearings were held by the special Texas legislative committee formed "to investigate juvenile delinquency" in 1977 and 1978. Many advocates for abused children turned out to testify in Houston, San Antonio, Austin, and Fort Worth and spelled out the ways minors were being exploited by Texas pornographers who produced films and magazines and operated through clandestine venues and the U.S. mail. Texas strengthened its child porn law, making it illegal to sell, distribute, or possess any video or still image of any person under seventeen engaged in sexual conduct. But as of January 1977, only six states outlawed child porn and many did not classify sexual abuse of teenagers as a felony.

The Texas law making child pornography a third-degree felony took effect four years after Corll's murders came to light. Still, no one discussed the links between Ames and the victims of Dean Corll, who remains one of America's most prolific killers. Roy Ames pleaded guilty to conspiracy to mail obscene material and three counts of distribution of obscene material in 1975 and ended up in a sex offender program in Springfield, Missouri. In 1981, he was indicted on more mail-order porn charges and earned another five-year sentence. But by 1986, he was released and resumed his public role as a Houston music producer, though he was later civilly sued by the families of musicians who claimed he'd illegally profited from some recordings. For years, Ames lived in the West University area and rolled around the city in a Jaguar. He never gave any published interviews about his relationship with Dean Corll before his death in 2003.

In early June 1973, Billy Lawrence turned up again unexpectedly at the house that Wayne Henley sometimes shared with his mother, grandmother, and little brothers on West 27th Street. Wayne often entertained his pot-smoking friends in a front bedroom. When Billy arrived, a small group was already passing around a joint. "He had a bloody nose, busted mouth, and both eyes blackened, like he'd gone through several rounds with a prizefighter," recalls Gary Gibson, who was partying at the Henleys' place again that day.

Though Billy Lawrence's father by then held a respectable job as a pressman, he was tough and had done prison time for bank robbery, Billy told the others. Billy was determined to run away; Gary tried again to change his mind. "You only have a little while longer now before you can leave and be an emancipated minor," Gary recalls saying. "Just go home, finish school. It can't be that bad. The streets are worse."

Wayne Henley had a different idea: "I'm going to take him to Dean."

Gary didn't know what that meant. He only knew that Wayne considered Dean Corll a protector and a sugar daddy. He had met

Corll at the Henley house once or twice; Corll sometimes stopped by for a meal or chatted with Wayne's mother and grandmother. But Gary didn't like or trust Corll. It wasn't because Corll was gay. Gary had nothing against homosexuals. Corll seemed cordial on the surface, but Gary sensed dangerous undercurrents. "He was one of those men who watched you."

Later, Gary came to wish he'd never met Corll or Wayne Henley. Wayne seemed to have a secret life; Gary suspected he was turning tricks at a bar called the Palace in Montrose, and stealing and doing illegal favors for Corll to earn cash he brought home to his mama. At that time, Wayne seemed constantly in motion between his house, Corll's place, and the home of a college student who worked at the Palace as a bartender. His mother, Mary Henley, pushed him to bring home cash, cigarettes, and beers and either didn't notice or didn't care that her son spent so much time quaffing beer, popping pills, huffing paint fumes, or smoking dope that he often couldn't string a sentence together.

By June 1973, even Wayne's little brothers began to talk about how many neighborhood kids had run away or disappeared. One day, one of the boys said: "Pretty soon there's going to be no boys in the neighborhood. They're all leaving and they don't come back." He threw out a number of twenty missing kids, Gary Gibson recalls. Gary grew up in Houston's Northside and did not know those missing boys, but the numbers seemed shocking. Looking back, he realizes that Wayne kept his friends compartmentalized, perhaps so no one would notice if someone suddenly vanished. After their second brief meeting, Gary never saw Billy Lawrence again, but he didn't know Billy well enough to wonder where he'd gone.

ENGROSSED IN HER OWN world of nine-year-old playmates, Michele Boudreaux didn't notice right away when her teen idol Billy Lawrence vanished in June 1973. She didn't see him every day and none of the adults in Garden Oaks openly discussed his running away. His father did not report him as missing until after the terrible discoveries in August 1973.

Jimmy Lawrence told police then that Wayne Henley had be-friended his son that spring. He explained that he'd not reported his youngest's disappearance because Billy phoned after leaving home in June to explain that he'd gone fishing with friends at Lake Sam Rayburn, where Corll's family had a cabin and where Billy's body was later found. His father had been fooled by a letter, postmarked June 6, that captors likely compelled his son to write. Some of its words rang true: "I think we should stay apart for a while since we've been having trouble," Billy wrote. He told his father he'd gotten a summer job but promised to be home in time for school in August. He also told his father he loved him.

Horace J. Lawrence Jr., 310 W. 31st, 862-9947. Mr. Lawrence stated that on June 4th, 1973, his son, BILLY RAY LAWRENCE WM15, had left home. The night he left Billy called his father and told him that he was going to lake Sam Rayburn to go fishing. On June 11th, Mr. Lawrence received a letter from his son that was postmarked June 6th. In this letter Billy told him that he thought that they should stay apart for awhile as rhhey had been having trouble and that he was in Austin and would work there for the summer. He also stated that he would come back to Houston between 8-1-73 and 8-15-73. Mr. Lawrence has not heard from Billy since this letter.

Billy Lawrence contacted his father, likely at his killer's request

CORLL APPARENTLY GENUINELY LIKED Billy Lawrence. David Brooks met Billy during the three days the fifteen-year-old was living at Corll's house in Pasadena. Corll introduced Billy as "sort of a friend." Prosecutors later said Corll kept Billy Lawrence alive in captivity longer than any other known murder victim—long enough that it seems Billy might have seized an opportunity to try to escape.

MICHELE BOUDREAUX WAS PLAYING outside with some Garden Oaks neighbor boys one afternoon when Billy showed up on the path only local kids used. This time, he was walking by without stopping—though he hadn't visited their house in a while—and she felt of-fended. "Hi, Billy!" she called out, her voice tinged with hope that he would notice her.

Billy didn't smile or stop. He was surrounded on both sides by strangers who seemed to be clinging tightly to each of his arms. That seemed weird, but Michele didn't know what to make of it. Billy didn't reply, only briefly glanced back over his shoulder with a helpless expression. The others ignored her; one was a thin blond boy close to Billy's height. The other was a dark-haired adult whom she now believes was Dean Corll.

For months, Michele was offended that the teenaged boy she dreamed about had snubbed her. But after she learned about his murder, she saw their encounter in a different light. "I think he went home and they came back to get him . . . and that look was his way of saying 'Help.' And I didn't know what to do. And I have to live with that . . ." She remembers telling her parents that she'd seen Billy. But she didn't know where they took him, and Billy hadn't shouted for help. She never saw him again. Decades later, Michele remains convinced that if, as a child, she'd managed to make her voice heard, she could have saved Billy.

Her father, who is still alive, does not remember her story; perhaps no one believed her.

Years later, she ended up owning the house where Billy had lived. Inside the garage, she found his name still spray-painted on the wall. She never covered it up.

In a 2019 study, researchers for the National Center for Missing and Exploited Children found that many boys who were sexually abused and exploited were too afraid to speak out or had their cries for help go unheard. There's a misperception that only girls are sold for sex, writes Staca Shehan, who oversees the center's efforts to combat child sex trafficking. "The rape or sexual exploitation of boys? How often do you hear about that? There's a gap in knowledge with males." The stigma of being outed as a sexual assault victim and the fear of confronting predatory adults remains strong.

Looking back, Michele Boudreaux says: "I think people were scared. Some people just wanted it to go away because it was so painful. It was very painful. Some people felt like justice wasn't done." In the 1970s, authorities never publicly discussed the issue of how members of a Houston-based porn ring had targeted and exploited Billy Lawrence and other of Corll's victims. At some point, the family of another murdered boy was quietly informed that he too had been photographed and exploited by the same group: That boy's name was Willard K. "Rusty" Branch, Jr.—and he was the son of a Houston police officer.

CHAPTER 35

THE POLICE OFFICER'S SON

HOUSTON, 1971–1995

SUSAN MCLEMORE, A COP'S daughter, always thought there had to be more victims—and unidentified accomplices—of Dean Corll's 1970s rape and murder spree. She had good reason for her suspicions: For about two years before her big brother Rusty disappeared in February 1972, she'd accompanied him to parties at Corll's place. Rusty often had to babysit her while his dad was working long shifts as a supervisor in the Houston Police Department's communications division. But Rusty didn't particularly like being stuck at home with a little kid. Her brother, like other teens, had met Wayne Henley at the SPJST—the Czech fraternal order's Olympic-sized swimming pool in the Heights—and through Henley, he'd met Dean Corll. "And when Rusty was supposed to be taking care of me, he'd take me over to Dean's," she remembered.

Their parents were already divorced by the early 1970s, and the oldest Branch siblings, Rusty, Doug, and Susan, split their time between their father's place in Houston and their mother's in Texarkana, a grueling day-long Greyhound bus ride. She was eleven when her teenaged brother first took her along to party at Corll's. Even then, the girl with wavy brown hair was small for her age, and she perched under a Formica kitchen table, watching the action unfold. She eyed older teens who smoked pot, sniffed glue, and "bagged paint," spraying paint fumes into a paper bag and then sniffing the vapors. Sometimes they handed her bongs or bags too. "All these kids knew each other, [and] knew Henley or Brooks," she told a *Houston Chronicle* reporter in 1993. In the back bedrooms at those parties were older men who took photos and did other things that little kids, like her, were not allowed to see. As an adult, Susan insisted that she and her brother both attended Corll's parties and that their father, a hard-drinking HPD officer named Willard K. Branch, Sr., knew that. By 1972, her brother Rusty, seventeen, had dropped out of high school, gotten a job, and begun feuding more violently with their dad. Some of those battles involved Dean Corll, Susan said. She claimed their father knew Corll was regularly hosting parties attended by teenaged boys and got angry when he heard Corll had propositioned his son for sex and taken pictures.

Willard K. Branch, Sr., never attended the police academy, rising up through HPD's ranks because of his radio skills. He'd been a ham radio operator before joining the department. Although he became head of communications for the Houston Police Department and made captain before retiring, he displayed poor communication skills with his children. The eldest three Branch siblings had a rough childhood. As a small boy, Rusty Branch fell out of a two-story window and cracked his skull. By the time he was seven or eight, his little brother Doug, eighteen months younger, was already sniffing paint and glue fumes out of bags. After their parents divorced and their mother moved away, the children stayed behind with their dad, who promptly remarried and had a fourth child, a half sister the others nicknamed Sprout. That marriage didn't last either. (In fact, all three of Willard K. Branch, Sr.'s marriages involved domestic violence and ended in divorce, though the divorce from his third wife was not yet final when he died.)

His stepson, Ray Hunt, whose mother was Branch's third wife, later became a prominent police officer and union leader. Hunt said he joined HPD because he wanted to be the opposite of Branch, who represented everything a cop should not be. "He took Pearl beers in his lunchbox in the morning and often stayed drunk all day," Hunt remembers. Hunt emphasizes that his stepfather lacked the formal academy training required of all HPD officers today. Hunt serves a much different department, which reformed and modernized under a succession of diverse police chiefs and mayors.

In the 1960s, the eldest Branch brothers' largely unsupervised lives in Houston were broken up by summers at their paternal grandparents' dairy farm near the village of Saltillo in East Texas. The journey took eight rugged hours from Houston then—on highways that literally ran over the Trinity River and through the woods. After passing the city of Tyler, those roads undulated and towns got progressively smaller. Road signs for communities out that way reflected the flavor of the forest: Woodsboro, Pine Mills, and Shady Grove. The last stretch from Saltillo required a jagged turn down a single track barely the width of the family car and then another down the farm lane that dead-ended at Papaw and Granny's place. In the days before the region's factory chicken farms arrived, the Branches pastured their cattle in meadows hewn out of this hilly timber country, with its mixed stands of oak, pine, and elm that glow golden and auburn in the fall. There was always plenty to do each summer: muck out the barn, mow the grass with the push mower, and other chores on Papaw's long list.

Their cousins, who had stable homes and more traditional lives, remember Rusty and Douglas Branch as wild. They were sometimes appalled at stories the Branch boys shared of roaming urban streets and taking police cars for joyrides (and never getting arrested, since they were the sons of a cop). In the summers, their Papaw kept a tight rein, until his death in July 1970. Still, the brothers sometimes scandalized their rule-following relatives by loudly swearing and pulling stunts. One Sunday at the farm, Rusty whipped out his penis and took a whiz on his cousin's new corduroy wraparound skirt, which she'd donned for services at Greenwood Baptist Church.

Back home in Houston, Willard K. Branch, Sr., tended to target his current wife or his sons for punishment whenever he became intoxicated. Susan and her younger half sister were usually spared. The girls would pile into a bedroom and shut the door whenever the screaming began. Together they would recite the Twenty-third Psalm, until it stopped. "The Lord is my shepherd; I shall not want /

He maketh me to lie down in green pastures: he leadeth me beside the still waters / He restoreth my soul . . ." The girls found those verses reassuring, not knowing how commonly they are recited at funerals.

Branch Sr. didn't report his son Rusty missing right away in February 1972. "When Rusty disappeared, we thought he would be back," Susan later recalled in an interview. "He'd left before, so I wasn't surprised. But then I didn't hear from him and I knew something was wrong." Her father initially assumed his eldest had run away, possibly to California. But Rusty never returned. Susan went to live with her mother in Texarkana after that. Her father, his third wife, and her boys remained in Houston.

Susan was in Texarkana watching TV on August 8, 1973, when news broke about the Houston murders and the bodies in Corll's boatshed. She remembered Corll's parties and immediately assumed her brother had been killed too. But her father assured Susan by phone that he'd reviewed the evidence about the bodies and bones pulled from clandestine graves and stored in the Harris County morgue. Rusty simply wasn't there, he said.

In August 1973, the elder Branch went public with the story of his son and defended his department's inaction on reports of so many other missing teenagers. He didn't mention in interviews that Rusty had attended Corll's parties, known Wayne Henley, and likely been murdered too. In the late 1970s, with his third marriage on the rocks, Officer Branch still claimed to be looking for Rusty. His children had different ways of coping with their father's drinking and their brother's disappearance. Doug Branch kept using drugs and breaking the law, and ended up in prison. When they drove up to visit, Doug's family members were startled to see Elmer Wayne Henley, Jr., incarcerated at the same prison, talking with his relatives at the window of another visitation booth.

For years, Susan argued with her father about her missing brother. She and her siblings and some cousins figured Rusty must be among Corll's victims, but for some reason Willard Branch, Sr., didn't want to admit it. *Was it too painful? Too embarrassing? Or perhaps too potentially damaging to his career?* Susan told others that their dad was involved in a "cover-up."

In February 1978, Susan Faye Branch married her sweetheart, Robert McLemore, took her husband's last name, and established her own Houston home. She still believed that Rusty's body was in the morgue waiting to be identified, and she became even more certain after her surviving brother, Doug, told her not to contact the ME because the truth would only hurt her. "Doug's fears were that we would find out Rusty was killed by a homosexual," Susan Branch McLemore once explained. "The fact that Rusty was tortured was what bothered Doug. He told me to leave things alone." Susan never said whether Doug Branch had attended Corll's parties too.

Her father and brother's hesitation to discuss Rusty's fate reflected a deep divide in 1970s America over who and what was responsible for all those appalling serial rapes and murders of teenaged boys in Houston. The candor with which Susan and a few other victims' family members spoke about the adults who photographed boys in back bedrooms at Corll's parties was unusual. Surviving victims, like Tim Kerley, Billy Ridinger, and others, received limited protection as grand jury witnesses, but no other real support, despite signs that they were struggling after traumatic ordeals. The case continued to haunt survivors and shorten lives. Kerley did a few short interviews in 1973 on his feelings about surviving Corll's torture board but avoided the press after that. In 2008, Kerley gave his first in-depth TV interview, speaking for more than an hour with investigative reporter Paige Hewitt of Channel 13, Houston's ABC affiliate. In some ways, it seemed like he'd never left the house at 2020 Lamar. Some of his words were chilling: "It's just one day in fifty-five years of my life," he said, ". . . and I have two choices—either accept it and move on or kill myself." He died abroad in March 2009, apparently of a sudden heart attack, only a few months after that interview.

IN MARCH 1982, SUSAN McLemore began to phone the Harris County ME's office, contacting investigators and urging them to identify her brother's remains, which she was certain were still stored in the morgue. By that time Susan no longer had to worry about upsetting her father or brother Doug. Both were dead. Her father had undergone an innovative heart operation with pioneering Houston heart surgeon Denton A. Cooley. (He'd then been warned to stop drinking and smoking, but never quit, another family member recalls.) In 1980, Officer Branch died from cardiac arrest at age forty-nine. Next to his body were his last cigarette and a Tom Collins cocktail, ice cubes still melting in the glass. Doug Branch passed away in 1981 at age twenty-five; heart problems also contributed to his early death.

Susan arranged for Douglas Branch to be buried in the Old Saltillo cemetery near her paternal grandparents. She reserved an extra plot for herself and for Rusty beside him. Their father was interred elsewhere.

SUSAN MCLEMORE HAD BEEN only thirteen when her big brother Rusty vanished. When she contacted the ME's office in 1982, she was twenty-four, but looked much younger. She wore her chestnut hair in a poofy modification of the feathered haircut made famous by Texas native Farrah Fawcett in an alluring 1976 bathing suit poster used to decorate many teenaged boys' bedrooms in that era. Despite her girlish looks, Susan also suffered from heart problems that seemed to run in her family, as well as lung issues that made breathing difficult. Still, she was surprisingly tough. Susan McLemore made her quest very public, giving multiple interviews to Houston newspapers and TV stations. This small woman seemed determined to break the wall of silence, to publicly recognize her brother as a victim of sex crimes and murder and provide him with a proper burial. If possible, she wanted Henley—and others who'd never before been named—prosecuted for that.

By the time the tenth anniversary of the Houston Mass Murders arrived in August 1983, Dr. Joe had testified in hundreds of murder cases and become so well known as a chief medical examiner that he'd be called to provide insights for the popular detective novelist Erle Stanley Gardner. But even Dr. Joe lacked answers for Susan McLemore. After a decade, Harris County still kept six of Corll's unidentified victims in cold storage.

Then the ME's office caught an unexpected break in a different Lost Boy's case. Jo Anne Kepner, a forty-seven-year-old airport parking lot cashier who lived in a north Houston subdivision, saw the anniversary stories and belatedly realized that her nineteen-year-old son's 1972 disappearance could be connected, given that some of Corll's known victims were his age or older. (She had previously assumed Corll targeted younger teens.) She dug up dental records, including a root canal, for Richard Alan Kepner, a Humble High School graduate who vanished in mid-November 1972 after walking to a pay phone in the Heights to call his fiancée. His ID, announced on September 15, 1983, made news as the oldest set of remains ever identified in Texas. After that, only five other unidentified victims remained—at least as far as ME officials knew then. (Derrick would later find more.) Receiving that tragic notification released her from a "state of limbo," Kepner said. "You can't believe they're alive, because part of you says they're not. And you can't believe they're dead, because part of you says they're alive."

Energized by the discovery, Dr. Joe and others devoted more efforts to the Rusty Branch ID. Rusty had disappeared after visiting an aunt in East Texas. He left with another boy to try to hitchhike to Houston. And his sister named his last known companion as Elmer Wayne Henley, Jr., though Henley had never admitted to knowing Rusty.

From 1982 to 1985, Susan McLemore kept hounding Harris County's ME investigators, demonstrating a force of will that belied her small size and fragile health. She made call after call to Cecil Wingo, a veteran cop who had worked as chief deputy in Brazoria County and as an elected constable before joining the ME's office as chief investigator. Experienced and stubborn, Wingo hated to give up on cold cases, but he knew more than one set of unidentified 1973 remains could belong to Rusty Branch, given pathologists' estimates of the victims' ages and heights.

Susan repeatedly visited the ME's office, still located in the crowded county hospital basement. In those cramped quarters, she reviewed the "hair board," a large piece of wood that Pat Paul and others had assembled in 1973 with rows of locks of hair trimmed from the murdered boys' skulls to create a kind of color palette. The unusual display contained rows of swatches like those used to advertise dye at hair salons; the same technique, though primitive, had proven useful for IDs involving victims of plane crashes. Unfortunately, many Lost Boys had been buried so long that their hair had radically changed by absorbing colors from soil and lime heaped upon them. Rusty Branch's hair had been black; Susan selected two of the darkest samples. One possibility was quickly eliminated. That hair belonged to Johnny Delome—Billy Baulch's childhood buddy from the Heights who'd been identified in August 1973 through dental and X-ray records. The other dark lock of hair, marked Swatch #12, came from an unidentified boy buried near the back of the boat stall. This boy's body lacked any clothing or possessions, aside from a braided leather bracelet tied around his right wrist. But the remains in ML 73-3350 had a particularly horrifying feature: The killers had severed the victim's penis and testicles before death and placed them in plastic bags. That detail, which authorities did not attempt to hide, only reinforced Susan's belief that her father's unwillingness to accept that Rusty had been raped and tortured likely kept him from making this ID. This boy had been shot in the head; the fatal bullet had traveled through his skull and lodged in his shoulder. She took some comfort in learning that the end, at least, had likely been swift.

Part of the problem, Wingo confided, was that her father never supplied any dental records for Rusty to enable comparisons to the charts and X-rays of teeth from unidentified bodies. Hair color was hardly enough evidence for an ID. The investigation also had been hampered by the photo of Rusty they'd received, which showed a boy of only ten or eleven.

Susan McLemore told Wingo her brother had fractured his skull as a kid, as well as injured his shoulder. She launched a search for his 1960s medical records. If they still existed, perhaps X-rays of his cracked skull could provide answers. For two years, from 1983 to 1985, McLemore worked so hard on trying to identify her brother that her health suffered. She sometimes fought with her husband over the toll her mission was exacting.

Pat Paul assisted with those ID efforts. In 1979, she had finally been named as the morgue's first female investigator—though winning that promotion had taken a real battle. Dr. Joe initially balked, saying "I'd be so afraid you'd get hurt!" and claiming "I'd worry about you" at crime scenes late at night. "I had to do some tall talking," she recalls. Even some other women in the office, all assigned secretarial or administrative assistant roles, got angry. "This isn't a job for a female and if it were—it wouldn't be you," one said.

From the beginning, her fellow investigators, even those Paul considered friends, teased and pranked her. For her first case, she was deliberately assigned to a badly decomposed body, a so-called suicide stinker. Later colleagues publicly hazed her as she investigated a death in a store's men's room. For years, Paul would show up at crime scenes wearing her thick blue coat with white lettering that said "Medical Examiner Investigator" and encounter male officers who refused to allow her onto the crime scene until she presented her county ID.

Pat Paul did that job for the next twenty years, eventually becoming the chief investigator and paving the way for other women. She stubbornly ignored the machismo and graduated from the University of Houston police academy in 1980. Paul remained dedicated to identifications, and to that end became certified as a fingerprint expert and earned certificates in child deaths, medicolegal death, homicide investigations, serial killers, cults, and forensic entomology. By the time Derrick joined the office in 2006, Paul had retired, but other forensic employees and investigators were female. Some things had not changed: The top bosses were still men and some of Corll's victims remained unidentifed.

IN THE 1980s, PAT Paul and chief investigator Cecil Wingo made at least five trips to the Texas Department of Public Safety's crime lab in Austin in efforts to identify Rusty Branch and other Lost Boys. On one trip, they loaded up the mandibles and craniums of three unidentified teens in order to try an ID technique called photo superimposition. DPS had recently invested in a sophisticated new projector that could be used to resize and then superimpose missing persons' photos onto skulls. Despite the fact that the only picture they had of Rusty was so outdated that it didn't reveal the oval face and strong chin he'd acquired at seventeen, Paul and Wingo hoped that the projections could help them determine whether Rusty Branch's dark eyes, pug nose, and generous mouth matched the proportions of one of these skulls.

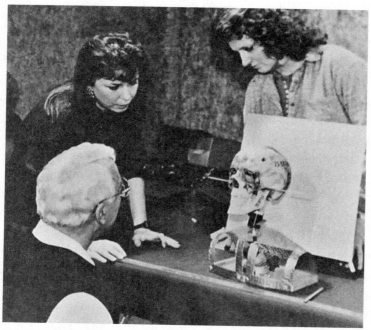

Pat Paul (right) at the state police lab in the 1980s with Cecil Wingo and a forensic artist

They were planning to attempt the same technique with photos of Mark Scott, whose father was still pressing for an ID, and of Norman Prater, a missing Dallas teen who'd last been seen in a white van, and whose mother and sisters were still seeking answers. In 1985, Susan McLemore, Rusty's sister, had been a particularly persistent visitor, often demanding to speak to Wingo in person and haranguing him about why it was taking so long to make an ID. Paul and Wingo hoped this new projection would provide a solid lead.

At the state police lab, Pat Paul and Cecil Wingo were greeted by

DPS artist Karen Taylor, a University of Texas at Austin fine arts major who'd once sculpted wax busts for Madame Tussaud in Europe before getting homesick and returning to Texas. Taylor ushered them into a photo studio. They unloaded the skulls and mounted each one on a stand that Wingo had customized, adding hinges that allowed the skull to be swiveled or tilted. The ability to make adjustments was important since school portraits used for IDs often showed an individual's head fashionably bent to one side. Behind each mounted skull was a small white screen.

Taylor often created charcoal portraits of criminal suspects and of the unidentified dead, gaining acclaim for an inexplicable ability to render accurate sketches of people she'd never seen in life. In preparation for the photo overlay procedure, she placed a wooden dowel through the skull's external acoustic meatus—the ear canals—to aid in the comparison process. As a precaution against any mix-ups, each skull had its case number scrawled on the bone. Before they began the first projection, Cecil Wingo crouched down to adjust the skull, trying to get the angle right. Wingo relished his role, confident that as a veteran lawman he could find clues others had missed.

Then they dimmed the lights. In the darkened lab, Pat Paul got excited when she saw the enlarged image of Rusty Branch projected over the skull in Case No. ML 73-3350. They were using a slide made from the only image they had—that little boy's school photo. Behind the project, another DPS employee attempted to shift, resize, and focus the enlarged image. But it just didn't work. This teen's skull was obviously too big to fit the face of such a small child.

Paul had repeatedly pressed for alternatives: "Hadn't this boy gone to school? Wasn't there a high school annual photo?" But even if that outdated picture had shared the skull's outline and contours, Paul knew that a match would be insufficient evidence to confirm an ID. Photo superimposition was more often used to rule out missing persons as candidates for unidentified remains. Dr. Joe had hoped the new technology would generate leads. They did think Mark Scott's photo corresponded with the skull of another unidentified boy—though later that turned out to be a false match. None of the other missing boys' photos seemed to fit.

By the 2000s and 2010s, photo superimposition techniques had improved through the use of three-dimensional imaging, but remained controversial tools for identifications. Derrick, like other experts, opted not to use them. By that time, independent research had revealed a high potential for false matches since many unrelated people have faces with similar shapes and proportions. When done right, though, the techniques were considered most useful for ruling out false matches. Researchers in Arizona who, as part of a multinational effort, were trying to identify migrants whose remains were found in the Sonora Desert, had found them helpful, particularly when family or friends knew the identities of people traveling together and DNA was not readily available. In a 2003 case, the bones of a group of Mexican men and women were found by a passing hiker on "a remote trail near the lower slope of a mountain, dotted with mesquite and palo verde trees." A Pima County Sheriff's Office search team discovered "five human skulls, numerous human postcranial skeletal elements, five backpacks, four personal identification cards and clothing scattered over a fifty- [to] one-hundred-yard radius." Three men were identified through dental work or DNA, but two younger women were not. Superficially, their remains were hard to tell apart; they were similar in age and stature, and both wore shoulder-length dark hair.

A family photo provided the key clue. It revealed a pretty woman in a pantsuit with her brown hair styled and her mouth parted in a smile, a sparkling diamond wedding ring on her finger and her feet in fashionable high heels. When analysts at the Michigan State University Forensic Anthropology Laboratory zoomed in on her face and attempted to overlay the image over one skull, the task proved impossible. This woman's face had been longer and thinner. In contrast, her eyes, nose, and mouth aligned with openings in the other skull. The results allowed both women's bones to be returned more quickly to their families. But even with advanced computers and projectors, the process depends heavily on the analyst's skill. The risk remains that investigators who want to help find missing persons may inadvertently tweak comparisons—enlarge or enhance images to make them fit or ignore gaps where the soft tissue of a face extends beyond a skull's outlines.

In 1983, while Harris County investigators were still comparing photos to skulls, Susan McLemore managed to find the family doctor, Dr. Thomas H. McGuire, M.D., who was no longer in practice but retained patient records from the 1960s. McGuire had cared for Rusty Branch when he fractured his skull at age six. A letter the doctor supplied from April 17, 1961, began: "Your courtesies in allowing me to see and examine this very nice child with you in Memorial Hospital are greatly appreciated." His notes described a "three inch linear" skull fracture, Rusty's "fairly high cheek bones," oversized front teeth, and another childhood shoulder injury. Susan passed everything on to ME investigators, and pressed again for an ID.

Susan was getting impatient. "Why is it taking so long?" she yelled more than once at Wingo, her voice echoing through the halls. Once or twice, their exchanges got so heated that the tough chief investigator asked someone else to escort her out.

ME officials were excited about the prospect of identifying another Lost Boy, but the potential ID of Rusty Branch posed problems. In the original 1973 autopsy report for Case No. ML 73-3350, the most likely candidate, pathologists had detected no skull fracture and had estimated the victim to be twenty to twenty-four years old; Branch was just seventeen. One issue seemed resolved when a new round of X-rays revealed a healed fracture. Still, it was challenging to compare those images to 1960s records, especially since children's bones rapidly alter. Wingo and Dr. Joe eventually concluded that Case No. ML 73-3350 was a match. Wingo prepared a one-page chart summarizing the attributes of the remains and of the known characteristics of Willard Karmon "Rusty" Branch, Jr. Based on that data, Dr. Joe and other pathologists made a "presumptive identification."

The 1985 ID made more front-page news. "Now I can bury him and put him at rest with his family instead of leaving him in the morgue. I think he deserves that in spite of how he was killed or what he was involved in," Susan McLemore declared.

FOR YEARS AFTER HER brother was identified, Susan McLemore kept speaking out. She was photographed looking fragile and feminine in a blouse with a high-necked collar, with her hands folded, fingernails painted, and a crucifix worn at her throat. But her voice remained firm: She wanted Wayne Henley to be denied parole and be prosecuted for her brother's murder—and she provided Houston police with names of adult accomplices whom she claimed had never been investigated. When the twentieth anniversary of the murders rolled around in 1993, McLemore gave more angry interviews. This time she pointedly asked why only Brooks and Henley—two teenagers—had been arrested and questioned but none of the men she'd seen at Corll's sex and drug parties had been publicly named as suspects.

In a rambling 1993 discussion with *Houston Chronicle* reporter Evan Moore, McLemore described four adults who remained in Corll's bedroom during the parties she'd attended with her brother over a two-year period before he disappeared. McLemore believed those men were all part of the organized crime ring that took photos and videos of the naked boys—and performed sex acts on teens.

She shared one particularly troubling party memory. "I remember, once, sitting under the kitchen table and there were four boys sitting under the other end, nude, smoking marijuana," she told Moore. "Dean came walking in naked and I said, 'Dean, I'm hungry.' He put some mayonnaise on a piece of bread and handed it to me and I started eating it and one of the boys started laughing at something." The boy kept laughing until he choked, turned blue, and fell to the floor. "I said, 'Dean, there's something wrong with him,' and Dean picked him up over his shoulder and started walking out of the room toward his bedroom with him. The boy was throwing up then and his bladder emptied. He was overdosing, but I don't know what Dean did with him back there. I remember I thought, *He's dying.*" Susan never knew that boy's name or what happened to him.

Corll, who had a younger half sister of his own in Colorado, was kind to her, Susan said. He once gave her a ride to the store in his van and bought her a dress. During the ride, she spotted a wooden box behind a curtain separating the front seats from the cargo bay, though she had no idea whether a body was inside.

McLemore supplied the names of three adults she'd seen in bedrooms at Corll's parties to HPD and to the *Chronicle*. Those men must have known about those boys' disappearances and murders, she said. "It would have been hard to be back there without knowing something was going on," she told the newspaper, which didn't print the names. One man had been murdered, the second died from a fatal overdose, and the third was doing prison time for sexual assault of a child. In a 2022 interview, reporter Evan Moore, long retired, didn't have his notes. But he thought one name, listed in 1973 police records, sounded familiar: Roy Ames.

PART VI

THE LAST UNSOLVED MYSTERIES

CHAPTER 36

LETTING GO

HARRIS COUNTY MEDICAL EXAMINER'S OFFICE, 2014

W HEN JENNIFER LOVE LEFT Houston in 2014 to become the very first forensic anthropologist for the District of Columbia Office of the Chief Medical Examiner in Washington, D.C., Derrick knew she would miss her. Though a decade younger, Love had been a valuable mentor, as well as a national trailblazer for women forensic anthropologists. Over time the two women had become friends and allies in the struggle to make more identifications.

As she began her new job, Love explained to a *Washington Post* reporter that relatives of unidentified people whose cases she worked on often got locked in a "horrible" state of limbo without an opportunity to grieve. "You would not have rest," Love said. "I don't pretend what I do provides closure. But it is certainly providing them answers."

Derrick hoped to replace Love and head up the county's forensic anthropology team at last. Instead, Sanchez recruited another outsider: Dr. Christian Crowder, another Ph.D. who'd played a prominent role in the years-long efforts to identify the 9/11 terrorist attack victims in New York City. Crowder was among the team of scientists who'd devised ways to scour Manhattan rooftops looking for biological material that might contain victims' DNA. He had an impressive résumé that included seven years as deputy director of the Forensic

Anthropology Unit of the Office of Chief Medical Examiner–New York City and shorter stints with the elite Armed Forces Medical Examiner System and the Joint POW/MIA Accounting Command Central Identification Laboratory. To her surprise, this impressive young forensic anthropologist had a kind and respectful manner with colleagues. (It didn't hurt that he too was an Aggie, having earned his undergraduate degree from Texas A&M in 1996 before racking up more degrees at the University of Texas at Arlington and the University of Toronto in Canada.) Derrick, initially miffed, found she enjoyed working with Crowder, a native Texan who'd taken the job partly to be closer to family in Dallas.

She liked most of her colleagues. For a while, her youngest daughter, Cristine, worked at the ME's office too, in quality control. Still, Derrick began to sense that it was time to move on. Her progress on trying to identify her very last big Lost Boys case—the one the press still called Swimsuit Boy, over her protests—seemed to have stalled.

Derrick tried to maintain her sunny disposition and sense of humor in the face of Harris County's crushing caseloads and increasing pressure for rapid yet high-quality forensic work. Most mornings, she guzzled coffee from her mug bearing an image of yellow crime scene DO NOT CROSS tape and a small body in the background. She felt satisfaction in knowing that thanks to federal grants, and to initiatives by her and other "anthros," the office had made a great deal of progress. Although one of the Lost Boys cases remained unsolved, Derrick and her colleagues had made dozens of identifications in cold cases. The publicity and data available on NamUs and other online search sites were encouraging more people to provide tips. One ID gave Derrick particular satisfaction. In 2013, Penny Penwell, one of many armchair sleuths who review online missing persons databases and cold case blogs, emailed Derrick about a teenaged girl whose remains had been unidentified since 1982, suggesting she might be Michelle Angela Garvey, a missing fifteen-year-old from Connecticut. (Penwell, who is autistic, later explained her unusual ability to see patterns offered her an advantage in spotting links between missing and unidentified persons lists.) Thanks to the NIJ's grant program, Harris County already had exhumed that unidentified girl's body and obtained a DNA sample. Derrick used her own investigative skills to locate Michelle's parents; both were still alive. The DNA they contributed matched the teen in a brown fringed cowgirl outfit whose body had been found in a field thirty-one years before.

The ID was announced in January 2014. On her office wall, Derrick still keeps a framed portrait of Michelle Garvey, a smiling redhaired teen, as a reminder that no cold case is impossible. "That was huge for me," she says. "Her mom and dad had divorced over this because they were so devastated. When we got her ID'd, it was just amazing. . . . They got back together. That's what we do this for—we do this for the families because it means so much to them and because everybody deserves to have their name in death."

After Garvey's identification Derrick got another great tip to the resolution of a case involving a woman killed in a 1980 hit-and-run pedestrian accident. (That woman, like Garvey, shared a unique facial feature: FRECKLES HELP ID WOMAN WHO DIED IN TEXAS, read one headline.) Her grateful sister suggested Derrick organize an event like one held in her home state, "Missing in Michigan Day." Derrick reached out to law enforcement and nonprofit partners and in April 2015, organized the first "Missing in Harris County Day." The inaugural gathering prompted 146 relatives of missing persons to submit DNA samples and as a direct result eight people were identified. More importantly, the event, supported by a diverse group of advocates, police, government, and nonprofit groups, raised awareness among elected officials about the ME's ID work. "One of the reasons all those bodies had backed up was because of a lack of funding and a lack of understanding from politicians how important it was to send these people to their final rest and let their families know," Derrick wrote in a 2016 article for the *Journal of Academic Forensic Pathology*. Derrick co-wrote that article about the ten years of progress she'd witnessed with Benjamin Figura, a New York–based anthropologist. They described leaps that Harris County and New York City had made by integrating forensic anthropology into identification protocols.

New York City, like Houston, had its share of difficult IDs, including the unknown slayer of eighteen women known as the Lost Girls, whose bones had been scattered in remote Long Island beaches and marshes from 1996 to 2011. But the Big Apple had become a world leader in forensic anthropology because of its work after the September 11, 2001, terrorist attacks. Forensic anthropologists, city and state investigators, and scientists collaborated for years on the immense task of finding, testing, and identifying even minute fragments of human remains left after the plane crashes and subsequent infernos, an even more daunting task since DNA can be destroyed by fire. A National Institute of Justice report defended those sweeping and costly efforts, declaring it essential to broaden ID work when "a mass fatality incident is so large and devastating that it affects the psyche of a community, a country, or the world."

Despite all that progress, Houston and New York City, bustling crowded metropolises filled with immigrants and newcomers, still had backlogs of cold unidentified cases and frequent arrivals of "initially unknown decedents." In 2015 alone, NYC was investigating 400 new unknowns and Harris County 226. Yet each place had adopted innovative techniques to tackle them: using 3-D printers to make copies of skulls for forensic artists instead of shipping out originals, enhancing ways to capture fingerprints from decomposing bodies, deploying anthropologists to reexamine remains to improve estimates of age and other characteristics, and regularly uploading case information and DNA profiles to national databases.

Derrick felt proud of how Harris County's pace of identifications was increasing and the backlog shrinking. Both offices had "successfully integrated forensic anthropologists into their offices to supervise routine identifications, direct resolution efforts in complex identification cases, manage disaster victim identification efforts, and organize community outreach events focused on identification," she and Figura wrote. Those forensic anthropologists "had streamlined identification procedures and increased identifications." Both offices had made dozens of IDs through the NIJ's "Using DNA Technology to Identify the Missing" grant programs. By 2016, Harris County's two grants had resulted in forty-six IDs in what had once been considered impossibly old cases.

IN SEPTEMBER 2016, DERRICK won a promotion to the post of Identification Manager. Her feelings were mixed. She appreciated the gesture, but felt she should have received that title years before. She still hoped one day to direct the Forensic Anthropology program, but worried that would never happen. The Harris County ME's office was still led by Luis Sanchez, the forensic pathologist who'd hired her, but it had grown tremendously, reinventing and rebranding itself as the Harris County Institute of Forensic Sciences. Derrick had labored for a decade in an outdated office built to accommodate the ME's 1985 caseloads and technology (though a big improvement over the original hospital basement). In 2017, she and her colleagues moved into a brand-new nine-story office with state-of-the-art labs, a dedicated forensic anthropology research area, and 210,000 square feet of space, including an indoor firing range for ballistics tests. But her work was complicated by the operation's increasing bureaucracy, Houston's growth, the hectic pace, and the pressure to meet deadlines for criminal cases and to present findings in scientific conferences and academic journals. The office's combination of eccentric personalities, brilliance, and big egos required tact, patience, and political skill to navigate. Over the years, other HCIFS employees had bristled, fled, or filed lawsuits after clashing with its intricate hierarchy and strict protocols. Most of the time, Derrick could get along with or win over colleagues through careful work and creative approaches. Sometimes that process took time; she could be patient and tried to remain upbeat. But occasionally the internal fire that enabled Derrick to thrive in her demanding career threatened to engulf her in frustration or, more rarely, in anger.

She was intrigued when in 2019 she spotted the announcement of a new forensic science position at Texas A&M University's campus in Corpus Christi, the place where she and Al had honeymooned and had taken their three children for beach vacations on the barrier islands across the city's long causeway: Mustang and Padre, the latter including a vast national seashore. She interviewed and received a tempting offer to join the faculty. This new adventure, she thought, would provide a different challenge, teaching aspiring young forensic anthropologists, but would allow her to occasionally moonlight on bone cases for Nueces County and smaller South Texas counties that had no forensic anthropologists at all.

Plenty of ID work beckoned beyond the bounds of Harris County. Across Texas, more than seventeen hundred unidentified bodies were listed in the NamUs database by 2024—about 12 percent of the national total. Though many Texas cases were linked to the deaths of migrants who too often perished in remote places after crossing the border, the entire state had more than its share of missing and unidentified persons. In the academic world, Derrick figured she'd still have plenty of interesting work and far more control over her schedule. She felt excited about building a new forensic program for a campus that was part of the Texas A&M system.

Leaving behind the case of the Lost Boy with the striped swimming suit hurt, but Derrick felt she could entrust that ID to Deborrah Pinto. The promising young woman who had initially been hired as a fellow to assist with grant-related identifications had seemed nervous in her early days. But she and Derrick had literally stood shoulder to shoulder at the Baulch boys' exhumations. Since then, Pinto had become an accomplished forensic anthropologist, attaining her place as a Diplomate with the American Board of Forensic Anthropology in 2017. Derrick hoped that even in Corpus Christi, she could consult from afar on the remaining Lost Boy mysteries. Before moving on, Derrick and Pinto discussed an intriguing strategy. Derrick believed that genetic genealogy—a type of sophisticated research made possible partly because of Americans' growing fascination with consumer DNA tests—might finally help resolve that boy's identity.

Interest in consumer genetic testing was expanding rapidly in the 2010s. By 2020, an estimated 30 million people had voluntarily submitted samples to consumer DNA companies like Ancestry.com and 23andMe through home kits—tests based on saliva collected in a plastic vial. Most consumer companies were now using more robust tests that allowed comparisons of the possible kinship between all kinds of distant relatives—not just along the paternal line, as was true of Y-DNA, or the maternal line.

Those developments greatly increased the power of researchers using what they called genetic genealogy to collaborate with investigators to help solve mysteries involving DNA, even though only a fraction of consumer DNA data could be tapped for forensic research. Just two consumer DNA companies allowed access to portions of their databases: GEDmatch, a company that offers free uploads to consumers, and the Houston-based Family Tree DNA. Over time, each company adopted a procedure to allow customers to opt to be included or excluded in searches by forensic investigators, who were generally restricted to seeking matches of relatives for unidentified dead persons or for suspects whose DNA was linked to unsolved murders or rapes.

Even with those limitations on access, pioneering genetic genealogists were proving that it was possible to restore the names of unidentified decedents even in cold cases where no close family members, such as siblings or parents, had ever provided any reference DNA samples. A far-flung and growing network of genetic genealogists, many of whom started by tracing their own family trees or helping adoptees find birth families, were forming teams, partnering with police and ME's investigators, and employing complex strategies to deduce the identities of unknown deceased persons starting with matches generated from open-source consumer DNA databases. They often began with a few distant relatives and then conducted additional research to create elaborate family trees—always looking for a connected person who suddenly disappeared from public records and might be a match for the unknown decedent. Those methods were providing new hope for seemingly unsolvable cases like Derrick's Lost Boy with the striped swimming suit.

But those techniques had made international news in 2017 with another kind of breakthrough: the unmasking of a notorious serial killer.

That year, Barbara Rae-Venter, a California-based pioneer in genetic genealogy, helped police identify the Golden State Killer, a man linked to at least twelve murders and forty-five rapes whose crimes had gone unsolved since 1984. That breakthrough had been made possible because of a series of behind-the-scenes collaborations. First, Dr. Pete Speth, M.D., a retired medical examiner, had managed to safeguard a back-up copy of a rape kit from a 1980 double murder linked to the killer. Then an offer of help came from the founder of Houston-based Family Tree DNA, a business located in an unassuming lab filled with computers and secure processing equipment just off the 610 Loop. The company, which typically provided services for consumers looking for living relatives and ancestors, quietly agreed to help generate a usable genetic profile from the murder victim's rape kit and then search for the suspect's possible relatives. Initially, Family Tree CEO Bennett Greenspan kept his decision to cooperate with police private, though he later told *The Wall Street Journal:* "If we can help prevent violent crimes and save lives and bring closure to families, then we're going to do that."

The lead detective then contacted Rae-Venter, who searched for more of the unknown suspect's relatives through GEDmatch, a clearinghouse created in 2010 that already allowed people to upload genetic profiles they'd obtained through commercial services to conduct additional genealogical research. Slowly, she constructed family trees that might ultimately reveal the assailant's identity. She needed to find a Californian—a man of about sixty or seventy who'd lived in or near the nine counties where his victims had been raped and murdered. At first, she spotted only fourth or fifth cousins with Italian origins. Slowly, she and a small team of investigators traced the distant relatives' family trees, verifying connections through birth and death certificates, marriage licenses, gravestones, and other sources. She wanted to learn how these family trees might connect—a trail that might lead to the suspect's parents or grandparents.

A breakthrough came when Rae-Venter managed to find a second cousin: a woman who, based on the percentage of DNA patterns she had in common with the unknown killer, likely shared a set of great-grandparents with him. By focusing on that woman's

male relatives—and drinking lots of espresso during all-night research binges—she developed a list of nine Californians who could
be the raspy-voiced masked man who had stalked and killed women
and couples, invading homes and terrorizing communities. Another
DNA research tool unlocked the suspect's likely eye color—blue—
narrowing her list to one man: a former police officer named Joseph
DeAngelo. Buried in newspaper databases, Rae-Venter found an article that revealed DeAngelo had been fired from the Aurora police
force for shoplifting a hammer and mace from a store near where
the Golden State Killer committed his first known crime in 1976.

Incredibly, DeAngelo's name had never appeared on any suspect
list generated by Michelle McNamara, the crusading journalist who'd
coined the name Golden State Killer, or by committed California detectives who had worked these cases for decades. Undercover police
shadowed DeAngelo, wiping the door handle of his pickup for touch
DNA and collecting a tissue he discarded. Additional DNA tests verified the match. And news of the breakthrough exploded.

Half afraid DeAngelo would go free and come after her, Rae-
Venter initially took no credit for using genetic genealogy to help
crack a case in four months that had gone unsolved for four decades.
She was floored by the publicity—and by the subsequent backlash.
"I felt a profound sense of pride, not just in myself but also in science
itself. We had solved one of the most notorious U.S. criminal cold
cases and dragged a truly heinous monster out of his hiding place
and into the light," she later wrote in a book about her work. Despite
the incredible results, privacy advocates attacked leaders of DNA
services who had agreed to allow the serial killer suspect's genetic
profile to be uploaded and compared to other customers' profiles,
calling them unethical. Rae-Venter had no doubt what they'd done
was right: "We had made history," she wrote. "Joseph DeAngelo simply did not exist as a suspect until DNA told us he was the killer."

SHARON DERRICK DIDN'T KNOW Rae-Venter, but she knew another genetic genealogist, Colleen Fitzpatrick, who was using her own impressive skills to help track murder and rape suspects—and to research

362 | THE SCIENTIST AND THE SERIAL KILLER

unidentified decedents. They'd met through the American Academy of Forensic Sciences, an organization whose six thousand members come from all fifty states and dozens of foreign countries. In 2014, Derrick had been invited to deliver an update on the Lost Boys for the AAFS's sixty-sixth annual conference in Seattle. By then she'd made six IDs, including Donnie Falcon, though she could not publicly discuss his case. Derrick ran into Fitzpatrick, who had come to deliver a talk about the relatively new field of forensic genetic genealogy, by chance in a crowded auditorium. Derrick was used to having to look up to the men in her field, literally, since some were more than a foot taller. Fitzpatrick was petite, and Derrick picked up on a familiar accent: Even after years in California, Fitzpatrick retained the accent associated with residents of Irish origins in her native New Orleans. Fitzpatrick remembered the Corll murders, which made news during her time as an undergraduate at Houston's Rice University. More importantly, she shared Derrick's commitment to cold case identifications. The two exchanged emails and agreed to keep in contact.

In 2017, Fitzpatrick went on to co-found a nonprofit called the DNA Doe Project together with Margaret Press, a Ph.D. linguist and mystery writer. The organization focused exclusively on using genetic genealogy to help investigate long unsolved cases of the unidentified dead, and it quickly got results. In April 2018, the group's research helped unlock the identity of a young woman previously known only as "Buckskin Girl." She was Marcia L. King, a twenty-year-old who disappeared in 1980 after leaving her Arkansas home, one of seven cold case IDs the group announced in its very first year. In 2019, the group made headlines again by participating in a team that resolved the long-lost identity of the victim of a 103-year-old homicide: John Henry Loveless, the man initially thought to be a recent murder victim when his torso was found in 1979 in an Idaho cave. Loveless, a bootlegger born in 1870, had perished there in 1916, after murdering his wife with an ax and then breaking out of jail. That identification seemed to suggest an almost unlimited potential for genetic genealogy to resolve U.S. cold cases. But the process had been complex. To unlock his name, a team of genetic genealogists had collectively constructed family trees charting thirty-one thousand relatives and probed hundreds of public records, including an Old West WANTED poster that showed the sweater Loveless had still been wearing when he died.

By the time Derrick reached out to Fitzpatrick about her Lost Boy case in 2019, Fitzpatrick had begun to shift her focus away from the DNA Doe Project and concentrate on running Identifinders International, her separate for-profit company that billed itself as "investigative partners—collaborating with our law enforcement clients until the case is solved." The DNA Doe Project focused exclusively on the unidentified, but Fitzpatrick also relished helping police search for suspects in cold rape and murder cases by using genetic genealogy research. Identifinders handled both kinds of projects. Before Derrick left Harris County in the summer of 2019, Fitzpatrick agreed to help tackle the mystery of Swimsuit Boy.

BY THE FALL OF 2019, Derrick was busy with her new job teaching the next generation of forensic scientists at Texas A&M–Corpus Christi, a campus built on an island that jutted into Nueces Bay; recruiters bragged about its palm-tree-lined paths and its classrooms with waterfront views. Still, Derrick wept over leaving her last Lost Boys case unsolved in Harris County. Late at night, she still sometimes hunched over the screen of her laptop, searching for boys who could be "Bobby French." She still pondered the teen's facial reconstructions and wondered about his identity. But she gradually came to terms with the idea that solving this remaining mystery would largely fall to someone else. Derrick had faith that Deborrah Pinto, in collaboration with Colleen Fitzpatrick, would reveal the identity of the boy with the striped swimming suit at last.

Then in 2020 a worldwide pandemic began. And Deborrah Pinto, a young mother as well as a dedicated scientist, decided to take a job in Dallas to be closer to extended family.

If the last Lost Boys cases were going to be solved, Derrick would need more allies. But she no longer felt that it was appropriate for her to reach out to police and other forensic investigators to press for answers. So I began to do so.

CHAPTER 37

A FRUSTRATING SEARCH—AND A BREAKTHROUGH

PASADENA, TEXAS, 2022

SGT. JAMES ANDERSON, A white-haired officer in a trim blue uniform, arrived for our meeting on the Dean Corll murder cases in August 2022 toting two binders that together were at least four inches thick. They were his copies of the homicide reports from both the Houston and the Pasadena police on the Corll case, all of the records he could find nearly fifty years after one of the biggest murder cases in local history.

Anderson is a pleasant man with a ready laugh and a knack for navigating police politics and for getting people to say more than they mean to. He hunkered down with me at a conference table in a Pasadena training room at police headquarters to discuss these murders, as well as other unresolved missing persons cases that remain fascinating and confounding to him, even after all this time. "The approach back then was a little different than we have now," he says. "That number of boys all disappearing from the same neighborhood—the Heights—would have been flagged."

Anderson's agency, the Pasadena PD, took the lead on the Corll murder cases in 1973, which were solved in large part because of Detective David Mullican's efforts to get Henley to confess and to help recover bodies. But when Anderson decided to reopen the cases in August 2021, it had been a struggle even to obtain a copy of

HPD's full file. Reading through the reports from both departments, he found that the murder cases had been closed surprisingly quickly and that many tips remained unexplored. Even in the 1970s, some HPD supervisors had seemed happy to allow Pasadena, a smaller department, to take charge of the massive homicide case, though it was immediately clear that fewer than a quarter of Corll's victims—approximately eight of the known twenty-seven victims—had been slain while Corll lived at 2020 Lamar in Pasadena's jurisdiction (police never determined exactly where each had been killed). Many more had been kidnapped, killed, and buried within the Houston city limits. "I noticed that HPD was like, 'Hey, let's just write this up, get it out of here. And I mean, we'll be happy.'"

I'd reached out to Anderson and arranged to meet that summer because I'd read about his interest in the Corll case. I knew he'd never spoken to Derrick, who had information I thought he'd want to know. Derrick felt uncomfortable reaching out directly, since by 2022 she had no official role in Harris County cases anymore. It fell to me to contact him, since I was writing about her discoveries and reinvestigating leads about the Lost Boys.

These days, Anderson calls himself the department's "old man"—the longest-serving officer, with decades of service. He's a senior sergeant and has served as a union leader too. "This case has always intrigued me. And I can tell you why," he said. Back in 1973, he was an eighteen-year-old Pasadena High School graduate when news broke that a man who'd been living in his hometown had murdered twenty-seven teens. That summer, Anderson had gone away on his very first out-of-state road trip with his brother and another friend. The trio headed to Tennessee, where his grandmother owned a place on the mountainside. "We stayed there for a week or so. Had a great time. It was the first time out and about on our own." They were just outside Great Smoky Mountains National Park when they stopped at a log-cabin store in Pigeon Forge for Pepsis. Anderson quickly spotted screaming headlines in a row of Southern newspapers displayed near the cash register of what he remembers as "a hillbilly souvenir shop." The front page of every paper had "pictures of all of these murders." Anderson gazed in shock at the faces of murdered

Texas schoolboys about his own age. He scrambled for change and fed a stream of dimes into a pay phone outside the store until he finally summoned up the total necessary for a long-distance call home.

"What's all this about Houston?" he asked his mother, who was relieved to hear from him; her two boys had been unreachable when those bodies were found. None of his own friends were missing, but the address on Lamar where Corll had been killed—and where his victims had been tortured—was near his childhood home and the area where his girlfriend (and "future ex-wife") lived. As a boy, he'd played in that neighborhood along Vince Bayou. His mother promised to save all the articles. At that time, Anderson was headed to San Jacinto Community College and thinking of becoming a journalist. A few years later, Anderson chose policework over reporting and joined the Pasadena PD.

Anderson heard a lot more about Corll and Henley while serving alongside Det. Mullican, the canny lead investigator on those cases. It was largely due to Mullican's skill that Henley had kept talking and leading police to more victims. He'd arranged to have Henley and his friends formally advised of their legal rights by a magistrate judge who held an impromptu hearing in the detective squad room on the morning of Corll's murder. Then he'd proceeded to obtain multiple confessions from the seventeen-year-old. The fatherly and affable homicide detective with expressive eyes had a smile that could break open wide or twist in a smirk. Mullican, originally from Teague, a town of three thousand, quickly gained the trust of Henley, who also had East Texas roots. Early on, Henley had even consulted Mullican about which reporters to speak with when Mullican squired the teenaged killer to graves in the boatshed, in the woods, and on the beach.

Mullican had been so well respected as a detective that from 1980 to 1984, he'd been promoted to serve as Pasadena's police chief. But the general opinion at the cop shop was that he'd been better suited for soliciting confessions and solving cases than pushing papers and administering policies. Mullican liked to reminisce about Henley and Corll, the most infamous case of his career. He'd told Anderson he figured more victims' bodies were still out there. Like some other investigators, he believed Corll and Henley had killed thirty-five or more people. Mullican considered writing a book after he left the Pasadena PD in 1990, but continued working at other investigative agencies instead. By the time he fully retired in 2002, he'd lost enthusiasm for the project. Mullican spent his last years with his wife of more than half a century, focusing on being a grandfather.

IN THE SUMMER OF 2021, Anderson got a call out of the blue from another senior Pasadena officer, Lt. James Holt. While working off duty at a local gun show, Holt told Anderson he had met up by chance with Tim Miller, the fast-talking and determined head of Texas EquuSearch, a nonprofit that specializes in searching for missing persons. Miller founded Texas EquuSearch in the 1980s after his teenaged daughter had become one of the four victims of an infamous unsolved serial murder case known as the Texas Killing Fields, and local police had failed to find her body for months. Now, phone conversations with inmate Wayne Henley had prompted Miller to try to reactivate the search for Corll's teenaged victims' long-lost graves.

Anderson consulted with the department's chief, who promised to provide support for Miller's group and the families of missing or murdered boys from the 1970s. He'd already heard about Texas EquuSearch's accomplishments, but when Anderson met Miller, he was impressed with the seemingly endless energy of the man. Well into his seventies, Miller remains a hyperactive heavy smoker (though he sometimes quits) with a construction worker's deep tan and the zeal of a vigilante whenever he takes on the topic of missing persons and murder victims.

Texas EquuSearch is based in Dickinson, a rural community south of Houston, and its members use horses in some search and recovery efforts, but by 2021 Miller had accumulated a barnful of equipment, including speedboats and ATVs, and had an agreement with a company that provided ground-penetrating radar. He and his volunteers had already hunted for hundreds of missing kids and dead bodies nationwide and occasionally abroad. Miller had gained a reputation for having a sixth sense about where a living child might be lost in an impenetrable thicket or a body might be hidden under murky swamp water. As the leader of a frequently cash-strapped nonprofit, Miller had to seek the limelight to survive, and he decided to kick off the high-profile search for the Corll victims with a splashy press conference.

Anderson agreed to join him in uniform on Silver Bell Drive, outside the metal shed that Corll once used as a stash house for corpses. On August 9, 2021, Anderson stood beside Miller on the dead-end public street with their backs to the boat stalls as a phalanx of reporters from Houston's major TV stations and newspapers arrived, setting up a row of oversized cameras. The two men reminded the reporters, most of whom were too young to remember, that this metal building was where the remains of seventeen victims of a serial killer had been recovered in August 1973.

Miller, who had already spent months trying to extract clues from Wayne Henley, proposed using his access to ground-penetrating radar to search for more buried bones, a tool detectives hadn't even dreamed of in 1973. "Unfortunately, many of the parents have passed away never knowing where their child was," he told reporters, as the cameras rolled. "Hopefully there are brothers and sisters out there that can reach out to us."

Back in 2000, this same location had been featured in *The Collectors,* a film about murderabilia fanatics that contained footage of a grinning trespasser pocketing gravel from outside Corll's boatshed. But by 2021 the property, then owned by a mom-and-pop landscaping company, was ringed with a steel fence, security cameras, and signs that read KEEP OUT.

FOR MONTHS AFTER THE August 2021 press conference, Anderson scrounged for clues about other hidden burial grounds by tracking down officers who worked the case and by reading investigative reports. Meanwhile, Miller kept interviewing Henley by phone. The trouble was, by the time Miller began those discussions, many places where Corll had once lived, tortured and killed victims, or sold candy had been repeatedly flooded, paved over, or redeveloped into towering condominiums. Miller proposed to offer Henley an incentive—$1,000 for his commissary account—if he could provide solid leads on locations that could still be searched. That money could buy Henley a lot of Cokes, stamps, books, and other items that might improve his prison life.

"He'd be a king," Anderson figured. It was too late to reach David Brooks, who died in May 2020 as the COVID-19 pandemic was ravaging Texas prisons. Brooks's corpse, unclaimed by relatives, had been buried in Captain Joe Byrd Cemetery in Huntsville, Texas, the nation's largest prison graveyard.

In our first meeting, Anderson described how he had carefully reviewed all of the incriminating statements made by Wayne Henley and by David Brooks in 1973, including many reports signed by David Mullican. Mullican had once told Anderson that Wayne Henley knew the location of six or seven more bodies, but Henley's defense lawyer had shut down their conversations. Mullican had died in 2014, so Anderson reached out by phone to Sidney Smith, a long-retired Pasadena detective, who insisted that police had long ago found every grave Henley knew about.

Anderson told me he was surprised by other things he read in 1973 homicide reports, including a tip that Paul Gale, the older brother of one of his high school classmates, had shared about Corll hanging around the Pasadena Skate Ranch in 1969. (Anderson hung out there too as a teen.) By August 1973, Gale had been deployed overseas, but Gale's mother had shared a letter from him informing Pasadena investigators that a man resembling Dean Corll had tried to abduct him. Gale's letter also mentioned that the group might also have been responsible for the disappearance of a Pasadena girl. Later, Sgt. Gale gave a follow-up interview in Guam to military police in which he insisted that "more people were involved than just Henley and Brooks" and shared the girl's name. But Anderson couldn't find the military police report or any information about the missing girl.

Other tips came from people known to police as hippies, drug users, or suspected homosexuals, many of whom were treated with skepticism or suspicion and whose information generated little follow-up. One officer described a man attending Corll's memorial service at Niday Funeral Home as obviously effeminate, implying he must be gay. "The subject had feminine mannerisms," the report said.

Anderson sighed, reflecting back on those times: "I mean, you know, that's what the vernacular back then was."

Not much physical evidence from the murders remained in storage. Houston PD seemed to have purged items that had been photographed for trial exhibits, though the torture board remained in a district court locker and served as an informal courthouse curiosity for years. Anderson learned that the Pasadena department retained the .22 caliber blue metal pistol that Henley used to kill Dean Corll. He also discovered a pair of boys' pants in a size far too small to belong to any of the known victims, yet marked as evidence recovered from the boatshed. The youngest victims buried there were thirteen. Officers had collected rumors about a nine-year-old who Corll supposedly killed, but no solid leads surfaced about that child's identity (though police reports refer to the "little Albright boy").

Anderson was surprised when I told him that Derrick had discovered that a part of a cranium of a boy about that same age had been recovered in the boatshed and stored in the ME's office for decades.

By the 2020s, complex murder investigations in cities like Pasadena or Houston might take years to prepare for trial, even when arrests were made quickly. Anderson was astonished to read in the records that Henley's pretrial hearing had begun less than five months after Corll's murder. "That was kind of like, 'Hey, we got our guy. He confessed,'" Anderson reflected. Even though many officers had been initially deployed during the body recovery phase, and had collectively interviewed dozens of witnesses, the leaders at HPD and in the Harris County DA's office seemed to have little interest in following up on allegations that Corll participated in a larger criminal organization with other co-conspirators and accomplices, based on the 1973 homicide files. Anderson read reports that showed how investigators and tipsters from Dallas, Los Angeles, San Diego, New

York, and elsewhere had contacted Houston or Pasadena officers describing links between porn rings or teen murders in their cities that should be explored. Those tips had arrived nearly two years before Roy Ames, a known associate of Corll's, had subsequently been arrested with pornography that featured eleven of Corll's murder victims.

After reading such tantalizing details, Anderson became convinced that Corll had been involved in organized crime, including theft, drug dealing, and pornography, as well as abduction and murder, just as Henley and Brooks had claimed. Then, as now, local police agencies lacked jurisdiction and resources to investigate multi-state criminal organizations, but what about the FBI? Perhaps powerful people who were important enough to pull strings had been customers of the magazines, films, and services provided by Corll and his associates, he speculated. "I think when Corll was killed, a lot of people breathed a sigh of relief. . . . He's not going to talk. He's dead," Anderson said. "In the back of my mind is [the idea] that maybe somebody was uncovered in that investigation that had some ties politically. And it's like, 'Hey, we've got to squash this.' So that's probably what happened."

ANDERSON HAD WATCHED A special report on the Corll cases by Jessica Willey for Channel 13, the Houston ABC affiliate, in November 2021, and learned for the first time from her investigation that Henley had approached Harris County assistant district attorney Doug Shaver in 1979 and offered information on additional victims' graves. Anderson was a little shocked that Henley's offer had been so swiftly rejected. But already by the 1970s, Harris County had been known for its aggressive murder prosecutions. "And, you know, to me, it's almost like more of a conservative, tougher approach to law enforcement back then," Anderson told me. Looking back, Anderson wonders what would have happened if prosecutors had negotiated with Henley. "The death penalty at the time was off the table. So, he wasn't going to get death. And I'm thinking like, 'Hey, dude, if you've got some information that can help some people find a loved one let's work with it.'"

AS ANDERSON WAS DOING his own research, a member of the Texas EquuSearch team began to use computer mapping programs to overlay police officers' hand-drawn outlines of burial sites over modern maps to try to pinpoint victims' original grave sites along the beach near High Island. The coastline where at least seven murder victims had been buried (counting Allen Lyles, whose body had been found and identified ten years after the rest) spanned five miles in Chambers and Jefferson counties. Because of sea level rise, storm surges, and tidal action, all those locations were now permanently underwater, according to the volunteers' comparison of police reports, historic shoreline maps, and modern satellite and survey data.

Another known burial ground hadn't changed much since 1973—the Angelina National Forest, a vast wooded area that spans four East Texas counties more than one hundred miles northeast of Houston. Texas EquuSearch volunteers drove through Harvey's Lakeview Estates, the rural subdivision where Corll's dad once owned a log cabin. The family had owned that property (and the house on Vince Bayou in Pasadena) for decades. But no one they met seemed to remember anything useful beyond a weird story about a stranded hitchhiker carrying a messy hot dog.

When Anderson made inquiries in San Augustine County, he was surprised to find that no records remained. Newspapers nationwide had published photos of Sheriff Hoyt, a former Texas Ranger who personally accompanied Henley and oversaw searches. Hoyt, wearing his white cowboy hat and flanked by other officers and journalists, stood triumphantly over a hole as a body was being unearthed in one photo. But Hoyt was long dead, and Anderson could find no current county employee who admitted to recalling anything about the celebrated case.

Anderson made more calls and learned that forest rangers could assist, but without precise coordinates the task seemed daunting even for Miller's EquuSearch. The Angelina National Forest includes 153,179 acres of towering longleaf, loblolly, and shortleaf pine, tangles of brambles, and groves of ferns, all poking up from gently rolling sandy soil. The Pasadena PD's hand-drawn map of the forest burial sites revealed an irregular-shaped rectangle, an area bordered on the east by Highway 147, on the south by a creek, and by unmarked dirt roads to the north and west. Even Henley struggled to find four graves there in August 1973, though he'd helped kill and bury victims in those woods only a few weeks before.

EVEN ON HIS HOME turf in Pasadena, Anderson managed—barely—to obtain access to search the yard of 2020 Lamar Drive, Corll's last known address, by persuading the property owner. "We ended up getting permission and got pictures of the inside and the outside of the house." No bodies had ever been ever found in Pasadena, but Anderson had reason to suspect that Corll could have kidnapped or killed more victims there—and perhaps used his father's place along Vince Bayou to hide remains. Besides Paul Gale, whose harrowing 1969 experience was included in the Pasadena PD report, others mentioned meeting Corll or his henchmen in Pasadena.

In 2021, a fellow Pasadena PD officer shared a personal story. One afternoon, the officer's relative, kind of a hippie in the early 1970s, "was standing near the intersection of Peachwood Drive and Allendale Road when a couple of teens in a van stopped to talk."

One teen hollered out, "Hey dude, do you want to get high?"

He answered: "No man, I'm good. I already got high." At the time, the encounter seemed funny. But in 2022 the former hippie still felt frightened whenever he thought about it. That party invitation, he believes, came from Corll, Henley, and Brooks.

Anderson noticed that street corner was near where James Stanton Dreymala, thirteen, had been picked up by the killers while riding his bike in August 1973. Stanton was Corll's last known murder victim.

In our first meeting, I told Anderson about an unsolved missing persons case from Pasadena from 1971, involving a young man whose body had never been found. Old Harris County deed records showed that the Waggoners, a married couple from Rockport, Texas, were among Arnold Corll's neighbors in Pasadena's Vince Heights subdivision from 1971 to 1973. On October 1, 1971, their son David Waggoner, a twenty-three-year-old Marine, disappeared under suspicious circumstances. Waggoner's keys were found lying on the seat of his car just outside his Pasadena apartment complex—as if someone had surprised him there.

Anderson dug up the department's missing persons report on Waggoner. The original reports from the 1970s had been lost. But he learned that the case had been reopened in the 1990s at Waggoner's sister's request. Progress reports showed that Detective Smith, who worked with Mullican on the Corll case, believed the twenty-three-year-old to be one of Corll's victims. Although Corll's oldest known victim was twenty, Waggoner looked younger than his years. Like Dean Corll, he was a handsome, muscular military veteran who rode a motorcycle. A few weeks after his disappearance in 1971, Waggoner's red Honda CB350 was found in trees off of Highway 59, along the route Corll and the others often took to the cabin on Lake Sam Rayburn.

IN NOVEMBER 2021, MILLER and Anderson began their search at 2020 Lamar, even though Henley told Miller he knew of no one buried there. A group of volunteers ended up tramping around the yard and poking holes in the ground with shovels. One team deployed ground-penetrating radar and was excited when they identified three hot spots, indicating the ground had previously been disturbed. "We found all three anomalies and it turned out to be nothing," Anderson recalled in our August 2022 discussion. One held a trash pile, another a piece of concrete, and the third an old T-shirt. The T-shirt initially generated some excitement until a searcher spotted a phone number on a scrap of paper beside it: a ten-digit phone number beginning with 832. That Houston metro area code didn't exist in the 1970s (it was introduced in 1999).

I was surprised when Anderson told me he and Miller never tried to get permission to search the boatshed, across the street from where they'd announced their search. In fact, the boatshed's current owners, a married couple who own and operate a landscaping company there, had been visibly angry about the press conference on Silver Bell Drive, Anderson told me. One of the owners confronted Anderson, who was wearing his police uniform, and claimed he was trespassing.

"He was very mad," Anderson recalled. "I said 'Number one—we're not on your property—this is a public street.'"

Gradually, the man calmed and began to talk to Miller. He explained he and his wife were not informed when they bought the landscaping company and industrial property, with its sheds, a small house, and a no-frills office building, that a serial killer had once stashed murder victims inside one of the storage units. They found out when a customer dropped by and said: "You know all about the bodies?" But the owners would not allow Miller or Anderson to view the contents of the shed, ringed by razor wire, warning signs, and security cameras. Anderson and Miller didn't push for access; they figured the place already had been thoroughly searched.

Anderson had read about Derrick's efforts to identify Corll's victims, and he knew that one boatshed body remained unidentified: the teenager nicknamed Swimsuit Boy.

But I shared information with him that the Harris County Medical Examiner's Office had never posted on its website. Sharon Derrick had identified a few bones found in that shed as belonging to seventeen-year-old Donnie Falcon, a likely Corll murder victim whose name had never been made public and whose sister Dana was still living in Corpus Christi. Anderson's eyes widened when I told him that Derrick believed more bones belonging to Donnie Falcon and perhaps those of that much younger boy might still be buried there.

Unfortunately, I told him, the owners had refused a formal request to allow forensic anthropologists or other experts access for a new search, a request I had made along with an attorney named Scott Durfee on behalf of Donnie's sister, Dana Falcon Jones. When we first contacted the current owners in 2022, they had refused to meet to discuss the matter in person or by phone. Later, in response to a follow-up email, they declined to grant permission for an excavation. The storage shed's co-owner emailed me on August 12, 2022:

"We sympathize with the Jones families and all families involved, we cannot imagine what they have gone through. When we purchased the Silver Bell property, we had no knowledge of its history 50 years ago.

We realize if any additional information could be obtained that confirmed your inquiry it would give the Jones family some comfort however it is with great compassion that we cannot allow any excavations to be performed. The storage units are occupied and daily operations cannot be suspended. We respectfully decline your request."

ANDERSON AGREED THE SHED still needed to be searched, but that would be more difficult without the owners' agreement. He immediately thought of the pants of a small boy that had been stowed away in Pasadena's evidence lockers. He and I both wondered: *Could those belong to the boy whose frontal bone Sharon Derrick had found stored in the ME's office?* Anderson was busy supervising the Pasadena team that served a steady stream of felony warrants, among his other duties, but in between, he kept poking around on the Corll cases. He told me that he'd explore the possibility of seeking a search warrant for the boatshed. The trouble was, these murder cases were all closed. Typically judges need an affidavit of probable cause involving an active criminal investigation before agreeing to authorize a search by police officers; instead, this request would be for a body recovery mission overseen by forensic anthropologists looking for additional victims in a closed serial murder case.

After I returned home from the Pasadena PD in August 2022, I sent two emails to Anderson. One contained a summary of Sharon Derrick's findings in the Donnie Falcon case, including a request we'd sent to the property owners outlining why their boatshed likely needed to be searched again. In the second, I told him I'd just learned some astonishing news.

Swimsuit Boy had been identified.

I drove back to the brick Pasadena PD headquarters on a rainy afternoon in October 2022 to follow up with Anderson about the surprising revelation in that boy's case. He and I met in the same training room, which had been gussied up with a mural that included scenes from the happier side of life in Pasadena: its strawberry festival and a cowboy competing in the local rodeo. For Anderson, 9 A.M. was practically midday, since he supervised serving warrants, a potentially dangerous task best begun at dawn. He arrived toting an extra-large Diet Coke in an oversized Styrofoam cup, his usual morning pick-me-up. He'd grown a trim mustache and goatee since I'd last seen him.

Anderson grew visibly excited when I told him that a team of genetic genealogists had determined the name of the boy thought to be the last unidentified Corll victim, Case No. ML 73-3356. Colleen Fitzpatrick and her team at Identifinders International had used a genetic profile developed from that boy's bone to search for relatives in open-source DNA databases and then had quickly deduced his likely identity. In fact, they had provided a name for Swimsuit Boy in mid-2021. But officials at the Harris County Medical Examiner's Office had not yet contacted his family or announced that news.

There were complications.

CHAPTER 38

SWIMSUIT BOY REVEALED?

ORANGE COUNTY, PHILADELPHIA, AND
HOUSTON, 2007–2021

IN 2019, THE SAME year Colleen Fitzpatrick agreed to work on Harris County's Swimsuit Boy case, Identifinders International also had been asked to assist with Philadelphia's oldest unsolved child murder, a case known as the Boy in the Box. The body of the unidentified boy, four to six years old, had been wrapped in a blanket and then abandoned by a roadside in 1957. He'd been malnourished and abused, an autopsy showed. More than four hundred thousand flyers were distributed and information was tucked inside Philadelphians' natural gas bills. Hundreds of tips arrived, but no one claimed him, and he was buried in the city's potter's field.

Unknown child murder victims remain rare in America, and for decades that Pennsylvania boy was the oldest unsolved case tracked by the National Center for Missing and Exploited Children. In the 2010s, an artist created a lifelike reconstruction of a tot with wide eyes and a homespun haircut as part of an effort to generate new tips. None materialized. The boy had been exhumed before, but an earlier attempt to develop a DNA profile had proven unsuccessful. This time, Philadelphia leaders contacted Fitzpatrick to see if her team could help, and in April 2019, the little boy's remains were exhumed again.

Part of the problem was that the boy's bones had been buried so long that it was difficult to extract enough DNA to develop a genetic profile sufficient for genetic genealogical research. Fitzpatrick turned to one of the world's leading labs. "I sent the remains to the International Commission on Missing Persons. I needed help," she said. Fitzpatrick decided to see if the famous lab would agree to help on two cold cases—the Boy in the Box, found in Pennsylvania in 1957, and Swimsuit Boy, found in Texas in 1973. "At the time, I asked 'Would you do more than one case?' And Swimsuit Boy went along for the ride."

The International Commission on Missing Persons, an intergovernmental organization based in The Hague in the Netherlands, has considerable skill in extracting DNA from bones recovered even many decades after military battles, massacres, and natural disasters. Still, even its experts struggled to obtain enough DNA from a bone belonging to the Boy in the Box to produce the information needed to enable investigators to search open-source consumer DNA databases for his relatives. The boy's DNA "was shot, all that was left were little pieces like confetti," Fitzpatrick later explained to a Philadelphia TV reporter.

A bone from the body of Swimsuit Boy proved easier for the lab to analyze. The lab obtained a strong DNA profile from a sample of his left femur, which had been retained before his 2009 reburial. His profile was submitted to publicly available consumer DNA databases and quickly turned up promising matches. Fitzpatrick assigned the genealogical detective work to Gretchen Stack, a senior Identifinders researcher from the Houston suburb of Katy.

Gretchen Stack was thirteen when news broke about the teenagers' bodies inside Corll's boatshed in August 1973. She grew up in Houston's Spring Branch area, near where at least three of Corll's victims lived—Danny Yates and Jim Glass, reported missing in December 1970, and Allen Lyles, who vanished in February 1973. Fitzpatrick considered Stack a "force to be reckoned with." In her time with Identifinders, Stack also used her research skills to help identify a serial rapist who had terrorized the Washington State

University campus nearly twenty years before. Stack was passionate and brought a sense of urgency to her assignments. A terminal cancer patient, she knew she had little time left on earth to make a difference.

EXPERTS IN GENETIC GENEALOGY can't magically solve cold case mysteries. Even after a list of matching relatives is produced through a computerized comparison to an unknown decedent's DNA profile, the search process is complex. Most begin with distant kin, third or fourth cousins, whose names provide cryptic clues to a larger puzzle: Who are the common ancestors that link matching relatives to the DNA of this unidentified dead person? Finding the answers often involves creating a forest of family trees. Tracing connections between those family trees can eventually lead to common sets of great-grandparents, to grandparents, to parents, and finally, with luck, to the name of a missing person. Fitzpatrick compares the process to an expert level sudoku puzzle. Stack's search for this Lost Boy went faster than other assignments she had undertaken. Although the process of extracting DNA and getting a usable profile from his bone had taken months, Stack completed her research in only weeks.

ON MAY 12, 2021, Stack sent an email to Pinto, the Harris County forensic anthropologist, to say she was almost sure of Swimsuit Boy's identity. "The genealogy database returned some very good DNA matches to the unknown victim's DNA, the highest being a first cousin once removed. This gave me a good dataset for my analysis and to begin building out the tree." An even stronger match turned up later: a first cousin who shared a set of grandparents with the unidentified victim. Soon, Stack identified a probable candidate: a young man whose death was recorded in February 1972. That month stood out, since she already knew Corll's known murders spanned December 1970 to August 1973.

In fact, the boy Stack identified was already known as one of Corll's victims.

Stack linked Swimsuit Boy to the relatives of a teenager who had previously been linked to another body buried in the boatshed in 1985, before DNA tests were available. "In conclusion, based on my experience, I believe the DNA sample given to Identifinders International is that of Willard 'Rusty' Branch," Stack wrote.

It appeared the Branch family had also been given the wrong murder victim's remains to bury.

Pinto seemed gobsmacked by the news that a DNA profile produced from the bone of Swimsuit Boy had matched Rusty Branch. She recalled past mix-ups in the case—she had worked on the exhumation of the body misidentified as Michael Baulch in October 1973—but knew much less about the Lost Boys than her former colleague Sharon Derrick.

Pinto didn't know how to answer a question Stack posed: "Could there have been commingling of DNA between bodies found in the boatshed—Case No. ML 73-3350, the remains given to the Branch family, and Case No. ML 73-3356, the Swimsuit Boy?"

"I am stumped," Pinto replied via email on May 13, 2021. "I don't have anything in my records [to] indicate commingling." But Pinto told Stack she'd searched HCIFS laboratory files and discovered that a tissue sample had been retained before those other boy's remains had been released to the Branches for burial in 1985. "If we are able to get a DNA profile, we can compare it to ML 73-3356 and see if we have a commingling issue. I will keep you posted."

Though DNA from Rusty Branch's relatives had matched a bone from Swimsuit Boy, Pinto, a by-the-book scientist, wanted to hold back the news and ordered tests on another 1973 lab sample to try to determine whether remains buried in the county cemetery or in the Branch family plot might contain a mixture of two different boys' bones. She dispatched the additional sample to UNT for more DNA testing on June 8, 2021. "It will be a while before we have an answer due to their backlog," Pinto wrote Stack.

Pinto didn't try to locate Rusty Branch's family. She didn't have Derrick's knack for searching online databases. Nor did she know about the issues of overlapping graves and extra bones associated with the boatshed where these murder victims' bodies had been buried.

MEANWHILE, THE LAB WORK for the case of Philadelphia's Boy in the Box continued. It took two and a half years to generate a DNA profile usable for forensic genealogical research. "This was the most challenging case of my career," Fitzpatrick later said.

As soon as she got that profile, Misty Gillis, another researcher for Identifinders International, began tracking distant relatives linked to the Boy in the Box. "When that data came in, she worked night and day to get that boy his identity back," Fitzpatrick said. Gillis took the task personally: She had children about the same age as that boy had been when he was killed. Working with Philadelphia police, the closest matches Gillis initially found were second cousins. Gillis carefully constructed those relatives' family trees, and the likely identity of his deceased birth mother came to light first. Once Gillis supplied the birth mother's name, Philadelphia police obtained court orders to review all birth certificates, including any closed ones for adoptions, linked to that mother in the early 1950s. They found three responsive records. Among them was the January 13, 1953, Pennsylvania birth certificate of Joseph Augustus Zarelli.

IN DECEMBER 2022, PHILADELPHIA PD scheduled a news conference to announce a breakthrough in the case of "America's Unknown Child."

Philadelphia Police Commissioner Danielle Outlaw stood proudly in uniform at a podium before a row of cameras and a crowd of local and national correspondents.

"In his very short life, it is apparent that this boy experienced horrors that no one, no one should ever be subjected to," she began. "For sixty-five years, the story of who would come to be known as America's unknown child has haunted this community, the Philadelphia police department, our nation, and the world. When people think of the boy in the box, a profound sadness is felt. Not just because he was murdered but because his entire identity and his rightful claim to his existence was taken away."

Joseph Augustus Zarelli was this child's name. Though his parents were dead and the four-year-old child's murder remained unsolved, Outlaw declared that progress in such an extremely cold case brought new hope for all of America's unidentified. "The science and technology that were instrumental in the identification of this child, one of our oldest unsolved homicides, give me hope that we can continue to identify unknown victims of crime, and that no one will ever again have to wait this long for their name and the story of their life to be told."

BACK IN HARRIS COUNTY, the long-awaited identification of Swimsuit Boy remained unannounced. In January 2022, Forensic Anthropologist Deborrah Pinto left to accept a job at the Dallas Medical Examiner's Office. After more than ten years in Houston, she would now lead Dallas efforts to build an electronic database with information on its five hundred unidentified decedents—a backlog even larger than Harris County's. The Lost Boys cases would no longer be her responsibility. Later that same year, in November 2022, Gretchen Stack, the Identifinders researcher who'd used genetic genealogy to help restore this Lost Boy's name, died of cancer. And Dwayne Wolf, the deputy medical examiner who'd championed these cases for so long, retired and moved to Ohio. Other forensic anthropologists and pathologists in Harris County were overwhelmed by an unexpected rise in deaths of all kinds that accompanied the pandemic.

Even in December 2022, the identification of Swimsuit Boy as Rusty Branch had never been announced to the public—and no one had contacted his next of kin. No current or former Harris County official I interviewed seemed to know whether Rusty Branch had any close relatives left: His police officer father died of a heart attack in 1980. His only brother, Doug, died a year later. His most outspoken advocate, his sister Susan McLemore, who'd helped ME's officials make the 1985 ID, died in 1998. His mother, Bonnie Sue Sherman Clark, died in 2005.

Deep in the Harris County archives, a handwritten message showed that in 1987, Bonnie, who lived in Beckville, Texas, then, harbored doubts about whether the right remains had been shipped home. She was concerned enough to consider exhuming the body in Rusty's grave, according to a phone message Susan McLemore left Dr. Joe in December 1987. "She advised decedent's mother is going to get a court order . . . if her call is not returned. The mother is NOT convinced that is him and they would like to reclarify some things."

Despite the mother's doubts, the body sent to the Branches in 1985

One of many messages McLemore left at the ME's office

stayed in the family plot in Old Saltillo Cemetery, a rural graveyard beside a country church on the site of a former railroad whistle-stop.

Rusty Branch's grave site

Rusty has his own full-sized tombstone in a grave beside his brother Douglas's. The graves of the siblings and of their grandparents all seemed to share that peaceful meadow dotted with tombstones. But forensic evidence suggests that Rusty Branch's real body lies in a government-owned graveyard nearly 270 miles away. His DNA matched remains interred in 2009 in the Babyland section of the Harris County Cemetery as Case No. ML 73-3356. Exhumations are expensive—and resolving this Lost Boy's case would likely require two.

THE LOST BOYS

THE SEVENTH ID:

Willard K. "Rusty" Branch, Jr., 2021 (unannounced)

Rusty Branch, 17, who grew up in Houston, disappeared in February

Rusty Branch, portrait by Nancy Rose

1972 after visiting family in East Texas. According to his sister, his last known hitchhiking companion was Elmer Wayne Henley, Jr. He was previously identified in 1985 as Case No. ML 73-3350, a body recovered from Corll's boatshed, but that ID was not confirmed through DNA or dental records. In 2021, new DNA tests and genetic genealogical research linked Rusty Branch to Case No. ML 73-3356, another boy whose remains were recovered from Corll's boatshed alongside a striped swimming suit. The true identity of the boy still buried in Rusty Branch's grave remains unknown.

CHAPTER 39

THE FAMILY PLOT

HOPKINS COUNTY AND HOUSTON, 2022

R USTY BRANCH'S FAMILY HAS scattered since the 1970s, but they turned out to be fairly easy to find. His grave in Old Saltillo is a five-minute drive from the dairy farm where Rusty spent many summers with his grandparents. When I visited there in December 2022, the leaves were turning and cattle grazed on verdant pastures. By that time, his sister Susan had been buried in an unmarked grave beside her brothers, but one of Rusty's first cousins still lived on his grandparents' farm.

Rusty Branch's youngest sister is still alive, too. She was named as one of Willard K. Branch, Sr.'s heirs in his 1980 typewritten will that I found in the probate department of the Harris County District Clerk's Office, housed inside the high-rise courthouse complex that long ago replaced the cramped quarters used for Henley's hearing and Brooks's trial. One of Rusty Branch's stepbrothers, Ray Hunt, also was listed as an heir. I couldn't believe the coincidence when I spotted his name. I knew Hunt, a well-known Houston police officer, who serves as executive director of the powerful Houston Police Officers' Union. In a few minutes, I reached him on his cellphone. Hunt didn't have Rusty's little sister's contact information, but he knew a cousin in Dallas who did.

When I finally reached Rusty's only surviving sibling, she was not as surprised as I expected her to be. "Somehow I always thought this was not over," she said. She'd read about the Golden State Killer, and she understood when I explained how research by another genetic genealogist had helped link the unidentified remains of Swimsuit Boy—a known Corll victim—to DNA profiles in consumer databases supplied by his (and her) relatives. Those researchers had determined that the DNA from Swimsuit Boy belonged to her male sibling. Her only other brother, Douglas, lived into the 1980s, so this body had to be Rusty's.

Rusty's little sister no longer lives in Texas and wasn't interested in having her name published, but remembers her big sister Susan's struggle to reclaim Rusty's body very well. She supported an exhumation and began pushing for answers. "That's what Susan would have wanted," she told me. After we got off the phone, she looked up information on the internet about the Swimsuit Boy case. The reconstruction done by the FACES lab in Louisiana resembled Rusty, she thought. "The artist did an incredible job. She captured the shape of his face and eyes and the unusual shape of the lips that runs in our family," she later told me.

In a follow-up conversation, I told her that James Anderson, the Pasadena police officer who'd already spent more than a year looking for missing persons and bodies related to the Corll case, had taken an interest in Rusty Branch's mistaken ID. There was a possibility, based on information in a 1973 autopsy report and in missing persons files, that David Waggoner, the Marine from Pasadena who disappeared in October 1971, might be buried in the grave marked with Rusty's name. Waggoner's sister had been looking for him for decades—and had reached out to Sharon Derrick and provided her DNA, though none of the Lost Boys had matched.

Anderson arranged a meeting in early 2023 with a group of Pasadena PD officers who agreed to help Rusty's little sister and simultaneously investigate whether the mistake in the Rusty Branch ID might provide a break in one of the department's oldest missing persons cases. Several details from the reports on the ME's 1973 autopsy for Case No. ML 73-3350, the body identified in 1985 as Rusty Branch, stood out to him and other officers. The 1973 report said these remains likely belonged to a man of twenty-two to twenty-four, around the age of David Waggoner, and not a boy of seventeen.

In the mid-1980s, pathologists had taken new X-rays and found that this particular murder victim had suffered a skull fracture. Rusty Branch had fractured his skull falling out the window of a house as a small boy. But the age and other details in the autopsy report seemed to better fit Waggoner, who had fractured his skull as an adult in a 1967 motorcycle accident while he was home on leave from the Marines.

IN THE FALL OF 2022, I had traveled to Rockport, Texas, to meet David's sister, Diana Waggoner Shurbet. Both she and David grew up in this Gulf Coast city known for its fall hummingbird festival. Those small birds, with their bright feathers and flitting wings, converge here by the thousands to feed and rest every September before making the journey across the Gulf of Mexico to their wintering grounds. We shared steaming cups of coffee, eggs, and homemade biscuits in a busy small-town café adjacent to the local Walmart. Diana had similar features to her brother on missing persons pages. She talked with vigor about how she'd never given up on finding out what had happened to him. "He was a wonderful person. We hardly ever fought when we were kids. He was a good human being and he served our country. And I miss him terribly," she told me, in one of several conversations we'd have.

In October 1971, the year he'd vanished without leaving any word, their parents lived in a house only blocks from Corll's place on Lamar—a five- or ten-minute walk down the bayou. David often visited them, though he had his own apartment in a new complex overlooking Pasadena's bustling Strawberry Park. At that time, Diana was already married and living elsewhere, but she never believed her brother would leave without telling her or anybody else where he'd gone. She knew from police reports that David's keys had been found in his car, which remained in the lot in front of his apartment. She also knew his motorcycle had been found later in the woods off Highway 59—with the helmet still on the seat. She'd always suspected he'd been murdered, but had never lost hope that his remains might be recovered.

Diana had kept in touch with the Pasadena PD for decades, repeatedly calling to update her address, as her husband's job in emergency management kept them on the move. As part of her efforts, Diana had tracked down her brother's military dental and medical records; provided her DNA sample to the Harris County ME's office; appeared on a podcast; done interviews with Texas newspapers; and added her brother's case to every missing persons database and online forum she could find: the Doe Network, the Charlie Project, NamUs. For a while, she'd been convinced he'd been killed by a notoriously corrupt former sheriff who ran a mafia of highway robbers in the 1970s based in Coldspring, Texas, a small town near the woods where David's motorcycle had been found. But she'd also suspected he'd been killed by Corll.

David never mentioned meeting Dean Corll, as far as she knew. Her brother had been slightly older than Corll's known victims, but like Corll he rode motorcycles and played trombone in his high school band. Before his disappearance, he frequently visited the Pasadena neighborhood where Corll's father lived. She didn't know whether he was gay, but told me he'd never really had a girlfriend.

At Christmas 2022, I saw a poignant note she posted on Facebook about how she always missed her brother more during the holidays. I knew that if there was any chance her brother's body might be buried in the Branch family plot, she would want to know. We talked again, and I connected her with Rusty Branch's little sister so they could exchange information and coordinate next steps with police. In January 2023, Diana Waggoner Shurbet, who'd moved back to her hometown of Rockport, Texas, and Rusty Branch's little sister, who had left Texas for a job out of state, met via email and decided to join forces. If things worked out, the sisters hoped that together they might be able to right old wrongs and reclaim their brothers' real bodies at last.

Sharon Derrick wasn't part of that process—and it frustrated her. Derrick had been elated when she heard from former co-workers in 2022 that her final push to solve this case through genetic genealogy had gotten results, but she'd largely been kept out of the loop. Derrick never complained to former colleagues, but privately she told her husband that she found their silence heartbreaking: "I submitted this DNA and didn't hear anything back."

With Derrick on the sidelines, it seemed to be up to these sisters to call for justice for the Lost Boys. Perhaps two determined women could help accomplish something no investigator on the case had managed to do: identify the very last unidentified body hauled out of Corll's boatshed in August 1973.

I hoped in 2022 that Sgt. James Anderson and other officers in Pasadena would assist them. But one of the hurdles was the expense: Solving this mystery, determining whether David Waggoner—or some other murder victim—was in Rusty's grave, and fixing the mix-up would require two exhumations in two different counties, including a state permit and a private undertaker's assistance, as well as additional forensic anthropology work and genetic tests.

Without Sharon Derrick around, Anderson and other Pasadena police officials weren't sure they could persuade the Harris County ME's office to help—even though the Pasadena police still had an active missing persons case for David Waggoner.

For the next year, there were no updates. The fiftieth anniversary of the discovery of Corll's crimes arrived in August 2023 without any word. To mark the occasion, the Harris County ME's office worked with the National Center for Missing and Exploited Children to issue yet another revised sketch of the unidentified Corll victim still known as ML 73-3356 or Swimsuit Boy.

No Harris County official said anything publicly about the fact that this boy might actually be Rusty Branch. The news remained, quite literally, underground.

CHAPTER 40

THE PRISONER'S STORY

HOUSTON, 1973–1998, AND ANDERSON
COUNTY, TEXAS, 2023

IN AUGUST 1973, HARRIS County DA Carol Vance sought a speedy investigation of Corll's murders and a rapid prosecution of Brooks and Henley, an efficient approach that left many leads unexplored. Vance's style stood in contrast to that of Los Angeles County prosecutor Vincent Bugliosi, who devoted more than a year exploring bizarre motives and searching for additional victims of Charles Manson and the Manson family and then co-wrote a potboiling bestseller called *Helter Skelter*. (Both approaches generated criticism.) In 2010, thirty-one years after he left the DA's office, Vance produced a blander book about his career called *Boomtown DA*, with a chapter on the Corll case. In his book, Vance proudly declared that Houston, despite its size, had virtually no organized crime at all.

Unfortunately, the systematic exploitation and mass sexual abuse of teenaged boys in Harris County did not end with Dean Corll's corpse being hauled out of a house in Pasadena in August 1973. Paper trails of documents, newspaper articles, and the tales of surviving victims suggest that other players linked to Corll's schemes continued to exploit and sexually assault teens for decades, and indeed retained a strong presence in the Heights.

Headlines that appeared in Houston newspapers in February

1975 seemed explosive. JUVENILE OFFICERS SAY 11 BOYS WHO WERE VICTIMS IN THE HOUSTON MASS MURDERS CASE ARE PICTURED IN SEXUAL MATERIAL SEIZED IN WHAT POLICE CALLED A HOMOSEXUAL RING, read one. That cache of items seized by Houston police and by federal postal investigators included ten thousand photos of naked teens, a thousand reels of film, and two hundred magazines, the newspapers reported. "Some of the boys in the photos are now legal adults, leading officers to believe the businesses had been going on locally for some years," one story said. Many of the ring's living victims had been sexually assaulted; some told police they were being paid $15 to $30 for "being in a movie," HPD investigator Johnny Freeman told the *Houston Post* in February 1975. Some he identified were only eight or nine years old. But Freeman quickly went quiet. Freeman, part of a small group of officers assigned to investigate which juveniles had been exploited by those pornographers, did not respond—even as recently as 2022—to further questions. The official explanation for that silence in the 1970s was that dedicating more time and attention to the sexual exploitation of Corll's murder victims by a porn ring would only worsen the suffering of their grieving parents.

Only Ames, the alleged ringleader, was charged in federal court for distributing those pornographic images nationally and internationally and went to federal prison (though related state charges were dropped). Other Houston men, including Leonard Edward Cunningham and Bryant A. Burch, who were arrested in February 1975 and named by police as collaborators in the 1970s boy porn ring, mostly managed to avoid publicity. Those two men ended up being convicted in Harris County of what back then were deemed lesser crimes, including sexual abuse of a juvenile. Neither seems to have been questioned about how or why the pornography contained Corll's murder victims' photos.

I tracked down a teenaged boy identified in court records as one of the group's living victims. That former Heights resident, a sexual assault victim I won't name here, still suffers from frightening memories. He believes he narrowly avoided being murdered and that his life was spared partly because of a warning from Billy Baulch, who was killed by Corll and Henley in May 1972. And yet, he still became ensnared by Ames who, according to court records, sexually assaulted him and paid many Houston teenagers to pose for nude photos and films.

Ames's dual role as an abuser and a pornographer was well reported in Texas—though his association with serial killer Dean Corll was not. His activities as one of America's major commercial child porn dealers became notorious, the subject of state and federal government hearings. But long after Ames went to federal prison, Ed Cunningham and Bryant Burch, identified as Ames's alleged partners in that same juvenile porn ring, kept on operating in Houston Heights. Court records, deeds, and documents show the pair collaborated in legitimate businesses—as well as clandestine criminal activities. Over the next two decades, they amassed more criminal charges for juvenile sex crimes, thefts, and drug offenses, court records show. Yet they prospered, acquiring real estate and running a car painting business called Houston Auto-Bake, Inc. Among other things, Burch was convicted of crimes linked to his operation of a storehouse filled with stolen goods, including art taken in a heist from a local gallery. But Burch never seemed to stay locked up long. In fact, Burch and Cunningham together and separately seemed to have continued a cycle of abusing teenaged boys, dealing drugs, fencing stolen goods, and distributing child porn, though neither man was ever implicated in any murder. Cunningham died of natural causes.

In an eerie echo of the Dean Corll murder case, Burch's long criminal career ceased only when Burch, then fifty-five, was shot and killed in 1998 in a small house he owned on Prince Street in the Heights by a boy he'd sexually exploited: eighteen-year-old Anthony John Mendez.

ANTHONY MENDEZ, A SLIGHT man who stands only five feet four and speaks in a soft, smooth voice, is still serving out a life sentence for killing Burch. In 2023, he was doing time inside a prison that is part of the Tennessee Colony complex, factories and farmland in rural

Anderson County. In the visitation room of that high-security prison, a copy of the unit that houses Texas's death row, a talented incarcerated artist has created elaborate cartoon characters to disguise otherwise dull concrete block walls. In one corner, the artist painted an oversized version of the Incredible Hulk doing something most prisoners must dream about: breaking free. Mendez wore handcuffs on his wrists and fumbled with the receiver as we talked via phone, separated by a thick plate of glass in one of the visitation booths that bisect that room. Even with the barriers of glass and an intercom phone line between us, his soft-spoken words seemed to echo loudly.

Mendez readily admits that in 1998 he deliberately planned to kill Burch, who had been providing housing for him that year in return for sexual favors. He regrets this because, he says, Burch was "not a bad guy. He was really a sweetheart." But the story Mendez tells about how he met Burch and Burch's friend Cunningham suggests that the pair who'd been named as accomplices in the "boy porn" ring that had distributed images of some of Corll's murder victims continued to collect and exploit teenaged boys long after Corll died.

Mendez, born in 1980, more than seven years after Corll was killed, had heard about the Lost Boys. But he didn't know of the connection between Burch, Cunningham, and the porn ring that traded in explicit photos of eleven boys murdered in the 1970s, until I held up court papers to show him through the plate-glass window in the visitation booth.

"I didn't know anything about any of his dark past," Mendez says, seeming astonished. Mendez, who weighs less than 150 pounds, appears to swim in his white inmate's coveralls, bound by a thick leather belt prison officials use to attach handcuffs to when transporting inmates. The belt and cuffs make it hard for him to handle the phone we use to communicate.

Mendez looked much younger when he was arrested in October 1997 at seventeen for joyriding in a friend's car and charged as an adult with unauthorized use of a vehicle, a misdemeanor. He was unable to post a $2,000 bond and ended up in Harris County Jail, one of the nation's largest local lockups. He remembers standing in the recreation yard outside when an older inmate named Ed Cunningham approached him and other teenaged prisoners and offered to pay $50 or $70 for a hand job or other sexual services. Mendez, raised mostly in foster homes, had heard that Cunningham had been jailed on child pornography charges, but he needed money. Others also accepted Big Ed's offer.

When Mendez was released a few months later, he had nowhere to go. He'd aged out of foster care, where he had also been sexually abused, and had lost touch with most of his relatives. Cunningham handed him a phone number and suggested he contact his business partner, Bryant Burch.

Burch seemed nice at first, Mendez recalls. He allowed the teenager to stay with him rent free in the 2016 Main Street Condominiums, a high-rise Houston complex with valet parking. But there was a price: Burch, who told Mendez he was HIV positive, asked the teen to sleep with him. Mendez said Burch asked him to "spend the nights with him, to hang out with him, and sleep on the bed together." Mendez initially agreed. The condo faced Houston's busy downtown Greyhound bus station, a congregation point for homeless teens and runaways. Other youth hanging around the condo seemed to be working for Burch or Cunningham in various businesses, which included drug dealing. Burch initially treated him well, Mendez said. But Mendez suffered PTSD from being sexually abused by a foster father. As a child, he says he'd been forced to testify against that predator. Ultimately, he couldn't stomach his sexual arrangement with Burch. One day when Burch was away, he grabbed some cash, fled the condo, and bolted for the bus station.

Burch soon caught him. "I made him mad," Mendez tells me. For the first time, Burch's menacing side showed and Mendez feared for his life. "He wanted his money back [and] he was willing to do whatever. He was talking about getting one of them youngsters to hurt me or make me disappear." So, Mendez returned the money.

AFTER THAT, MENDEZ WAS still expected to sleep with Burch, but was relocated to another house in the Heights, a gray hovel on a side street with asphalt shingles and burglar bars on the windows. Some Heights teens knew that Prince address as a dealer's house, a sort of dark hole. Mendez believes he was being punished: He was locked inside the house on the 1300 block of Prince Street "because I had stolen from him that one time and tried to get away." That place, long since demolished, contained an ordinary-looking bedroom where he and Burch slept together and a TV room with a large projector and library of hard-core porn. Other rooms were filled with stashes of marijuana and cocaine.

It took a while before Burch agreed to let Mendez out again. But when he eventually did, Mendez snapped. "The next time, I decided to take [his money] and kill him."

On the night of August 19, 1998, he went to dinner with Burch at Houston's retro 59 Diner, secretly packing a gun he'd taken from his brother. He waited until later, when Burch fell asleep in the bedroom of the house on Prince with the covers pulled up to his neck. Then he shot Burch in the head. Mendez swiped Burch's Rolex watch and his money, then sped away in the dead man's pickup, which he later abandoned. He returned to the Greyhound station and hopped a bus to San Antonio.

It was not a well-executed plan. Mendez was the obvious and only suspect. Mendez had left his ID and an extra pair of pants next to Burch's body. "Everything was pointing in my direction," Mendez recalls. "I was the only one there. I was the only one locked in a house with him. I was only really lucky enough to get the key and open the door and get out."

Houston police issued a warrant for his arrest. On October 21, 1999, Mendez was captured in San Antonio, brought back to Harris County, and charged with capital murder. Prosecutors considered seeking the death penalty, though Mendez was eighteen at the time of the crime and had only one prior misdemeanor conviction. He pleaded guilty to first-degree murder and was sentenced to life on March 30, 2001. For several years, Mendez did time with another prisoner who seemed like a celebrity. "He used to live with us. Not the serial killer, but his crime partner. Elmer Wayne Henley . . . And I've met him. Actually, he never really talked to me about his crimes, but I knew why he was here, and I knew that his case was high profile," Mendez says.

Our society judged these teenaged killers worthy of a similar punishment. Though Henley received multiple life sentences for six murders, he was not prosecuted for killing Dean Corll, the unarmed older man who had abused and exploited him. For years, Henley kept serving time with Mendez in the same high-security facility.

Prior to his sentencing, Mendez's court-appointed attorney, apparently grateful to have avoided the death penalty, made no attempt to convince the court that Mendez, still a teenager, had taken responsibility for his crime, but might merit a lesser sentence, given that he'd been sexually abused as a child and then allegedly threatened and exploited by the man he killed. In fact, Mendez says he didn't discuss being sexually abused with his lawyer. Aside from a pro forma direct appeal, he's never had any assistance from an attorney to challenge his sentence or to address the parole board.

Into the 2020s, many missing and endangered teens reported to the National Center for Missing and Exploited Children are still believed to be exploited (or killed) by sex traffickers. Yet even later in life, male victims of sexual assaults rarely come forward, as psychiatrists Joan M. Cook and Amy Ellis wrote in an article entitled "The Other MeToo: Male Sexual Abuse Survivors." "Men who have been sexually assaulted may have concerns about their masculinity as well as their sexual orientation; they struggle intensely with shame and self-blame. They are less likely to report sexual abuse, to identify experiences they have had as abusive, and to seek support or formal treatment for these experiences."

As of 2024, the revelation that Rusty Branch, a victim both of a pornography ring and of a serial killer, had been linked through DNA to the unidentified remains dubbed Swimsuit Boy remained under wraps. Pasadena PD detectives had few updates for Rusty's little sister. Officials from the Harris County Institute for Forensic Sciences declined interviews and seemed uninterested in exhuming the body buried in the Branch family plot. Given the need for permits, the complexity, and the costs, the process appeared stalled. Part of the problem came down to money: Who would pay for exhumations, related reburials, and complex DNA tests? Harris County, the leaders in the forensics on the Corll cases? The Pasadena PD, who had an open missing persons case? The families? Some other donor?

IN AUGUST 2023, ANOTHER Pasadena city official pushed for a very different initiative to mark the fiftieth anniversary year of the discovery of the murders: razing Corll's house at 2020 Lamar Drive and erecting some kind of memorial to honor the victims of these terrible crimes who otherwise seemed forgotten.

CHAPTER 41

THE HOUSE FALLS

PASADENA, TEXAS, 1974 AND 2023

I N THE WINTER OF 1974, Truman Capote stood in front of the house at 2020 Lamar Drive, breathing in its "chemical-scented air." He came to Houston that January intending to cover Henley's trial for *The Washington Post* and decided, on a side trip, to seek out the spot where Dean Corll had been gunned down. By then obsessed with murder, Capote had been lured here by the idea that this horrifying case might explain why so many Americans seemed lost and were losing faith in their own society. But Capote quickly abandoned the project called the "Houston Diary." Years later, only a few pages of notes about his visit to Corll's working-class neighborhood in Pasadena were rediscovered: They'd been stashed and forgotten in a closet of a house he'd rented in 1976 in Santa Fe, New Mexico.

Capote's contemplation of Corll's last address, and murder scene, handwritten in pencil on a yellow legal pad, was the only surviving Houston Diary entry. He'd been looking for Lamar Street, rather than Lamar Drive. And he'd had trouble finding the place:

> In search of it, I consulted a cruising police car with some hesitancy, for the Pasadena police, like so much of the Texas constabulary has a reputation for being a bit . . . over-zealous. But the young officer driving the car was a model of helpfulness—after studying a

street directory his instructions on how to arrive at 2020 Lamar Street could not have been clearer. The surprising part was he didn't recognize the address.

After all, it was at 2020 Lamar Street and only a mere [five] months earlier that the ultimate scenes of the largest mass murder in modern American history had been enacted.

From the outside, Truman Capote found the house itself unremarkable: a flimsy wood-frame affair painted a "bilious green" that seemed interchangeable with the others, although the neighbors' choices in exterior colors and garden statuary varied: "here a gnome, there a flamingo." He observed nothing unusual, jotting down notes about "neighborhood kids biking and skating" and "rolled-sleeved men leaning around a car collectively listening to a football broadcast" and "housewives bustling past in bursting slacks."

Yet to him, this ordinariness itself seemed ominous. "How was it possible that these gregarious people living in their thin-walled, so closely assembled homes, how is it conceivable that they would have been unaware of the outcries, the gunshots, the traffic in corpses at number 2020?"

ON FEBRUARY 22, 2023, long after Capote's brief visit, Corll's old house remained at 2020 Lamar. Only it was now government property, recently acquired with taxpayers' funds on behalf of the City of Pasadena Public Works Department. At first glance, the block's boxy houses and yards seemed unchanged, compared to Capote's impressions, though the house, freshly repainted, was now an innocuous gray rather than that "bilious green." Today, Dean Corll's last home, a place some considered an unofficial monument to a serial killer, was about to disappear.

Sgt. James Anderson stands on Lamar Drive and watches white dust billow, forming clouds as the house falls nearly fifty years after Dean Corll was hauled out of it as a corpse. That thick mist hovering over this place can surely be no more than pulverized Sheetrock—fragments of modern walls from a recent real estate flipper's remodel. But somewhere embedded in these bricks and boards there may be some lingering memory of horror, some remnant of the souls of boys tortured and killed here in the summer of 1973.

With those thoughts in mind, Police Chaplain Kathy M. Pratt holds a brief ceremony on the cement driveway on this February morning. She bends her head in prayer, long curly hair folding in around her face. She prays for the Lost Boys' friends and for their families. She pleads for peace and for release from terrible memories, for them and for first responders who found Corll's crumpled and lifeless body in the hall of this house in August 1973. She remembers others who recovered remains of the boys murdered here. There were at least seven: James Stanton Dreymala, thirteen; Billy Lawrence, Michael Baulch, and Homer Garcia, all fifteen; Charles Cobble and Marty Jones, seventeen and eighteen. And Ray Blackburn, a twenty-year-old father nabbed as he tried to hitchhike home to Baton Rouge to see his wife and meet his newborn. She prays for the victims killed elsewhere. And for the police, pathologists, and witnesses who viewed so many bodies in clandestine graves and on steel autopsy tables and who never forgot how violence marked and marred them. The gags, nooses, bullet holes, and horror . . .

Sgt. Anderson waits, wondering when her prayer will end. Then he and two other Pasadena City employees amble to the center of the front yard, where morning sun still streams through the house's three east-facing windows. Anderson and two others heave bricks through the glass of each window, sending shards into the living room. Breaking windows feels strange to Anderson, who in his career has arrested vandals for less. But that act seems necessary to Assistant Public Works Director Mark Gardemal, who assembled the funds, permits, and heavy equipment needed to tear down this house. "I'm not a fan of religion but I think we leave a residual of ourselves behind," he says, soon after throwing his brick. "I had to find a way to release them. We did that by breaking glass. . . . But the last guy to die here was Dean Corll, so I have to be careful who I release."

For him and other officials in the City of Pasadena, this brick home was a dark, unwelcome tourist attraction and a blight on a working-class neighborhood; a house of horror, an embarrassment that even Google eventually turned into a blotch on its maps.

Houston TV crews have visited there to film stand-ups on nearly every significant anniversary of August 1973, the month when Corll was killed and those murdered boys' bodies were discovered. Gardemal talks of placing a pergola and benches at this location, as part of a planned trail along Vince Bayou. He hopes city officials will agree to erect some kind of a sign dedicated to the memory of these boys, and to other murdered and missing children.

For Chaplain Pratt, who regularly studies the Bible, the revamped bungalow seems like a pagan temple. She believes that not even gleaming unused appliances nor the newly installed AC unit should be spared. Pratt trained for five years before being approved as a voluntary chaplain in 2022. Too often she mourns and comforts. Today she rejoices, watching walls fall. "I think it's going to be very healing, not only for those involved but for the city."

ONLY NINETY MINUTES AFTER the brick-throwing ceremony, one man operating a single yellow excavator claws down the house's walls, its ceilings, its essence. The living room goes first, then the hall where Corll himself fell, sending more puffs of pulverized Sheetrock skyward. The kitchen and bedrooms are last. The operator works efficiently right to left, steadily churning his loudly humming machine with its caterpillar feet as its oversized shovel arm tears through all 1,231 square feet. Finally, the big digger pauses as the driver pivots his shovel in order to tamp down debris into manageable piles. By midday tomorrow, dump trucks will haul it all away.

This is mostly a Mexican American neighborhood now. This block of modest houses is filled with hardworking people who mostly rent and can't afford to own. From across the street, Paulino Rodriguez Garcia pauses to watch the demolition. He used to live at 2020 Lamar, and his driver's license still shows that address. For seven years, he sensed nothing evil inside those walls. No lingering sign of suffering, pain, or violence. None of his neighbors ever spoke of the murders. Only the internet revealed that the address was a serial killer's former home. The house itself is guilty of nothing and Rodriguez Garcia regrets that it will be erased. When asked if this seems wise, he reveals doubt: *"La verdad que no."*

Sgt. James Anderson grips a floorboard he retrieved on the day Corll's former house was torn down.

Sgt. James Anderson walks toward his Pasadena PD SUV, marked with the slogan TO PROTECT AND TO SERVE. He has watched the house fall not with glee, but with obvious satisfaction. After ninety minutes of demolition, he strides in his stiff blue uniform through the front yard to survey the rubble piled on a slab that since 1952 had been a home. He does not expect to find undiscovered corpses or clues. This house had been gutted and updated many times since 1973. Surely if Corll's trophies or relics remained, they would have long ago been recovered. In a few strides, Anderson reaches the spot where Corll's spare room once stood. From the area where Corll kept his torture board, Anderson retrieves a piece of wood from the original floor. He hefts the darkened panel, shiny with what seems like original stain, and totes it back to his police cruiser. He will store it in his office. A few days hence, he will show it to a classroom of teenagers at the Pasadena Junior Citizens Police Academy. Those students were not alive in 1973, the year Anderson turned eighteen.

He thinks a new generation of kids should hear this story. This piece of wood is a piece of history, but predatory pedophiles are still around.

From a Pasadena hospital room, Michelle Dreymala Wilson returns my phone call. She is relieved to hear that the house where her brother died is coming down. But she's too busy to ponder the news. Her mother, Elaine, and father, James, are the last remaining pair of Lost Boys' parents. Last year, her father suffered a stroke. Only eleven days ago, her mother was rushed here with a cerebral hemorrhage, and she's recovering slowly. In the hospital, Michelle is once again in charge of her parents' care. She's struggling to decode her mother's condition, her parents' wishes, the doctors' orders, and the nurses' instructions.

It's another of too many times in Dreymala family life when her big brother's company would have been welcome. But Stanton Dreymala died in the house at 2020 Lamar. As a girl, Michelle loved and idolized her brother. Now she sometimes struggles to remember him. For so long, she has been the only child. On the phone, Michelle sounds spent, but she is still glad to hear that house has been demolished. "I think it's probably a good thing," she says.

The Dreymalas still live only minutes from 2020 Lamar, but they have never once visited this house. Maybe she'll tell her parents whenever her mom feels better. Or maybe she won't.

Elaine and James Dreymala—shown at home with their adult daughter Michelle and a photo of Stanton— prefer to share happier memories of their lost boy.

SHARON DERRICK'S 2023 CASE LIST:

THE LOST BOYS

30 MURDER VICTIMS; 7 NEW IDS (INCLUDES 3 CORRECTED AND RE-IDENTIFIED), 1 ID CORRECTED AND 1 ID PENDING—SHADED AND SHOWN IN BOLDFACE

ORDER	NAME	AGE	DATE
1970			
1	Jeffrey Alan Konen	18	9/28
2 & 3	Danny Michael Yates	14	12/13
2 & 3	James "Jimmy" Glass	14	12/13
1971			
4 & 5	Donald Waldrop	15	1/30
4 & 5	Jerry Lynn Waldrop	13	1/30
6	**Randall Lee Harvey**	**15**	**3/9**
7 & 8	Gregory "Malley" Winkle	16	5/29
7 & 8	David William Hilligiest	13	5/29
9	**Donald "Donnie" Falcon**	**17**	**7/1**
10	Ruben W. Watson (Haney)	17	8/17

1972			
11	Richard Alan Kepner	20	1/19
12	Willard K. "Rusty" Branch, Jr.	17	2/1
13	Exhumation & DNA tests pending	unknown	unknown
14	Frank Anthony Aguirre	17	3/24
15	Mark Scott (body unrecovered)	17	4/20
16 & 17	Billy Gene Baulch, Jr.	17	5/21
16 & 17	Johnny Ray Delome	16	5/21
18	Steven Kent Ferdig-Sickman	17	7/20
19	Roy "Ikie" Bunton	19	8/21
20 & 21	Wally Jay Simoneaux	14	10/4
20 & 21	Richard Edward Hembree	13	10/4
1973			
22	Joseph Allen Lyles	17	2/1
23	William "Billy" Lawrence	15	6/4
24	Raymond Stanley "Ray" Blackburn	20	6/15
25	Homer Louis Garcia	15	7/7
26	John "Johnny" Manning Sellars	18	7/12
27	Michael Anthony "Tony" Baulch	15	7/18
28 & 29	Marty Ray Jones	18	7/25
28 & 29	Charles Cary Cobble	17	7/25
30	James Stanton Dreymala	13	8/3

A NOTE TO READERS FROM SHARON DERRICK

A S YOU FINISH THIS book, but before you place it back on your shelf or loan it to others, I'd like to share a personal note about my need to contribute, through scientific evidence, as much justice as I could to these young men and boys after they had been tortured and killed in what should have been the prime, most joyous years of their lives. I feel so close to them, even though we are not actually family.

I was born and raised in Austin, but I have deep roots in the Houston Heights. Both my maternal and paternal grandparents settled in Houston when they were starting their families. My mother and her siblings grew up in the Heights. My father and his little brother moved near the Heights after my grandfather was shot and killed while arresting a criminal—Grandpa McCormick was a deputized lawman in a rural area. After his death, Grandma McCormick needed to work to raise her children, but she also needed a husband to help support her. She found one in Houston and my father grew up there. Later he met and married my mother. They moved to Austin, or, as my father called it, escaped to "God's Country."

Eventually, both sets of grandparents moved to Austin, but my mother's brother stayed in Houston, married, and had three sons.

These cousins of mine were very close in age to Henley and Corll's victims, and their neighborhood was near the Heights. One of them actually met Henley—said he was "creepy," and he stayed away from him. Good thing.

ACKNOWLEDGMENTS

I AM GRATEFUL TO Dr. Sharon Derrick for sharing her story, and to Dr. Derrick and Pat Paul for their years of dedication to these cases and their contributions to this book. You gave these boys back their names and helped tell their stories.

I deeply appreciate friends and family of the Lost Boys who shared their memories, including Bernie Milligan, Bradley Yates, Donna Robbins, Dana Falcon Jones, the Dreymala family, Robert Rose, Michele Boudreaux, Nita Bodiford, Daniel Vancura, and many others. I am grateful to everyone named in the notes that follow and to others who preferred to be unnamed.

Nancy Rose, a talented Houston artist who grew up in the Heights, drew marvelous portraits to honor the memory of the seven teens whom Derrick helped identify and of murder victim Mark Scott, whose body remains missing.

The assistance and advice I received from Skip Hollandsworth of *Texas Monthly*, Caroline Grist of First Story Productions, and Ted Oberg and Paige Hewitt, both formerly of ABC13, was invaluable. A shoutout to the many current and former journalists from the *Houston Post* and the *Houston Chronicle* who graciously shared their own stories.

Thanks to Sgt. James Anderson who reopened this murder case and continues to keep an eye on the Lost Boys. I am grateful to Colleen Fitzpatrick and to many investigators and attorneys who provided recollections and records, as well as those who handled research requests in the New York Public Library archives as well as in various Harris County archives where the process was complicated by the age of the documents and the COVID-19 pandemic. More thanks to Scott Durfee, who has helped advocate for a more thorough search of Corll's boatshed.

Many writer friends reviewed passages and offered suggestions (and support): Mimi Swartz, Andrea White, Maggie Galehouse, Laura Callaway, Sophie Novack, Kema Geroux, Nanci Wilson, Patricia Kilday Hart, Renée Ashley, Rene Steinke, Josette Huber, Katie Iles, and Margie Seaman. A shoutout to Idra Novey, whose wise counsel supplied a metaphor I would otherwise have overlooked.

More thanks go to Angela Tanzillo-Swarts, a forensic molecular biologist and expert in human identity testing, who generously reviewed several passages and offered advice.

I feel incredibly lucky to have found agent Susan Canavan at Waxman Literary Agency, who has advocated for me even in extremely difficult times. Thank you, Susan.

I have been treated wonderfully by all of my editors at Random House. Thanks to Clio Seraphim, Leila Tejani, Mark Warren, and to Alistair, the latest addition to the team.

My friends Lewis Kamb and David McCumber, former colleagues at the late great *Seattle Post-Intelligencer,* introduced me twenty years ago to the world of America's unidentified dead. Together we produced a series that led to several astounding IDs, including a mother and child murder victim from the 1980s: Raj Mati and her daughter Kamnee. That series inspired this book.

I am forever grateful to all who helped tell the Lost Boys' stories so that in these pages, they could live again. Perhaps their tragic experiences may motivate others to act.

Above all, thanks to my family: Ron, Jeremy, and Gabriel, and to my parents, Duane and Carolyn.

NOTES

THE JOURNEY TO WRITING this book began with a conversation with Dr. Sharon Derrick, then a Harris County forensic anthropologist, about the perplexing identity of a teenager's torso, clad in a purple surf shop T-shirt, that had been found floating in a murky lake in 1971. Those remains were originally labeled male. But a homicide detective believed they belonged to the fifteen-year-old victim of a serial killer who targeted surfer girls in the 1970s. Who was right?

The answer is not as simple as you might expect, Derrick explained. Young girls and boys can be hard to tell apart from bones alone. Her tone was unexpectedly warm—this skilled scientist cared deeply about restoring the identities of the long dead. In fact, she'd already reviewed that case as part of her quest to identify the Lost Boys. Between September 2020 and February 2024, we had dozens of conversations about her efforts and reviewed hundreds of photos and documents for this book. Unless otherwise noted, quotes attributed to her come from these interviews.

When an individual is quoted, I am drawing from interviews, emails, court documents, Facebook posts, or texts. When possible, I interviewed more than one participant in a conversation. Quotes are attributed, unless a source requested not to be named. Some asked to be identified by the name used in the 1970s. Given the passage of time, I verified dates, names, addresses, and events through case files, deed records, marriage licenses, and Houston City Directories, among other sources.

Many friends and the families of the murdered and the missing victims assisted efforts to re-create the world of 1971–73 Houston and the lives of the Lost Boys. Bernie Milligan gave more than a dozen interviews, shared difficult experiences and investigative insights, and toured me around the Heights. Others shared painful memories for the first time, convinced that some secrets kept in the dark fifty years ago must at last be aired. Some stories come from siblings who still grieve: Bradley Yates (brother of Danny Yates); Donna Robbins, Cindi Michalk, and Jimmy Lyles (siblings of Allen Lyles); Dana Falcon Jones (sister of Donnie Falcon); and James and Elaine Dreymala and Michelle Dreymala Wilson (the family of Stanton Dreymala). Friends of murder victims gave interviews: Robert Rose, Michele Boudreaux, Nita Bodiford, Daniel Vancura, and Johnny and Cindy Holton. The Holtons provided insights into 1970s hippie Houston as well as a driving tour of homes, schools, and teen hangouts.

The world-class journalist and author Skip Hollandsworth provided his September 2010–11 research for his April 2011 *Texas Monthly* story, "The Lost Boys," including unpublished recollections from victims' relatives who are no longer alive. The investigative reporter Ted Oberg facilitated access to recordings of two in-depth interviews aired on ABC13 in Houston, one Oberg conducted with Rhonda Williams in 2008 and one investigative reporter Paige Hewitt conducted with Tim Kerley in 2013. (Williams and Kerley are both dead; as agreed, the station is credited for quotes.)

All chapters rely heavily on primary sources, including interviews with more than a hundred other people from September 2020 to February 2024, court records and hearing transcripts, statements given to Pasadena and Houston police in 1973 and 1974, crime scene photos and diagrams, emails and correspondence, unpublished memoirs, and recordings. Many documents and photos were obtained through public records requests and archives; others were shared by sources. I benefited from the trove of Harris County Medical Examiner's records retained by the Harris County Archives, which include autopsies and forensic anthropology reports as well as photographs, newspaper clippings, and scrapbooks. Pat Paul, who worked in the ME's office when these murder victims' remains arrived in 1973, pored over files and shared her own scrapbooks, photos, and memories. Forensic anthropologists Jennifer Love and Deborrah Pinto and genetic genealogist Colleen Fitzpatrick provided interviews and insights. I also consulted journal articles and books, attended one of Derrick's classes, and visited the "Body Ranch," Texas State University's Forensic Anthropology Research Facility.

The Pasadena Police Department's report on the Homicide of Dean Corll (et al.) 8/8/1973, and Houston Police Department's report on the Homicide of James Stanton Dreymala (et al.) 8/8/1973 are key documents. In response to records requests, the Harris County District Attorney's Office and the Pasadena Police Department provided additional key documents and crime scene photos. Court records came from Harris County district clerks' archives and from Nueces County district clerks' archives in Corpus Christi. For the chapters on the Houston porn ring, I reviewed records of the state prosecutions of Roy Ames and his accomplices and found government records on the related congressional and legislative hearings in archives online. In the New York Public Library archives, I found notes and records that Truman Capote and journalist Arthur Bell kept of their visits to Houston to cover these cases. Bell saved a recording with grieving mother Dorothy Hilligiest and a copy of Houston police chief Herman Short's controversial speech. The Truman Capote Papers include a scrapbook and photos of Dean Corll.

The competitive and thriving media world of 1970s Houston produced a wealth of coverage, which I found in former Harris County district attorney Carol Vance's scrapbook (Harris County archives); in the Houston Mass Murders files (Houston Public Library archives); in the *Houston Post* and the *Houston Chronicle* archives; in Capote's scrapbook; and in the Dolph Briscoe Center for American History at the University of Texas at Austin.

I witnessed some events: I was there when Dean Corll's house was torn down; I interviewed Anthony Mendez in prison; I tracked down Rusty Branch's family, visited Corll's boatshed, and interviewed Sgt. James Anderson at the Pasadena PD and at Corll's former home.

These and other sources are cited in the following notes and bibliography. These abbreviations are used:

Harris County District Attorney: HCDA

Harris County Archives, medical examiner's records: HCME

Houston Police Department: HPD

Pasadena Police Department: PPD

New York Public Library Archives: NYPL

PART I: DISAPPEARANCES AND DISCOVERIES

CHAPTER 1: The Death of a Killer

3 **Elmer Wayne Henley, Jr.:** Descriptions and details based in part on affidavits by Elmer Wayne Henley, Jr., Tim Kerley, and Rhonda Williams included in the PPD "Report on the Homicide of Dean Corll et al.," 8/8/1973, Case No. J-12, 345.

5 **"ten-speed society":** Williams, recording of interview by Ted Oberg, ABC13 Houston, excerpts aired as "Serial Killer Dean Corll's Lone Female Survivor Recalls Attack," 11/1/2013, abc13.com/archive/9308674/.

7 **"I'm not going to let you do this":** Henley, affidavit to PPD, 8/8/1973.

7 **"I saw him change":** Kerley, interview by Paige Hewitt, ABC13 Houston, excerpts, "Surviving a Serial Killer," originally aired 8/10/2008, abc13.com /archive/6316179/.

9 **"the decedent was having a sex party":** Investigator's Report, Case No. ML 73-3329, Dean Corll, HCME 8/8/1973, HCME.

CHAPTER 2: A Roomful of Mysteries

15 **"the victim's last chance to be heard":** Douglas Ubelaker and Henry Scammell, *Bones: A Forensic Detective's Casebook* (Lanham, Md.: M. Evans, 1992), p. 286.

17 **"In my heart of hearts":** J. R. Gonzales, "Old Stubby Is Finally Laid to Rest," *Houston Chronicle,* 11/28/2014.

18 **"Each of them said 'Houston Mass Murders'":** Sharon Derrick, interviews by author. All Derrick quotes in this book are from author interviews unless otherwise noted.

19 **killing fourteen and wounding another thirty-one:** Gary M. Lavergne, *A Sniper in the Tower: The Charles Whitman Murders* (Denton: University of North Texas Press, 1997). Whitman separately killed his wife and mother, committing a total of sixteen murders.

20 **Some of her classmates:** "Bus crash remembered 50 years later," Yahoo News, 12/27/2022.

CHAPTER 3: The Bodies in the Boatshed

26 **Detective David Mullican pulled up:** Crime scene photos and diagrams of boatshed; PPD and HPD homicide reports, 8/8/1973 and 8/9/1973.

27 **"forget about Frank":** Rhonda Williams, statement to HPD, 8/16/1973.

27 **"I knew Dean":** George Flynn and Kathy Lewis, "'I'd Love to Forget It,' Witness Says," *Houston Post.*

31 **Wayne Henley blanched:** HCDA report, 1/10/1974.

32 **"tied together in a single piece of plastic":** Ibid.

32 **Another homicide detective:** Skip Hollandsworth, "The Lost Boys," *Texas Monthly,* April 2011.

35 **"Mama?" he said:** Wayne Henley to Mary Henley, conversation recorded by Jack Cato, Channel 2, 8/8/1973; video and other August 1973 footage available on the Texas Archive of the Moving Image website, texasarchive .org/2022_00177.

37 **"She invited me in":** Craig Smyser, interview by author, 12/9/2022.

38 **"Dean treated Wayne like a son":** Craig Smyser and Rad Sallee, "He Was a Polite Man, Loved to Be Around Kids," *Houston Chronicle,* 8/9/1973.

38 **"She was a nice woman":** Smyser, interview by author.

38 **Dorothy, an organized mother of six:** Dorothy Hilligiest, recorded interview by Arthur Bell, August 1973, Arthur Bell Papers, Billy Rose Theatre Division, NYPL. Portions of this interview published in Bell, "The Fate of the Boys Next Door," *Esquire,* March 1974.

39 **"I'll never give up":** Ibid.

39 **"It's David's birthday":** Ibid.

39 **"No," she answered, explaining why:** Ibid.

40 **"Why?":** Ibid.

41 **"No matter how much you talked to him":** James Conaway, *The Texans* (New York: Alfred A. Knopf, 1976), p. 207.

45 **"If there's nineteen in here":** George Flynn and Ann James, "Police Hunt for Graves as 19 Bodies Unearthed," *Houston Post,* 8/16/1972.

48 **"We have X-rays":** "Youths Feared Among Mass Murder Victims," *Houston Chronicle,* 8/12/1973.

CHAPTER 4: The Boy on the Bike

52 **"angelheaded hipsters burning":** Allen Ginsberg, "Howl," *Howl and Other Poems* (San Francisco: City Lights Books, 1956).

53 **Inspired by W. B. Yeats's:** W. B. Yeats, "The Second Coming," *The Dial,* November 1920.

53 **The hippie movement:** Joan Didion, "Slouching Towards Bethlehem," *Saturday Evening Post,* 9/23/1967, republished online 2017, saturdayeveningpost .com/2017/06/didion/.

53 **"Adolescents drifted":** Ibid.

54 **"where even if you only had a dollar":** Johnny Holton, interviews by author, 5/1/2022 and 7/10/2022.

55 **"It killed your brain cells"**: Cindy Bazar Holton, interviews by author, 5/1/2022 and 7/10/2022.

57 **"Subject missing for 2 days"**: HPD missing persons report, Randell Harvey, 3/11/1971.

58 **"I am not a Klansman"**: Mimi Swartz, "The Louie File," *Texas Monthly*, October 1985.

58 **"I hate my hair!"**: Monica Rhor, "Victim's Family Finally Has Answer," Associated Press, 10/27/2008.

58 **"All I can say is"**: Ericka Mellon, "Heights Teen Slain by Notorious Serial Killer Remembered," *Houston Chronicle*, 11/22/2008.

58 **"Sometimes, somebody would come along"**: Michael Morse, interview by author, 1/28/2020.

60 **"Dean Corll knew all the boys"**: Selma Winkle, interview by Bell, Bell Papers, NYPL. A portion published in Bell, "The Fate of the Boys Next Door."

61 **"They weren't lured away"**: Bradley Yates, interview by author, 2/13/2024.

61 **Everett Waldrop immediately told police**: Smyser, "Father of 2 Slain Boys Critical of Police Effort Here," *Houston Chronicle*, 8/14/1973.

61 **"But all they did was say"**: Ibid.

63 **By 2023, that system had contributed**: Kayla Clarke, "Who Did This to Amber?" ClickonDetroit, 6/2/2022.

65 **"Everyone knew"**: Stanley Hilligiest, interview by Hollandsworth, notes for "The Lost Boys," September 2010–April 2011.

Chapter 5: The Chief Strikes Back

67 **"No pattern was evident"**: Herman Short, speech, Bell Papers, NYPL.

68 **"It might make a better story"**: Sam Fletcher, "Short Defends Police Policy on Runaways," *Houston Post*, 8/14/1973.

70 **"As you may have noticed"**: Luis Garcia, father of murder victim Homer Garcia, in a note on Short's press conference in a self-published memoir for his family. Luis Garcia died in 2022.

71 **"every police trick"**: Tommy Miller, "Finding Missing Children Mostly Matter of Luck," *Houston Chronicle*, 8/10/1973.

71 **He did so**: Amended Autopsy Report, ML 73-3350, 8/12/1973, identified as Willard Karmon "Rusty" Branch, Jr., 7/3/1985, HCME.

71 **"does everything they can"**: Miller, "Finding Missing Children."

71 **He claimed to still be doing so**: Ray Hunt, interview by author, 11/30/2022; Rusty Branch's surviving half sister (who asked not to be named), interview by author, 12/22/2022.

71 **His children did not think**: Ibid.

Chapter 6: The First Mysterious Box of Bones

73 **Sharon Derrick had always had lofty goals**: Derrick, interviews by author; Al Derrick, interview by author, 4/22/2023.

75 **"He sang around the office"**: Ubelaker and Scammell, *Bones: A Forensic Detective's Casebook*, p. 24.

76 "Not many people have our kind of experience": Ibid., p. 163.

76 "Every one of these lessons": Bill Bass and Jon Jefferson, *Death's Acre: Inside the Legendary Body Farm Where the Dead Do Tell Tales* (Newburyport, Mass.: Berkley Publishing Group, 2003), p. 21.

78 She had already pulled related files: Autopsy Report, ML 73-3349, 8/12/1973 (Unidentified), HCME.

80 Based on measurements: Derrick interviews; Amended Autopsy Report, Randell Harvey, ML 73-3349, original 8/12/1973, updated 10/16/2008, HCME.

CHAPTER 7: The Parade of Bodies

83 For two full days: Pat Paul, interviews by author, 4/23/2021 and 2/10/2023.

84 "whether they like to admit it or not": Al Reinert, "Ah Sweet Mystery of Death," *Texas Monthly*, November 1975.

85 "Some places are still pretty primitive": Ibid.

86 "If you want to get rich": Matt Wingo, interview by author, 12/4/2020.

88 "Nothing is ever obvious": Reinert, "Ah Sweet Mystery."

89 At times, he despaired: "Tedious Job of Identifying Bodies Called Difficult Task," *Houston Post*, 8/28/1973.

CHAPTER 8: The Boy and His Boots

91 DNA samples from inmates and crime scenes in CODIS: 1999, Jennifer Love, interview by author, 11/20/2020.

91 "Stacie vanished": Peggy O'Hare, "Body in Barrel ID'd with DNA from Twin Sister," *Houston Chronicle*, 4/12/2011.

95 Eventually, Derrick dug up: HPD missing persons report, Randell Harvey, 3/11/1971.

CHAPTER 9: Clues from an Accomplice

97 "Elmer Wayne Henley feels": Conaway, "The Last Kid on the Block," *Texas Monthly*, April 1976.

98 "Wayne is a media whore": Hollandsworth notes, 2010–2011.

98 Maybe David Brooks could better assist her: Derrick, interviews by author.

101 "a sickly kid who wore those hippie glasses": Hollandsworth, "The Lost Boys," *Texas Monthly*, April 2011.

101 "My first homosexual contact": Brooks, first affidavit, HPD, 8/9/1973, HPD and PPD homicide reports.

104 "I don't remember": Derrick, interviews by author.

104 "We left about 6 P.M.": Brooks's third affidavit, HPD, 8/10/1973.

105 She handed him a piece of paper: Copy of map drawn by Brooks.

CHAPTER 10: The Search

109 When Lenore (Harvey) McNiel: Derrick, interviews by author; Amended Autopsy Report, ML 73-3349, Randell Harvey.

110 "I wish Mama had been able": McNiel in Hollandsworth notes, 2010–2011.

113 "So, we had a big meeting": Derrick, interviews by author; Amended Autopsy Report, ML 73-3349, Randell Harvey; Derrick, "Recent Developments, The

Ongoing Saga of the Houston Mass Murders," presentation, American Academy of Forensic Sciences, 2009.

114 Randy "was all boy": Mellon, "Heights Teen Slain by Notorious Serial Killer Remembered," *Houston Chronicle,* 11/22/2008.

114 "We used to jump off my grandma's porch": Ibid.

114 She was sure that more answers would soon follow: Derrick, interviews by author.

PART II: SEX, DRUGS, AND OTHER PIECES OF THE PUZZLE

CHAPTER 11: The Candy Man

119 There were boys wearing swimming trunks: Corll's photos, reviewed by author.

119 "He was always buying things": "Corll Didn't Kill All of Those Boys, His Mother Claims," *Houston Post,* 8/19/1973.

120 "My son didn't kill all of those boys": Ibid.

121 "If you like we'll go down and kill him": W. B. Barrie, *Peter and Wendy* (original copyright 1911; reprinted by Suzeteo Enterprises, 2019), p. 5.

122 "When you wake": Ibid.

122 "He always had several pockets full of candy": Dorothy Ridinger, PPD homicide report.

122 It did seem "kind of strange": Ibid.

123 Billy Ridinger came to see: Billy Ridinger, affidavit to HPD, 8/10/1973, HCDA.

123 Ruben Haney: Autopsy reports, Ruben W. Watson (Haney) and Tommy Haney, HCME.

123 Billy claimed that Corll "never made": Billy Ridinger, affidavit to HPD, 8/10/1973, HCDA.

124 "I couldn't see anything": Ibid.

124 "We're thinking about letting you go": Ibid.

124 "I didn't tell anyone what had happened": Ibid.

124 "I believe the only reason": David Brooks's affidavit, 8/9/1973, to HPD.

124 "sole survivor of Corll's sexual fetish": Det. Sidney Smith, PPD homicide report.

125 "If Dean Corll had knocked on my door": Ed Deswysen, "Dean Corll, the Smiling Friendly Candy Man of the Heights," *Houston Chronicle,* 8/15/1973.

125 "Dean never showed any sign": Chuck Saad, "Mom Tells *Sun* in Local Interview: Mass Slay Suspect Tricked," *Colorado Springs Sun,* 8/19/1973.

126 "Checking out the local gay circuit": Bell papers NYPL, portions of interviews published in Bell, "The Swell Guy Murderer: Deep in the Dark of Texas," *Village Voice,* 8/30/1973.

126 "Like I say, the cops did not harass us": Ray Hill, oral history interview, 6/21/2016, from "Civil Rights in Black and Brown," the Texas Christian University Mary Couts Burnett Library, https://crbb.tcu.edu/clips/4438/police-and-law-enforcement-in-raids-on-lgbt-bars.

127 "In all instances, the gay angle": Bell papers NYPL, portions of interviews

published in Bell, "The Swell Guy Murderer: Deep in the Dark of Texas," *Village Voice*, 8/30/1973.

127 **Charles Berger:** Ibid.

127 **"Does Dean Corell [*sic*] represent homosexuals":** Unsigned editorial, "Post Reports & Prints Misleading & Offensive Copy," *The Nuntius*, January/February 1973, via Houston LGBT History website, houstonlgbthistory.org/.

127 **a "hothouse of a helltown":** Bell, "The Swell Guy Murderer: Deep in the Dark of Texas."

128 **"a gun stuck in my face":** Ibid.

129 **"Corll's father dished out macabre beatings":** Carol S. Vance, *Boomtown DA* (Houston: Whitecaps Media, 2010), p. 188.

130 **"He was just an average classmate":** Jerry Allen, interview by author, 10/24/2022.

131 **In that photo:** Dean Corll, Vidor High School Yearbook.

131 **"If a mother could have caused":** Judy Allen, 8/14/1973 interview, PPD homicide report.

132 **"Kids flocked around him there":** "Corll Didn't Kill All of Those Boys."

133 **claimed Corll was administratively discharged:** Vance, *Boomtown DA*, p. 189.

134 **"He'd let them in nights":** "Corll Didn't Kill All of Those Boys."

135 **"give the Homophile Society the finest club":** "Houston Boasts Finest Gay Club in US," *The Nuntius*, August 1970.

136 **"breastplate of righteousness":** Jane E. Brody, "Crimes Against Homosexuals Analyzed," *New York Times*, 9/17/1975.

136 **Humphreys titled his book:** Laud Humphreys, *Tearoom Trade: Impersonal Sex in Public Places* (London: Duckworth, 1970).

136 **A few closet queens:** Ibid., p. 128.

136 **"I just want to love every one of these kids":** Ibid.

137 **"He stepped out":** Tommy Railsback, interview by author, 5/19/2022.

137 **"His eyes would flash":** Smyser and Sallee, "He Was a Polite Man, Loved to Be Around Kids."

137 **"the boys on the island":** Barrie, p. 46.

137 **"He might have forgotten":** Ibid.

138 **"Society's attitude toward homosexuals":** Brody, "Crimes Against Homosexuals Analyzed."

CHAPTER 12: The Hunt

139 **Paul was seventeen:** Paul Gale, interview by author, 5/26/2022.

139 **"What he'd do is pull up":** Ibid.

140 **He sent a letter:** Gale's 8/11/1973 letter, PPD homicide report.

140 **In September 1969, Bernie Milligan:** Bernie Milligan, interviews by author, and visit to gas station site.

144 **"They asked us":** David Gibson, Facebook messages to author, 12/20/2022.

144 **And their bodies:** HPD homicide report, 10/1973.

145 **"We rode bikes":** Bradley Yates, interview by author, 2/9/2023.

145 **"That guy wouldn't let up":** Yates, interview by author, 2/13/2024.

146 **"Right when he disappeared":** Yates, interview by author, 2/9/2023.

146 **Jim Glass's mother drove them there:** Photos and descriptions of the Long Point Cinema and Thunderbird Twin Drive-In, via Cinema Treasures website, cinematreasures.org.

146 **"Get out of here!":** Yates, interview by author, 2/13/2024.

148 **Jim Glass's lists:** Photo of gravestone of James Eugene Glass, via Find a Grave, findagrave.com/memorial/8500128/james_eugene-glass.

148 **"The whole thing at the theater":** Yates, interview by author, 2/13/2024.

148 **The Harris County medical examiner opined:** Autopsy reports for James Glass and Danny Yates, August 1973, HCME.

148 **"I had taken him home":** Brooks's second affidavit, 8/10/1973, HPD homicide report, also published as "'I Never Actually Killed Anyone,' Youth Says," *Houston Post*, 8/11/1972.

CHAPTER 13: Who Knew?

149 **Bernie Milligan ran into his old buddy:** Milligan, interviews by author, 6/2021–2/2024.

151 **"When children disappeared":** Williams, interview by Oberg, ABC13.

151 **a "magical place to grow up":** Bernie Milligan, unpublished account, shared with author.

151 **He envisioned it as:** Ibid.

CHAPTER 14: Mapping the Murders

156 **Bernie Milligan had been quietly collecting material:** Milligan, interviews by author.

157 **At some point, Danny Furstenfeld:** Both men appear in *The Clown & the Candyman,* a 2021 limited docuseries originally aired on Investigation Discovery Network.

157 **Grist had met Danny:** Caroline Grist, interview by author, 4/12/2023.

158 **Bernie suggested that they begin:** Maps and timelines provided to the author by Milligan. Derrick provided a spreadsheet of known victims. The author compiled and mapped Dean Corll's known addresses from HPD and PPD homicide reports and other records.

158 **By the center's later reckoning:** Sebastian Junger, *A Death in Belmont* (New York: W. W. Norton, 2006), p. 81.

159 **Back in August 1985:** R. K. Ressler and A. W. Burgess, "Crime Scene and Profile Characteristics of Organized and Disorganized Killers," *FBI Law Enforcement Bulletin* 54, no. 8 (August 1985): 18–25. Summary online at ojp.gov/ncjrs/virtual-library/abstracts/crime-scene-and-profile-characteristics-organized-and-disorganized.

160 **After their initial meeting:** Roki Furstenfeld, interview by author, 1/25/2024.

163 **The duo were filmed driving by:** *The Clown and the Candyman,* 2021 limited docuseries.

163–164 **One key stowed inside a cigar box:** Investigator's interview with Scotts, 10/10/1973, HDCA.

164 **Two days later:** Tom Kennedy, "I Haven't Heard from Him Since," *Houston Post,* 8/12/1973.

166 **Then Corll moved into another unit:** Ibid.; lists of Corll's addresses and interviews with landlords in PPD and HPD homicide reports.

168 **"How are you, Dean?":** Saad, "Mom Tells *Sun* in Local Interview: Mass Slay Suspect Tricked"; Beverly Harris, "Corll's Mother Talks: Says Son 'Was Used,'" *Houston Chronicle*, 8/19/1973.

CHAPTER 15: The Uncounted Murder Victim

170 **In one of her first presentations:** Derrick, "Houston Mass Murder Victims: 33 Years Later," Abstract of presentation, American Academy of Forensic Sciences (AAFS), 2007.

171 **"Most people need the concrete experience":** Pauline Boss, *Ambiguous Loss: Learning to Live with Unresolved Grief* (Cambridge, Mass.: Harvard University Press, 1999), p. 26.

171 **"Even sure knowledge of death":** Ibid., p. 6.

171 **"a loss that goes on and on":** Ibid., p. 8.

171 **Donna Taylor Robbins:** Donna Taylor Robbins, interview by author, 1/28/2021.

172 **"I put down that my brother Allen":** Ibid.

175 **Donna, who was now living on family property:** Donna Taylor Robbins and Cindi Michalk, interviews by author, 1/28/2021; Jimmy Lyles, 12/1/2022; and follow-ups with Taylor Robbins.

176 **Lance Harris:** Lance Harris, interview by author, 12/19/2022.

CHAPTER 16: The Bodies on the Beach

178 **Wayne Henley arrived:** Description, photos, and diagrams in HPD and PPD homicide reports. Transcripts of testimony from Henley, Smith, and Mullican in *State of Texas v. Henley*, Case No. 01988950, January 1974 pretrial hearing in Harris County District Court, HCDA.

181 **"We're going to try to use a motor grader":** Dave Petro and Bill Coulter, "More Bodies Expected as Grim Search Continues," *Houston Post*, 8/13/1973.

182 **"Why, Maggie, you come right out of there!":** Bell, "Houston Murders: We Wrappin' 'Em in Saran," *Village Voice*, 8/23/1973.

182 **At one point, Chambers County:** Ann James, "Mass Slaying Death Count Climbs to 27," *Houston Post*, 8/13/1973.

182 **"This one was fresh":** Bell, "We Wrappin' 'Em in Saran."

182 **The eighteen-year-old boy:** Autopsy Report, ML 73-3408, Johnny Manning Sellars, 8/15/1973, HCME.

183 **"It always bothered me":** Hollandsworth, "Lost Boys."

184 **"There is a unique possibility":** Pete Wittenberg, "2 Extra Bones Prompt Search at High Island," *Houston Post*, 10/12/1973.

CHAPTER 17: An Unexpected Breakthrough

185 **The physical anthropology section:** 1992 list, Ubelaker and Scammell, *Bones*, Appendix.

186 **Both women had Ph.D.s:** American Board of Forensic Anthropology, list of active diplomates, accessed in 2023, theabfa.org/active-diplomates-by-state.

187 **"Every day at work":** Post about Dr. Jennifer Love, Forensic Anthropologist, Texas County & District Retirement System (TCDRS) Facebook page, 5/31/2011.

187 **"When you live it":** Love, interview by author, 11/20/2020.

187–188 **Since the 1990s:** Andy Nystrom, "MIHS Graduate and Forensic Anthropologist Kathy Taylor Passes Away," *Mercer Island Reporter*, 8/10/2021; Author interviewed Kathy Taylor for Lewis Kamb and Olsen, "Without a Trace," *Seattle Post-Intelligencer*, June 2003 series.

188 **Suspect Gary Leon Ridgway:** Elizabeth Svoboda, "Cold Case Is Closed by DNA Match: Green River Killer," *New York Times*, 5/11/2009.

188 **"We got word":** Nystrom, "MIHS Graduate and Forensic Anthropologist."

189 **The NIJ later established a task force:** Eric Martin, Dawn Elizabeth Schwarting, and Ruby J. Chase, "Serial Killer Connections Through Cold Cases," *National Institute of Justice Journal*, 6/20/2020, nij.ojp.gov/topics/articles/serial-killer-connections-through-cold-cases.

189 **On that list:** Lise Olsen, "21 Bodies No Clear Answers," *Houston Chronicle*, 7/24/2011.

189 **(Indeed, DNA evidence):** Olsen, "An Astonishing ID," *Texas Observer*, 7/9/2022.

189 **Love initially applied for:** Olsen, "Investigators Hope DNA Provides Answers in 30-year-old Murder," *Houston Chronicle*, 11/27/2011.

190 **Yet even in 2024, Cook County sheriff's officials:** Unidentified Victims John Wayne Gacy, Cook County Sheriff's Office website, accessed September 2024, cookcountysheriff.org/departments/c-c-s-p-d/unidentified-victims-john-wayne-gacy/.

190 **"Oh my gosh":** Love, interview by author, 11/23/2020.

190 **"It had the word 'Antiquities' on it":** Ibid.

190 **In one well-publicized blunder:** Bass and Jefferson, *Death's Acre*, pp. 68–70.

191 **He said it was "strictly his guess":** Ubelaker and Scammell, *Bones*, pp. 152–53.

191 **"I was going into the box":** Love, interview by author.

192 **In February 2008, Love shipped:** Amended Autopsy Report, ML 83-6849, Joseph Allen Lyles, 11/18/2011, HCME.

193 **"The plastic and the types of cord":** Ibid.

PART III: MISTAKEN IDENTITIES

CHAPTER 18: The Lost Brothers—Michael and Billy Baulch

199 **Michael Baulch was born:** Background from author visits to Baulch's former home in the Heights, visit to family graves, and HCME autopsy reports related to both brothers.

202 **He spoke politely:** Jack Olsen, *The Man with the Candy: The Story of the Houston Mass Murders* (New York: Simon & Schuster, 1974), p. 91.

203 **"In those days":** Nita Bodiford, interviews by author, 6/3/2021 and 12/8/2022.

203 **"My big brother":** Ibid.

204 **"Nothing worked":** Olsen, *The Man with the Candy*, p. 79.

CHAPTER 19: Graves in the Woods

206 **On the morning he shot:** From PPD homicide reports and Henley's affidavits, 8/8/1973 and 8/9/1973, and HCDA's 1974 report.

206 **"He was telling me":** Henley testimony, *State v. Henley,* pretrial hearing transcript, 1/1974, HCDA.

206 **"I didn't particularly want":** Ibid.

207 **"I killed several":** Henley, affidavit, 8/9/1973.

208 **"They were what I call rednecks":** Henley testimony, *State v. Henley,* pretrial hearing transcript, 1/1974.

208 **Soon after meeting Hoyt:** Ibid.

209 **"I couldn't let him come down":** Ibid.

209 **"Any time you've got a big crowd in East Texas":** Hoyt testimony, *State v. Henley,* pretrial hearing transcript, 1/1974.

210–211 **"He wanted me to grin":** Henley testimony, *State v. Henley,* pretrial hearing.

211 **"I done ruined his golf shoes":** Ibid.

CHAPTER 20: "Bones That's All They Were"

213 **The crowded cold storage vault:** Autopsy Report, ML 73-3333, 8/9/1973, misidentified as Michael Anthony Baulch, 10/9/1973, HCME.

214 **"I knew it right off":** King Waters, "Heart-Broken Parents Identify 2 Dead Sons by Studying Skulls," *Houston Chronicle,* 10/10/1973.

215 **"You don't know what it's like":** Ibid.

215 **"Bones," she finally said:** Ibid.

CHAPTER 21: A Motion to Suppress

217 **"serious reservations":** Ed Deswysen, "DA's Aide: It's Not in New Law," *Houston Chronicle,* 8/12/1973.

218 **Scott said the caller pressed him:** Waters, "Murder-for-Pay Offer on Henley," *Houston Chronicle,* 2/8/1974.

218 **"one of America's most distinguished writers":** "Truman Capote's Houston Diary," proposal to *The Washington Post,* 12/16/1973, Truman Capote Papers, NYPL.

218 **"incorporate a wider landscape":** Ibid.

219 **"Perhaps it could have happened anywhere":** Ibid.

219 **Capote planned to take the mystery:** Ibid.

219 **"Perhaps this is true":** Ibid.

219 **Capote told an interviewer:** Gerald Clarke, *Capote: A Biography* (New York: Simon & Schuster, 1988, 2010), p. 448.

219 **"looked more like an airport corridor":** Kathy Lewis, "Officials Screen Everyone Entering Henley Courtroom," *Houston Post,* January 1974.

220 **"I've seen this before":** Clarke, *Capote,* p. 448.

220 **Truman, he cabled, was hospitalized:** Ibid., p. 449.

221 **no memory at all of Capote's interest:** Lynn Wyatt, communication via journalist Andrea White to author, 8/31/2023.

221 **"It's gruesome":** Kate Donnelly, "At Home with Texas Philanthropist Lynn Wyatt," *Town & Country*, 10/19/2018.

222 **A few months later:** *State of Texas v. David Owen Brooks*, Case No. 198894, Harris County District Court, jury verdict, 3/4/1975.

CHAPTER 22: The Boy in the Silver Casket

224 **In 2010:** Barbara Gibson and Debera Phinney, "Forensic Anthropologist 'Digging' for Answers to 37-year-Old Murders," *Police News*, May 2010; Mike Tolson, "Remains Draw More Questions on '70s Corll Killings," *Houston Chronicle*, 9/18/2010.

225 **The Body Ranch:** Forensic Anthropology Research Facility, Texas State University website, txst.edu/anthropology/facts/labs/farf.html.

225 **At any given time:** Danny Westcott, interview by author, 1/19/2023; see also Olsen, "Learning from the Dead," *Texas Observer*, 3/28/2023.

226 **Flies and their offspring maggots:** Ibid.

226 **In January 2023:** Ibid.

227 **Upon examining them:** Derrick interviews by author and Derrick, "The Lost Boys of 1970–1973," presentation, the National Center for Missing and Exploited Children (NCMEC), 2012; Autopsy Report, ML 73-3333, remains of Roy "Ikie" Bunton misidentified as Michael Baulch, 10/9/1973, HCME.

228 **Dark-haired like her brothers:** Ibid., and Amended Autopsy Report, ML 73-3378, 1973 unknown, identified as Michael Baulch 8/10/2010, HCME.

CHAPTER 23: The Missing Missing

231 **"It's very frustrating":** Tolson, "Remains Draw More Questions on '70s Corll Killings," *Houston Chronicle*, 9/18/2010.

231 **On February 8, 2011:** Derrick interviews; Deborrah Pinto, interview by author, 7/15/2022; photos of exhumation; author visit to Woodlawn Cemetery; related autopsy reports.

235 **"I never heard the family speak about him":** Caryl Coronis, interview by author, 9/29/2022.

235 **Even in the 2020s:** James Dean, "Pillemer: Family Estrangement a Problem 'Hiding in Plain Sight,'" Cornell University website, 9/10/2020; article describes findings from Karl Pillemer, *Fault Lines: Fractured Families and How to Mend Them* (New York: Avery, 2020).

235 **Estrangement most frequently occurs:** David Brooks, "What's Ripping American Families Apart," *New York Times*, Opinion, 7/29/2021.

236 **The remains she'd exhumed:** Autopsy Report, ML 73-3333, 8/9/1973, HCME, and Olsen, "After Decades, Another Serial Killing Victim Identified," *Houston Chronicle*, 11/30/2011.

239 **Derrick had momentum:** Derrick, "The Lost Boys of 1970–1973," NCMEC, 2012.

CHAPTER 24: A Devastating DNA Mistake

241 **In her spare time:** Interviews with Derrick, Amended Autopsy Report, ML 73-3355, 8/13/1973 (misidentified as Mark Scott, January 1994), HCME.

242 **That agency's enormous mission:** "Partnership Critical to Mission Success," Department of Defense POW/MIA Accounting Agency Public Affairs Office News, 10/4/2019.

242 **Those forensics operations:** Earl Swift, *Where They Lay: Searching for America's Lost Soldiers* (New York: Houghton Mifflin Co. / Bantam Press edition, 2003).

243 **"They perform forensic detective work":** Swift, *Where They Lay,* p. 14.

243 **In 1994, the *Houston Post*:** Steve Olafson, "DNA Test puts face on '70s murder. Blood, bone help identify Corll victim," *Houston Post,* 1/6/1994.

243 **"The family's pretty well torn up":** Ibid.

244 **Over the years, researchers like Itiel Dror:** Itiel Dror et al., "Cognitive Bias in Forensic Pathology Decisions," *Journal of Forensic Sciences* 66, no. 5 (September 2021): 1751–57, pubmed.ncbi.nlm.nih.gov/33608908/.

245 **In 1987, American researchers announced:** Swift, *Where They Lay,* p. 237.

245 **MtDNA is both ancient and mysterious:** Bryan Sykes, *The Seven Daughters of Eve* (New York: W. W. Norton, 2001).

245 **It is found within the cells:** "How Mitochondria Evolved from Bacteria," *Nature India,* 1/27/2022, nature.com/articles/d44151-022-00006-8. See also Thomas Cavalier-Smith, "Origin of Mitochondria by Intracellular Enslavement of a Photosynthetic Purple Bacterium," *Proceedings of the Royal Society,* published online 4/11/2006.

245 **"These genes tell a story":** Sykes, *The Seven Daughters of Eve,* p. 2.

246 **"I have found DNA":** Ibid.

247 **At least three of his ribs:** Amended Autopsy Report, ML 73-3355, Steven Kent Ferdig-Sickman, 4/20/2011, and original autopsy 8/13/1973, HCME.

248 **"We want to make sure":** Derrick interviews; additional details from Hollandsworth notes, 2010–2011.

248 **"My brother knew":** Jeff Scott, Hollandsworth notes, 2010–2011.

248 **"He was afraid of them":** Derrick interviews.

249 **She'd named some birds:** Hollandsworth, "Lost Boys."

249 **"Wayne came over":** George Flynn, "Mom Couldn't Bear TV Reports," *Houston Post,* 8/11/1973.

249 **An investigator's report:** Autopsy Report, Ronnie Henley, 12/5/1975, HCME.

250 **Derrick walked up:** Derrick interviews; Hollandsworth notes, 2010–2011.

251 **Derrick didn't tell the Scotts she'd already collected DNA:** Amended Autopsy Report, ML 73-3355, Steven Kent Ferdig-Sickman, 4/20/2011, HCME.

CHAPTER 25: Party Time

253 **Luckily, he befriended:** Daniel Vancura, interview by author, 9/2/2022.

254 **"Everything's kind of blurry":** Ronnie Kettler, interview by author, 9/24/2022.

254 **"We were a typical brother and sister":** Mike Glenn, "Quest ends in Anguish for Sister of Serial Killer's Victim," *Houston Chronicle,* 7/30/2011.

255 **"He got some construction-type jobs":** Vancura, interview by author.

255 **"I always had a curfew":** Ibid.

256 **"He always said he was going to leave":** Kettler, interview by author.

256 **"At least in those days":** Vancura, interview by author.

256 **Erma Sickman called so often:** Glenn, "Quest."

256 **"But this was pre computers":** Vancura, interview by author.

258 **"All I'd like to know":** Mary Scott, Hollandsworth notes; Derrick, interviews by author.

259 **"He needs a memorial service":** Juliana Goodwin, "39 Years After Disappearance, Son's Ashes Are Returned," *Springfield News-Leader*, 8/6/2011, via AP.

259 **"Erma will be buried":** Erma Sickman's obituary, Legacy.com, 10/15/2017.

PART IV: PATTERNS AND CONTRADICTIONS

CHAPTER 26: A Killer's Revelations

265 **Sharon Derrick couldn't stop:** Derrick, interviews by author, and Derrick's contemporaneous handwritten notes on her meeting with Henley.

266 **"How are you doing?":** Mark Scott's postcard is described in police files and in Flynn, "Mom Couldn't Bear TV Reports."

268 **HANG HENLEY! NOT HIS ART:** Eric Hanson and Steve Brewer, "Buyers May Put an Early End to Killer Henley's Art Show," *Houston Chronicle*, 2/5/1997.

268 **The film includes footage:** *The Collectors*, directed by Julian P. Hobbs (New York: Magnet Media, 2000).

268 **In 2001, Texas adopted a law:** Andy Kahan, interview by author, 4/8/2022.

268 **Later, relatives shut down:** Robert Hurst, spokesman for the Texas Department of Criminal Justice, email to author on why interview requests with Henley were being denied, 8/9/2022.

CHAPTER 27: The Edge of the Knife

275 **"He was a really sweet person":** Cindy Bazar Holton, interviews by author.

275 **"You were lucky":** Ibid.

277 **He remembers Mark saying:** Robert Rose, interview by author, 4/14/2022.

278 **"Mark sometimes made crazy decisions":** Ibid.

278 **Even Mark Scott's little brother:** Jeff Scott, Hollandsworth notes, 2010–2011.

278 **"Houston's Left Bank":** Thorne Dreyer and Al Reinert, "Montrose Lives: There's Something for Everyone in Houston's Montrose, the Strangest Neighborhood East of the Pecos," *Texas Monthly*, April 1973.

279 **Mark began "rolling queers":** Rose, interview by author.

279 **Mark became afraid:** Jeff Scott, Hollandsworth notes, 2010–2011.

279 **"He wouldn't have told me":** Rose, interview by author.

280 **(HPD officers verified):** Police interview with Jeral McDaniel, 10/1973, HPD homicide report.

281 **"I wonder":** Rose, interview by author.

CHAPTER 28: Who Is Swimsuit Boy?

283 **"It breaks my heart":** Allan Turner, "40 Years After Death, Victim of Serial killer Is Laid to Rest," *Houston Chronicle,* 11/12/2009.

284 **"We don't know the name":** Ibid.

284 **"We are at peace":** Ibid.

285 **"It wasn't all that helpful":** Derrick, interviews by author.

286 **Essentially, Derrick was confronting:** Derrick, interviews by author.

CHAPTER 29: An Unexpected Offer

287 **A new trial was scheduled:** Doug Shaver, interview by author, 8/11/2022; former *Houston Chronicle* reporter Gary Taylor, interview by author, 7/8/2022 (Taylor also shared his trial coverage); Vance, *Boomtown DA;* and the *State of Texas v. Elmer Wayne Henley,* Case No. 79CR-260-E, in Nueces County District Court archives.

287 **The unexpected order for a retrial:** Lewis Dickson, emails to author, 5/30/2022.

288 **"I hoped they were a good shot":** Shaver, interview by author, 8/11/2022.

289 **Shaver had always believed:** Shaver, interview by author.

CHAPTER 30: Too Many Missing Persons

291 **In 2011, Sharon Derrick:** Derrick, interview by author, 9/18/2021.

292 **"And all the while":** Oscar Wilde, "The Ballad of Reading Gaol," 1898, available at poetryfoundation.org/poems/45495/the-ballad-of-reading-gaol.

CHAPTER 31: A Forgotten Call for Help on 9/11

297 **"I had two older brothers":** Dana Falcon Jones, interview by author, 5/20/2022.

298 **The family rented unit 16:** Falcon Jones, interviews by author in 2022 and 2023; Donnie Falcon's stepfather's profession and 1971 address verified in the 1971 Houston City Directory, R. L. Polk & Co.

299 **"The more time I spent with the science":** Tolson, "Remains Draw More Questions on '70s Corll Killings," *Houston Chronicle,* 9/18/2010.

CHAPTER 32: An Anonymous Tip

305 **Vargas began their first phone conversation:** Derrick, interviews by author.

306 **Decades after her son's murder:** Michelle Dreymala Wilson, James Dreymala, Elaine Dreymala, and Andy Kahan, interview by author, 5/20/2022.

306 **She treasures the memories of her son:** Elaine Dreymala, email to author, 5/31/2022.

307 **Then, in the 2010s:** Michelle Dreymala Wilson, interview by author, 12/9/2022.

308 **"Upon the unexpected notification":** Derrick, letter in support of the Randy Harvey Law, April 2009.

308 **"I knew":** Jef Rouner, "Real Horror: Local Filmmaker Brings Horrific Crimes of Dean Corll to the Silver Screen," *Houston Press,* 12/4/2013, and Rouner, interview by author, 6/17/2022.

309 "Whatever evil was": Hollandsworth, "The Lost Boys," *Texas Monthly*, April 2011.

309 "He did not meet with us": Elaine Dreymala, 2011 post on Facebook group of family and friends of victims (used with permission of Elaine Dreymala).

309 "I am so full": Elaine Dreymala, 2011 Facebook post.

310 "He emailed a few times": Derrick interviews, copy of photo of Boy in the Box.

311 As buzz about "the Boy in the Box" increased: Derrick and Yates, author interviews.

311 In July 2010, in her office mailbox: Copy of photos of envelope and "Bobby French."

PART V: PLAYERS IN A PORN RING

CHAPTER 33: The Accomplices in the Shadows

317 "Dean told me": Henley affidavits to PPD.

317 "During one of our conversations": Brooks's affidavit, 8/9/1973.

317 On the day of Corll's murder: Williams affidavit to PPD.

318 "I don't expect justice": Smyser, "Father of 2 Slain Boys."

318 "My personal belief": Selma Winkle interview, Bell papers, NYPL archives.

319 The grand jurors' report: Pete Wittenberg, "Grand Jurors Critical of Mass Slaying Probe," *Houston Post*, 11/2/1973, and John Durham, "Short Calls Grand Jury Silly, DA Says It's Second-guessing," *Houston Chronicle*, 11/2/1973.

321 "We knew that they were": "Possible Link Is Discovered in Mass Slayings," *Brownsville Herald*, via UPI, 9/24/1976.

321 Indeed, FBI agents had: FBI report on Roy Clifton Ames, 5/31/1968.

321 In September 1976: Follow-up report by Mullican dated 9/1976, PPD homicide report.

321 (St. John eventually): Eric Malnic, "Legendary Detective Jigsaw St. John Dies," *Los Angeles Times*, 5/4/1995, latimes.com/archives/la-xpm-1995-05-04-mn-62350-story.html.

322 "All that was true": Derrick, Hollandsworth notes.

CHAPTER 34: An Attempted Escape

323 "I had a crush on him": Michele Boudreaux, interview by author, 6/16/22.

324 Her dad, L. N. Boudreaux, Jr.: L. N. Boudreaux, emails to author via his wife, 2022.

325 Gary Gibson was hanging out: Gary Gibson, interview by author, 7/3/2022. (Gibson also testified to the Harris County grand jury in 1973 and communicated with Derrick.)

326 "To me it seemed dumb": Michele Boudreaux, interview by author.

326 Investigators in Houston: PPD and HPD homicide reports.

327 Yet the forty-five-year-old leader: Robert Finklea, "Criminal Record of Alleged Homosexual Ring Leader Revealed," *Dallas Morning News*, 8/16/1973.

327 Chicago police sergeant Ron Kelley: George Bliss, Michael Sneed, and

Greg Moseley, "Chicago Is Center of National Boy Porn Ring," part of the series "Child Pornography, Sickness for Sale," *Chicago Tribune,* 5/15/1977–5/18/1977.

327 **Reporters also discovered:** Caroline Grist, memo to author, 2/12/2024. *The Clown and the Candyman* reported a concrete link between Norman and serial killer John Wayne Gacy. While on the lam from his Dallas crimes and awaiting trial in Cook County, John Norman met a young man named Philip Paske, who helped him relaunch his mail-order child sex business in Illinois. Paske had a direct link to the Killer Clown—he worked for Gacy and had a key to Gacy's house in Norwood Park Township, a Chicago suburb.

327 **"not relevant to any fraud":** Bliss, Sneed, and Moseley, three-part series published in the *Chicago Tribune,* 5/15–5/18/1977.

328 **"This case probably earned":** "Interim Report of the Select Committee on Child Pornography: Its related causes and control," Sixty-sixth Texas Legislative Session, committee report, 10/19/1978, hearings: 4/9/1977, 9/13/1977, 11/17/1977, and 9/14/1978.

328 **"In spite of the fact":** "Sexual Exploitation of Children," hearings before the Subcommittee on Crime of the Committee on the Judiciary, House of Representatives, 95th Congress, hearings: 5/23/1977, 5/25/1977, 6/10/1977, and 9/20/1977; Lloyd testimony, p. 344.

328 **Corll's "unholy trio":** Robin Lloyd, *For Money or Love: Boy Prostitution in America* (Vanguard Press, 1976), p. 48.

329 **And the numbers of male teen hustlers:** Ibid.

329 **business "doubled":** Lloyd, *For Money or Love,* p. 48.

329 **"To my knowledge":** "Sexual Exploitation of Children," 1977 congressional hearings, Martin testimony, p. 67.

329 **"I will tell you that this problem":** Ibid.

330 **Roy Ames pleaded guilty:** Jim Sherman, "A Hard Case of the Blues," *Houston Press,* 4/28/1994.

330 **In 1981, he was indicted:** Ibid. and *U.S.A. v. Roy C. Ames,* 743 F.2d 46, First Circuit, 9/12/1984.

330 **For years, Ames lived:** Sherman, "A Hard Case of the Blues," *Houston Press,* 4/28/1994, and Obituary of Roy Ames, *Houston Chronicle,* 8/27/2003, via legacy .com.

330 **"He had a bloody nose":** Gary Gibson, interview by author, 7/3/2022.

330 **"You only have a little while longer":** Ibid.

331 **"He was the kind of man":** Ibid.

331 **He threw out a number:** Ibid.

332 **Some of its words rang true:** Tom Kennedy, "I Haven't Heard from Him Since," *Houston Post,* 8/12/1973.

333 **In a 2019 study:** See Patricia Davis, "Boys for Sale Too; Sex Trafficking: It Affects Both Genders," National Center for Missing and Exploited Children, 9/5/2019. Blog post describes NCMEC study on 565 missing boys between eleven and seventeen who were trafficking victims or at high risk.

CHAPTER 35: The Police Officer's Son

335 **"And when Rusty was supposed to be":** Evan Moore, "The Horror Remains 20 Years Later: Memories of Dean Corll Haunt Survivor," *Houston Chronicle*, 8/8/1993.

336 **"He took Pearl beers":** Ray Hunt, interviews by author, 11/30/2022 and 12/12/2022.

338 **"When Rusty disappeared":** Rob Meckel, "Body Identified After 12 Years in the Local Morgue," *Houston Post*, 7/4/1985.

338 **But her father assured Susan:** Barbara Linkin, "Victim's Sister Out to Keep Notorious Killer in Prison," *Houston Post*, 4/29/91.

339 **"Doug's fears were that":** Meckel, "Body Identified."

339 **"It's just one day":** Kerley, interview by Paige Hewitt, ABC13.

339 **In March 1982:** Amended Autopsy Report, ML 73-3350, 8/12/1973, identified as Willard K. "Rusty" Branch in 1985, HCME.

341 **"You can't believe":** Jack Douglas and Jerry Laws, "Decade After Slaying Discovered, 22nd Murder Victim Named," *Houston Post*, 9/15/1983.

341 **In those cramped quarters:** Pat Paul, interview by author, 2/10/2023, review of scrapbook, photos, and Amended Autopsy Report, ML 73-3350, HCME.

343 **In 1979, she:** Ibid.

344–345 **At the state police lab:** Evan Moore, "Round Rock Artist Puts a Face on Crime," *Houston Chronicle*, 5/2/2004.

346 **In a 2003 case:** Todd W. Fenton, Amber N. Heard, B. A. Norman, and J. Sauer, "Skull-Photo Superimposition and Border Deaths: Identification Through Exclusion and the Failure to Exclude," *Journal of Forensic Sciences*, 2/11/2008.

348 **provided Houston police with names:** Moore, "The Horror Remains 20 Years Later."

PART VI: THE LAST UNSOLVED MYSTERIES

CHAPTER 36: Letting Go

353 **"You would not have rest":** Keith L. Alexander, "She Doesn't Have Rest Until the Dead Have a Name," *The Washington Post*, 1/3/2017.

354 **(Penwell, who is autistic):** "A One-Woman CSI Unit: Penny Penwell Has Autism and the Passion to Solve Cold Missing Persons Cases," *Northern Express*, 6/1/2014.

355 **"That was huge":** Derrick interview in her office, where Garvey's portrait hangs.

355 **"One of the reasons":** Derrick and Benjamin Figura, "The Role of the Anthropologist in Identification at Two Urban Medical Examiner Offices: New York City and Harris County," *Journal of Academic Forensic Pathology*, 9/1/2016. Available via the National Library of Medicine: ncbi.nlm.nih.gov/pmc/articles/PMC6474562/.

356 **September 11, 2001:** "Lessons Learned from 9/11: DNA Identification in Mass Fatality Incidents," National Institute of Justice report, September 2006, p. 14.

356 **A National Institute of Justice report:** Ibid.

358 **Across Texas, more than seventeen hundred unidentified bodies:** NamUs search by author for unidentified decedents in Texas, 2/28/2024.

360 **That year, Barbara Rae-Venter:** Barbara Rae-Venter, *I Know Who You Are: How an Amateur DNA Sleuth Unmasked the Golden State Killer and Changed Crime Fighting Forever* (New York: Ballantine Books, 2023).

360 **Initially, Family Tree CEO Bennett Greenspan kept:** Amy Dockser Marcus, "Customers Handed Over Their DNA. The Company Let the FBI Take a Look," *Wall Street Journal,* 8/22/2019.

361 **"I felt a profound sense of pride":** Rae-Venter, *I Know Who You Are,* p. 132.

361 **"We had made history":** Ibid.

362 **In 2014, Derrick had been invited:** Abstract of presentation, American Academy of Forensic Sciences, 2014.

362 **In 2017, Fitzpatrick went on to co-found a nonprofit:** Background on DNA Doe Project website, dnadoeproject.org/andcasesummaries:dnadoeproject.org/cases-success/.

362 **In 2019, the group made headlines again:** Case summary of "Clark County John Doe," DNA Doe Project website, dnadoeproject.org/case/clark-county-john-doe/.

363 **By the time Derrick reached out:** From Identifinders website, accessed 2/28/2024, identifinders.com/about/.

CHAPTER 37: A Frustrating Search—and a Breakthrough

364 **"The approach back then":** James Anderson, interview by author, 8/25/2022. All Anderson quotes in this chapter are from author interviews in 2022 and 2023.

368 **"Unfortunately, many of the parents":** Press conference, 8/9/2021, videos posted on YouTube by FOX and KHOU and KTRK, excerpts on websites including abc13.com/texas-equusearch-elmer-wayne-henley-dean-corll-serial-killer/10938878/.

371 **Anderson had watched a special report:** Jessica Willey, "The Candyman Murders," *Texas True Crime,* ABC13 Houston, 11/16/2021.

376 **"We sympathize":** Lisa Laird, email to author, 8/12/2022.

CHAPTER 38: Swimsuit Boy Revealed?

378 **In 2019, the same year:** Colleen Fitzpatrick, interview by author, 2/1/2023. Background from Capt. Jason Smith of Philadelphia PD and others in press conference, 12/8/2022, streamed by CBS News Philadelphia, cbsnews.com/philadelphia/news/the-boy-in-the-box-to-be-identified-by-philadelphia-police/.

379 **"At the time, I asked":** Fitzpatrick, interview by author.

379 **The boy's DNA "was shot":** Joe Holden, Alyssa Adams, and Tom Dougherty, "What We Know About Joseph Augustus Zarelli," CBS News Philadelphia, 12/10/2022.

379 **Stack was thirteen:** Obituary, Schmidt Funeral Home, 11/9/2022.

379 **Fitzpatrick considered Stack:** Fitzpatrick, interview by author.

379 **In her time with Identifinders:** "'Like a Puzzle': How Pullman Police Identified a Rape Suspect in a near Twenty-Year-Old Case Using Forensic Genetic Genealogy," 3/21/2022, KHQ.com.

380 **"The genealogy":** Stack, email to Pinto, 5/12/2021.

381 **"In conclusion":** Ibid.

381 **"I am stumped":** Pinto, email to Stack, 5/13/2021.

381 **Pinto didn't try:** Pinto, interview by author, 7/15/2022.

382 **"This was the most":** Michelle Taylor, "Boy in the Box Is Identified as Joseph Augustus Zarelli," *Forensic Magazine,* 12/8/2022.

382 **"When that data":** Fitzpatrick, interview by author and follow-up emails.

382 **In December 2022:** Press conference, 12/8/2022, streamed by CBS News Philadelphia.

382 **"In his very short life":** Danielle Outlaw, press conference, 12/8/2022, Ibid.

383 **"The science and technology":** Ibid.

384 **"She advised":** Amended Autopsy Report, ML 73-3350, Willard K. "Rusty" Branch, Jr., original 8/12/1973, amended 7/3/1985, HCME.

CHAPTER 39: The Family Plot

387 **Rusty Branch's family has scattered:** Author interviews with Ray Hunt and two of Rusty's cousins and visit to the cemetery in December 2022.

387 **She was named as one of:** Last Will and Testament of Willard Karmon Branch, 1980.

388 **"Somehow I always thought":** Rusty Branch's half sister, interview by author, 12/22/2022.

388 **"That's what Susan would have wanted":** Ibid.

389 **In the fall of 2022, I had traveled:** Diana Waggoner Shurbet, interviews by author, 7/6/2022 and 9/2022.

391 **found their silence heartbreaking:** Al Derrick, interview by author.

CHAPTER 40: The Prisoner's Story

393 **"Some of the boys":** No byline, "Police say sex ring files include mass murder victims," *Houston Post,* 2/28/1975.

394 **Over the next two decades:** Author's review of state prosecutions of Cunningham and Burch in Harris County district court clerk archives and related HCDA files.

394 **In an eerie echo:** "Area briefs: Man gets life sentence for killing acquaintance," *Houston Chronicle,* 4/2/2001.

394 **Anthony Mendez:** Anthony Mendez, interview by author, 1/5/2023 (all other Mendez quotes from interview). Additional details from property and criminal records related to Mendez; Bryant Burch and Leonard Cunningham; Harris County clerk and district clerk archives.

397 **On October 21, 1999:** *State of Texas v. Mendez, Anthony John,* Harris County District Court, Case No. 08268050, filed 10/21/1999.

398 **"Men who have been sexually assaulted":** Joan M. Cook and Amy E. Ellis, "The Other #MeToo: Male Sex Abuse Survivors," *Psychiatric Times,* 4/8/2020.

CHAPTER 41: The House Falls

400 **In the winter of 1974:** Truman Capote, "Houston Diary," Truman Capote Papers, NYPL.

400 **Years later, only a few pages:** Katherine Ramsland, "Capote's Missed Opportunity: After 'In Cold Blood,' Capote Considered Another Unique Crime Story," *Psychology Today,* 12/14/2013.

400 **In search of it, I consulted:** Truman Capote, "Houston Diary," Truman Capote Papers, NYPL.

401 **He observed nothing:** Ibid.

401 **"How was it possible":** Ibid.

401 **On February 22, 2023:** Author witnessed demolition of the house in Pasadena.

401 **Sgt. James Anderson stands on Lamar:** Ibid.

403 **"I'm not a fan":** Mark Gardemal, interview by author, 2/22/2023.

403 **"I think it's going to be very healing":** Kathy M. Pratt, interview by author, 2/22/2023.

404 ***La verdad que no":*** Paulino Rodriguez Garcia, interview by author, 2/22/2023.

405 **"I think it's probably a good thing":** Michelle Dreymala Wilson, interview by author, 2/22/2023.

SELECTED BIBLIOGRAPHY

Bass, Bill, and Jon Jefferson. *Death's Acre: Inside the Legendary Forensic Lab the Body Farm Where the Dead Do Tell Tales*. Newburyport, Mass.: Berkley Publishing Group, 2003.

———. *Beyond the Body Farm: A Legendary Bone Detective Explores Murders, Mysteries, and the Revolution in Forensic Science*. New York: William Morrow, 2009.

Bell, Arthur. "The Fate of the Boys Next Door." *Esquire,* March 1994.

———. Houston file, Arthur Bell Papers, Billy Rose Theatre Division, NYPL archives.

———. "The Swell Guy Murderer: Deep in the Dark of Texas." *Village Voice,* 8/30/1973.

Bliss, George, Michael Sneed, and Greg Moseley. "Chicago Is Center of National Boy Porn Ring," part of the series "Child Pornography, Sickness for Sale." *Chicago Tribune,* 5/15–5/18/1977.

Boss, Pauline. *Ambiguous Loss: Learning to Live with Unresolved Grief.* Cambridge, Mass.: Harvard University Press, 1999.

Cato, Jack. Houston Channel 2, video recording and other August 1973 footage available via the Texas Archive of the Moving Image.

Conaway, James. *The Texans.* New York: Alfred A. Knopf, 1976.

Congressional Record. "Sexual Exploitation of Children." Hearings before the Subcommittee on Crime of the Committee on the Judiciary, House of Representatives, 95th Congress.

Douglas, John E. *Mindhunter: Inside the FBI's Elite Serial Crime Unit.* New York: Scribner, 1995.

Fitzpatrick, Colleen, and Andrew Yeiser. *Forensic Genealogy, Revised.* Fountain Valley, Calif.: Rice Book Press, 2013.

Goldfarb, Bruce. *18 Tiny Deaths: The Untold Story of Frances Glessner Lee and the Invention of Modern Forensics.* Naperville, Ill.: Sourcebooks, 2020.

Gurwell, John K. *Mass Murder in Houston.* Houston: Cardovan Press.

Hollandsworth, Skip. "The Lost Boys." *Texas Monthly,* April 2011.

———. *The Midnight Assassin: Panic, Scandal, and the Hunt for America's First Serial Killer.* New York: Henry Holt, 2015.

Humphreys, Laud. *Tearoom Trade: Impersonal Sex in Public Places.* Chicago: Aldine Publishing Co., 1970.

Johnson, Kirk Wallace. *The Fishermen and the Dragon: Fear, Greed, and a Fight for Justice on the Gulf Coast.* New York: Viking, 2020.

Kimmerle, Erin. *We Carry Their Bones: The Search for Justice at the Dozier School for Boys.* New York: HarperCollins, 2022.

Kolker, Robert. *Lost Girls: An Unsolved American Mystery.* New York: HarperCollins, 2013.

Lloyd, Robin. *For Money or Love: Boy Prostitution in America.* New York: Vanguard Press, 1976.

Manhein, Mary H. *Bone Remains: Cold Cases in Forensic Anthropology.* Baton Rouge: Louisiana State University Press, 2013.

McNamara, Michelle. *I'll Be Gone in the Dark: One Woman's Obsessive Search for the Golden State Killer.* New York: HarperCollins, 2018.

Olsen, Jack. *The Man with the Candy: The Story of the Houston Mass Murders.* New York: Simon & Schuster, 1974.

Rae-Venter, Barbara. *I Know Who You Are: How an Amateur DNA Sleuth Unmasked the Golden State Killer and Changed Crime Fighting Forever.* New York: Ballantine Books, 2023.

Roth, Mitchel P., and Tom Kennedy. *Houston Blue: The Story of the Houston Police Department.* Denton: University of North Texas Press, 2012.

Sherman, Jim. "A Hard Case of the Blues." *Houston Press*, 4/28/1994.

Sloan, Anne. *Houston Heights.* Images of Modern America series. Charleston, S.C.: Arcadia Publishing, 2016. (The author also reviewed the 2009 edition.)

Swift, Earl. *Where They Lay: Searching for America's Lost Soldiers.* London: Bantam Press, 2003.

Sykes, Bryan. *The Seven Daughters of Eve.* New York: W. W. Norton, 2001.

Ubelaker, Douglas, and Henry Scammell. *Bones: A Forensic Detective's Casebook.* Lanham, Md.: M. Evans, 1992.

Vance, Carol. *Boomtown DA.* Houston: Whitecaps Media, 2010.

Vance, Mike, and John Nova Lomax. *Murder and Mayhem in Houston: Historic Bayou City Crime.* Charleston, S.C.: History Press, 2014.

ABOUT THE AUTHOR

LISE OLSEN is an investigative reporter and editor whose work has appeared in the *Texas Observer,* the *Houston Chronicle,* and in documentaries on Netflix, Paramount+, A & E, and CNN. Her work has inspired reforms, contributed to the prosecutions of a former congressman and a federal judge, and restored names to unidentified murder victims. Her first book, *Code of Silence,* won awards from Investigative Reporters & Editors and the Texas Institute of Letters.

X: @LiseDigger
Instagram: @LiseOlsenauthor
liseolsen.info
Find Lise Olsen on Facebook

ABOUT THE TYPE

This book was set in Minion, a 1990 Adobe Originals typeface by Robert Slimbach. Minion is inspired by classical, old-style typefaces of the late Renaissance, a period of elegant and beautiful type designs. Created primarily for text setting, Minion combines the aesthetic and functional qualities that make text type highly readable with the versatility of digital technology.